THE MIND ALIVE ENCYCLOPEDIA
EARLY CIVILIZATION

CHARTWELL
BOOKS INC.

THE MIND ALIVE ENCYCLOPEDIA
EARLY CIVILIZATION

Edited by Jane Browne

Published by Chartwell Books Inc.,
a division of Book Sales Inc.
Distributed in the United States by
Book Sales Inc., 110 Enterprise Avenue,
Secausus, New Jersey 07094.

©Marshall Cavendish Limited 1968, 1969, 1970, 1977

Printed in Great Britain

This material has previously appeared in
the partwork *Mind Alive*.

This volume first published 1977

ISBN 0 85685 301 1
Library of Congress Number 77-73852

Pages 2 and 3: This bronze panel is from a
pair of doors by the 15th century artist Lorenzo
Ghiberti, known as the 'Gates of Paradise'.
The doors were badly damaged in the Florence
flood disaster of 1966 when flood waters
swept through the Baptistery in the Piazza del
Duomo, tearing off five of the carved panels.
Pages 4 and 5: This Assyrian bas-relief
(approximately 9th century BC) shows the
use of a four-wheeled battering ram with a
head in the form of a boar, an early siege weapon.
Page 6: When Howard Carter discovered the
tomb of the boy-king Tutankhamen in the
Valley of Kings near Thebes it was one of the
most exciting archaeological finds of the
century. Countless priceless artifacts were
buried with the young Pharoah to accompany
him on his journey to the next world. This
exquisite gold mask covered the head and
shoulders of Tutankhamen's mummified body.

Introduction

The history of modern times will be documented in minute detail in print, on film, on tapes and in computer records. Early history is different: our distant past, like a richly coloured mosaic, must be pieced together by archaeologists and scholars from surviving written records and the products of years of painstaking excavation. Many of the fragments of the picture are missing. New facts constantly come to light.

One thing is certain, that history is never dull. The pages of history are peopled with flesh and blood characters whose stories are by turns thrilling, romantic, comic, often tragic. The world's earliest known civilizations may have had some barbaric customs and primitive beliefs by modern standards, but they were frequently highly structured. The exquisite jewelry and artifacts excavated from Sumerian tombs, the staggering dimensions of the Pyramids, Roman roads and Greek temples, all bear witness to highly developed and sophisticated societies.

This entertaining and lavishly illustrated encyclopedia covers the whole span of ancient and medieval history from the earliest recorded civilizations right up to the relatively 'modern' times of Elizabeth I. It tells the story of the rise and fall of empires and the development of art and religion. To read it is to explore many different worlds and yet to recognize in all of them the foundations of our own age. We have our roots in history – and the pattern of history may well be the key to our future.

Contents

Picture Credits

The power of law in ancient empires

The people had no hand in the government of the Ancient Egyptian and Assyrian empires. Yet the Pharaohs in Egypt ruled for four thousand years; and law was first written down in Babylon.

GOVERNMENT IN the ancient empires took a form very different from the Athenian model because the pattern of life in these empires was so unlike that of Greece. The Athenian city state of the fifth century BC had a population of perhaps 300,000 and its whole territory of Attica covered a geographically varied region of little more than 800 square miles. In contrast, Egypt, Babylon, Assyria and Persia were vast, arid, geographically monotonous empires claiming dominion over millions of people.

The democratic way of life that Athens achieved for a third of its adult population could be lived only on the tiny scale of Attica. In the kingdoms and empires that stretched in a broad crescent from Greece through the Middle East to Egypt, huge populations and vast distances compelled a more bureaucratic, despotic kind of government.

More than 2,000 years before the golden age of Athens, Egyptians and Sumerians lived in settled communities based on the scientific understanding of agriculture and the seasons. Long before Socrates taught, Babylonians had recorded their laws, their knowledge of astronomy, mathematics and medicine, and their financial and economic transactions. Although neither Egypt nor Babylon were in the least democratic, they both developed into brilliant, stable and enduring civilizations with highly developed systems of law. This tends to suggest that their forms of government suited the conditions of time and place.

The most successful civilization

The Egyptian civilization lasted in total for nearly 4,000 years, beginning before 3100 BC and surviving (in fossilized form) until c. AD 500. That is, it lasted possibly three-quarters of the period between its earliest beginnings and the present day. What is even more remarkable is that throughout its history, through periods of rise, decline and recovery, from flourishing empire to foreign rule, through unity and disunity, Egypt kept its way of life and government comparatively unchanged, intrinsically Egyptian. There is no evidence that Egypt was indebted to any parent civilization, and no significant civilization branched from it. Since it was 'rediscovered' by French scholars in the late eighteenth century its greatest impact upon men's minds has been through its stereotyped art and hieroglyphic language, its colossal buildings, and its preoccupation with death.

The art of Egypt, though stiff and formal, gives a fascinating insight into the way the Egyptians – or at least the Egyptian ruling class – saw their own society. Egyptian art depicts a highly organized people dependent upon a life-

The Pharaohs of Ancient Egypt were supreme heads of state, but they depended on officials to carry out the complex task of governing the country. The vizier, or chancellor, as in England today, was responsible for regulating the state revenues and all matters concerned with internal economic matters. The picture shows the squatting figure of Sennefer, Royal Chancellor under Queen Hatshepsut and her stepson, Thutmose III (c. 1500 BC). This was a period in Egypt when peace reigned; much time was devoted to the arts; and the business of running the country proceeded free from internal strife. Officials of the treasury collected taxes which were paid in kind, since money in the form we know it was not invented. Taxes could take the form of grain, animals or other necessary commodities – which the Pharaohs then used as payment to their officials.

giving river and the supreme wisdom of a divine king backed by a multiplicity of deities. Today the fertile strip along the banks of the river Nile supports about 30 million people, and as early as 1200 BC it probably already sustained a tenth of that number. Their prosperity – their very survival – depended not only upon the mere existence of the Nile, but also upon the co-ordination of their efforts to put the vital river to greatest use.

At the top of Egyptian society was Pharaoh, a divine king who after death joined the pantheon of gods that watched over Egypt. Through his nobles and officials, led by the vizier, he imposed law and economic order throughout the land, employing a large army of priestly clerks called *scribes* as supervisors.

The conscientious scribes regulated agriculture, industry and trade. They set up Nilometers to measure the rise of the river, calculated the size of the coming harvest and the probable tax yield, and allotted funds to various government

'ministries' to finance the ambitious projects of Egypt's economic planners. By controlling traffic on the Nile – the only important trade highway – the scribes brought almost all internal and external trade under their scrutiny. Through their hands passed the precious imports that great economic developers such as Rameses II (who reigned through most of the thirteenth century BC) either purchased or exacted as tribute from Egypt's neighbours. Up the Nile came cedar wood from Lebanon, copper – probably from Cyprus – gold, iron, tin and wine from the Levant and Asia Minor.

Down the Nile from Nubia came amethyst, diorite and more gold; from black Africa, a great variety of animals and animal products. As agricultural production became more and more efficient and the output per head rose, so each generation spared more men to train as artisans. The cities of Egypt became treasure houses for the rulers; the temples, magnificent abodes for priests and gods.

9

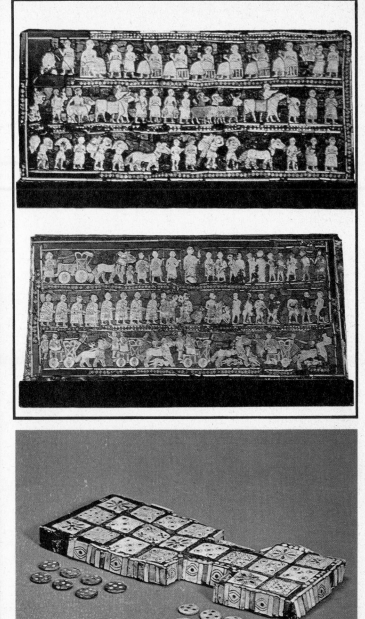

Above, a noble Sumerian lady once owned these jewels, and must have delighted in the beaten gold leaves and flowers, the gold ear-rings and the necklaces of lapis lazuli, cornelian and pearls.

This magnificent curly-haired bull's head adorned a lyre, like that being played at the court banquet on the 'Royal Standard', to the right of the highest row in our picture *top right.*

The famous box called the 'Royal Standard' of Ur, *c.* 2700 BC, shows scenes of peace, *top right,* and war, *centre right.* Some experts believe it was not in fact a standard, but the sounding-box of a musical instrument. *Above right,* some rich Sumerian must have spent many hours with this ivory board and counters for some unknown game – perhaps similar to our draughts.

was a step towards the system of writing we use today. By about 2500 BC they had evolved *cuneiform* (wedge-shaped writing) which they wrote on damp clay tablets with a sharpened reed. The Sumerian cuneiform was later taken over by the Babylonians, Assyrians, Hittites and Persians, who adapted it for their own languages. Thousands of Sumerian clay tablets and fragments have been recovered by archaeologists. Most of these are now in museums awaiting examination by scholars. The Sumerians also produced delicately carved cylinder seals which they used to roll pictures and writing on clay tablets, labels and stoppers. Most business documents were sealed as a matter of course.

In the nineteenth century archaeologists excavated the library of Assurbanipal, the last great king of the Assyrian Empire. Among the tens of thousands of clay documents and literary works unearthed was a poem, the *Epic of Gilgamesh,* written in the Akkadian Semitic language. This poem was found to be a translation from the original Sumerian. Gilgamesh, legendary king of the city-state of Uruk, is among the earliest-known human heroes. The Epic tells how Gilgamesh, distressed by the death of his friend, the divinely-created Enkidu, set off on the quest to discover the secret of immortality. After many adventures he came to the Ocean of Death, where he built a boat and persuaded a ferryman to take him across. Beyond the ocean Gilgamesh met Utnapishtim, a semi-divine immortal, who was a pre-Biblical Noah. Utnapishtim told Gilgamesh a divine secret concerning a great flood cruelly sent by the gods to destroy mankind. The gods planned this destruction to stop the perpetual noise and uproar of the human race which disturbed the sleep of

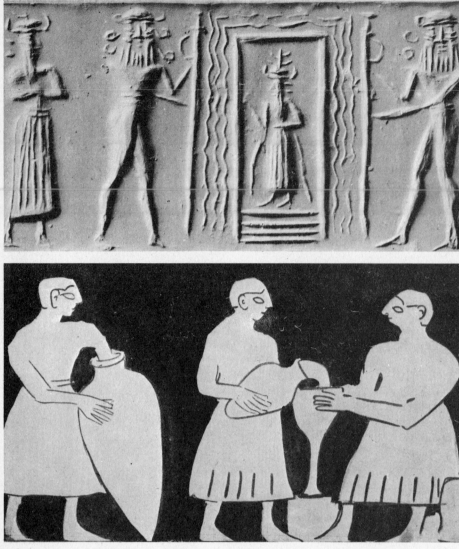

Top left, a version of the Great Flood myth occurs in the Epic of Gilgamesh, who here watches Utnapishtim; the Noah of the story, in his ark: an Akkadian seal carving dating from *c.* 2200 B C. *Above left,* the lively style of Sumerian art is seen in this vignette of servants busy with storage jars for wine and corn (called *amphorae*). *Top right,* a statuette like this was left in the temple during the donor's absence, to assure the god of his devotion at all times. *Above right,* a master goldsmith wrought this dagger and decorated sheath found in Ur.

their divine creators. But one of the gods, Ea, betrayed the plan of destruction to Utnapishtim, advising him to build a boat and take 'the seed of all living creatures' into it. The boat was built on schedule, and Utnapishtim and his family, together with other people and wild and tame animals, went aboard as the rain began to fall. Enlil, the warrïor god, at first enraged that any human should have escaped the deluge, was persuaded by Ea to relent and grant Utnapishtim immortality.

The plant of eternal youth

Utnapishtim then confided the secret of immortality to Gilgamesh, telling him that it resided in a plant at the bottom of the waters. Gilgamesh eventually procured the plant, planning to take it back to Uruk for old men to eat in order to regain their youth and vigour. Resuming his journey in company with the ferryman, Gilgamesh stopped to bathe in a well where a serpent stole the youth-restoring plant, sloughed its skin and disappeared into the water. At this point the tale breaks off, leaving Gilgamesh weeping with frustration: it is the will of the gods that man shall age and die.

Early Sumerian schools were run by the temple priests, but in time education became separated from religion. A small private school dating from about 1800 B C excavated at Ur, had accommodation for about 25 pupils. The curriculum of the school seems to have centred mainly on the 'three r's' – reading, writing and arithmetic – but the teachers treated these subjects fairly broadly. The ruined classrooms contained, when excavated, multi-

Sumerian picture-writing developed until it could express abstract ideas. A star first meant just 'star'; later, 'god' or 'heaven'; later still, 'high'.

plication tables and tables for working out square roots and cubic capacities. Education was of a practical nature, suitable for future scribes, traders, surveyors and businessmen.

North of the Sumerian city-states lay the territory of the Semitic Akkadians, united some time before 2300 B C by Sargon, a warrior chieftain who ruled Akkad for about 55 years. Many legends and mysteries surround the origins of Sargon and his rise to power. One account says that he was born of a temple prostitute, another that he was found exposed in a basket of reeds (centuries before Moses was said to be found in similar circumstances). Having mastered Akkad, Sargon marched southwards against the divided Sumerians, conquering them city by city. But the Sumerians, settling down under Akkadian rule, civilized their conquerors, who quickly absorbed Sumerian culture. Sargon, King of Akkad and Sumeria, extended his empire from present-day Iran to the Mediterranean. The Akkadian Empire disintegrated after the death of Sargon, under pressure of invasion by other Semitic peoples. About 600 years later, Hammurabi, King of Babylonia, incorporated the old Sumerian-Akkadian territories in his empire.

Man and the great river

Throughout history men have experienced the need to explore, to sail the seas, to build great empires, to expand their civilizations – as the people of the Indus did nearly 5,000 years ago.

IN 1856 two brothers, John and William Brunton, both railway engineers, were laying out the East Indian Railway from Karachi to Lahore. John was a very experienced engineer, having been in charge of some of the heaviest works on the London and Birmingham Railway, and hearing of a ruined city called Brahminabad near to the line of the railway, he plundered it ruthlessly for ballast. His brother William did the same with a shapeless heap of huge dusty mounds near the village of Harappa – and today, writes Stuart Piggott, 'the trains run over a hundred miles of line laid on a secure foundation of third-millennium brickbats'.

In fact William Brunton was plundering one of the two centres of what Sir Mortimer Wheeler calls the 'vastest political experiment before the advent of the Roman Empire'. It was not until 1922 that systematic excavation was begun of what we now call the Indus civilization, but since then more and more sites have been discovered until more than 60 are now known, covering half a million square miles of the Indus plain and the neighbouring regions of Pakistan and India.

'A mockery of snow'

The truly astonishing things about this civilization are, first, its extent; second, its complete uniformity; third, the fact of its being virtually unknown until under 50 years ago; and fourth, the almost complete absence of any evidence of gradual growth. Unlike the cities of Sumeria, those of the Indus plain seem to have sprung into being by some sort of ideological explosion.

Like Sumer and Akkad, the Indus cities were in a country which is today inhumanly barren and repelling – an arid salt desert where the stunted trees and shrubs are covered with what Piggott called 'a Satanic mockery of snow' and where the temperature rises to 120 °F. in the summer. The Indus has eroded another channel for itself and now flows several miles away. Yet this country must have been a flourishing jungle-clad land in the time of the great cities of Mohenjo-daro and Harappa (we do not know their ancient names; these are the names of the two villages now near the sites of the ancient cities), for both cities, each over a mile square, were built of baked bricks; this implies an unlimited supply of wood for fuel. Moreover, we know from designs on their seals that the Harappans knew the water-buffalo, the rhinoceros, the bear, monkey, squirrel, parrot and deer, to say nothing of various fish and crocodiles.

This problem of deterioration of climate confronts the geographer in many places, from Arizona to the Sahara and from Egypt to Turkestan. No one answer is satis-

Crude but lively clay figurines have been found on the sites of the once-great walled cities of the Indus valley. *Top left,* a double female head, the two faces exactly alike, separated by a projection probably representing the fashionable head-dress shown in the 'mother goddess' figure, *top right.* The goddess, with her short skirt, necklaces and remarkable headgear, is a distinctive personality – as is the alert little dog, *centre left. Above,* from the Indus, civilization spread eastward far over the plains, and westward to trade with the Sumerian cities of Ur and Akkad.

factory: here on the Indus plain, for example, there is evidence that the monsoon region has receded slightly, but human neglect and the denudation of the ancient forests must have been a major factor. At all events, the contrast between past and present is more striking here than almost anywhere in the world.

The earlier prehistory of India can tell us little or nothing to throw light on the sudden maturity and vast bureaucracy of the Indus civilization. There are as yet few prehistoric human remains in the peninsula, and as Wheeler puts it, Man's solitary memorial is an infinitude of stones, ranging from the great clumsy 'pre-Soan' stones of the Punjab to the puny little flaked stones of central India. We can deduce from the evidence of hand-axes and other implements that some of the great trade-routes round the Indian Ocean were known in prehistoric times, and the occasional Mongoloid skull at Harappa is evidence of contact with China, perhaps through the Burma passes to Yunnan and the Yang-tze; but this does not help us a great deal in our study of the Indus cities.

Identical cities

Nor are we very much nearer when we examine the village cultures of Baluchistan and the adjacent plain which flourished about 3000 BC, and which were the immediate precursors of the Indus civilization. These village cultures were in the valleys between massive hill-ranges, and were isolated rather like the early Greek city-states, each in its mountain fastness. These cultures are at present the subject of much archaeological activity, and are differentiated from one another largely by their pottery. The ware from the Nal and Amri districts is colourful and sophisticated with life-like representations of animals, while that from Kulli-Mehi seems to show the horror of vacant space which we associate with some early Greek vase-painting, and its main preoccupation seems to be with the Indian humped buffalo. From Zhob come various female figurines with a skull-like appearance, taking us into that weird world of magic and superstition which we surmise to have been behind the cultures of India as well as of Sumer, Egypt, Crete and America.

In contrast to this localized variety we have the complete uniformity of the Indus civilization over a vast area. The two great cities themselves, each over a mile square, were laid out on the same rectangular plan, rather like that of a present-day American city. Their great resemblance to one another has led to speculation whether they were the twin seats of government of this vast area. Each was dominated by a central citadel and in each the width of the streets, the dimensions of the bricks, the units of measurement, the drainage, the pottery, the script, all are uniform. Not only is this noticeable in space, but in time. Until towards the end of their existence there seems little discernible change or development.

And yet this civilization had some strange features. In some respects it produced workmanship that is unsurpassed –

Heavy, brutal and authoritative, this bearded man has a presence more impressive than pleasant. The trefoils on his robe – religious symbols – may indicate that he was a priest or even a god.

in seals, jewellery, bronze ornaments and the like – but in weapons we find nothing more advanced than the hill villages previously mentioned. The socketed axe, for instance, was never thought of. Clearly the Indus people were not particularly warlike, and it is difficult to imagine them arriving from the northwest and subduing a native people, in the way that they themselves were subdued or destroyed by the advancing Aryans. We are much hampered, too, by the fact that although we have abundant examples of their script, running to nearly 500 characters, no one has yet been able to decipher it.

What did the people look like in these far-off cities? The predominant type is the Mediterranean, of medium height, with olive complexion, a long head and face, a long narrow nose and dark hair and eyes – a type found in abundance in India today. Lower in the social scale were probably the proto-Australoid type with negroid features and bunched curly hair. This type is strikingly represented by the most charming of all the objects found at Mohenjo-daro, a bronze statuette of a dancing girl, with head provocatively tilted and right arm on hip as if about to do a suggestive body-shake (see vol. 2, page 561). A third or Armenian type is seemingly represented by the head of a bearded man wearing a trefoil-decorated robe. The religious symbolism of the trefoil may indicate that this man is a priest or even a god, but his low receding forehead, narrow eye-slits, jutting lower lip, shaven upper lip and stylized beard make him the sort of man one would hate to meet on a dark night, and render it difficult to place him in any racial category.

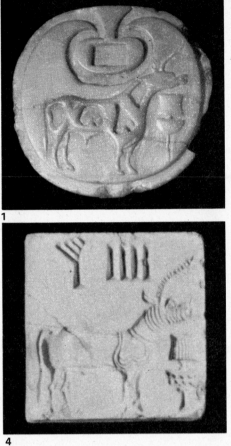
1

2

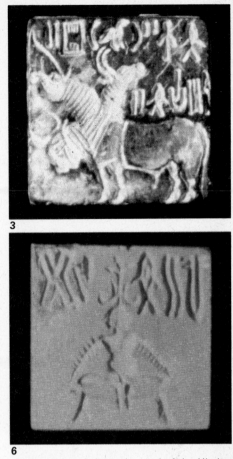
3

4

5

6

That the arid salt plains once teemed with life is seen from the many seals found in the city ruins. Their designs include bears, tigers, antelopes, rhinos, **5**, and – most common – an odd one-horned ox, **1, 2** and **4**. Some, like **3**, show 'fabulous monsters'. Particularly interesting is **6**, showing a seated cross-legged figure who may, even at this early date, represent Siva, the creating and destroying god of the Hindus. Inscriptions on the seals, in a language which still baffles the attempts of scholars to decipher it, are thought to be personal names.

Time has played some very queer tricks of survival in the Indus cities. All trace of properly laid-out burial grounds is lacking, probably because the earliest strata are below water level and it has so far been impossible to excavate them. Yet tiny things survive: traces of cotton cloth, for instance, at Mohenjo-daro through the creation of metallic salts – by far the

Laboriously made from bored and polished carnelian and steatite, these beads were a popular adornment for the ladies of the Indus civilizations. Similar ones were found in Sumer.

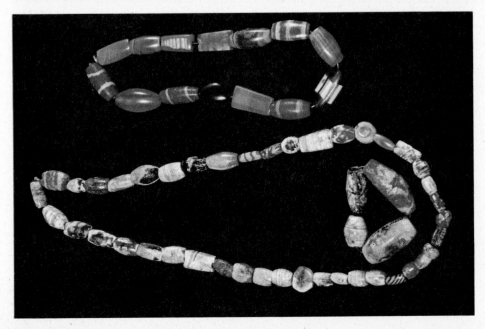

earliest known evidence of cotton; children's toys, some found in drains as if they had been washed away with the bath water, and also models of animals and movable carts, even a whistle and a monkey designed to run up a stick. There are the traces of rubbing on the corner of a building where pack animals have pushed along the street, the impression left by the mineral salts in a footmark near a well, even the paw-marks of a cat and a dog left on a drying brick at Chanhu-daro – we can tell that the dog was chasing the cat because the cat's paw-marks were spread out as if in headlong flight. Yet we still know nothing of what these people wrote and said, what they thought and believed.

We do know a little about their dress on ceremonial occasions. The women seem to have extraordinarily large, even grotesque, head-dresses like panniers, and the men long tunics, though of their everyday apparel we know almost nothing. Various kinds of hair arrangement are found: the bun, the pigtail, even a kind of permanent wave. Several razors have been found, also kohl-sticks (used as black eye-liners) and pots for make-up.

Vast civil service

The houses were on the average quite large, with a central court and with few or no street windows but with huts for watchmen rather like the *chaukidars* of modern India. Everything to do with furniture or indoor decoration is a matter of surmise. We may suppose that the Harappan sat cross-legged for meals, since this posture is well attested. Above all the Indus cities boasted splendid drains, better than anything to be found in India before the advent of Western amenities. These drains emptied into main sewers going the length of the streets and well covered, unlike those of eighteenth-century London, with manholes at intervals. Strangely enough, in spite of the elaborate bathrooms there is little evidence of privies – another example of the strange inequalities of this civilization.

We can picture to ourselves something of the everyday life of the Harappans,

peaceable civilization must have been given over to myth and ritual. Over each city frowned its central citadel, placed high on an elevated platform supported by great walls with access through great gates at the top of an inclined plane. On this high place at Mohenjo-daro, is a great bath, a group of buildings which has been tentatively identified as a priest's house or college, while near the bath are small rooms where probably the priests prepared themselves for their ritual. There is also a great hall and the remains of a vast building identified by Sir Mortimer Wheeler in 1950 as the city granary, with a landing stage down by the level where the Indus was. The size of the granary indicates that it was a main source of wealth, and below it in the city are the remains of rows of little rooms which may have been coolie-lines, for there are rows of circular platforms near them for the pounding of grain into flour for bread.

Death in the streets

No trace has been found of royal burials like those at Ur, but there is good reason to guess that these cities were utterly under the domination of their priests or priest-kings. Representations on seals suggest some sort of worship associated with bulls as in Minoan Crete, but most of the seal-representations are very mysterious. There is, however, one which depicts a man or god in the now familiar cross-legged posture, surrounded by animals, and it is very probable that this is a representation of the god Siva as Pasupati, lord of creatures. This leads to speculation as to how much of the indigenous Indian religion goes back to the Harrapans. Did they practise the caste system? Were their very sinister priests the earliest Brahmans? Were the yogi techniques of concentration and meditation already known so long ago? One is tempted to surmise that they were, for certainly the earliest parts of the Vedas, the hymns of the invading Aryans, show no knowledge of any of these things.

The end of the cities was abrupt and violent, but they had been falling away for some time from their earlier standards. There are smaller houses and even pottery kilns encroaching on the streets, and everywhere there are signs of overcrowding and deterioration. But Mohenjo-daro was apparently sacked and burnt in a final overwhelming attack. Men, women and children were massacred in the streets and houses and were left lying – a fairly sure sign that the city was at least temporarily abandoned. In one lane are nine skeletons, including five children, and in another place several people were apparently climbing steps from a well-room to the street when they were knocked over backwards and fell dead at the bottom of the steps. The weight of probability suggests that these invaders were the first wave of Aryans, whose onslaughts on the cities of the aborigines are celebrated in the Vedas. If so, then the peak of the Harappan civilization may be placed between 2500 and 1500 BC and its destruction at about 1500. We must hope that one day the decipherment of its script will tell us more about this enigmatic civilization.

Over Mohenjo-daro rose the citadel, a group of buildings on a huge man-made platform guarded by walls and towers, all built of baked clay bricks neatly laid, as the tower, *above,* and well-head, *right,* testify. The citadel's buildings included a large ritual bath, 39 feet long, for the priests, and a great granary, placed there to be safe from floods or attack.

because so much survives in the corresponding details of life today. We find wells in courtyards where servants gathered for gossip, and even one floor which may have been that of a restaurant. We can picture the men in boats like those of today, hunting and fishing, and we must imagine a vast civil service to organize the enormous labour involved in building and maintaining the cities.

A unique contribution of this culture to art is the vast number of steatite seals – over 1,200 have been found at Mohenjo-daro alone. Most of them are square in shape with sides of roughly an inch. They have a fine white lustrous surface and depict a wide range of animals, associated with signs in a pictographic script. The most common animal is an ox-like beast with apparently one horn, standing in front of a curious object which has been variously identified as a standard, a bird-cage and a sacred manger. We find the buffalo, tiger and rhinoceros all rendered

with astonishing vividness and actuality.

Apart from the idea of city civilization, in which Mesopotamia retains a world priority and which must have been taken from there by the Indus planners, there are few but quite definite evidences of contact between Ur and the Indus cities before the time of Sargon of Akkad (c. 2400 BC). These consist of Indus seals found at Ur and of fragments of Sumerian pottery at low levels at Mohenjo-daro. Later we find bronze or copper Indus knives at Hissar and pins and objects of lapis lazuli at Ur. But there is by no means as much evidence as might be expected.

Much of the leisure of this apparently

Death of a lost empire

In 1906 some 10,000 tablets were discovered by archaeologists working in Turkey. They revealed the incredible story of the Hittite Empire; powerful for six centuries until its destruction in 1200 B C.

IN 1200 B C the long northern reaches of the River Euphrates marked the barrier between two great empires – uneasy neighbours in the past, but now at peace and busily trading with each other to the profit of both. East of the great river lay Assyria, with its Semitic population; to the west was the land of the Hittites – hawk-nosed men of Indo-European speech. Their ancestors, some 800 or 900 years earlier, had come down into Turkey and settled in the upland plateau of Anatolia, east and south of the modern city of Ankara. Their history, like that of their neighbours in the Near East, had been a stormy complication of battles and treachery, alliances and retreats; but now they seemed to have reached a point of balance.

Flame went before them

Their security was an illusion. Gradually the empire began to crumble. The dependencies began to fall away. Then over the plateau swept a terrible horde. Who they were is still not known; the Egyptians called them 'the sea people'. But we do know that about 1200 B C they swarmed over Anatolia and through Syria. 'They swept on,' says an Egyptian chronicler with a vivid turn of phrase, 'flame going before them, onwards towards Egypt.' The lively description by the Pharaoh Rameses III of how the Egyptian army prepared to meet the sea raiders show the formidable nature of the threat: 'I made the river-mouths ready, like a strong wall, with warships, galleys and skiffs; they were manned fore and aft with brave fighters armed with their weapons, the pick of Egypt's infantry, like roaring lions on the mountain; able warriors were in the chariotry . . . their horses quivered in every limb, eager to crush the foreigners under their hooves.'

Egypt was saved – but the Hittite empire had disappeared, destroyed in a horror of looting and burning, of dead charioteers and razed cities. Its western boundary had been Arzawa, in the southwest of Asia Minor; its eastern, Carchemish on the Euphrates; its southern, the land of Kode or Kizzuwadna on the Cilician coast. It also ruled Alashya, the island of Cyprus conquered some decades earlier by the Hittite king. A great empire had fallen.

This empire, which had lasted six long centuries, had once comprised, at its greatest extent, an area of some hundred thousand square miles. Yet less than a century ago, its very existence was not known.

Then, in 1906, Dr Hugo Winckler, excavating in Turkey on behalf of the German Oriental Society, made a sensational

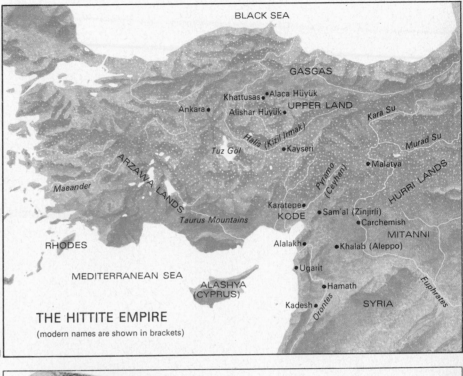

THE HITTITE EMPIRE
(modern names are shown in brackets)

1 A map of Asia Minor in the time of the Hittites. At its greatest extent, the Hittite Empire covered an area of some 100,000 square miles, roughly the size of Great Britain.

2 A neo-Hittite relief from Carchemish (c. 850 B C) showing a Hittite battle chariot and warriors. To the right stands a sphinx with two heads, one human and the other lion.

discovery. In the ruins of the citadel at Boghazköi, some 80 miles east of the present Turkish capital, Ankara, a hoard of clay tablets came to light. They were written in the cuneiform script of Babylonia. Some were in Akkadian, the language of Babylonia, and could at once be read. They revealed that the city in which they had been found was Khattusas, the capital of the land of Khatti, and that Khatti itself had been a great power hundreds of years before King Solomon's reign, in the second millennium B C. The majority of the tablets, however, though in the same script, were in an unknown tongue. This language when eventually deciphered turned out to be one of the great family of Indo-European languages of which Greek, Latin and Sanskrit are the best-known examples. It then became clear that although the clumsy hieroglyphic picture-writing had been used for monuments and although the language of diplomacy had been Akkadian, yet the normal language used for administrative and religious purposes had been the Indo-European tongue. They themselves called this language Nesite, after the city Nesas, an early capital. Having, it is assumed, no writing of their own when they first entered the area, they adopted the Mesopotamian habit of writing on clay tablets, and took over the cuneiform script, adapting it to their own tongue as best they could.

As the archaeologists and the philologists went to work, the story of the Hittite Empire gradually unfolded. It is still incomplete. Both its beginning and its end are shrouded in uncertainty; the exact number of its kings and the length of many of their reigns is uncertain. But every year fresh evidence comes to light – new texts are published, a little more is added to history. From the mists of oblivion, the Hittites are beginning to appear as a vigorous, intelligent people who played an important role as an imperial power in that first age of diplomacy, the formative centuries of the second millennium BC.

What kind of people were they?

The Hittites were not the first people in Anatolia. Exactly whence they came, and when, is still unknown; they appear to have had their origins in mountain country. They worshipped the forces of nature, gods of storm and wind and the heavenly bodies, the gods of the localities in which their settled and the spirits dwelling in springs on hilltops. All of these were counted among 'the thousand gods of Khatti'. By the seventeenth century BC they were well established in the area enclosed by the bend of the Kizil Irmak, the river which bounded the 'Upper Land', the core of the kingdom. Their capital had been moved from Nesas (in the region of modern Kayseri), to Khattusas, a fortress on a hilltop first captured by Anittas, an early king. It was probably a king named Labarnas who encircled the hill with a fortification wall (c. 1630 BC) and built his citadel on the highest point. His successors repeatedly enlarged it till Khattusas became one of the most remarkable cities of ancient times.

On a rocky spur between two mountain torrents, the site was a natural stronghold. The citadel, Kuyuk-kale, commanded a fine view of the valley and was protected on two sides by steep precipices. Crags and rocky gorges themselves provided defences to the inner city, and as the inhabited area increased, a massive double wall was built on the south and west of huge blocks of masonry, piled in haphazard fashion without mortar, punctuated by strongly fortified gates. Through a long tunnel under the ramparts, the defenders could make a secret sortie to

1 The Lion Gate at Khattusas — one of the five main gates which led through the massive wall of the outer city. Gaping mouths were intended to frighten away the powers of evil.

2 This procession of 12 identical gods (c. 1200 BC) was found carved on a wall of a rock chamber in the shrine of Yazilikaya dedicated to the cult of dead Hittite kings.

surprise their attackers. The great length of the wall (it was over two and a half miles long) and the huge area which it enclosed, must have made heavy demands on the national resorces in manpower for garrison duties. It was probably for this reason that the capital was more than once captured and sacked by fierce barbarians from the northeast, the formidable Gasgas.

The Hittite king was a warrior leader surrounded by a feudal assembly of nobles who advised him and even at times imposed their will. His position was not always secure, and a succession of regicides makes the early history of the kingship one of constant bloodshed and rebellion.

The order of succession, however, was fixed by royal decree in the reign of King Telepinus about 1500 BC and later Hittite kings enjoyed power which was little short of absolute: as army leaders, supreme judges and chief pontiffs they controlled every aspect of national life. An elaborate ritual governed their actions, and their presence as officiants at the chief religious festivals in the kingdom was regarded as essential. The queen played a prominent part in these ceremonies, and conducted her own diplomatic correspondence with the courts of allied countries. Several queens appear to have wielded considerable power and this confirms the impression, gained from legal

1 A neo-Hittite relief from the Lion Gate at Malatya (c. 850 BC) vividly captures the excitement of a lion-hunt. Details such as the elaborate mane are derived from Assyrian art.

2 One of the pair of great sphinxes which guarded the gateway of the Hittite city, Alaca Hüyük (c. 1300 BC). The head-dress shows evidence of strong Egyptian influence.

3 A relief from the sanctuary at Yazilikaya depicting King Tudhaliyas IV. His mother was a Hurrian princess, and during her lifetime the Hittite state cult was reorganized along Hurrian lines.

4 A neo-Hittite relief from Carchemish showing a procession of officers. The neo-Hittite kingdoms preserved the artistic traditions of the empire for centuries after its fall.

and administrative texts, that Hittite women enjoyed a more important position than in most ancient Oriental societies.

In appearance the Hittites were rather short, with high-bridged noses and strongly marked features; their warriors wore short belted tunics and boots of felt with upturned toes. Representations of the king on monuments, however, show him dressed in the long flowing robe of ritual with a shawl around his shoulders and a close-fitting cap, and carrying a long inverted crook at his side.

The growth of the empire from a small kingdom was achieved gradually and not without set-backs. The need for defence against the northern mountaineers, against Hurrian chariot-warriors from the east (who taught them the techniques of siege-warfare), and against hostile neighbours to north and west led them on their career of expansion. Crossing the barrier of the Taurus mountains, they

1 A basalt relief from Sam'al (*c.* 850 BC) shows a god in the traditional style — with thunderbolt, long plait, peaked cap and tilted boots. But the curls, anklet and sword are all Assyrian.
2 Jugglers and acrobats play and perform their tricks in a relief from the city wall of Alaca Hüyük (*c.* 1200 BC). Despite their crudeness and the flat relief, the works are very beautiful.
3 Another relief from Sam'al shows a man and his wife eating fruit.

found themselves involved in the struggle for the possession of the wealthy commercial kingdoms of North Syria. The capture of Aleppo and Carchemish by Khattusilis I and his son Mursilis at the end of the seventeenth century BC, and a surprise march down the Euphrates to capture the city of Babylon itself in 1595 BC, must have startled the ancient kingdoms of the Near East and warned them that a new power was about to enter the arena. But dynastic weaknesses for a time occupied the attention and sapped the strength of the Hittite kingdom and it was not until the end of the fifteenth century BC that the foundations of the later empire were laid.

With the accession of Suppiluliumas (*c.* 1380–1350 BC), an able diplomat and great warrior, the domination of the Hittites was extended over most of the Anatolian plateau and over the small kingdoms of Syria and the Lebanon which had been subjected either to Egypt or the chief Hurrian kingdom, Mitanni. He overthrew Mitanni, and a clash with Egypt became inevitable. In about 1315 BC direct encounters took place between Egyptians and Hittites, but a peace treaty was signed between King Sethos I and the Hittite Muwatallis. In the reign of Rameses the Great, however, hostilities broke out afresh, and in 1300 BC a large Egyptian army met the Hittite coalition

at the fortified town of Kadesh. Here, deceived by spies who proved to be 'double-agents' in the pay of the Hittites, into believing that the enemy had fled northwards, Rameses' army was ambushed and barely escaped annihilation. But the personal skill and bravery of the Pharaoh (or so he himself assures us in the many inscriptions which commemorate the battle) saved the day, and the Hittite army was thrown back in confusion. Whatever the immediate outcome of the battle may in fact have been, the Hittites seem to have gained rather than lost territory. Peace was cemented by the marriage of Rameses to the daughter of Khattusilis III, the Hittite king. The alliance lasted, so far as we know, until the fall of the Hittite Empire.

Khattusilis, like his predecessors, enjoyed a prosperous reign (*c.* 1285–1265 BC). His son governed the Syrian dependencies from Carchemish, where he ruled as viceroy; the western provinces were firmly held. But already in the reign of his successor, Tudkhalias IV, the empire had begun to crumble. Rulers of dependencies on the Mediterranean coast first broke away; to the northeast there was unrest and on the eastern frontier the Assyrians pressed hard.

The successor of Tudkhalias called upon his Syrian allies and dependencies for aid. One of these was the ruler of

Ugarit, a town whose ruins are still to be seen on the Mediterranean coast at a place called Ras Shamra. In the palace of the kings of Ugarit the excavators found large numbers of tablets; some of the tablets were part of the diplomatic archives, and these demonstrated clearly that since the early years of the fourteenth century BC Ugarit had been tributary to the Hittite Empire. There was ample evidence that the palace had been looted.

In one of the courtyards was a kiln which the royal scribes had used for baking their clay tablets. It was packed with documents, some of them copies of letters which had evidently been recently received and translated into the local language. Some speak of an approaching foe whose onslaughts were evidently causing grave concern. Others mention preparations for attack and one is an urgent call for a shipload of corn from a Hittite king facing famine. It appears very possible that we have here the last cry for help from an empire about to vanish.

The 'Neo-Hittite' kingdoms

Who were the destroyers? The answer to this question has yet to be found. Khattusas was rebuilt, but when it again became important, it was a Phrygian city. There were no more cuneiform tablets. No Phrygians are named among the pirate-adventurers who attacked Egypt, but the same migratory movement which impelled these raiders may have been responsible for the destruction at Boghazkoi. Certainly the years immediately after 1200 BC saw great upheavals in Asia Minor and the Levant, and when the dust of conflict cleared away, the political map was strangely altered.

But the Hittites did not disappear altogether. Driven eastwards by their conquerors, perhaps, many subjects of the erstwhile empire contrived to preserve their language and script and probably their ancient traditions in alien surroundings. Centuries after the fall of Khattusas, there were small states in southeastern Anatolia and in north Syria between the Gulf of Alexandretta and the Euphrates bend, whose rulers still wrote inscriptions in the Hittite hieroglyphic script. Some of these bore names similar to those of the ancient kings.

These small but prosperous 'Neo-Hittite' kingdoms had a significant part to play in the history of the centuries after 1100 BC. The Assyrians, striking southwards in their search for sources of metal and the need for a Mediterranean outlet for their commerce found that their advance was now opposed by the kings of Khatti – in particular by the kings of Carchemish. Even after the Neo-Hittite dynasties had been overthrown and Aramaean nomads had moved in from the Arabian deserts to take over political control, Hittites contributed a considerable element to the population. The sculpture which adorned the palaces of the kings of Sam'al and Carchemish, Hamath, Malatya and Karatepe, preserved to a late period some of the very finest artistic traditions of the great days of the mighty Hittite Empire.

'Like a wolf on the fold...'

The history of the Assyrian nation is one of violent oscillation between greatness and eclipse. For hundreds of years it dominated the Near East until its final defeat by the Medes and Babylonians.

IN AUGUST, 612 BC, Sin-shar-ishkun, the great king, the mighty king, king of the Universe, king of Assyria, lay beleaguered in Nineveh on the Tigris, capital of an empire which extended from the Mediterranean to Iran and the richest and most magnificent city of the Near East. For three months he had been under attack from the combined forces of his rebellious subjects, Kyaxares, king of the Medes, and Nabopolassar, king of Babylon. But the massive fortification walls had withstood their repeated assaults and there was as yet no shortage of food. Confidently he awaited the arrival of a relief force to raise the siege, his optimism strengthened, according to later legend, by the words of an ancient prophecy: 'No enemy will ever take Nineveh by force unless the river shall first become the city's foe.'

'They made a great defeat'

Suddenly and dramatically the prophecy was fulfilled. The Tigris, swollen by exceptional rains, rose in a flash flood and tore away a stretch of the fortification wall. Through this breach the Medes and Babylonians stormed into the city. In the terse phrases of a Babylonian chronicler: 'They made a great defeat of the chief people; they carried off the spoil of the city and temple; and they turned the city into a mound of rubble.' Sin-shar-ishkun perished with Nineveh. The classical historian, Diodorus, relates that, preferring death to dishonourable captivity, he built a great pyre in his palace upon which he heaped up his gold, silver and robes of state, and then consigned himself, the women of his harem, and his palace to the flames. With the fall of Nineveh, the Assyrian nation vanished from history. Its empire was divided up between Kyaxares and Nabopolassar. Many of its people were carried into captivity and those who remained became subject to Babylon. Despoiled and sacked, its great cities lay deserted except for a remnant of poverty-stricken inhabitants sheltering within the crumbling walls.

The empire which had been so dramatically overthrown by the Medes and Babylonians was the climax of a series of attempts by the Assyrians to dominate the Near East. Their past history had been one of violent oscillation between expansion and contraction. Brief periods of imperial power were succeeded by sudden collapse when their rule was reduced to the limits of their native land. This was small in extent, without natural frontiers and possessed of few economic resources apart from agriculture. It lay along the middle Tigris from the mouth of the Lower Zab River to the edge of the mountain zone of eastern Turkey. An undulating country of low hills, it was brilliant in spring with

A marble slab shows Ashur-nasir-pal (883–859 BC) receiving wine from an officer of his court: 69,574 guests were invited to the celebration feast when his palace at Kalkhu was completed.

growing crops and wild flowers, but parched and swept by dust storms in the heat of summer. To the east the horizon stretched away to the snow-capped Zagros Mountains of Iran; to the west the fertile land merged into arid steppe. Strung out along the Tigris River lay the great cities of Assyria. Furthest south was Ashur, the earliest capital, which gave its name to both the state and the national god, whose temple lay within its walls. This city was always the religious centre of the nation, an Assyrian 'Canterbury'; in the ninth century the capital was moved upstream to Kalkhu, and finally in the seventh century still further upstream to Nineveh.

The Assyrians themselves traced their history back to a time when they were a nomadic tribe roaming over the western steppe under the leadership of 'kings who lived in tents'. Towards the end of the third millennium BC they seized and settled in Ashur, an important commercial centre from which their merchants engaged in a lucrative and highly organized trading venture. Donkey caravans laden with woven fabrics and Caucasian tin trekked the long journey to Cappadocia, where their wares were exchanged for local products such as copper and silver. The first military expansion came under Shamshi-Adad I (c. 1813–1781 BC), who imposed his rule on the numerous small states of

25

upper Mesopotamia. This Old Assyrian Empire, however, did not survive his death for very long. His successors retained only the Tigris valley from Nineveh to Ashur and for over four centuries Assyria was an insignificant dependency first of Babylonia, its southern neighbour, and then of Mitanni, a state established in upper Mesopotamia in about the sixteenth century by Hurrian invaders from the mountains to the north.

The power of Mitanni, which at one time stretched from the Syrian coast to eastern Assyria, was seriously weakened by the Hittites of Anatolia about 1360 BC. Regaining its independence and showing the remarkable capacity for rapid recuperation which is so marked a feature of its history, Assyria embarked on a policy of foreign conquest which in the thirteenth century made it one of the greatest powers of the Near East. This was the formative period of Assyrian imperial power when the objectives of foreign policy were clearly defined. The practical means for their realization was provided by the development of an extraordinarily efficient military machine; and the psychological impetus for expansion by the concept that world domination was the will of the national god, Ashur. It was at his command that wars were fought and with his support that they were won.

Three theatres of war

With the intention of removing all danger of hostile attack against their exposed frontiers and of ensuring unimpeded access to the sources of metal and other raw materials in which they were deficient, the Middle Assyrian kings of the fourteenth to tenth centuries operated in three main theatres of war. Each pre-

1 A bronze relief from the ninth century BC shows a battering ram breaking down a wall. The Assyrians invented the ram and developed it into a highly effective siege-weapon.

2 A beautifully carved ivory fragment showing an Ethiopian being slain by a lion. Once richly decorated with precious stones and gold, it was probably plundered from the Phoenicians.

sented special problems of political and military strategy. The mountain zone which curved round from the northwest to the southeast had important resources of copper, semi-precious stones and timber but it was inhabited by fierce tribesmen, prone to pillage trading caravans and to

raid down into Assyria itself. The country was so wild and difficult of access that its permanent pacification was impracticable but punitive expeditions, especially if conducted at frequent intervals, could hold the inhabitants in check and could persuade them to send the products of their land to Assyria in the form of tribute.

With Babylonia, the Assyrians always had a peculiar love-hate relationship. On the one hand they were deeply imbued with the older culture of the south, speaking the same Semitic language, writing the cuneiform script on clay tablets and worshipping the same gods.

1 A panel from a royal tomb depicts the climax of a ritual lion-hunt. With the death-blow, the king fulfils his religious duty.
2 Pottery was one of the most ancient crafts of Assyria, but with the development of stone and metal work it became purely utilitarian.

On the other hand, their interests clashed with those of Babylonia, particularly in the eastern hills where each sought exclusive control of trade. In consequence wars were of frequent occurrence. Partly for reasons of sentiment but also because the burden of conquering the southern state was out of proportion to the advan-

3 Although the Assyrians seldom used religion as an art subject, they did sometimes depict benevolent winged genii for their protection.
4 A group of Assyrian archers: military conquests were a favourite subject for relief works, which are distinguished for their stylistic vitality.

tages gained, the Assyrians preferred to discourage it from hostile activity by limited demonstrations of force. When, however, the Babylonians became too obstreperous and more particularly when they made common cause with other enemies of Assyria, more drastic action seemed necessary. The first king to conquer and occupy Babylonia was Tukulti-Ninurta who by doing so advanced Assyrian power to the shores of the Persian Gulf. But the main direction of Assyrian conquest, both now and later was westward. The Hurrians of upper Mesopotamia, who had earlier reduced Assyria to submission and were still actively hostile, were finally defeated by Shalmaneser. Beyond the Euphrates lay the fabulously rich cities of Syria and Lebanon, great commercial centres on which converged trade routes from the Near East and the Mediterranean. They were a rich prize, but in the thirteenth century they were still firmly held by the Hittites and unattainable.

Political eclipse

The national strength had, however, been overtaxed by the effort of winning and administering an empire that extended from the Euphrates to the Zagros and Persian Gulf. After only seven years Babylonia and other lands were lost, Tukulti-Ninurta was murdered by his son, and for a time Assyria became subservient to Babylonia. There was a brief revival under Tiglath-Pileser I (1115–1077 BC) who not only re-established his authority over the lands held earlier but extended it to Syria and the Mediterranean where the Hittites, whose empire had fallen about 1200 BC, were no longer there to oppose him. Yet on his death, his country once again suffered disaster, this time as the result of an eruption of Aramaean nomads from the Syrian desert. They overran all the lands bordering the Euphrates and in two centuries they had established

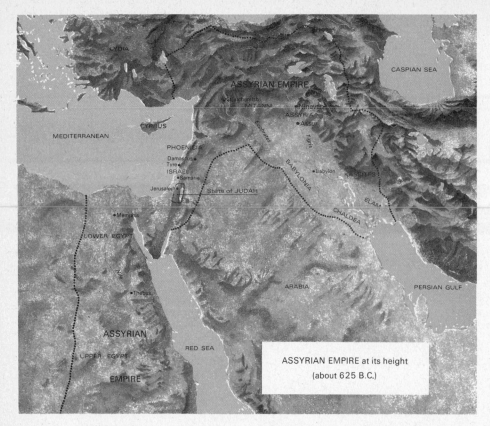

ASSYRIAN EMPIRE at its height
(about 625 B.C.)

and on the construction of great cities whose magnificence gave expression to the power of the Assyrian kings. Other kings displayed their personal grandeur in new palaces alongside those of their predecessors. These palaces functioned not only as a royal residence but also as the administrative centre of the empire and, as such, their completion was a matter for universal rejoicing. Ashur-nasir-pal (883–859 B C) celebrated the opening of his palace at Kalkhu with a great feast to which were bidden representatives of all his subjects and the 47,074 workers who had built the city.

The palaces, built of mud brick as was customary in Mesopotamia, were gorgeously decorated and sumptuously furnished, materials, artists and craftsmen being drawn from different parts of the empire. The entrances and principal doorways were flanked by huge sculptures of guardian genii such as winged human-headed bulls and winged lions. The walls of the throne-room, audience chambers and public courts were lined with limestone slabs, carved in low relief with scenes of the king fighting, receiving tribute, hunting and feasting.

The collapse

The kings who appreciated such works of art were often highly cultured men. Ashurbanipal (668–627 B C), for example, prided himself on being the equal of the best scribes in the art of cuneiform writing and amassed a huge and representative library of Babylonian and Assyrian literature. They made a practice of bringing back from their campaigns trees and plants unknown to Assyria, and Sennacherib (704–681 B C) introduced Indian cotton. Some kept zoos for strange animals such as the live crocodile sent by the king of Egypt as a present to Tiglath-Pileser I.

Despite its power and splendour the empire rested on insecure foundations. Because the population of Assyria was small in relation to the size of the territories governed, the army had to recruit large numbers of subject peoples. Tens of thousands of foreigners, mainly prisoners of war and deportees, were also brought to Assyria to labour on the royal building projects and then settled in the country. The loyalty of such people could not be depended on, especially when Assyria got into difficulties, and this dilution of native Assyrians with foreigners, both at home and in the armed forces abroad, was a major factor in the rapid collapse of Assyria following the death of Esarhaddon. His son, Ashurbanipal, lost Egypt and had to suppress a dangerous revolt by his brother the king of Babylon taking his city after a terrible siege. Weakened by these disasters, Assyria was unable to prevent the Babylonians and the Medes of Iran from regaining their independence and when in 614 B C these two powers made common cause against it, the fall of the empire was inevitable.

numerous small kingdoms in upper Mesopotamia and Syria as far south as the borders of Israel. Assyria was again reduced to its narrowest limits.

Recovery came slowly, but by the ninth century the Assyrians had begun to re-create the empire. This was only achieved after many years of bitter fighting. The wealthy Aramaean cities of Syria, supported by the Israelites and Phoenicians, put up a prolonged resistance. The strong state of Urartu, centred on Lake Van, not only opposed Assyrian expansion northwards but in the eighth century threatened its control of Syria and northwest Iran. Under Tiglath-Pileser III (745–727 B C), however, Urartu was crushed and Assyrian rule consolidated from Palestine and Cilicia in the west to Babylonia and western Iran in the east. To these conquests Esarhaddon (680–669 B C) added for a short time that of Egypt.

In some of the conquered lands, native princes ruled as Assyrian vassals, sending annual tribute and receiving in return promise of aid against external attack and internal rebellion. But vassals were prone to revolt and areas of vital importance, such as Syria and Palestine, were ruled directly through Assyrian governors, whose activities were closely supervised by the king and his ministers.

Assyria's administration

To facilitate communications between the capital and the provinces, the Assyrians developed an imperial road system with relay stations and guard posts, which was later taken over and extended by the Persians. The provincial administration was well organized and efficient and the subject peoples enjoyed the benefits of law, order, increased prosperity and peace, for the old interstate wars, such as those of Israel and Judah, had ended. The burdens of military service, forced labour

and taxation were, however, heavy and Assyrian rule was sternly enforced. Rebellious cities were sacked and their leading men executed or mutilated. Mass deportation was regularly used to break the resistance of persistently troublesome peoples, such as the Jews of whom 27,000 were transferred from Samaria to other parts of the empire in 722 B C. Such methods were customary in the ancient Near East but never before had they been so systematically employed or on so vast a scale.

Much of the wealth obtained by tribute and tax was expended on the upkeep of the armies and imperial administration,

The eagle-headed deity, Ashur – most powerful Assyrian god – holds a cone and a basket representing the receptacle for divine gifts.

Akhenaton, the heretic pharaoh

To the ancient Egyptians the gods controlled every event in life. Amenophis IV, set on changing his people's ways, had first to destroy the gods and then establish himself as god-king.

WESTERN MAN has 'compartmentalized' religion – that is, made it a thing apart. But to the Ancient Egyptian it was everything. Every event in his life – social, political, economic – was determined by the attitude of the gods. The rising of the Nile, the failure of the crops, the death of a dog – all could be attributed to the whims of the gods. But in the middle of the fourteenth century BC – during the period in Egypt's history known as the New Kingdom – a new pharaoh came to the throne. And Amenophis IV, as he was initially known, was determined on change. Paradoxically, though Egypt had grown in strength to become the greatest power in the civilized world, when Amenophis came to rule the power of the pharaohs had waned. Victories in the field were attributed to the gods. And it was the priests who served the gods – not the pharaohs – who reaped the rewards. Amenophis, determined to restore the power of the pharaohs, had to break the clergy. To do this he had to destroy the gods.

King's son dies

In the year 1400 BC, the civilized world was effectively bounded by the Black Sea and Persian mountains to the north and east, and by the Arabian deserts and adjoining seas on the south, while to the west it extended no further than Crete and the shores of Greece. Within this ancient Near Eastern world the word of Egypt's kings was law northward through Syria almost to the Euphrates, and southward for over a 1,000 miles along the valley of the Nile. In the Levant, two other great powers courted Egypt's favour and coveted her rich Syrian provinces, namely the kings of Mitanni and the kings of the Hittites.

From about 1402 to 1364 BC, Amenophis III 'the Magnificent' ruled in the utmost splendour. Egypt's future seemed brilliant and assured, and to rest with the king's eldest son Tuthmosis. But the premature death of Tuthmosis meant that it was his younger brother, the Prince Amenophis – a young man of peculiar physique and determined character – who inherited the throne instead, and as Akhenaton, the name he was to adopt, he made a unique impression on Egyptian history.

But this splendid realm was no overnight creation, nor was life at its court just one long, carefree idyll. By 1400 BC, Egypt had witnessed over 16 centuries of alternating achievement and eclipse. From about 1550 BC on, the Princes of Thebes in Upper Egypt had expelled a line of foreign rulers, reunited Egypt, recovered Nubia, and even extended their rule into Palestine and Syria. As a result, the wealth of Western Asia and Africa poured into

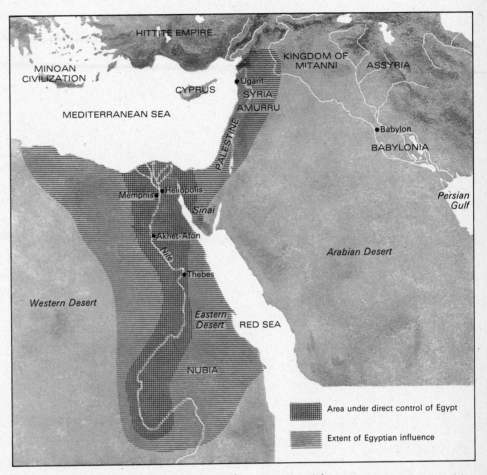

The empire at its zenith. The pharaoh Akhenaton, determined to break the power of the old gods' priests, ignored the wiles of Egypt's greedy neighbours – to the country's cost.

Egypt, and much of this was presented by the pharaohs to the giver of victory – Amun, god of Thebes. Soon, Amun's splendid temples in Thebes, especially Karnak, and his ever-growing wealth far outstripped those of any other god or institution except for the pharaohs themselves. Ancient Memphis in the north was the real capital, but Thebes served as sub-capital for Upper Egypt, as leading religious centre, and burial-place of the pharaohs.

The successors of Tuthmosis III were not prepared to risk their authority being overshadowed or undermined by either the bold theology or the economic strength of Amun. They therefore transferred some of their patronage to the two 'senior' gods, Ptah of Memphis and Re of Heliopolis, and hand-picked loyal supporters to fill the post of high priest of Amun. Amenophis III combined these policies with an outward generosity towards Amun in the form of the most impressive temple-buildings so far erected in Egypt, but with special favours going to Memphis and its notables. Thus Prince Tuthmosis served

as high priest of Ptah, and Memphite dignitaries were given the highest posts in Thebes itself. However, in court circles, greater devotion was affected for the sun-god Re, particularly as manifested in the sun's disc under the name Aton. Such was the background and atmosphere against which the younger Prince Amenophis grew up. When the time came to effect his reforms Amun and his priests were the pharaoh's first target.

At first, the new king ruled as Amenophis IV, outwardly a traditional New Kingdom pharaoh. But behind the scenes, there were tensions within the state. In his father's closing years several prominent dignitaries fell into disgrace, and their sumptuous Theban tomb-chapels were defaced. In a later inscription, Amenophis IV refers to 'evil things' occurring under Tuthmosis IV, Amenophis III and in his own first and fourth years of reign. Moreover, the new king was not content merely to juggle with priestly appointments and to favour other gods within the court circle. By Year 4, he had resolved on more direct policies. He openly promoted the worship of the sun-god above all others, Amun included. One quarry-inscription even assigns to the king the remarkable title of 'High Priest of Harakhte [the sun-god], rejoicing in the horizon in his name of Shu who is Aton'. From the same quarry came the stone for a vast temple of Aton due east of Amun's own great Karnak temple. Upon his new temple, the pharaoh conferred rich endowments of offerings and personnel; grain was issued for every god by strict ration, but for Aton with heaped-up measures! At Karnak, sun-worship assimilated to that of Amun was one thing, but a vast rival establishment was quite another matter. The resulting tensions by Year 4 simply strengthened the king's resolve to reduce the status of both Thebes and Amun.

In his fifth or sixth year, the king celebrated in Thebes a 'jubilee' or feast of the renewal of kingship, and used the occasion to make a double break with Amun and Thebes. Henceforth he called himself not *Amenophis* ('Amun is content') but *Akhenaton* ('it is well with Aton'), and he founded a new southern capital to supplant Thebes. About halfway between Memphis and Thebes, on the east bank of the Nile, Akhenaton selected for the new city a superb desert plain bounded by cliffs, with rich agricultural land on the west bank to feed its populace. Here, and here only, proclaim the boundary-inscriptions, was Akhet-Aton, Horizon of the Disc. It is known in modern times as Tell el-Amarna.

Symbol of life

The buildings of the city, which were largely mud-brick, mushroomed so rapidly that king, court and dependent populace were able to move in by Year 7. Its main roads ran north-south, parallel to the Nile; the central city was the official quarter. Close to the river rose the endless courts and reception-halls of the official palace. A bridge over the main street connected it to the king's private residence which Akhenaton shared with his queen, Nefertiti, a woman as beautiful as her origins remain mysterious – and with their six daughters. Hard by were the great open-air temple and sanctuary of Aton, the police and military headquarters, and the records office for the 'Foreign Office' archives. The tombs of the court were cut in the cliffs, their chapel-rooms enlivened with reliefs of Akhenaton and the royal family in the service of Aton.

The worship of Aton was simply that of the sun-god manifest in the solar disc, and thus depicted as a disc with rays ending in hands that present the symbol of life to the king. The main emphasis was on the creative and sustaining power of the sun, as can be seen from the great Hymn to Aton, perhaps composed by the king himself. We find a general care for nature, and for Egyptians and foreigners alike, but no profound philosophy or moral concern. The superstitions of the old cults and all the deeper values of a long-developed civilization were largely discarded and nothing put in their place. Atonism thus remained a court fad, and never stirred the Egyptians as a whole.

Through Atonism, the king claimed a more exalted role. The people had no direct access to the god. The king and his family could worship Aton but the people

were meant to worship the pharaoh – the god-king. He both served Aton and was identified with him, and they shared each other's attributes; other mortals served the king as embodiment of Aton on Earth. 'Living in truth' was simply maintaining the world-order as Akhenaton conceived and decreed that it should be. In art, this meant discarding conventional idealization of the king, so that at first the artists produced works which exaggerated the

abnormal features of Akhenaton's physique – long jaw, effeminate torso, heavy hips, symptoms of perhaps a glandular disorder. But as the artists recovered their poise, they produced a series of remarkably naturalistic statues and paintings. The latter, and the incised reliefs which adorned tomb-chapels and temples alike, were executed according to the basic conventions of Egyptian drawing, but with the addition of many lively details in the

1

2

official usage alongside the classical idiom of centuries.

In Year 9, it seems that Akhenaton held a further jubilee of himself and Aton. This time, he gave a stricter form to the titles of Aton, eliminating names like Harakhte and Shu which were common also to the discarded mythology of the rest of the gods. The persecution of Amun was especially severe, and, it may well have been at this juncture also that Akhenaton took the final step of closing the temples of Amun and ordering the destruction of the name and image of Amun (and of other gods) throughout Egypt. By this act, Aton became in practice sole recognized god, and his worship a form of monotheism. Even the name of Akhenaton's own father was not exempt; his titles of Nebmare Amenophis III were altered on the monuments to Nebmare Nebmare. Doubtless, the estates of the older temples were simply annexed to the service of Aton for his temples at Akhet-Aton and other centres. Now, it seemed, Akhenaton's triumph was complete.

Year 12 witnessed a splendid Pageant of Empire, at which the king and royal family reviewed from a pavilion a grand parade of tribute from Syria and Nubia, symbolic of the royal power. But the bustling display was in truth little more than a showy façade, for the Syrian provinces were in a state of jeopardy; nor was all well in Akhet-Aton itself.

Akhenaton did almost nothing to cultivate the alliance with Mitanni or to quell the growing local strife between rival client-princes of Palestinian and Syrian city-states, who bombarded Egypt's foreign office with claims and counterclaims. Some tried to procure the support of particular Egyptian officials for their cause, to influence the king in their favour. But Akhenaton's interest was centred upon Aton alone. The long-standing enmity between the Hittite and Mitannian states erupted into open war, and by Year

3

1 Colonnade at Deir el Bahiri showing the head and shoulders of Amenophis IV. He later changed his name to Akhenaton when he established himself as a god-king.
2 The ruins of Karnak, the great temple of Amun, the god most Egyptians thanked for their victories. Akhenaton's prime task was to break the power Amun's priests held over the people.
3 Nefertiti, the wife of Akhenaton. She was considered a great beauty of the time and this limestone bust is one of the most admired examples of Egyptian art.
4 This picture of a goose rising from a papyrus thicket is a good example of the break away from tradition by artists during Akhenaton's reign. Formality gave way to naturalism.

activities of lesser characters, in settings, and in plant and animal life. One sees the aged vizier panting along by the royal chariot, the reactions of bystanders at the reward of a high official, the layout of the palace or the great temple, waving heads of grain, or the spirited canter of chariot-horses. In language, the new movement brought about the use of current, colloquial speech, 'late Egyptian', and forms in hieroglyphic inscriptions and

4

12 or 13 of Akhenaton, the wily Hittite king Suppiluliuma had defeated Mitanni, taken over northernmost Syria, and imposed a Hittite protectorate upon the wealthy seaport of Ugarit – formerly a client of Egypt. Meanwhile, at home, the death of Akhenaton's second daughter was probably followed by that of his beautiful queen, Nefertiti. For a time, his eldest daughter became first lady and by her Akhenaton had a further daughter. But his constant failure to obtain a son, and, perhaps, failing health, led him at last to marry her off to Smenkh-ka-re (probably his half-brother) and to appoint the latter as joint-king.

Abroad, Akhenaton finally exerted the maximum diplomatic pressure to bring to

heel Aziru, ruler of the key-state of Amurru in Central Syria, whose loyalty to Egypt was more than suspect. Both the solutions to Syria and the succession were tragically short-lived. Probably within the last 18 months of Akhenaton's life and reign (Years 16–17), Aziru became closely involved with Ugarit, now linked to the Hittite Empire, with the result that Suppiluliuma imposed on him also the status of subject-ally. Thus, at one blow, the important province of Amurru and all its allied territories were lost to Egypt forever.

At home, the machinery of government was creaking under the strain of graft and petty abuse of power. Discontent was no doubt rife at various levels, particularly

among the dismissed priests and the military who had to watch the Egyptian Empire in Asia disintegrate for lack of military intervention. Economic decline probably was setting in due to the internal dislocations and the falling-off of Syrian tribute. At all events, as the reins of kingship passed from the dying hands of Akhenaton into those of Smenkh-ka-re, a youth of about 19, the open worship of the discarded gods – not least Amun – was resumed. In the young co-regent's name a funerary temple for the cult of the king and of Amun was built in western Thebes as of old. With the death of Akhenaton in Year 17, Aton's outright supremacy was over. And with the death of Smenkh-ka-re perhaps only a few months before or after Akhenaton's own decease, the royal succession was again crucial. The throne passed to a nine-year-old boy, Tutankhaton, the last royal prince.

Great adventure over

For some three years, the boy-king reigned at Akhet-Aton and Memphis, with Aton and Amun uneasily sharing the headship of the gods. Finally, in ancient Memphis, the young king issued a decree for the full restoration of the temples and cults of all the gods of Egypt from Amun downwards; Aton goes unmentioned, and the sun-god is once more Re or Harakhte. The great adventure was over.

Now known as Tutankhamun, the young king died prematurely as a mere youth; the throne then passed briefly to Ay, a close associate of the royal family, and then to Ay's Deputy of the Realm, the general Haremhab whose queen Mutnodjmet may have been the last heiress of the old royal line. He took in hand the internal renewal of Egypt, and it was left to a new dynasty of kings – the Ramessides – to attempt recovery of Egypt's role abroad. They at last brought the wheel full circle, destroying the monuments of the Aton-kings, eliminating them from official records, and grudgingly referring to Akhenaton only as 'yon criminal of Akhet-Aton'. Thereafter, the Horizon of the Disc remained almost undisturbed until, as El Amarna, its ruins, art and archives came back into human knowledge hardly a century or so ago.

What, then, did the Amarna episode achieve? Politically, it was a setback for Egypt at home and abroad. In art, its adventurous developments led to the panoramic depiction of events like the Battle of Qadesh. In language, there followed a flow of short stories and lyric poetry composed in the colloquial idiom. Culturally, older values had been challenged, but not worthily replaced. In religion, Atonism merely gave an outwardly extreme form to concepts long known and which long continued in Egypt; only the short persecution was untypical. The cult had neither a foreign origin nor any farreaching effects. In a wider context, the age of Akhenaton is one of the most complex and difficult to evaluate in all of antiquity, not least for the interaction of a powerful individual with his society; but its fascination still grips the modern imagination.

1 Another example of the 'naturalistic' art of the period – this time of Akhenaton, its patron. The new movement also saw colloquial language put on a par with the classical idioms.
2 Akhenaton's eldest daughter whom he married after Nefertiti's death. But he did not have the son he longed for by her, only a daughter.
3 The royal family making offerings to the sun. Atonism, the worship of the sun-god, was very much a court fad and never captured the enthusiasm of the people, who reverted to the old gods after Akhenaton's death.

Phoenicia sails west

Courageous travellers, shrewd merchants, the Phoenicians planted vigorous and wealthy colonies across the ancient world. But for their descendants in Carthage, a savage fate awaited.

Once the market place of the Mediterranean, the Phoenician city of Tyre was an island fortress that withstood a 13-year siege by Nebuchadnezzar. It fell in 332 BC to Alexander, who smashed an entry with the help of 334 ships and rams mounted on floating batteries.

MANY ANCIENT PEOPLES have left us traditions of art and culture: mighty monuments, elaborately decorated, attest their interests and ability; scrolls, preserved by dry climates, contain detailed written records of their thoughts and ideas, their literature and their religion. From the Phoenicians and the Carthaginians no such legacy has come, and one reason is that their energies were devoted largely to trade and manufacturing.

Theirs was a commercial pattern of society, which afforded little time for artistic achievement. For example, their position on a narrow strip of fertile coast meant that expansion was easiest by sea; they had timber for ship-building and for export, and their trading acumen was highly developed. Commerce and colonization became their main activities. Finally, such architectural and written achievements as they had were almost entirely destroyed, as warrior peoples greedy for their wealth swept over them.

The Canaanites were a Semitic race and came to the strip of land we know today as Israel, Lebanon and the coastal part of Syria, from the area of either Arabia or the Persian Gulf. Unlike most ancient peoples, they were not primarily farmers, but already, from the beginning of their known history, some time after 2900 BC, city dwellers and sailors. As sailors the Canaanites of the coastal strip are better known by the name the Greeks gave them: *Phoenicians*. This name may have come from the Greek word *phoinos* (blood red). Probably the Greeks called the Phoenicians 'red men' either because of their sea-swept, ruddy complexions, or because only they provided the 'Tyrian purple' – the red-purple dye praised and prized through the ancient world.

Possibly the Phoenicians first launched their rafts and boats into the Mediterranean in search of food for an expanding population. Their land, though fertile, was tiny, but the sea was rich in fish.

Fortified cities

In time, between 2900 BC and 1500 BC, the Phoenicians built a chain of ports with natural harbours along the 200-mile coastline that they occupied. Their chief ports, Aradus (Ruad), Byblos, Berytus (Beirut), Sidon and Tyre, were fortified cities either built on islands or backed by headlands that gave defence from land attack. Each city was an independent state ruled by a merchant-king rather than the warrior-kings of neighbouring societies. Although the cities occasionally united to form a single Phoenician state these unions never lasted long. But the cities co-operated with each other and never fought among themselves.

In addition to shipping and selling cedar wood, the Phoenicians became highly skilled at working it. The Old Testament tells several stories of trading between the Phoenicians and Israelite kings. About 950 BC, Phoenicians provided the timber to build the palace of King Solomon and the famous temple in Jerusalem. Hiram, king of Tyre, provided skilled shipbuilders to construct a fleet for Solomon, and entered into a trading alliance with him. According to the Old Testament the combined fleets of the two kings visited the land of the Queen of Sheba and brought back gold, silver, ivory, spices, precious stones, monkeys and peacocks.

The Phoenicians added to their reputation as navigators and traders by turning their cities into great manufacturing centres. They learned the techniques of neighbouring peoples, particularly the Egyptians, and adapted them for their own purpose. With great acumen, the Phoenicians imported from Europe and Africa materials such as ivory, gold, silver and silk, and worked them into furniture, jewellery, cloth and other saleable items

In 1920, archaeologists discovered thousands of earthen vessels buried in Carthage. All contain the ashes of burnt children. The Romans were horrified by the cruelty of Carthaginian religion. It derived in part from ancient Phoenician worship of such gods as the *baal, left,* and the goddess of fertility, *right.* But the urge to sacrifice came from a deeply held belief that without it the city of Carthage would fall.

for export to other Mediterranean countries. They also exported glassware, and cotton and linen cloth.

Sidon and Tyre were the main centres of the dyeing industry for which the Phoenicians were famous. Only they knew the secrets of how to produce the purple-red dye used for the robes of kings and nobles in many countries. They took the secretion from a particular sea shell called *murex,* and from it obtained purple-toned dyes of varying shades. Because the murex secreted its dye only when dead and decaying, the smell of Phoenician cities was often far from pleasant.

Papyrus for books and documents was produced at Byblos, and from the name of this city, the Greeks derived the word *biblion* (book), from which came our words *bible* and *bibliography.* Besides adopting and improving other peoples' techniques, the Phoenicians were great communicators of information. As merchants and traders they kept accounts and records, and developed an alphabet of 22 consonants. This alphabet was developed between 1600 BC and 1100 BC; some of its symbols derived from Egyptian hieroglyphics. The Greek and Roman alphabets developed from the Phoenician system.

The Phoenicians had two main kinds of ships: 'round' ships for trading and 'long' ships for war. An Assyrian wall relief from Nineveh which tells the story of the flight from Tyre of Luli, king of Sidon and Tyre, in 701 BC, shows both kinds of vessels. The *long ship* had a vertical prow and the keel of the ship extended forward below the prow to form a protruding point for ramming enemy vessels. The stern was curved. The long ship had two banks of oars, and soldiers' shields lined the side of the ship, near the deck. The ship had a central mast from which a sail could be hoisted to supplement the energies of the oarsmen. The smaller, *round ships,* used for trading, had rounded prows and sterns. They had two banks of oars, but no sails. Up to about a dozen men are shown in each ship. Later, the Phoenicians built *triremes* (galleys with three banks of oars). The sailors and ships of Phoenicia commanded great prestige for hundreds of years, and countries at war eagerly sought their aid. Phoenician ships acting as mercenaries helped the Persians in their war against Greece (499–479 BC). In the combined fleets of Persia and its allies (according to the Greek historian Herodotus) the king of Sidon ranked second in status to Xerxes, king of Persia.

Dido and the ox hide

Phoenician ships carried their trade westward to the Mediterranean coasts and islands, sometimes substituting slave-raiding or piracy for trading, according to which yielded the best profit.

Motivated perhaps by the pressure of an expanding population, the Phoenicians established scores of colonies throughout the Mediterranean. They founded Gades (Cadiz) on the Atlantic side of southern Spain, and settlements in Malta by 700 BC, and Massalia (Marseilles) by 600 BC. They established their colony of Utica (in present-day Tunisia) at about the same time as they built Gades. They may also have reached the Canaries and the west coast of Africa, and sailed round Spain to Cornwall, although Lord Leighton's famous painting showing Phoenician merchants visiting Britain (kept in the Royal Exchange, London), like so many nineteenth-century ideas about the Phoenicians, is unsupported by evidence.

In 842 BC Assyrian armies captured the cities of Phoenicia, which then declined in influence and prosperity. In Phoenician tradition, Dido, a princess of Tyre, led a mass emigration from that city westward in search of a new home. Traditionally she founded Qart Hadasht (New Capital), which we call Carthage, in 814 BC. According to legend, Dido acquired the site for Carthage by a trick of bargaining worthy of the daughter of a Phoenician merchant-prince. She struck a bargain with the existing inhabitants for a piece of land on a hill, as big as could be covered by an ox hide. Cunningly, Dido sliced the hide into thin strips and strung them out end on end to encircle the base of the whole hill, which she then claimed as the area agreed in the bargain.

The Phoenicians chose the site for Carthage carefully, and constructed its harbour skilfully. The harbour had two sections connected by a narrow channel: a roughly rectangular outer harbour about 1,600 by 1,000 feet, and a roughly

Top, the blue sea beyond Tyre yielded shells which helped to found the fortunes of Phoenician traders. They were the source of a red-purple dye prized throughout the ancient world. More talented in trade than art, the Phoenicians copied freely from neighbouring cultures. The beaten masks, *above left,* were made in Byblos; the glass paste bead, *above right,* in Carthage. Popular ornaments, the beads were worn on cords.

circular inner harbour about 1,000 feet in diameter. The inner harbour was kept for ships of war. On an island near the centre of the inner harbour was the naval head-quarters, a tall building which afforded an unobstructed view of the sea. But the secrets of the naval harbour were cunningly hidden from the prying eyes of visiting foreigners by a high double wall. More than 200 warships could be docked in the inner harbour. Ships entered both harbours direct from the sea through a single entrance about 70 feet wide, which for security could be closed with heavy chains.

The oldest district of Carthage contained the citadel. Between the citadel and the port lay a great public square similar to a Roman forum. The Carthaginian Senate stood near this square. The main city was a maze of narrow, winding streets, crammed with houses up to five or six storeys in height.

The main city covered about 30 square miles, and its 22-mile boundary was protected by a massive wall. Not until the last day of Carthage was this wall penetrated, and then only at great cost of life by invading Roman soldiers. One vital section of this wall stood about 400 feet high and 30 feet thick and was surmounted by tall military towers. Within the wall at ground level 300 elephants of war were stabled. At a higher level, approached by ramps, were stables for 4,000 horses. About 20,000 infantry and 4,000 cavalry soldiers guarded the city, and lived in barracks also built in the wall. Cunningly constructed ramparts and also a 60-foot-wide trench guarded the approaches to the outer wall.

Like their Phoenician ancestors, the Carthaginians were sea-going townsmen who lived by trade and piracy, and had little time for artistic and cultural activities. They tilled the land beyond the city and by the sixth century BC brought more than 20,000 square miles of Africa under their control. The crowded city contained up to about 200,000 people, but the whole territory of Carthage had a population of perhaps 700,000. Continuing their Phoenician tradition, the Carthaginians gradually planted colonies in the western Mediterranean and in time brought Sicily and the greater part of Spain under their control.

The Greeks and Romans had a poor opinion of the Phoenicians generally, and the Carthaginians in particular. This may have been prejudice based on jealousy of trading rivals in the case of the Greeks, who certainly admired the Carthaginians' constitutional organization (of which few details have survived) and it may have been fear of a powerful enemy in the case of the Romans. But the Carthaginians did value human life cheaply, inflicting cruel tortures not only on their enemies but on their own people, too, often in the name of religion.

A terrible religion

The migrants who founded Carthage took the Phoenician religion with them and set up temples to their gods throughout the city. Removed to the west, many Phoenician gods changed their form and took new names. One of the leading Carthaginian deities was Baal-Hammon, a horned and bearded old man, god of both sky and fertility. In later times, Baal-Hammon became fused with Kronos (the Greek god who devoured his own children). Closely associated with Baal-Hammon was the goddess Tanit – probably the Carthaginian version of the Phoenician Astarte, the Babylonian Ishtar and the Greek Aphrodite (all goddesses of love and fertility).

The sacrifice of living creatures to appease wrathful gods was fairly widespread in ancient times, including, in some places, human sacrifice. The Carthaginians acquired special odium, because they regularly practised human sacrifice and self-mutilation, long after neighbouring Mediterranean people had abandoned it. Through an error of translation nineteenth-century scholars 'discovered' a fearsome god, Moloch, thought to have been fed by the Carthaginians with live babies of noble families in exchange for his protection of the city. The concept of Moloch fired the imagination of the French writer Gustave Flaubert, who, after extensive research, completed in 1862 *Salammbô*, a novel about Carthage. In the

Phoenician cities are named in italic type

Unique among Semitic peoples, the Phoenicians took boldly to the sea. Their trading empire covered the length and breadth of the Mediterranean, and established far distant colonies.

Their greatest single legacy to history, the Phoenicians' alphabet had 22 consonants. From it, the Greek and Roman alphabets derived.

No city suffered a more savage defeat than Carthage. Three years' desperate and hopeless resistance ended in almost total destruction.

following passages he visualized the scene when the huge brass god had been dragged from its temple to the main square of Carthage for a mass sacrifice to save the city from the Romans.

'The priests of Moloch paced about on the flagstones, scanning the crowd. They needed an individual sacrifice, a voluntary offering which would spur others on. . . . To encourage the crowd, the priests drew bodkins from their girdles and slashed their faces. . . . Finally, a pale, terror-stricken man tottered out clutching a child; the small, black bundle lay briefly in the hands of the colossus before it sank into the dark opening of the god's belly. . . .'

Sacrifices to Tanit

Flaubert was mistaken: Moloch never existed. The word 'moloch' (MLK in the vowel-less Phoenician script) meant 'sacrificed offering', and in Carthage offerings were made to Baal-Hammon and Tanit. In other respects, Flaubert's dramatic account may have been nearer the truth. Diodorus, a Sicilian-Greek historian who lived at about the time of Julius Caesar, gave an account of a desperate Carthaginian sacrifice of 500 children of noble birth in 310 BC when the city of Carthage was under attack by the Sicilian Greeks. Diodorus' history is not altogether reliable, but other, more recent, evidence is

more conclusive. In a shrine to Tanit at Salammbô (near the city of Carthage) excavators found thousands of jars containing the cremated remains of children. Most of the children were under two years old when they died, but some were as old as 12. Cremated birds and animals were also found. Probably animal sacrifice gradually replaced human sacrifice in Carthage, as much earlier it had done elsewhere.

In time, the trading and colonial interests of Carthage were challenged by the rising power of Rome. In 264 BC the rivalry of the two powers exploded into bitter and desperate warfare. Three wars were fought – the *Punic Wars* – and Rome won each of them. (The word *Punic* is Latin for Phoenician.) In 146 BC Rome gained the final victory, and showed no mercy to the vanquished enemy. Those who resisted the Romans were slaughtered: those who surrendered were sold into slavery. The mighty city, set on fire during the fighting, was deliberately razed to the ground. Scipio, the conqueror of Carthage, then took the final dreadful vengeance on behalf of Rome. He cursed the ruins, and at his command a plough was symbolically drawn over the site of the city and salt dropped into the furrow. The Carthaginian way of life was dead. It was cruel and tasteless; few have mourned its passing.

Persia bursts into history

Out of the East came the Persian hordes, dispensing mercy or murder as suited them best. Great Babylon, Egypt, Greece herself paid forced tribute to the high kings in Persepolis.

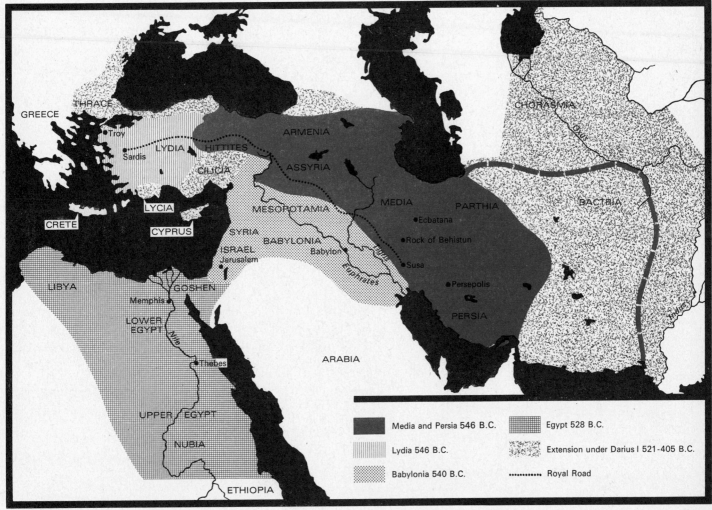

Media and Persia 546 B.C.

Lydia 546 B.C.

Babylonia 540 B.C.

Egypt 528 B.C.

Extension under Darius I 521-405 B.C.

·········· Royal Road

TO THE ORACLE at Delphi came messengers bearing gifts of gold from Croesus, King of Lydia, said to be the wealthiest man in the world. 'Should Croesus make war on the Persians?' they asked. The oracle replied: 'If Croesus should make war on the Persians, he would destroy a mighty empire.' Delighted with the reply, and failing to perceive the ambiguity in it, Croesus in the spring of 547 BC sent his armies to attack Persia. By this move he doomed his own kingdom to defeat and extinction.

Later in the same year the Persian armies swept into Sardis, capital of Lydia, and it is at this stage that Herodotus, the lively Greek chronicler, introduces to history the character of Cyrus, founder of the Persian empire. According to his account, Persian soldiers captured Croesus and brought him for judgement to Cyrus the Great, first king of Persia. Cyrus condemned him to be burnt alive. As the flames crackled at the base of the high-piled faggots, Cyrus watched the unhappy face of his fallen enemy. Suddenly Croesus groaned, and cried: 'Solon! Solon! Solon!' Cyrus commanded his interpreters to ask Croesus whom he called upon. 'I name a

man,' said Croesus, 'whose counsel I wish that all tyrants should hear.' Pressed to explain, Croesus went on to say that Solon, the great lawgiver of Athens, had once visited him and, having inspected the king's treasures, commented that wealth was of little account because no living man could be justly called happy.

A storm from Apollo

Cyrus was touched. He reflected that, being but a man himself, he was about to burn a fellow man once as powerful as himself. Relenting, Cyrus ordered the fire to be quenched, but the flames were by this time too fierce to be extinguished. Becoming aware that the Persians now had the will to reprieve him, Croesus cried out for help to the Greek god Apollo, who sent a storm to douse the flames. Cyrus, seeing that the gods favoured Croesus, liberated him, and sat him by his side as a friend.

Later, watching Persian soldiers sack Sardis, Croesus asked Cyrus what they were doing. 'Sacking your city and plundering your riches,' answered Cyrus. 'Not so,' replied Croesus. 'They are ravaging what now belongs to you.' Cyrus, ready to

At its height, the vast Persian empire extended beyond the Aral Sea in the northeast to distant Ethiopia in the southwest, from the Balkans in the northwest to the Indus in the southeast.

profit from another's wisdom, ordered his soldiers to stop the sack of Sardis. There is, however, a Babylonian account of Cyrus' war against Lydia which says of Cyrus, 'he killed its king'.

The Persians suddenly burst into history at the beginning of 547 BC (the year of Croesus' defeat) when Cyrus, king of Anshan, of the Achaemenian family, united the Medes and Persians (both Iranian peoples) into the single empire of Persia. The speed with which Cyrus defeated Croesus, whose domains he immediately annexed, took Lydia's allies (Babylon, Egypt and Sparta) by surprise. Too late to save Lydia, they nevertheless remained Cyrus' enemies, powers which, if unchecked, might destroy the rising power of Persia. Cyrus therefore decided upon a preventive war. In 540 BC he struck at mighty Babylonia, took Babylon itself in the following year, and annexed the Babylonian empire. As a result of this action Persia extended from the borders of India to the Mediterranean and Arabia. Its might appeared as a direct threat to Egypt, which was fast sinking into decline. Cyrus had created this vast empire in little more than seven years. How had he done it?

Some insight into Persian policy and diplomacy may be gained from the character of Cyrus as portrayed by Herodotus in the story of Croesus. The Persians could be ruthless in the pursuit of empire, but by comparison with their neighbours they were seldom cruel. Cyrus avoided serious revolts in his conquered territories not by instilling terror into his subjects, but rather by pursuing a policy of toleration. He ruled Babylonia with the acquiescence of a large proportion of the population, who preferred his rule to that of Nabonidus, the king whom he supplanted. Nabonidus was opposed for his earlier neglect of the New Year Festival at Babylon and for his interference with the established religion. In particular, the priests of Marduk, Babylon's city god, felt threatened by the prominence given to the god Sin. Cyrus shrewdly appeased the priests and the people by revoking the religious changes.

Conqueror of Egypt

Cyrus also earned the undying gratitude of the many Jews who had been forcibly transported to Babylon over the years. He freed from their 'Babylonian captivity' all those Jews who wanted to return to Palestine. Following a policy of assimilation rather than domination, Cyrus made Babylon one of the four capitals of his empire, took over Nabonidus' palace, and styled himself *King of Babylon*.

Cyrus long had the ambition to subdue Egypt, but the consolidation of his empire absorbed his energies for the ten years that followed the conquest of Babylon. In 530 BC he hurried eastwards to defend the Persian frontier against savage attackers. The eastern frontier held, but Cyrus was killed defending it. It was Cambyses, Cyrus' son and successor, who finally launched the attack on Egypt. Weakened by treason within its own armies, Egypt capitulated in 525 BC and was reduced to the status of a Persian province. Cambyses' thoughts then turned westward to the conquest of Carthage, but he had to abandon this ambition because his fleet was manned by Phoenician mercenaries who would not fight their Carthaginian kinsfolk. Instead, advancing up the Nile the Persian armies entered Ethiopia, but failed to capture Meroe, its capital, and had to withdraw. Towards the end of Cambyses' reign, rebellions broke out in various parts of the empire. One Gaumata, a *magian* (priest of a Median cult), usurped the throne, by impersonating Bardiya, the dead brother of Cambyses. In 521 BC, having consolidated Persian power in Egypt, Cambyses turned back to Persia. But he never reached it, and scholars think he committed suicide on the way.

After Cambyses' death, Darius, who came from another branch of the Achaemenian family, killed Gaumata and crushed the rebellions before establishing himself as King Darius I (521–486 BC). Darius was a great organiser. Over each of the empire's

satrapies (provinces) Darius set a *satrap* (governor), a general, and a secretary of state. Each acted independently of the other and reported direct to the king. Inspectors, acting for the king, visited each satrapy regularly, accompanied by troops. They were empowered to investigate the conduct of affairs as they thought fit, and to punish abuses of power by the satrap, general or secretary of state. All the satrapies (except Persia itself) paid taxes to the central government. It has been estimated that Darius received in taxes each year the equivalent of 3,500,000 gold sovereigns in cash alone. Considering the size of the empire, this amount of tax was hardly oppressive.

Darius was the first Persian king to mint money. His gold coin, the 'daric', passed as currency in many countries even outside the Persian empire. (The first king to have minted gold coins was the un-fortunate Croesus of Lydia.) Apart from monetary taxes, each satrapy had to supply a stipulated quantity of goods to Persia's central government. Egypt, for example, had to provide corn for Persia's soldiers. Darius constructed good roads throughout the Persian empire, particularly the Royal Road between Sardis and Susa, which extended for 1,500 miles. Along these roads travelled not only soldiers and traders, but mounted couriers organized in relays, who sped royal dispatches to the remotest part of the empire in less than 15 days. By order of Darius a canal (begun and abandoned by the Egyptians) was completed to link the river Nile with the Red Sea, near the present town of Suez. The Persians also kept in good repair the Egyptian-built dam at Memphis. The empire of Darius stretched from Ethiopia to China, from the south-eastern corner of Europe to India.

Following the policy of Cyrus the Great, the Persians ruled their empire from more than one city: Susa was the main capital, Ecbatana the summer capital, and Babylon the winter capital. Pasargade was also a royal capital. In these capitals each king constructed new palaces and administrative centres, improving upon the work of his predecessors. Darius I began to build his imperial capital in about 520 BC, but it took about 150 years to complete; he called it Parsa, which meant 'Persian', so the Greeks who later conquered it called it 'the city of the Persians' – Persepolis. To build Persepolis, workmen constructed a terrace about 40 feet high, covering an area about 1,500 feet by 1,000 feet. Here, Darius began the construction of palaces, audience halls, administrative buildings and monuments, all to the glory of the Achaemenian kings. Its largest buildings were the *Apadana* (audience hall of Darius) and the Hall of a Hundred Columns (the throne hall of Xerxes I, Darius' son and successor). Persepolis was built not as another political capital, but rather as a ceremonial shrine. It became the main centre of the New Year festival, held each spring.

Vines, doves and peacocks

To this festival came representatives of 28 subject peoples bearing tribute to Darius, 'king of kings'. Sculptors chiselled their images on the stone walls of the two staircases of the terrace, where they can still be seen. From Africa came Ethiopians bringing a giraffe, Somalis guiding a horse-drawn chariot, and Egyptians leading a bull. From the east came Bactrians with a two-humped camel; Indians with a donkey, axes and other gifts carried in a pair of baskets suspended from a pole across a man's shoulders; and Scythians from Samarkand, bringing daggers, bracelets and a horse. From Persia's Greek possessions came Thracians and Macedonians bringing shields, spears and another horse. From nearer territories, came Arabs offering cloth and a one-humped camel; Assyrians with a bull; Elamites with bows, driving a lioness with two cubs; and Babylonians bearing gifts of gold and silver.

The Achaemenian kings took a personal interest in forestry and agriculture. In the conquered Mediterranean lands the Persians exploited the timber, but replanted trees systematically. Darius ordered fruit trees from the fertile areas west of the Euphrates to be transplanted to Persia's eastern satrapies. The Persians experimented with the vine, and introduced pistachios into Syria. They planted sesame in Egypt, and rice in the Tigris-Euphrates area. In the wake of Persian soldiers, white doves and peacocks made their first appearance in Europe.

Persia's food was produced mainly on large estates worked by serfs, who were bound to the land and purchased or sold with it, and by slaves captured in war. Barley, wheat, olives and grapes were grown, and rich and poor ate fish, bread and oil, and drank wine. Cattle, sheep and goats were bred for food, and horses, mules and donkeys for the army or for trans-

Guarded by a pair of huge, man-headed bulls, the gate-house of Persepolis, **1**, led to a city whose ruins, **2**, rising from the dusty, windswept plains of today's Iran, still convey the might of the Persian empire in its glory – a power deliberately symbolized in the relief of a lion slaying a bull, **5**, from the Great Staircase. The many columns of the king's palace were topped by pairs of animals like these fierce griffins, **3**, set back to back and brilliantly painted. The Persians borrowed freely from the nations they conquered; their pillared palaces were inspired by Egyptian architecture, the double animals follow old Elamite and Babylonian traditions, while the masons were probably Greek. Among the most skilled of native craftsmen must have been the goldsmiths who made the griffin armlet, **4**, found in the famous Oxus treasure and now in the British Museum, and the gold buckle, **6**, set with turquoises, which belonged to Darius I. **5**

Decorative but highly formal, the spirit of Persian art is clearly shown in the vase mounted on kneeling rams, *top left,* and the subtly smiling winged Sphinx, *right.* The gaiety of the great New Year festival at Persepolis, however, comes through even the stylized frieze, *top right*: long rows of Medes, in round head-dresses, and Persians, in fluted ones, some carrying lotus-flowers, are holding hands or touching each other's shoulders in a friendly fashion. But the great feature of that festival was the arrival of delegations from all the 28 subject nations to pay homage to the king. *Far right,* up the Great Staircase to the Audience Hall of Darius I troop for ever tribute-bearers bringing animals and gold – though now the palace is ruined and weeds grow on the stairs.

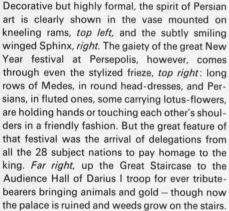

portation. Bees provided honey for sweetening matter.

The large estates were mainly self-sufficient. Some of the serfs made clothing, furniture and other items of everyday life. Under the Achaemenian kings the standard of living rose in most parts of the empire. Babylon, for example, probably had a higher standard of living than Greece did at that time. Internal and external trade expanded fast as money came into general circulation. At the beginning of Xerxes' reign (486 BC), workmen at Persepolis received a third of their pay in cash and two-thirds in goods; by the end of it (465 BC), they received two-thirds of their pay in cash.

Magic and fire worship

The empire was self-sufficient not only in timber but also in metals, particularly copper, iron and silver. Large quantities of stone, quarried in the mountains of Elam (north of the Persian Gulf), provided the material to build the royal capitals. Shipwrights constructed Persian vessels of up to 200 tons that could sail up to 80 nautical miles a day. These plied up and down the Nile, Tigris and Euphrates rivers. The Achaemenian kings developed Persia's ports and regulated shipping. Captains had to carry ships' documents, and sailors were given ranks that corresponded with their skill.

Persia rose to political supremacy before it developed its own distinctive art. At first the Persians borrowed and skilfully adapted the arts of other peoples – particularly the Babylonians and Greeks. Later, in Persepolis and other royal cities, they developed a Persian style of architecture – sculpture favouring particularly the use of columns. They painted this stonework in bright colours. The Persians borrowed the cuneiform (wedge-shaped) writing of the Babylonians and improved it for their own use. This particular writing (which did not survive the Achaemenian dynasty) is recorded in a historically important document carved on the inaccessible Rock of Behistun (near present-day Kermanshah). This document shows Darius standing before defeated rebel chiefs and traitors. Ahura-Mazda, god of the Achaemenian family, dominates the scene.

The Persian religion in Darius' time was a complex amalgamation of Babylonian and Aryan beliefs, together with earlier, local cults. The Magi (from whom the word *magic* comes) were a sect of priests who practised magic rites and ceremonies. They were probably Median rather than

Persian in origin, and became important for a while when Gaumata usurped the throne of Cambyses. They declined in influence under the Achaemenian kings whose own god, Ahura-Mazda, is quoted and portrayed in practically every document and sculpture that has survived the Achaemenian period. As Darius was king of kings, so the winged Ahura-Mazda was gods of gods, and was worshipped as 'protector of the just king'.

Towards the end of his reign, Darius was increasingly preoccupied with campaigns against the Greeks. After his death in 486 BC his successors became embroiled in wars with Greece for more than 150 years. Alexander of Macedon finally defeated Darius III, the last Achaemenian king, in 330 BC. Darius III was killed by one of his own generals, the Achaemenians disappeared from history, and the Persian domains became part of Alexander's empire. A year before the final defeat, Alexander committed an act of vandalism uncharacteristic of him. Having taken Persepolis, he destroyed its magnificent palaces by fire. Only the stones endured to remind future generations of the glory of the Achaemenians – the kings of kings.

China burns her books

'History', said the Emperor, 'begins with me.' The wisdom of China flamed under his soldiers' torches. But a long-dead philosopher, Confucius, had left a legacy which was indestructible.

Master K'ung to his pupils, Confucius to the Western world, the philosopher of ancient China, *above*, was to outlast the fury of the emperor who built the Great Wall, *right*. Imperial efforts to smash Confucianism failed absolutely.

IN THE third century BC the efficient military state of Ch'in defeated and crippled its neighbours Han and Wei. Having annexed much of the Han-Wei territories, Ch'in struck at Chu and Chi and further expanded its territory. Contemptuously marching through Han territory, the Ch'in armies turned against the mighty state of Chao, which threw 450,000 soldiers into the desperate defence of a threatened border town.

By a combination of intrigue and tactics the Ch'in ruler lured Chao's soldiers away from their fortifications, encircled them, and slowly starved them out. The Ch'in armies then fell upon the emaciated Chao soldiers and cut them down, putting every prisoner to the sword. The way lay open for the achievement of Ch'in's ultimate ambition. Between 230 and 221 BC Ying Cheng, Prince of Ch'in, finally annexed the remaining territories of Han, Wei, Chu, Chi and Chao; together with those of the only remaining state, Yen. The enfeebled 800-year-old Chou dynasty had finally disappeared in about 256 BC. By 221 BC Ch'in incorporated the six conquered states into a single empire that we have since called, after Ch'in, *China*.

The civilizations of Egypt, Sumeria, Babylon and Greece had already passed their zenith; Indian culture flourished; Rome was locked in its long struggle with Carthage. But to Ying Cheng, China was the world: beyond its frontiers lived only barbarians. To keep them out he constructed across northern China the Great Wall, linking earlier walls into a 3,000-mile system (allowing for the twists and turns of mountains and valleys). Ying Cheng decreed that work on the wall should never cease and that his dynasty should last for ever. He commanded that henceforth he should be titled *First Emperor* and his successors *Second, Third* and *Fourth Emperors,* and so on.

Advised by his Grand Councillor, Li Ssu, a scholar who had risen from poverty, the Ch'in Emperor decided that history began with himself. He set himself the task of reorganizing China and stamping out all marks of the past. Local boundaries disappeared and statues toppled, but ideas were not so easily disposed of. Stung by a scholar's criticism of his flattery of the emperor, Li Ssu retaliated by striking at scholarship itself. In a memorandum to the emperor he observed that as the world had been unified and brought under a single law it was now the business of the common people to concentrate their efforts in agriculture and industry, while the role of scholars was to apply their intellect to law and administration. Instead of attending to their proper business, complained Li Ssu, scholars were probing into the past in order to criticize the present. This, he claimed, caused distrust and confusion in the land.

Li Ssu then came quickly to the point. 'I advise your majesty to have destroyed, all ancient records (other than those of Ch'in), and all books on poetry, history, and philosophy except those in the royal library. Furthermore, I recommend that all who recite or discuss these subjects, be executed, and that those who complain against your majesty's government, in the name of tradition should, together with their families, be beheaded.' The Ch'in Emperor accepted this advice, which was codified, issued as an imperial decree, and put into effect.

A great burning of books followed. Much of the wisdom of ancient China, preserved so carefully for generations on bamboo and wooden tablets, disappeared in smoke. Then the public executioners busied themselves, ridding China of hundreds of its greatest scholars and sages. But the greatest atrocity was yet to come.

It had long irked Li Ssu, a scholar of the *Legalist* school, that followers of Master K'ung, a philosopher who had died more than two and a half centuries before, commanded more influence among intellectuals than did the Legalists. The Grand Councillor therefore advised the Ch'in Emperor that the K'ung scholars were dangerous subversive men whose sly tongues could bring down his dynasty. The Emperor took little convincing: a year after the burning of the books he had 460 K'ung scholars rounded up and buried alive. That, thought the Emperor, was the end of them and their ideas!

In fact he was mistaken. The Emperor and his Grand Councillor had succeeded in destroying neither all the K'ung scholars nor their books. The philosophy that the Ch'in Emperor feared and hated was to survive his dynasty by more than 2,000 years.

Who were these K'ung scholars? Their history had begun more than three centuries before. In about 551 BC in the town of Tsou in eastern China there was born to the wife of an elderly minor official surnamed K'ung, a second son whom she called Ch'iu. K'ung Ch'iu grew up with a serious view of life and at 15 decided to devote his life to learning. His father had died when he was only three, his mother when he was 17. K'ung Ch'iu set up a school in his own house. His scholars called him K'ung Fu Tzu (K'ung the Master). Today he is better known in the West by his Latinized name, Confucius, and his followers are called Confucians.

A ceremonial code

Confucius advocated the six traditional branches of learning, which were: archery, carriage driving, mathematics, writing, music and ritual. Innately conservative, Confucius was fascinated by the last of these disciplines. He believed that, as the ideally perfect society was unattainable, the next best thing was to organize social relationships through a complex code that laid down strict rules of behaviour for each kind of person.

Confucius did not accept the religious ideas of his times, and was sceptical of the supernatural. He told his scholars: 'We have not yet known life; how can we know about death?'

Confucius was the ultimate conservative. He was not so much the creator of a new system of ethics and behaviour as a systematizer of old ones. He practised *Li*, a ceremonial code of social and religious behaviour, and maintained that it was the true code for a gentleman to follow. The Li code embraced beliefs, ethics, manners, deportment, social behaviour, ceremony and statecraft. Many of the students who came to Confucius for instruction profited so much from his teaching that they gained high places in government service. After Confucius' death in 479 BC, his students collected his sayings in the *Lun Yü (The Analects)*.

It was important for a man to study, taught Confucius, not merely to gain knowledge but rather to improve his character. Learning was not an end in itself; when a man had taken the trouble to learn something, he should put it to practical use. The man who sought the good life should be ready to learn from anyone, irrespective of whatever he ranked higher or lower socially than himself.

Confucius taught that in all things a man should be a *chüntzu* (gentleman). Whether or not a man was a chüntzu depended upon his character and his behaviour; it had nothing to do with his birth. The chüntzu would never allow his desires to deflect him from doing what he thought was right. His conduct would be prudent and cautious; neither extreme nor ostentatious. He would be known as an honest man who kept his promises and remained true to his principles. To others he would be scrupulously fair. If others refused his advice he would not lose his temper. He would in any case always strive to be calm and avoid demonstrative words or behaviour.

The chüntzu would naturally follow the rules and etiquette of *Li*. But he would observe the principle rather than the form; he would act intelligently rather than mechanically. He would meticulously observe and practise the correct rituals and ceremonies and adjust his behaviour according to what was appropriate for each class and rank of person. But he would do this not because convention demanded it, but rather because he genuinely believed that this was the best thing to do.

The true chüntzu would, by example, civilize and educate those he met, and persuade through his superior moral power. He would be courageous, calm and self assured, but neither pompous nor hypercritical. Whatever task he undertook he would carry out to the best of his ability. He would be a natural leader, but if none recognized his worth and he went unrewarded he would not be resentful. Such was the ideal gentleman, taught Confucius. Few could reach such perfection but all might strive towards it.

Besides propagating his ideas by teaching, Confucius turned to writing. Ever a lover of the past, which he tended to idealize as a golden age, he revised and edited a book of history, *Spring and Autumn Annals*. He probably also edited a collection of earlier writings: the *Book of Changes*, the *Book of History*, the *Book of Songs* and the *Book of Rites*. These four books and the *Annals* are still known to the Chinese as 'The Five Classics'. It was two of these classics, the *Book of History* and the *Book of Songs* which incurred the

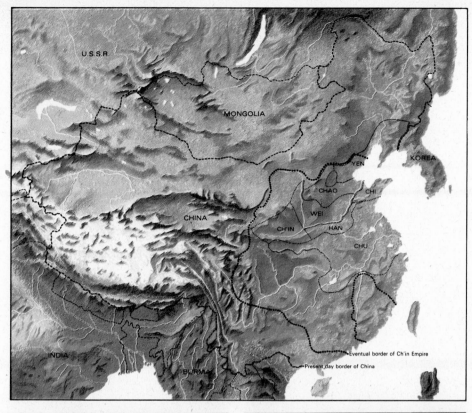

special wrath of the Ch'in Emperor nearly three centuries later.

In propagating the good life and pushing forward his views on how rulers should go about their business, Confucius cared less for power than for doing what he thought was right. He filled with distinction various government posts in Lu, his home state, including that of magistrate and Minister of Justice. His fame spread and he travelled far and wide for about 13 years, but never gained a post of great power. Not everyone agreed with his views.

One tale about Confucius – possibly no more than a legend – tells how he once met Lao-tzu. This sage (whom some scholars regard as a mythical character) is the reputed founder of *Taoism,* which alongside Confucianism has been a Chinese religion and philosophy for about 2,500 years. According to the story, Lao-tzu, the older of the two sages, thought very little of Confucius. The old man upbraided Confucius for harping on the past, expressed his disbelief in the virtues of learning and advised him to stop meddling in other people's affairs.

After the death of Confucius in 479 BC, his fame spread; his followers grew in number and influence and modified his

One of a handful of warring states in China's third century BC, Ch'in fought its way to supremacy over its neighbours. Its name survives, as China, today. Warriors of ancient China, such as the horseman, *far left,* dealt savagely with defeated enemies. But the artists and craftsmen of the country were masters of a delicate and civilized workmanship which closely reflects the values of contemporary thinkers and philosophers. *Centre,* this ritual vessel, created in the eighth century BC, pre-dates Confucius but shows in its formal interlacing ribbon decoration the same concern with rational processes that the philosopher shared. *Left, below left,* and *below right,* are three carvings in jade – regarded in China as the most precious of stones. The White Tiger, carved in white jade, was a mythical beast symbolic of the West. The *pi* disc symbolized heaven, with the sun its centre. Both artists and philosophers believed that jade has virtues closely comparable to human virtues. A dictionary of the second century AD described jade as a stone that is beautiful. 'There is warmth in its lustre and brilliancy, this is the manner of kindness . . . it may be broken but cannot be twisted, this is the manner of bravery.'

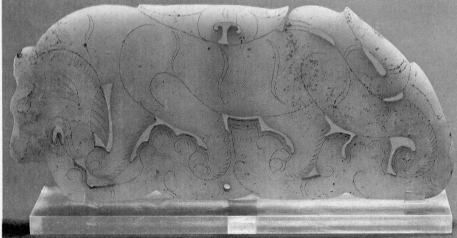

While the Han dynasty ruled in China, from 206 BC to AD 220, Confucian scholars were influential both in government and education.

The bronze bear, *top,* and warrior leading a bullock cart, *right,* date from this period. Simple and clear-cut art forms characterize

the epoch, in contrast to the more magical quality of bronze work of the fourth century BC, from which the bull's head, *left,* derives.

doctrines. The greatest disciple of Confucius, Meng K'o (*c.* 370–*c.* 290 BC), better known by his Latinized name, *Mencius,* expounded Confucianism about 200 years after the death of Confucius. Although he had advised against ostentatious behaviour, Confucius had never been a puritan and he abhorred asceticism. Not so Mo Ti, a peasant philosopher born at about the time that Confucius died. Mo Ti also drew his inspiration from the past, but despised the ceremony-loving Confucianites. Mo Ti championed the cause of the peasants and puritanically stressed the virtues of hard work. He also stressed the ideal of universal love. If everyone loved others as himself, taught Mo Ti, the troubles of society would disappear. He strongly opposed the ceremonial pomp of the Confucians.

Another of the many schools of philosophy that flourished in China between the sixth and third centuries BC was the *Legalist* school, of which mention has already been made. The Legalists rejected both the moral standards of the Confucianists and the democratic leanings of the Mohists (followers of Mo Ti's doctrines). The Legalists believed that power should be exercised by a strong man – a benevolent and efficient dictator who would rule with a rod of iron. To Legalists

like Li Ssu, Grand Councillor of the Ch'in Empire, the First Emperor was the ideal ruler, whose dynasty should last for ever.

The Ch'in despotism tore the peasants from their farms and families and sent hundreds of thousands of them to build the Great Wall and to construct new military roads. Other peasants slaved at building the Emperor a sumptuous palace, one floor of which could hold 10,000 people. Still more conscripts, organized into gangs like convicts, sweated at constructing for the Emperor, a magnificent tomb 500 feet high and 1½ miles in circumference. Hatred of the régime grew.

Fall of the Ch'in Empire

In 209 BC, during the reign of the Second Emperor, 900 conscript soldiers bound for the frontier to take up general duties, found their route blocked by floods. To be late in reaching their destination would bring the punishment of death. In desperation they killed their commander and raised the cry of revolt against tyranny. The revolution spread like wildfire from province to province as peasants armed themselves with sharpened bamboo sticks and joined the fight. Three years later the capital of the mighty Ch'in Empire fell to soldiers led by Liu Pang, a junior official. In 202 BC Liu Pang took the title of Eminent

Emperor, and became first Emperor of the Han dynasty which was to last more than 400 years.

The tragedy of the burning of the books at the orders of Li Ssu and the Ch'in Emperor had an even more disastrous sequel. When Liu Pang's peasant armies stormed the Ch'in capital, the royal library – the only surviving complete collection of China's ancient classics – caught fire. It burned for three months and all its treasures perished.

The first Han Emperor was a man of action who came from an illiterate family. He had scant respect for the pedantry and ceremonies of the Li scholars and – so the records tell – showed his contempt by urinating in their high hats. But, conqueror though he was, Liu Pang could not govern an empire competently. Nor could his quarrelsome, uneducated soldier-ministers. The Han Emperor soon found himself obliged to call in the Confucians to establish a court procedure. Their success in doing this ensured a stable government; as a result they came back into favour.

Emperors of the T'ang dynasty (AD 618–907) built temples for the worship of Confucius. Even the Manchu emperors, last rulers of China, publicly worshipped Confucius as a god. When their empire collapsed in 1911, his cult went into decline.

Ancient India's modern king

A youthful Greek conqueror, a magnificent Eastern monarch and an Indian philosopher who anticipated Machiavelli all combined to produce a truly great civilization of the ancient world.

IN 330 BC, Alexander the Great, king of the ancient Greek land of Macedonia, finally defeated the mighty empire of Persia and annexed it to his own domains. Fired with the ambition of further conquest, he turned eastwards into Parthia, Bactria, Sogdiana (Bokhara), and finally, India. In 326 BC his troops crossed the river Indus into the Punjab.

For four years (330–326 BC) his army marched through unknown mountains and deserts, braving burning heat, biting snow and disastrous floods, fighting fiercely all the way. The young conqueror would have pushed further eastwards, perhaps to China or south-eastern Asia, but in the Punjab his own troops forced Alexander to halt. The Macedonian army then returned to the Indus, and leaving garrisons behind, followed the river southwards to Pattala, near the Indian Ocean. There, the Macedonian army split into two. Part of its forces put to sea and sailed to the Persian Gulf. The main body marched back across the mountains of Persia. The two forces linked near Susa, the old Persian capital, and pressed on to Babylon. There, in 323 BC, at the age of only 33 and at the height of his power, Alexander died of malaria.

Chandragupta gains power

The departure of Alexander from India caused a power vacuum into which stepped Chandragupta Maurya, an adventurer from a low-caste family. From the time of Chandragupta, a reasonably reliable history of India begins to take shape.

According to the works of Greek and Roman historians, including Plutarch, Chandragupta as a youth helped the Macedonians in their invasion of India, but later spoke too boldly to Alexander, who ordered him to be put to death. The story continues that Chandragupta escaped and mustered an army which drove the remaining Greek garrisons out of India. In about 321 BC, Chandragupta defeated the Nandas, a dynasty which ruled the state of Magadha in modern Bihar, and captured their capital of Pataliputra (now Patna). Soon, Chandragupta brought most of northern India under his control, and he went on to capture state after state southwards as far as the Narbada river.

In about 305 BC, when Seleucus Nicator, the Macedonian governor of Babylon, crossed the Indus from Bactria, Chandragupta met and fought him with a vast army. Some sources say that Chandragupta mustered 600,000 infantry, 30,000 cavalry, 9,000 war elephants and many chariots. Chandragupta seems to have got the best of the encounter, but the affair ended amicably. Seleucus ceded parts of present-day Afghanistan to Chandragupta

The North Torana, sculpted sometime between the second century BC and the first century AD, is a remarkable example of how the techniques of the woodcarver can be applied to solid stone. The work is covered with reliefs and sculptures in the round. The North Torana stands at Sanchi.

in exchange for 500 elephants, and later Chandragupta married a Macedonian woman who may have been Seleucus' daughter. In all these adventures and achievements Chandragupta was assisted and advised by his minister, Kautilya, a shrewd brahman often called 'the Machiavelli of India'.

Kautilya, it is said, had deserted Pataliputra after being insulted by the Nanda king. Kautilya is believed to be the author of the *Arthasastra* (Manual of Politics), a treatise instructing a would-be king how to gain and hold power. The *Arthasastra* reads strangely like Machiavelli's *Prince,* which was written about 1,800 years later. The man who aspires to be king, advised Kautilya (if indeed he was the original author) should always act according to what is expedient in particular circumstances. He should not consider himself bound by the prevailing moral code. Kautilya laid down in detail the discipline that an efficient king should follow. The king, he said, should be energetic. His subjects would then respond to his example by being energetic in turn.

The *Arthasastra* laid down a strict code of conduct for the king, including a time-table of how he should spend his time. The king's day should begin with a visit from the priest. The king should allot one and a half hours to religious observances, three hours for bathing, taking meals and private study, and four and a half hours for sleep. If he so wished, the king should spend up to an hour and a half in recreation, and the remainder of his time should be given to affairs of state. His day should end with evening prayers.

India – land of villages

Much of our knowledge of Chandragupta's India comes from fragments of accounts left by Megasthenes, Seleucus' ambassador at Chandragupta's court. Unfortunately only parts of Megasthenes' records are now known. Contemporary Indian accounts, particularly dates, are not very reliable. All accounts suggest, however, that Chandragupta's government was very efficient for the times, even though the king ruled despotically and his officials could not be cured of corruption.

Many of the tasks that Chandragupta's government tackled parallel administrative problems faced by India's present government. Then as now, India was a land of villages, each with its headman and *panchayat* (council of elders). Officials of the central government supervised groups of villages and organized irrigation systems. The government built new villages in remote areas in order to bring about a more balanced distribution of the population. It also stockpiled food to give relief in times of famine. Farmers paid taxes to the central government, and provided most of its income.

Pataliputra, the capital, was run by a board of 30 members which enforced strict regulations to control social and economic life. The city had administrative departments for finance, harbours, public buildings, sanitation and water supply. City officials carried out censuses, kept records of property dealings and ownership, and generally busied themselves with the tasks of government much as local government officials do today. As Indian houses and public buildings were constructed almost entirely of wood, fires broke out frequently. To guard against this hazard, officials enforced elaborate fire precautions. They kept water containers in the streets and forced householders to keep fire-fighting appliances ready in their houses. People who littered or dirtied the streets were liable to be fined. The government officials issued coin money and levied a five-per-cent tax on gambling, which was permitted at hotels and inns. Its officials collected heavy taxes which paid the costs of administration and supported Chandragupta's large standing army.

Patterns of administration

The *Arthasastra* laid down rules of military strategy and tactics, and several other books were written on the art of war. The ministry of defence had various departments to control the infantry, the cavalry, the elephants, the chariots, the navy, supply and so on. It was laid down that the lives of prisoners captured in war should be spared.

Chandragupta's engineers and surveyors constructed and maintained roads and canals. They surveyed land and erected signposts and distance indicators. Like the Achaemenian kings of Persia (whose dynasty was destroyed by Alexander the Great) Chandragupta had his own Royal Road constructed. This highway linked Pataliputra with the northwestern outposts of his empire. A special task of the administrators was to supervise and regulate occupations bound up with the land, such as mining, tree-felling and woodworking.

Justice was efficiently dispensed, consistent with Kautilya's doctrine that none should be allowed to oppress the people except the king himself. Chandragupta often judged cases personally, and by all accounts his judgements were generally fair. The law punished serious crimes with death or mutilation. But corruption was widespread in the administration and so firmly rooted that it baffled even the intelligence of Kautilya, who confessed himself unable to prevent it.

Rice was the staple food, and rice beer was a popular drink on festive occasions,

when a little drunkenness was socially acceptable. Meat was eaten in Chandragupta's India to a far greater extent than it is today. Even brahmins ate meat, but not the flesh of horned cattle. According to Megasthenes, a caste system based on occupations had already formed, but it was more fluid, less set, than it later became.

Although Chandragupta seems to have profited by Kautilya's advice in statecraft, the king certainly did not live a life of austerity. Megasthenes recorded that Chandragupta's palace, set in an ornamental park, was more magnificent than the most splendid palaces of Persia. The king's palace, like all early buildings of northern India, was built of wood, so no part of it survives. The king loved the company of women. He kept a plentiful harem, and teams of girls danced and played music for his entertainment. Slave girls prepared and served his food and drink and attended to his every whim. Other slave girls humoured him by perpetually massaging his body with ebony rollers while he attended to affairs of state and received officials and ambassadors. Tough, trained women guards protected his palace.

When the king went hunting, mounted on an elephant and dressed in splendid clothes, he was inevitably accompanied by teams of women attendants. Soldiers escorted the royal procession and drummers gave warning of its approach. The route was cleared and cordoned off in advance of the royal party and any people who strayed in the king's path risked the punishment of death. Gladiatorial contests were staged for his amusement, and bulls, elephants and rhinoceroses were set to fight for the entertainment of the king and his court.

Peace under despotism

Under the despotic but efficient rule of Chandragupta and Kautilya, India prospered and enjoyed comparative peace. The king employed agents to spy on his officials and report to him any suspicions they had of disloyalty or corruption on the part of his administrators. Chandragupta ruthlessly punished those suspected of disobeying his will. Not surprisingly, he made many enemies. He took elaborate precautions against assassination. Official tasters tested his food and wine against poison and it is said that he changed his bedroom every night to avoid being murdered in his sleep.

In the time of Chandragupta and his immediate successors India passed through a period of great religious experiment. Hinduism, already very old, was challenged by three vigorous sects: Jains, Ajivikas and Buddhists. These three sects stemmed from the doctrine of three great teachers who lived about 300 years before Chandragupta's reign: Mahavira, Gosala Maskariputra and Siddhartha Gautama, called the *Buddha* (Enlightened One). The three sects came to possess great influence during the period of the Maurya dynasty.

The Jains, who believed their religion to be extremely old, held that time was divided into immensely long eras, and that in each era 24 perfect beings, called *Tirthankaras*, or *Jinas*, appeared on Earth. According to Jain tradition, Mahavira (Great Soul), who lived between about 599 and 527 BC, was the 24th Tirthankara of the present era. The Jains opposed all

2

3

4

The history, thought and culture of a people is often more expressively revealed through its art than by any other means. As in the West, themes of religious worship and awe for the king permeate Indian art. The Lion Capital of Asoka (1) surmounted a column on the shaft of which was carved an edict of the emperor. The lions may have had a religious significance as well as being dramatic symbols of royal power. Among the architectural forms adopted by the Buddhists was the *stupa* (2), which served as a storehouse for religious relics and was designed to represent the cosmic mountain, the pivot of the world. This stupa, located at Sanchi, is known for the exceptional beauty of its sculptures and *torana*, or gateways. The partially destroyed relief (3) is representative of the Gandhara school, and depicts the future Buddha as a student. Before him a worshipper prostrates himself. The themes depicted by the pediment of the Gandhara school (4) are obviously Indian, but the influence of Hellenistic concepts in a work produced hundreds of years later shows the role played by Alexander in the creation of an Indian empire.

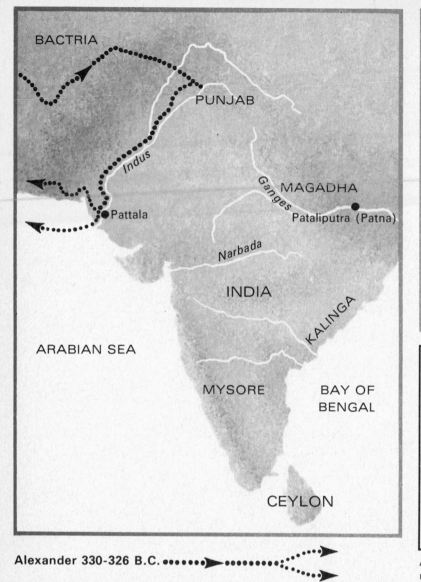

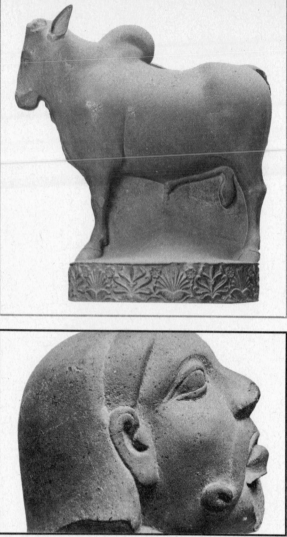

Alexander the Great's invasion of the Punjab and his subsequent retreat, *left*, laid the groundwork for an indigenous empire. The sandstone statues, *top* and *bottom*, date from this period.

kinds of killing, lived as ascetics, and renounced unnecessary material possessions to the point of abandoning clothing in favour of nudity. They became very strong in eastern India, and Chandragupta himself became a Jain. Towards the end of his reign, so many Jains had withdrawn from society to live in monasteries that the starving people of India could no longer support them. The Jain monks therefore moved south, possibly led by Chandragupta himself, and established themselves at Sravana Belgola in Mysore. This place became a great shrine of Jainism and remains so to this day. It is known to many visitors by the massive image of a Jain saint, cut from rock in the tenth century AD. According to Jain tradition, Chandragupta died a penitent at Sravana Belgola, slowly starving himself to death (in 298 BC) as was the custom of Jain saints.

The Ajivikas also became prominent in Maurya times. Their leader, Gosala Maskariputra (who died about 484 BC), was a contemporary of both Mahavira and the Buddha. Ajivikas and Jains had much in common. Both sects believed that their religions dated from extremely ancient times. Both practised asceticism and nudity. The Ajivikas were complete determinists who believed that nothing could

alter the course of destiny. They therefore disagreed profoundly with Hindus who believed that a man's deeds in this life determined the shape and circumstances of his next life on Earth. If the Ajivikas recorded their belief and doctrines, none of their scriptures have survived. Unlike the Jains, the Ajivikas did not flourish for long. After Maurya times they survived in a small area of eastern Mysore, but disappeared in the fourteenth century AD.

Figs, wine and a sophist

When Chandragupta died he was succeeded in 298 BC by his son, Bindusara. Little is known for certain about this king, but according to Athenaeus (a Greek writer) he once requested from Antiochus I, the Greek king of Syria, gifts of figs, wine and a *sophist* (Greek philosopher-teacher). The story tells that Bindusara received his wine and figs, but Antiochus did not send a sophist. The tale suggests that Bindusara, like other kings of the Mauryan dynasty, wished to keep up with the philosophies of the time. Bindusara extended the Maurya empire further into southern India, and Tamil poets refer to his chariots speeding across the land with white pennants reflecting the rays of the sun. Most of southern India surrendered to Bindusara without a fight.

At Bindusara's death in 272 BC, his son Asoka became king and began the conquest of Kalinga (now Andhra Pradesh and Orissa) in eastern India. According to Asoka himself, he killed 100,000 Kalingans, deported 150,000 and brought about the death of hundreds of thousands of others. The terrible carnage finally struck the king with remorse. In expiation of his crimes he turned to meditation, and within three years became a zealous Buddhist. The transformation of this remarkable king from ruthless warlord to near-pacifist is one of the strangest events in history. Asoka became the ideal philosopher-king. His domains included parts of present-day Afghanistan and most of Pakistan and India (except the extreme south). Until his death in 232 BC the vast empire was governed according to the doctrines of Buddhism – the most influential of India's non-Hindu religions and philosophies. In his reign, a highly important council was held in Pataliputra to define the exact beliefs of Buddhism, and the first stirrings of Buddhist missionary activity are recorded at this time.

After Asoka, the empire of the Maurya kings began to break up; finally, the commander-in-chief of the last Maurya assassinated his master in 185 BC, to found a dynasty of his own.

The land that Cleopatra lost

Under the Ptolemies Egypt boomed as a trading nation. State-run banks, scientific agriculture, a splendid library stored with half a million books lay to its credit. But it was not to last.

Timeless symbol of the desert, the camel, *left,* was introduced into Egypt by the Ptolemies, and has been stalking over her hot sands ever since.

Its ability to carry goods across the desert between the Nile and Red Sea turned Ptolemaic Egypt into a great trading nation. *Right,* crumb-

ling heads of the cow goddess Hathor surmount columns of her vast temple at Dendera, begun under the Ptolemies and completed by Augustus.

INTO MEMPHIS, capital of Egypt, rode Alexander the Great, joyfully hailed as liberator by the people. The year was 331 B C. Most of the vast Persian empire already lay in Alexander's hand; now he had come to claim its most eastern province. The delighted Egyptians crowned him pharaoh; he in turn paid homage to their gods.

Alexander went on to Siwa, an oasis in the Libyan desert, where he is said to have consulted the oracle of Ammon, who to the Greeks was the same god as Zeus. There, the priest of the oracle is said to have greeted him as 'son of Ammon'. This would be the normal greeting to a king of Egypt, but Alexander appears to have been profoundly impressed. Later he left instructions that at death, his body should be buried in the temple of his father Ammon-Zeus. After his death at Babylon in 323 B C, his body was borne to Egypt in accordance with his wishes. But Ptolemy, Alexander's ambitious *satrap* (military governor) in Egypt, realizing the mystical power which possession of the body would bring, seized the body and buried it in Memphis. Ptolemy's son later transferred the body to a magnificent

tomb in Alexandria, the Greek city in Egypt built by the dead king. In 306 B C Antigonus, a Macedonian general, proclaimed himself king of the whole of Alexander's empire. But Cassander, satrap in Macedonia, Seleucus, satrap in Syria, and Ptolemy refused to recognize Antigonus' authority and each declared himself king of his own satrapy.

In Egypt the king was pharaoh, and to the Egyptians, a god. But in fact Ptolemy was a practical soldier, shrewd and genial. He was also a cultured man who valued literature, and himself wrote a book on Alexander's campaigns. This book, now lost, was used as a source by later historians whose work remains.

The despised cities

While Seleucus, following the example of Alexander, founded many cities, Ptolemy founded only one, Ptolemais, on the west bank of the Nile in southern Egypt. This city, together with Naucratis (in the Nile delta) and Alexandria were the only self-governing cities in Ptolemy's Egypt. Early in his reign, Ptolemy transferred the capital from Memphis to Alexandria.

Alexandria, Naucratis and Ptolemais

were Greek in character, governed almost as autonomous city-states. Although ultimately under royal control, they had their own laws, one of which forbade intermarriage between Greeks and Egyptians. The other cities of Egypt, though often quite large, had no such freedom. Lacking any form of self-government, popular assembly or senate, these cities were to the minds of the Greeks little more than villages, despite their size.

Alexander had been welcomed as a liberator in Egypt partly because his reputation as a believer in racial equality had preceded him. Ptolemy I departed from Alexander's policy of equality, and allowed special privileges to all his mercenary soldiers, who came to include Persians and other west Asians as well as Greeks. For example, the mercenaries, who in time settled on the land, were excused the normal liability of farmers to carry out work on irrigation canals and embankments. This inevitably created a class distinction along racial lines, but it is doubtful whether such was Ptolemy's intention. While Egyptian farmers had to give their labour as rent, the farmer-mercenaries had to be on call for military service. He needed soldiers and brought into Egypt as many mercenaries as he could. With an eye to security against possible revolt Ptolemy settled them, not in the Greek cities but among the Egyptians either in the countryside or in the capitals of the *nomes* (provinces). The governor of each nome was also the military commander of the district.

Revolts by Egyptians against their alien masters did in fact break out as early as the third century BC, and recurred throughout the Ptolemaic period (306 BC–30 BC). A patriotic literature existed, together with a 'nationalist party' which looked to the ultimate ejection of the alien ruling class. But no mass rising ever occurred, and most Egyptians apparently accepted their position passively. Some learned to speak Greek and even took Greek names, adapting to the prevailing situation. Others scorned the ways and habits of the Greeks, or showed only a sullen hostility which the Greeks repaid with ill-disguised contempt. The Egyptians lived in social and economic inferiority to the Greeks who administered and directed society. The class-race gulf never hardened into a rigid caste system, however, and from early Ptolemaic times onwards a few Egyptians did fill important posts and enjoyed a high status. They wore Greek dress and spoke *Koinê*, an international form of Greek. In the countryside, although the foreigners had more land and privileges than the Egyptians, they came more and more to share life in common. Inter-marriage took place, and the foreigners were gradually assimilated.

A take-over of gods

The Egyptians held their own in one important field: religion. Unlike the last Persian rulers of Egypt, the Greeks did not despise a religion which had a multiplicity of deities. Indeed, they could hardly do so; their own religion was polytheistic, and all the Ptolemies, like Alexander before them, accepted the status of gods even in their lifetimes. The Ptolemies respected Egyptian religion, and confirmed the priests in their positions. They built new temples and repaired and improved old ones. The city Greeks identified Egypt's gods with their own, and the country dwellers came to follow local cults. In the countryside, worship of Greek gods probably ceased.

Egypt was legally the king's estate, and everything in it was subject to his will. Most of his land was leased to 'royal tenants'. These farmers, although technically free men, could not leave their holdings of their own accord, but could be compulsorily moved to other holdings or have their leases ended. The state took over control of land once held by the temples, but ran it for the benefit of the temples and priests. The king also made gifts of land to favoured officials and courtiers. The military settlers held their land on the understanding that they had liability for army service. Officially, the king leased them land for their lifetime only, but the custom developed whereby the son of a deceased soldier-farmer inherited his father's holding. Clearly this

Of all the Ptolemies, only the last, Cleopatra, learned to speak Egyptian. But native culture continued under the alien kings. The broad river Nile shines beyond the walls of Kom-Ombo, **1**, a unique 'double shrine' to the god Horus and a local crocodile god, built at this time. The invaders quickly identified some Egyptian gods with their own. Thoth, **2**, here seen as a blend of his two symbols, the baboon and the ibis, was to them Hermes, for both were lords of language. Many small statues of this period survive, including that of a priest holding a shrine to Osiris, **3**, and this charming, sad-faced official, **4**; the sphinx, **5**, had the head of a Ptolemaic king. Preferring the new 'Greek' city of Alexandria, the Greeks left to the natives the ancient capital of Memphis, **6**, which had seen the crowning of Alexander as pharaoh; gradually it fell into ruins.

was in the interests of the Ptolemies. As time went by, the vigorous soldier-farmers extended their holdings by reclaiming land from the fringes of the desert.

The Ptolemies' officials knew well the value of trees in a desert land, and caused many to be planted. They encouraged the application of science to the land, and brought agronomists into the country. The Greeks developed improved varieties of wheat and introduced garlic and new varieties of cabbage into Egypt. They planted many kinds of fruit trees and cultivated flowers. They brought new breeds of sheep and other domestic animals into Egypt to replace earlier, inferior breeds, as a result greatly improving the quality of wool. While the Egyptians regarded pigs as unclean, the Greeks enjoyed pork as a delicacy, and established pig-keeping as an important part of farming. They sweetened their food with honey, and greatly extended bee-keeping in Egypt.

The Egyptians drank mainly barley-beer, but the wine-bibbing Greeks planted vineyards on irrigated but less fertile land. The Greeks also extended the cultivation of olives. Before Ptolemaic times the Egyptians grew olives as food, but the Greeks needed them for olive oil. Vine and olive growers were protected by tariffs against cheap imports of wine and olive

oil. The economy of ancient Egypt was based largely on corn which, in a barter society, had formed the basic currency; under first the Persians, then the Ptolemies, however, money more and more replaced barter. Gold, silver and copper coins circulated. A well-organized banking system developed as a state monopoly, although some of the banks were handed over to private concerns to run.

The old economic system existed alongside the new. Farmers on the royal land still paid rent in commodities, and some salaries and some business transactions were still settled without money. The government kept granaries which operated like banks, accepting private 'deposits' of grain. In time (possibly after the Ptolemaic period) payments in both grain and money were made by book-keeping transactions, without physical movement of either taking place, and papyrus prototypes of the present-day cheque were in use – both highly sophisticated concepts.

An income from oil

Much of the government's revenue came from taxes, which included land tax, property tax, purchase tax and a form of poll tax. Tolls and various customs duties brought further income. Some taxes were payable in commodities, and state officials collected these for the king. Money taxes

were collected for the government by strictly-controlled private contractors. At first aspiring contractors fiercely competed for the business but later, possibly because the remuneration was low, few people came forward to volunteer as tax-collectors. Apart from taxes, duties and land rents, the state (theoretically Ptolemy, the king) received a large income by operating monopoly control of certain projects and services.

Various oil-producing plants had been grown in Egypt long before Ptolemaic times. The Ptolemies controlled the sowing, cultivation and gathering of these plants, and laid down the area to be sown in each nome. They supplied the seeds to the farmers, calculated the likely yield, and charged one quarter of it as taxes. The growers sold the rest to contractors at state-determined prices. The oil was extracted in government mills by workers who could not leave their homes during the work season. The only non-state mills allowed to operate belonged to temples, which for two months in the year could produce their own oil. The government licensed wholesalers and retailers of oils, and controlled prices. The state made high profits on the oils – possibly as much as 300 per cent in some cases. Other state monopolies included linen, wool and hemp. Again, the temples had a concession.

city of the western world. Alexandria's main thoroughfare, Canopic Street, ran east to west along the length of the rectangular city, and other streets branched off it. The original fishing village of Rhacotis was the Egyptian district. The city was divided into five parts, each called after a Greek letter: Alpha, Beta, Gamma, Delta, Epsilon.

Alexandria's population was cosmopolitan, but mainly Greek. The Greeks were full citizens, with their own system of government resembling that of a Greek city-state. The Jews lived in their own district, Delta, but later spread throughout the city. Jews were denied citizenship but allowed special privileges, including the right to their own courts. The port of Alexandria was a crossroads of most of the known world, a meeting point of peoples. In Ptolemy II's time, two Buddhist missionaries arrived, sent by King Asoka of India, but they appear to have made little impact upon the pleasure-loving city.

A causeway connected the offshore island of Pharos with the port, creating a large western harbour and an adequate, safer one to the east. On Pharos stood the famous lighthouse, one of the 'seven wonders of the world'. Alexander's body lay in the *Sema*, the great tomb built at the order of Ptolemy II. In the Greek fashion the city had its stadium, gymnasium, hippodrome, and theatre, as well as its fine temples and the royal palace.

Two spell-bound soldiers

But above all, Alexandria was a great centre of learning and scientific inquiry. Its royally endowed library contained half a million papyrus 'books'. Its Museum, the 'shrine of the Muses', which fulfilled the function of a university, dominated the cultural life of the eastern Mediterranean and under its aegis a burst of scientific activity occurred. Many great scientists, including Euclid, the 'father of geometry' and Archimedes, studied there.

Under the first three Ptolemies Egypt prospered; its culture thrived and it had stable government. But life for the mass of the people changed little. They lived as far removed from the luxury of the upper class as they always had done, with the added irritation that the new upper class were foreigners. With the fourth Ptolemy, two centuries of decline set in. The last effective Ptolemaic ruler was a clever and able woman, Queen Cleopatra, who used her wiles to try to save Egypt from the ambitions of Rome. She became mistress first of Julius Caesar and later of the Roman commander Mark Antony, whom she married. When Antony committed suicide after defeat by Octavian (later Augustus), Cleopatra sought to conquer yet a third time. But at 39 she could not turn the head of the cold, austere, young Octavian. When she failed to seduce him, she committed suicide in 30 B C by allowing an asp to poison her by its bite; a death most significant to her subjects, who believed the snake to be the minister of Ammon. Her son by Julius Caesar, Caesarion, was executed by the Romans. Egypt became no more than a province of Rome.

The island of Philae in the Nile, *above,* covered with Ptolemaic temples, is now under water for 11 months of the year because of the Aswan dams; in the 1970s it is hoped to protect it by coffer dams. This old photograph shows the little temple called 'Pharaoh's Bed' before the waters closed over it. *Left,* most famous of all the Ptolemies – a contemporary portrait of Cleopatra. *Below,* Greek face, Egyptian headdress – a bust of Ptolemy Apion shows the twin influences which shaped the dynasty.

Priests were allowed to make their own linen, but had also to provide a stipulated quantity for export. The government kept monopoly control of beer, salt and natron (sodium carbonate used in the preservation of mummies).

Ptolemaic Egypt was a great trading nation. Into the Red Sea ports from Asia came cotton, silk, special woods, ivory, spices, pearls, precious stones and gold. Camels, introduced into Egypt by the Ptolemies, carried these imports across the desert to the Nile, to be transferred to boats. Some of the goods were directly exported at a profit. Craftsmen worked on other imports, processing or improving them into more valuable goods for export or for consumption inside Egypt. Other imports into Egypt included cheese, wine, olive oil, fruits, timber, metals, horses and slaves. Ptolemaic Egypt paid for its imports in the way that ancient Egypt had done; mainly by exporting corn. Other exports included linen, papyrus, alabaster, various kinds of stone and coloured glass – a much prized product of Alexandria.

The city of Alexandria, transformed by Alexander the Great from a fishing village into Egypt's greatest port, was also the country's capital and chief commercial and manufacturing centre. It soon outgrew Carthage and became the largest

Han emperors at China's helm

An army of desperate, yellow-turbaned peasants, the schemes of palace eunuchs, invasions by the Huns — these were the perils that beset the Han dynasty in their 400-year rule of China.

WHEN THE short-lived Ch'in dynasty (221–206 B C) which unified China collapsed, the soldier Liu Pang, the son of a peasant, became first emperor of the Han dynasty. Like all succeeding emperors, he is known to history by the name given to him after death. Liu Pang's posthumous name was Kao Tzu. After early difficulties in setting up his new government, the Han emperor succeeded in recruiting a number of competent administrators. At his command, one of his ministers wrote a report setting out the reasons why the Ch'in dynasty fell. The report concluded: 'The more powerful the armies of Ch'in grew, the more its enemies multiplied. The government was too harsh towards the people and punishment was too severe.' Liu Pang took note of this, and made concessions. He set free all people who had sold themselves into slavery for food during the Ch'in-Han war, and ended punishment by mutilation. He exempted demobilized soldiers from forced labour for up to 12 years, and reduced the need for conscript labour by cutting back the Ch'in dynasty's vast building projects.

Most people, including soldiers, came from peasant families, and agriculture was therefore extremely important socially as well as economically. Artisans had made

Cliff sculptures of Buddhas in the caves in Honan testify to the influence of the Buddhist faith. It reached China from India during the Han dynasty in the first century after Christ.

iron tools centuries before Han times but now their use became widespread. Privately owned factories each employed up to a thousand men making iron agricultural implements. As a result of peace, efficient government and technological advance, food production increased, the population grew, remoter regions were developed, and life became a little more endurable for the peasants.

Driven to slavery

The peasants remained desperately poor, however, producing just enough to keep themselves above famine level. When disaster came to a family, such as illness, death, drought or flood, they had to borrow from the money-lender, at interest rates which often reached 100 per cent a year. When this crippling burden became too heavy to bear, the peasants had either to sell their land to pay their debts and work for a landowner, or – the ultimate stage of misery – sell themselves into slavery in exchange for food.

Meanwhile the state itself prospered.

Coin money accumulated in the treasury and new grain was stockpiled on top of the old, which, not being distributed, lay rotting underneath. Flood and drought, the twin calamities of China, were vigorously tackled by the Han emperors. Many irrigation canals were dug, and flood defences kept in good repair. Records tell that Emperor Wu Ti (reigned 141–86 B C) himself went to a work-site on the Hwang Ho (Yellow River) and ordered the officials with him to help repair a breach in the river defences. Finding that timber was short, he ordered bamboo to be cut and brought from his own estates. No serious flooding occurred in the lower Hwang Ho for the next 80 years. Wu Ti patronized scholars and kept a library of 13,000 books.

North of China, presenting for hundreds of years a terrifying threat to the empire, lived the Hsiung Nu (Huns). It was to protect China against these 'barbarians' that the first Ch'in emperor had built the Great Wall. The first Han emperor had bought off a threatened attack by 300,000 Hsiung Nu horsemen early in his reign, but these soon returned to the attack, daringly raiding the land as far south as the capital, Ch'ang-an. Emperor Wu Ti decided to make a stand, and in three great clashes in 127, 121, and 119 B C, Han armies

Its banks heavily wooded, the river Fuchan, *left*, flows towards the East China Sea as it has done through centuries of upheaval. The pottery model of a watch-tower, *right*, made during the Han dynasty, must be typical of many constructed to warn against the invading Huns, the Hsiung Nu.

drove the Hsiung Nu north of the Mongolian desert.

In 138 BC, before these bloody battles began, Wu Ti had sent an ambassador to Tukhara (now part of Afghanistan) to propose an alliance against the Hsiung Nu. The ambassador was captured by the Hsiung Nu and held for ten years before he finally escaped, reached his destination, and after a stay of a year, returned to Ch'ang-an. The ambassador's mission failed, but he brought back a report on the lands westward as far as Parthia and Ferghana (now parts of Iran and the U.S.S.R.). For the first time, the Chinese court learned the secrets of the extensive and profitable trade carried on between China and western Asia. Wu Ti's fertile mind saw the immense value of this trade, and regularized it. Chinese silks and metal-ware flowed westwards; and the caravans returned to China bringing luxuries such as coral and jade.

Peaches and pomegranates

Wu Ti coveted the fine horses of Ferghana, and requested the ruler to send him some. When his request was refused, he dispatched 100,000 soldiers 4,000 miles to Ferghana to punish the country. Nearly half of this vast army perished from thirst, hunger and exposure in the remote mountains and deserts of central Asia, but the survivors returned with the emperor's horses. Following this high-handed action, east–west trade increased, as did the flow of ideas. Grapes, peaches, pomegranates and clover were introduced into China along with the music and dances of central Asia. In return, Chinese 'know-how' in well-sinking and iron-smelting was communicated to central and western Asia.

From the end of Wu Ti's long reign onwards, the plight of the peasants deteriorated. In one year alone, 2,000,000 peasants lost their land and became wandering beggars. Floods and drought bore heavily on the farmers, many of whom died from starvation and lay unburied in the barren fields. By the end of the first century BC, peasant revolts became frequent and more and more dangerous to the régime.

After the Emperor Yüan Ti died in 32 BC, four boys came to the throne one after another. The last, a one-year-old baby, was dethroned by the regent, Wang Mang, who then usurped the throne, declaring himself first emperor of the Hsin (New) dynasty. Wang Mang sought to placate the peasants by sharing out the land more equally. The rich and powerful opposed him, however, and his land laws were repealed. Wang Mang forbade trade in private slaves, but kept the official slaves unfreed. In fact he increased their numbers by several hundred thousand by officially enslaving coin forgers and their households.

Some of Wang Mang's policies such as the attempt to control prices and the granting of low-interest loans to needy people, if successful, could have gone far to relieve the distress of the peasants. But the benefits of these measures were lost because corrupt officials pocketed much money which should have gone either to the state or to the people. Wang Mang brought much of the economy under state control, but this did not help the people, because they had to pay taxes to the government for 'privileges' which had formerly been free. For example, they had to pay for the right to fish, and to collect firewood. A large proportion even of this revenue found its way into the pockets of the officials.

Wang Mang planned the final destruction of the Hsiung Nu in order both to annex their lands and to distract the minds of his own subjects from the distress

During the span of the Han dynasty the empire was united after the disastrous era of the Ch'in. With peace new trade routes were opened and new influences penetrated to enrich the quality of Chinese life and art. *Left,* a bronze clasp encrusted with turquoises. *Left below,* a sceptre like this, whose shape is known as a *ku kuei,* was used by the emperors in court and religious ceremonies. *Right and right below,* a pottery and a porcelain *hu,* used for storing wine.

group and forced the southern Hsiung Nu to seek the protection of the Eastern Han emperor.

Following the pattern of the first Han emperors, the first Eastern Han emperor made concessions to win popular support. He freed the slaves, carried out flood and irrigation projects, and reduced taxes and forced labour. Forty years of peace brought prosperity and added strength to the empire. In AD 73, 89 and 91 Han armies dealt crushing blows to the northern Hsiung Nu and steadily pushed them further to the northwest. There they were contained, and when they rode out again 250 years later it was not into China, but Europe – led by the terrible Attila. They defeated the Goths and Gauls and came near to destroying the eastern and western Roman empires. Then the people they subjugated rose in revolt, and in the mid-fifth century the Huns disappeared from history, becoming assimilated into the various ethnic groups of Europe.

Almost simultaneously with his success in the first battle against the Hsiung Nu, the first Eastern Han emperor sent an ambassador off to the western regions as Emperor Wu Ti had done more than 200 years earlier. In the following 30 years, Chinese diplomacy was studiously applied throughout the western regions, and more than 50 small states came under Han influence.

Revolt of the Ch'iang

In northwestern China, in the provinces of Kansu and Chinghai, dwelt the Ch'iang, warlike nomads living under the suzerainty of the Han emperors. In AD 107 the Ch'iang armed themselves with bamboo spears and attacked Han officials and landlords who oppressed them. Many Chinese colonists who had moved into the area threw in their lot with the Ch'iang. Fierce fighting continued for about 60 years. During this period Han armies also clashed with another nomadic people, the Yao of southern central China, who twice defeated the emperor's troops. The Han government finally won, but the long exhausting wars brought the Chinese economy to the brink of disaster.

After the first three Eastern Han rulers, a succession of boy emperors came to the throne. Regents exercised power and they and their supporters exploited the nation in their own interests. One regent, Liang Chi, appropriated for himself land and possessions equal in value to six months' taxes for the whole of China. He forced thousands of people into slavery, claiming that they had sold themselves voluntarily.

During the reign of Han Shun Ti (AD 126–144) a strange corruption crept into government, a weakness that was ulti-

in China. He goaded the Hsiung Nu to attack China by calculated insults, demanding that they change their name to *Hsiang Nu* (subjugated slaves). While a vast Chinese army gathered on the border of the Hsiung Nu territory, Turkestan slipped away from Chinese control.

The Lulin army

In Hupeh and Shantung provinces, drought again ruined the land, and locusts devoured what crops there were. Starving peasants gathered in the Lulin Hills and organized themselves into a huge army. This force was whittled down by plague, but others flocked to its banner. In time, the Lulin army came under the control of Liu Hsiu, a prince of the deposed Han dynasty. The Lulin army dispersed a large army sent against them and advanced to Ch'ang-an. But in the capital Wang Mang was already dead, killed by rebels who opened the gates of the city to the besiegers. Meanwhile, the Lulin army had

split into rival factions. Eventually, in AD 25, after much confusion, Liu Hsiu proclaimed himself emperor. He set up his capital in Loyang, crushed the peasant armies, and unified China under his new dynasty, the Eastern Han. After his death, Liu Hsiu was called Emperor Kuang Wu.

The civil wars ended Chinese suzerainty over the western trade routes, which fell into the hands of the resurgent Hsiung Nu. People in the western regions appealed in vain for protection to the powerless Eastern Han emperor, much as Britons were to appeal in vain to the dying power of Rome for protection against the Anglo-Saxons, four centuries later. The triumph of the Hsiung Nu was short-lived, however. Large numbers of them, together with the livestock by which they lived, died from the effects of drought and locusts. As if the troubles inflicted upon them by nature were not enough, the Hsiung Nu drifted into a debilitating civil war that left the predominance of power with the northern

mately to bring about the ruin of the Han dynasty. The numerous eunuchs who attended the women of the harem began to wield political power through their influence over the emperor. This came about because court etiquette kept the emperor secluded, mostly confined to the palace. Even his audience with ministers became so formal that they had to speak to him through a court official. The eunuchs were the only men allowed to live in the palace. Living in such close association with the emperors, knowing their weaknesses and foibles, screening them from the outside world, the eunuchs came to dominate them, and through them, to control the government of the empire.

Puppets of the eunuchs

This had not happened under the first three Eastern Han emperors because they were experienced men of the world before they ascended the throne. But the boy emperors, born and brought up in the palace, became the puppets of the eunuchs. Emperor Han Huan Ti (146–167), helped by the eunuchs, killed all the members of a powerful family called Liang who had tried to dominate him, and had indeed poisoned the previous child emperor. In gratitude to the eunuchs for their help in these murders, the emperor heaped wealth and honours upon them, and accepted their advice in all matters of state.

The scholars of China, a hereditary class, which traditionally provided the officials to govern the empire, banded together to protect their own interests against the eunuchs. They achieved some initial success, but the eunuchs struck back savagely. When the 12-year-old emperor, Han Ling Ti, ascended the throne in AD 168, they

Much of our knowledge of life during the Han dynasty is gleaned from engravings in tombs. *Left,* decorations on this stone slab include depictions of warriors galloping to battle. The

persuaded him that the scholars were plotting treason. With his acquiescence, all the leading scholars and officials who opposed them were arrested and executed. The entire administration of the country then fell into the hands of the eunuchs and those whom they appointed or confirmed in office. Again a great weight of oppression fell upon the poverty-stricken peasants.

While these events were taking place, a popular magician called Chang Chiao roamed the countryside, building up a huge following from his reputation as a curer of diseases. The peasants came to look upon Chang Chiao as their deliverer, and joined with him in a secret society formed to secure the overthrow of the eunuchs. Chang Chiao and his chief lieutenants drew their inspiration from a cult called 'Taiping Tao' which derived from Chinese Taoism, Persian Mazdaism and local superstitions. He and his lieutenants made preparations for the peasants to rise in arms all over China on the fifth of March, in AD 184. But a month or so before this date their plans were betrayed to the eunuchs, who arrested and killed a thousand of the conspirators.

Chang Chiao acted swiftly. He mobilized the peasants in February. They donned yellow turbans as a 'uniform', rose as one army, and conquered city after city, killing all officials who did not flee in time. But Chang Chiao – the healer of others – died of illness in August. In November, the Yellow Turbans lost their main army in

horse was very highly prized: *top,* this model is made of grey clay. *Above,* camels browse over vast Mongolian steppes across which swept the pitiless Mongol horsemen who invaded China.

merciless battles against the combined armies of the eunuch-government, local warlords, and the landlords, now allied because of their common terror of the peasants' vengeance. But the fight continued for another 20 years. In Hopei province alone, the Yellow Turbans mustered a million men. Finally, however, their enemies destroyed them.

During this long war, real power gradually passed into the hands of the generals, who were commanding vast armies. These generals came to despise and hate the eunuchs who presumed to give them orders. But the eunuchs would not surrender their claim to power easily. When the commanding general surrounded the palace with his army, the eunuchs lured him inside, killed him and defiantly exhibited his head over the gate. The enraged army then burst into the palace and killed every eunuch. The reigning emperor – another puppet – became the personal prisoner of a brutal general named Ts'ao Ts'ao. China then disintegrated into anarchy. In AD 220, the pitiful Eastern Han emperor finally abdicated in favour of Ts'ao Ts'ao's son, Ts'ao P'ei, who controlled northern China, which became the kingdom of Wei. Southeastern China broke away as the kingdom of Wu, and southwestern China became the kingdom of Shu-Han. In this way, China, after four centuries of union under Han rule, disintegrated, and was ruled for the next three and a half centuries by contending dynasties controlling rival states.

Freedom in the golden age of Athens

Greek democracy sums up the faith in the common people and the sense of freedom and power underlying the greatness of Periclean Athens. How did the democracy arise? Why did it ultimately fail?

EXILE – OR DEATH: Socrates could choose. Escape was possible – his friends had seen to that – but the 'wisest and justest and best' of the Athenians preferred to stay and drink the deadly hemlock prescribed by the State. He believed that the good citizen unjustly condemned should uphold the laws of his country and so die willingly. At the cost of his life, Socrates underlined a paradoxical truth about human freedom, law and society: it is only in a society that men can hope for any true and lasting freedom, and it is only where law prevails that a society can exist. That is why there are societies and laws, and why all societies revolve around a law-giver.

Who shall be the law-giver? How shall the laws be made? Who shall govern? Men have debated these questions down the ages, and history has put many of their answers to the test. This article describes one of those answers in its historical setting, the first great experiment in majority rule.

Men of restless and fiercely independent spirit, the Greeks had originally migrated from their earliest home possibly somewhere near the Caspian Sea. By c. 1200 BC, they had crossed the river Danube and settled in the southern Balkans. There, partly because of their temperament and partly because of mountains which virtually isolated one settlement from the next, they formed over a hundred self-sufficient city-states (*poleis*). One of them was Attica; its centre, the city of Athens.

The reforms of Solon the Wise

The four tribes of Attica had originally been brought together under a monarchy by Theseus (legendary. vanquisher of the Minotaur) but by c. 700 BC, power was in the hands of a class of hereditary nobles, the Eupatridae. Now an aristocracy, Athens was ruled by nine *archons* (chief rulers) elected from among the nobles by an Assembly (*ecclesia*) of citizens of property. Poor men, women, children, slaves and resident aliens, had no political rights. After their year of office, archons automatically joined the Council of the Areopagus, a powerful senate which also acted as a law-court.

The Eupatridae were selfish rulers. Forcing peasants into debt, serfdom and sometimes slavery, they seized most of the land for themselves. But they only sowed the seeds of economic disaster and hardened the common people against them.

In 621 BC came the first concession. The noble, Dracon, was asked to codify the laws. This helped to check the arbitrary justice of the nobles as, for the first time, it extended knowledge of the laws to all Athenians.

Set in the plain of Attica, Athens, capital of the Greek kingdom since the Bronze Age, is today still dominated by the Acropolis. A modern aerial photograph shows many features of the city's golden age. Most striking is the Parthenon, built under Phidias's supervision.

A final crisis point was reached in 594. In desperation the Assembly elected Solon as Archon of Athens with the widest possible brief to reform the constitution and save the economy. Of royal descent and also a successful merchant, Solon had recently distinguished himself by recapturing the island of Salamis from the Megarians, and his sharp political verse in defence of the poor had enhanced his popular appeal. All Athens swore to carry out his demands.

First he freed enslaved debtors and abolished the law permitting their enslavement, restricted the accumulation of land, and promised citizenship to aliens who brought their trades to Athens. Having laid the foundations of material prosperity, Solon turned to the constitution. In future, all men of property could become archons, and even the poorest citizen could vote in the Assembly, though they were not expected to hold office. Archons were chosen by lot from 40 candidates elected by the four tribes. A Council (*boule*) of 400, elected from all but the poorest class prepared the agenda of the Assembly. A new court of justice (*Heliaea*) was formed in which the judges, acting as a jury, were chosen by lot from the whole citizen body. The new laws were written down and ratified by the Council. Any archon infringing them would have to raise a life-size golden statue at Delphi.

Birth of a national spirit

His task done, Solon travelled abroad for ten years. Although unable to ensure that his constitutional reforms were properly carried out, the seeds of the democracy to come were slowly beginning to germinate: 'I gave the people such power as sufficed, neither taking from them their due honour nor giving yet more than was due. . . . I stood with my shield held aloft to guard both the rich and the poor, nor did I permit either to triumph

wrongfully.' Paradoxically, Athens was on the threshold of her 'age of despotism'.

Almost immediately feuding broke out among the nobles, and the nobleman Pisistratus, who was to dominate the period between 560 and 510 BC, was able to seize power by controlling elections in the Assembly from a 'back seat'. An enlightened tyrant (the word did not yet imply

disapproval), he stood by the working classes, and fostered trade and industry. His chequered rule – he was twice expelled from Athens – was a period of great prosperity and culture. For the first time Athens became an Aegean power to be reckoned with. A national Athenian spirit at last began to overtake tribal loyalties.

The true founder of Athenian democracy was probably Cleisthenes, a nobleman at odds with his class. Recalled from exile in 508, he broke the power of the four ancient tribes by dividing Attica into ten new tribal districts (*trittyes*). Cleverly included in each district was an urban, a rural and a coastal area, each further subdivided into parishes (*demes*). Every one of the tribes thus embraced a whole cross-section of Attic society and could meet as a unit only in Athens itself. Membership of the Council was raised to 500, each tribe contributing 50 members who acted as the Council's executive committee for one month in ten. Moreover, Assembly, Council and Law Court found that their powers were effective at last. An unpopular or power-hungry individual could be *ostracized*, banished from Attica for ten years – he had only to top the poll in a vote of not less than 6,000 citizens, each of whom would write the name of the man they hated most on pieces of pottery (*ostrakon*). By 487 the power of the archon had virtually become that of a chairman. The fledgling democracy was ready to spread its wings and its flight was assured by war.

Victories of the common people

The most glorious pages in Athenian military history were to hasten the full self-discovery of the common people. At Marathon, in 490, 20,000 Persians under Darius were overwhelmed by an Athenian army half as strong. And ten years later the mighty fleet of Xerxes, sent to avenge Darius, was routed in the Straits of Salamis by the fleet of Athens under

The theatre at Epidaurus, situated on the slopes of Mount Cynortium, is the greatest of ancient Greek theatres and the most beautiful. Its acoustics are so perfect that a speaker in the orchestra can make himself heard throughout the auditorium without raising his voice. Each summer thousands of visitors still come and listen to the tragedies of Aeschylus, Sophocles and Euripides.

Part of the Erectheum, Temple to Athena (*c.* 421 BC), viewed from the Parthenon. The famous caryatid porch can be seen with its six female draped figures (caryatids) replacing the usual columns.

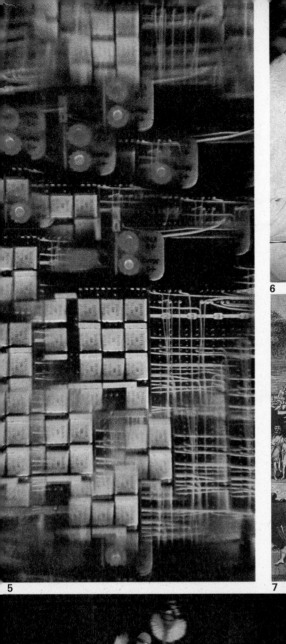

that to remove or change the order of any one of them will dislocate the whole. This axiom is still used as a guide in criticism, especially of mystery and crime fiction.

Tragedy depicts incidents arousing pity and fear. A bad man must not be shown passing from misery to happiness, nor an extremely bad man falling from happiness to misery, since such stories would not arouse us to pity and fear. Pity is occasioned by undeserved misfortune and fear by the suffering of one like ourselves. The hero must be a good man shown falling from happiness to misery, but his fall must be caused by some error on his part.

Aristotle's *Poetics* advocates the 'dramatic unities', the unities of action, place and time. Plays should have only one main action, and this action should happen in one place and in a time not exceeding that taken to perform the play. The dramatic unities influenced later writers, in particular the French seventeenth-century classical dramatists Corneille and Racine, although the latter stretched the unity of time to 24 hours, and place to cover a whole house or town rather than a room or street. The *Poetics* is still read by many students of literature in the course of their studies.

The function of the state

In his *Politics*, Aristotle's approach was quite different from that of Plato. Plato started with the idea that the state's function is to achieve justice, and he constructed his famous Ideal State round this notion, paying little attention to the operation of existing states. Aristotle was also interested in the idea of the best possible state, but for him the search for the system of running it necessitated the examination of forms of government in past and existing states. Like Plato, Aristotle bases his theories on a state which will have something in common with the Greek city-state, and so the Lyceum students took part in a research project in which were investigated the constitutions of 158 Greek cities. He regards the Greek city-state as being about the right size; the state he envisages, therefore, would be far smaller than modern states. Athens, for example, had something over 300,000 inhabitants, so that Aristotle's state would be only the size of one of many cities in a single modern state.

Aristotle regards the state as a natural institution. He says that the natural objects of procreation and self-preserva-

expressed a humane attitude towards his own slaves, none of whom were to be sold, while some were to be given their freedom.

Aristotle wrote a treatise on literature called his *Poetics*. In talking about poetry, Aristotle was covering the whole field of literature since, in his time, the writing of prose literature was a comparatively recent innovation. The *Poetics* we have is not his complete work – his treatise was in two parts, one dealing with Comedy and other subjects. We possess only the part dealing with Tragedy and Epic, which has

merely passing references to Comedy. These references are interesting. Aristotle regards Comedy as an imitation of men worse than the average in that they are ridiculous. Tragedy and Epic poetry, he says, are imitations of serious subjects. The story or plot of a tragedy is its most important element, and the characters are included for the sake of the action. A well-constructed plot must have a beginning, a middle and an end.

The incidents of the plot, declared Aristotle, must be so closely connected

An unbroken chain of writers and scholars pursued the study of Aristotle's thought throughout the course of European history. In the West, only a fraction of his work was available, in a Latin translation made by the fifth-century Roman philosopher Boethius, *left*. But by 1300 his rediscovery put him at the summit of medieval intellectual interests: the poet Dante, *above centre*, described him as *'the philosopher'*. Later, the Renaissance was to bring a reaction against his influence on the academics. The Reformation leader Martin Luther, *above right*, condemned 'Aristotelianism'. Beyond the main intellectual centres of Europe, Arabian philosophers made important commentaries on Aristotle's philosophy – they had the benefit of familiarity with the complete texts of his writings. *Right,* the doctor, statesman and lawyer Averroës was a Spanish-Arabian of the twelfth century. He was born at Cordoba, a major centre of Aristotelian study. Later, both Christians and Jews in the West were deeply influenced by Averroës' commentaries.

tion both lead men to form associations – the family for the producing and rearing of offspring, and the village to supply the wants and needs of a larger group.

By 'nature', he means something different from the present meaning. All natural things, he says, have ends or subjects to which they aspire – the end of a seed, for instance, is to become a plant. All natural things are in a process of movement towards their end, and their nature is their end. The end of the state is a similar but higher end than that of the families and villages which are its parts. Its end is the preservation not just of life but of the good life. The point about the idea that the state is natural is that Aristotle thinks of the state as a positive thing. Some later thinkers, Hobbes for instance, took a more negative view, regarding the state as an arrangement to limit each man's activities and so prevent him injuring his neighbours, which he would be naturally inclined to do, and to protect him from being injured himself.

As with Plato, ethics and politics are connected in his thinking; the good man and the good citizen are the same, in the ideal city. He also thinks, like Plato, that education should be the concern of the state rather than the responsibility of the individual. Aristotle holds that law must be the ultimate sovereign in the state – the rulers like the subjects must be ruled by law. Good law, for Aristotle, has been gradually discovered through experience.

This gives him a bias in favour of existing law which has been tested. He is unwilling to cast aside the experience of history. His positive views on Man's social and political life are again discernible in his regard for law, which he says is an intrinsic part of good government and not just an unfortunate necessity for restraining men's actions.

The one, the few, the many

He lists various possible forms of government. They fall into three classes: government by the one, government by the few and government by the many. It is possible to find good and bad forms of government in each class. He himself tends to favour a form of government by the many, since he thinks they are less likely than the few to approve a wrong policy.

Bad government furthers the interests of the rulers at the expense of the rest, and it is possible in government by the many just as it is with the one and the few. Aristotle thinks that government by the many will entail government by the poor, since they are more numerous than the rich, and bad government by the many will take into account the interests of only the needy. Democracy is this kind of bad government in Aristotle's view, and it also makes the mistake of regarding each individual as equal, rather than different and meriting differing rewards. He calls good rule by the many a *polity*, and says that a polity will be in the common interest of all members of the state. Perverted forms of government are despotic and place the subjects on the level of slaves.

Here, although it is not explicitly stated, Aristotle seems to have grasped what is regarded as a fundamental principle of the modern democratic state, the idea that the subjects should freely consent to the authority of the rulers.

The world and Man's activities in it have not so far been shown to conform to a convenient set of general principles. On the contrary, life seems full of variety and complexity, and these aspects are reflected in Aristotle. Yet he succeeded to a surprising degree in elucidating important elements implicit in our thoughts and actions, and most philosophers find it worth while to discuss and criticize Aristotle at some stage in their careers. In doing this, they need to make remarkably few allowances for the fact that Aristotle was writing over 2,000 years ago.

When the Italian poet Dante called Aristotle 'the master of those who know', he was summing up the genius of the philosopher for organizing *knowledge*. The campaigns of Alexander brought back to Athens a wealth of new and strange information about the wonders of the world. Aristotle was portrayed by Raphael in *The School of Athens*. Plato is shown pointing towards the heavens. Aristotle points to where his deepest interest lay – earthwards.

The Eagle over Italy

Some 2,500 years ago, the young city of Rome expelled its foreign king and embarked on the mammoth task of uniting all Italy under its dominion. A maxim of 'divide and rule' realized this ambition.

'Thou, Roman, rule, and o'er the world
proclaim
The ways of peace. Be these thy victories,
To spare the vanquished and the proud
to tame.'

So sang the poet Virgil, basking in the glory of an empire that stretched from the Euphrates to the Danube, from the Rhine to the Sahara, and whose ruler, Augustus Caesar, had restored peace and harmony to the Roman world after years of strife. Even in his moment of exultation, however, the Roman poet recalled the humble beginnings of the Eternal City, how it had risen from the insignificant position of a minor city-state near the coast of Latium to dominate first the Italian peninsula and then the Mediterranean basin.

Yet all this was only made possible by Rome's initial extension of its power and influence throughout Italy, the land that became the core and vital hub of the Roman empire. From a political point of view, Roman expansion in Italy was of a prophetic character, since the statesman-like policies the city adopted in these early centuries became the general rule in its expansion overseas. And most important of all the facets of Roman expansion was the young republic's peculiar ability to incorporate alien nationalities within its system without demanding harsh cultural uniformity. By sparing the vanquished as well as taming the proud, Rome was able to build up a secure foundation for its empire.

A matter of guesswork

The traditional date of the founding of the city of Rome, used by Romans to date all subsequent events, is 753 BC. In actual fact, Rome was probably not founded until around 600 BC; but a precise historical date is still a matter of guesswork. A monarchy for around the first 100 years of its existence, it expelled the last of its kings at the end of the sixth century BC and instituted a republic in which the real power lay in the hands of the aristocracy. Roman expansion, however, did not really begin in earnest until over 100 years later, and there were to be a number of set-backs. For Rome was not alone in ancient Italy: there were many potential rivals to be found throughout the peninsula.

To the north of the Tiber on the coastal plain of Etruria, there existed the strange and, in some respects, mysterious civilization of the Etruscans. Until recently it was believed that the Etruscans had arrived in Italy from Asia Minor at the dawn of history, but it is now thought that they were merely an eccentric outgrowth of the native Italic race. The Etruscans appear mysterious because scholars are still unable to decipher their language which is preserved in innumerable inscriptions; further, there is the weirdness of Etruscan art – particularly of their sculpture and the paintings in their underground burial chambers, and a strong Eastern flavour that often takes a strangely sinister form. The Etruscans inhabited 12 main cities scattered throughout Etruria which were federated in a loose league, whose main functions were religious rather than political. A fundamental weakness of the Etruscan league, and one which was to be of immense value to Rome, was its inability to unite for concerted action against the foreign invader.

At the southern tip of the Italian peninsula a different civilization was being established at the same time as Etruscan influence flourished in the north. This was the colonization undertaken by

1 A medallion with the heads of the twin brothers, Romulus and Remus, believed by Romans to have founded their city in 753 BC, although the actual date was probably some 150 years later.

the city-states of Greece from the eighth and seventh centuries BC. As these colonies grew in power, they were able to subdue the hinterland and establish a powerful sphere of influence, eventually coming into conflict with the Etruscans. The Greeks of southern Italy were proud of their own cultural heritage and tended to despise native Italic civilization. Of all their cities, Tarentum, situated on the inside of the 'heel' of Italy, was the most powerful, and it was to offer Rome her final challenge for supremacy within the peninsula.

The Etruscans, and the Greeks of southern Italy, were the most advanced peoples that Rome was to deal with in its expansion throughout Italy. Yet there were other equally dangerous people scattered throughout central and southern Italy.

The Samnites, a tough hardy people who occupied the mountainous areas to the south and east of Rome, resisted Roman arms longer than any other group; living in the mountains they made excellent guerilla fighters. Immediately south of Rome lay the plain of Latium where a number of cities had been founded by various Latin tribes: they provided Rome with its first challenge, and it was to Latium – with its fertile plain – that Rome was initially attracted. Lastly, and most dangerous of all, were the various barbarous Germanic tribes (known to the Romans as the 'Gauls') who inhabited the extreme north of Italy; these tribes were unstable and nomadic, moving on as soon as a locality had been fully exploited. The Gauls were to pose the greatest threat to

2 Once Etruria was absorbed by Rome, its culture quickly disappeared. Many beautiful works have been preserved, however, like the two wrestlers from the Tomb of the Monkey in Chiusi (c. 480 BC).

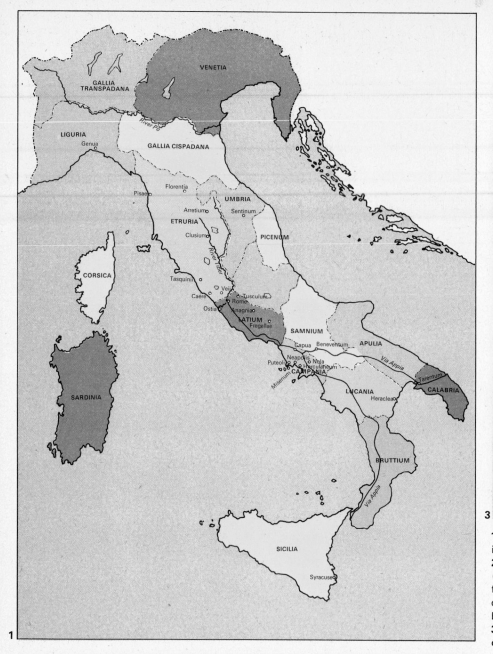

1 A map of Italy, during the period of Rome's initial expansion in the peninsula.
2 The Tomb of Hunting and Fishing at Tarquinii (c. 520–510 BC), with its striking medley of figures and subjects, rates as one of the most original of all Etruscan tomb paintings. A haze of broken colours indicates the surface of the sea.
3 The Roman forum, centre of business and judiciary, and meeting place of the Roman senate

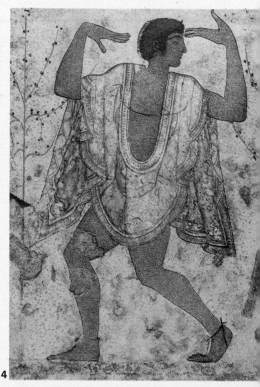

where members discussed the affairs of the republic and its government. Later, under the empire, a number of forums were built to accommodate the expansion of the city's affairs.

4 A young male dancer from the Tomb of the Triclinum in Tarquinii. Such decorations provide valuable documentation on the Etruscan way of life.

5 As the Greek states of southern Italy came under Roman control, their civilization and culture were adopted and absorbed. This Greco-Roman vase shows the grace and quality of their art.

6 A vivid Etruscan bronze of an archer loosing an arrow from his horse. It demonstrates a high level of skill and a strong Eastern influence.

7 Bucchero, the black glazed Etruscan pottery – widely found because of its use as a cheap replacement for more valuable articles. The bull's head, with its big oval eyes, was a popular theme.

the city of Rome that it was to face for 1,000 years.

The last of Rome's kings had been an Etruscan – the tyrant Tarquinius Superbus; Rome's initial task as a republic was to repel Etruscan expeditions sent in support of its ex-monarch. This successfully achieved, Rome spent several decades strengthening its position on the plain of Latium so that it could gain control of the loose federation of city-states which inhabited the plain. Rome's defeat of the ravaging tribes of the Volsci and the Aequi – in 431 BC – greatly enhanced its position and it was soon acknowledged as the leading city on the plain: it alone had the military strength and organization to protect Latium from the hill-tribes. Towards the end of the fifth century, therefore, Rome felt powerful enough to attack the strongest city of southern Etruria – Veii – which was finally captured by the Roman hero Camillus in 396 BC; already Etruscan power was on the decline, and Veii was left heartlessly to its fate by its fellow city-states in the Etruscan league. Why, remains an unanswered question, but it conforms with our knowledge of a streak of

fatalism in the Etruscan character.

At this juncture, Rome was all but submerged by a barbarous wave that very nearly engulfed the whole of the Italian peninsula. In 391 BC the nomadic Gallic tribes of northern Italy marched south through Etruria and savagely defeated the Romans close by their city, which was sacked in 390. Despite this blow to both its military and political influence, Rome immediately showed the iron will that was to maintain it in succeeding centuries against similar disasters. Re-establishing control over southern Etruria and Latium, Rome defeated further Gallic incursions, and in 332 BC was able to conclude a permanent peace treaty with the Gauls. Next, Rome turned its attention to the fertile plain of Campania, which lay along the coast south of Latium: Roman arms moved into the major cities of Campania in 341 BC to protect these communities from the ravages of the Samnites. In earlier times, Etruscan rulers had protected Campania from these tribes, and now Rome was needed to fill the vacuum created by Etruscan withdrawal.

Fighting Rome's wars

This move on Rome's part, however, brought it into direct conflict with its allies in Latium, who questioned why they should be obliged to fight Rome's wars without a major share in its political institutions. After a bloody battle near Mount Vesuvius, the cities of Latium were defeated and brought under complete Roman control, but on extremely generous terms: certain cities were even given the full privileges of Roman citizenship.

Rome now turned to the problem it had originally entered Campania to deal with – the Samnite hill tribes. From 327 BC to 290 BC, Rome fought a series of desultory campaigns against the wily mountain men; at one stage a Roman army was hopelessly trapped in a defile by the Samnites and compelled to surrender. Other Roman setbacks followed, and by the beginning of the third century BC, its troubles were aggravated by a fresh incursion of the Gauls, but at the crucial battle of Sentinum in 295 BC, both Gauls and Samnites were utterly routed. The resistance of the latter collapsed and peace was made six years later. A short while after this, a final Gallic invasion, aided by the last independent cities of Etruria, was decisively defeated and the threat from northern Europe eliminated for over 200 years. Rome took this opportunity to finally bring all the cities of Etruria under its control, though Romans still remained suspicious of the strange Etruscan tongue and oriental peculiarities.

Rome was now practical master of all Italy south of the River Po, with the exception of the independent Greek city-states in the south. It seemed inevitable that a conflict should develop, especially when Rome began to intervene in the disputes between certain cities and the tribes of the interior. Eventually the powerful city of Tarentum challenged Rome by refusing to allow a Roman squadron into its harbour and hurling abuse at Roman envoys. It then hired a strong army of

Greek mercenaries under the redoubtable general-king Pyrrhus of Epirus, whose forces included an extremely effective corps of elephants. But despite technical defeat in a number of battles, by 275 BC the Roman army had sufficiently weakened Pyrrhus to be able to vanquish his forces and drive him back to Greece. Undefended, Tarentum and the other Greek cities came under Roman control, thus completing Rome's sphere of influence throughout the whole peninsula.

The story of Rome's unification of Italy seems, in the light of its later expansion, almost inevitable. But it was an arduous process, helped without doubt by both Rome's peculiar characteristics as an expansionist power and certain natural factors. Rome was geographically placed in an ideal position for the extension of its power: the city was situated almost in the centre of Italy, on a navigable river whose estuary provided a natural harbour. From its central position, Rome could dispatch its forces north or south along the long coastal plain that extended from Campania, through Latium to Etruria. This natural factor Rome enhanced by its policy of strategic road building, which made the business of troop-movement much easier, particularly through the Apennines – the central range of mountains that forms the backbone of Italy.

Militarily, Rome was always willing to learn from its defeats and to improve its fighting ability accordingly. For example, in their struggle against the Samnites the Romans found that the heavy *phalanx* formation they had adopted – via the Etruscans – from the Greeks, was ineffective against small mobile groups attacking from several angles. Accordingly, the Romans reorganized the structure of the legion – their basic fighting unit – by dividing it into several 'maniples', each 120 men strong. These were formed in

1 Throughout its expansion, Roman discipline and tactics were vital keys to military success. Around 312 BC the army was radically reorganized to give it greater mobility and striking power.
2 By treating its subjects humanely, Rome assured itself of their support, particularly during the titanic struggle against Carthage. This relief shows the fleet Rome sent against the Carthaginians.

three successive lines, so that if the first line's attack failed there was always a line behind to take its place. This flexible organization was further improved by the introduction of both short swords and the long spear or javelin, which made the Roman army effective at any range. And throughout the period Roman discipline was unequalled amongst its enemies, with perhaps the one exception of Pyrrhus's mercenary force.

Far-sighted policies

Even more important in the long run was Rome's ability to conciliate the peoples over which it had established its rule. Time and again, when Rome was threatened, its conciliatory policies were to pay dividends in maintaining the loyalty of its allies. Rome's remarkable foresight in pursuing this policy had begun when it had assumed control of its immediate neighbours on the plain of Latium; these cities were given the same private rights enjoyed by Roman citizens – the guarantee of private contracts, marriage agreements, testaments, and other personal affairs by the Roman constitution. In time they came to be known as 'Latin rights' and were used by the Romans as a halfway stage in the granting of citizenship to subject peoples, while areas which contained towns with a tradition of self-government were treated with respect. Often, after the fourth century BC, Rome would grant the inhabitants of a town complete citizenship which meant that such a city would be incorporated into the Roman state, but that local affairs re-

mained in the hands of its citizens. The greatest burden of Roman citizenship came to be the war-tax, little indeed when every citizen was eligible to stand for any office in the Roman magistracy.

Naturally this was a gradual process: Roman citizenship was not the automatic prerogative of every conquered tribe. Rome was careful to phase its policy, so that by the time it had completed its expansion throughout Italy, it found itself at the head of a confederation made up of peoples at various stages of Romanization and with varying rights. The Samnites, for example, were not an urban dwelling people – they had no tradition of community self-government – and were obviously unripe for citizenship; they were therefore given the status of 'allies' until the process of Romanization should fit them for the duties of the full franchise. Such a federation of widely differing peoples with varying degrees of citizenship was to some extent an unwieldy body; to make it a more coherent whole and to establish order in recently conquered territories, the Romans dispatched groups of landless citizens (of which there were all too many) to establish colonies throughout Italy.

By the middle of the third century BC, Rome was indisputably the master of all Italy south of the Po. Taking advantage of the decline of Etruscan power, it had used its natural advantages to great effect, pursuing a constant policy of 'divide and rule'. By treating its subject peoples with sensible humanity, Rome protected itself against the threat of an unbeatable alliance against its suzerainty; in each such successive struggle, a high proportion of its allies stood firm and repudiated the temptations of revolt. In the titanic struggle against Carthage that was to engulf the Roman world in the following decades, Rome was time and again to be rewarded with loyalty for its statesmanlike policies.

Men who steered the might of Rome

Caesar, Augustus, Nero, Trajan, Hadrian, Diocletian, Constantine, Justinian – their names resound like drumbeats over the centuries. What were they like? How well did they rule Rome?

WHEN KING ATTALUS died in 133 BC his will contained a most extraordinary bequest: he left his entire kingdom – the Asia Minor city-state of Pergamum – to the Roman Republic. That the king of the most outstanding surviving centre of Greek culture should voluntarily cede his state to the Romans was perhaps the finest tribute ever paid to the new power from the west that was already in possession of almost all the Mediterranean coastline.

In one and a half centuries the disciplined legions from Rome had established Roman rule from north-western Europe to Arabia, and from Mauretania to Dacia (now Rumania). But the conquered territories had been won at a cost. Roman society was irreconcilably divided into the affluent, who grew richer year by year, and the deprived, who grew poorer.

Roman society was based upon the family and divided into various classes which included the *patricians* (old families of noble birth) and the *plebeians* (commoners). Members of the wealthy patrician families dominated the government. From

their ranks came the two chief executive officers, called *consuls* (who held office for one year) and the members of the Senate, which exercised supreme legislative power. Rome had gained enormous wealth through its conquests and most of this had gone to enrich the senators and their families. The senatorial families came to possess great estates which they worked with gangs of slaves, and they continually extended their land by evicting peasant proprietors. Thus deprived of both land and work, the peasants became an embittered, impoverished class.

Some members of the patricians felt that this situation was dangerous because it threatened the stability of society and thereby weakened the state. Prominent among them was Tiberius Gracchus, a man of good looks and personal charm who was the grandson of Scipio Africanus, an out-

This beautiful frieze executed in bas-relief is known as the Ara Pacis (Altar of Peace) and is found in the Vatican Museum in Rome. It shows senators making their way to the senate and was executed in 13-19 BC during the rule of Octavian.

standing general whose armies had finally crushed Rome's most formidable enemies, the Carthaginians, in 146 BC. Tiberius was himself a distinguished soldier with an apparently brilliant future in government. When he applied his mind to the problems of peace, it was the hopeless poverty of thousands of Roman citizens that weighed on his mind.

The cunning of Caius Gracchus

In 133 BC (the same year that Pergamum acceded to Rome) Tiberius became a *tribune* – one of ten officials elected to protect the interests of the plebeians against the patricians. Tiberius proposed that the state should repossess much of the public land and redistribute it among the poor. This drastic proposal frightened the majority of the senators, and to protect their land they persuaded another tribune to attempt to veto the measure. But Tiberius highhandedly overrode his fellow tribune, and his land measures were passed. Enraged and terrified of losing their land, some extremist senators stirred up a riot in

which Tiberius and 300 of his supporters were killed. With their champion dead, the plebeians appeared to lose hope of their land, and the senatorial families saw no need to placate them.

Ten years after the death of Tiberius, his brother, Caius Gracchus became tribune. Caius shared his brother's impassioned hatred of injustice but was a better politician and organizer, who knew that he could not beat the patricians merely by having the support of the plebeians. Proceeding with cunning, Caius sought ways of broadening his support among both rich and poor. On the one hand he proposed that jurors in the high courts, (traditionally senators), should be chosen from the lesser aristocracy, who were mostly merchants, and on the other that the poor should be found work on building new roads throughout the Italian peninsula.

Caesar crosses the Rubicon

Appalled by this attempt to gain the sympathies of the middle class as well as the poor, the Senate again provoked violence in the city. They blamed Caius for the riots and proclaimed him a public enemy. Once again the supporters of the Gracchus family were massacred, and to avoid the disgrace of capture and public execution Caius forced his own slave to kill him.

The killing of Tiberius and Caius Gracchus did not end the class struggle, which broke out anew – this time within the regular army. Rival generals emerged as the champions of either the Senate or the plebeians. Marius, a popular general who had saved Italy from invasion by the Gauls, took up the cause of the poorer citizens, but he was finally defeated by Sulla, an aristocratic general who in 83 BC made himself absolute dictator. Sulla packed the Senate with his friends and curtailed the power of the tribunes. When he died in 78 BC, supreme power passed to a triumvirate of Pompey (one of Sulla's outstanding generals), Crassus (a wealthy senator) and Julius Caesar (an aristocrat who had already held several government posts).

Caesar was a scholar, an orator and a lover of literature. Though an aristocrat, he had, as a young man, criticized the idleness and corruption of his class and built

A contemporary gold coin inscribed with the image of Octavian Caesar, emperor in all but name, who ruled the Roman world after the humiliating defeat of Antony and Cleopatra at Actium in 31 BC.

up a popular opposition to the senatorial oligarchy. He organized and paid for games and other entertainments for the people, getting into debt to do so.

Caesar became commander of the province of Gaul (present-day France) in 58 BC, when he was well over 40 and despite the fact (unusual for a senator) that he had never fought in a battle. Rather to the Senate's surprise, Caesar proved himself a brilliant soldier, conquering all Gaul right up to the Rhine, and landing two expeditions in Britain – then a virtually unknown island.

Meanwhile, Crassus had also been given a military command, but was killed in the east in 53 BC. Pompey remained in Rome and became jealous of Caesar's power. He allied himself with the aristocrats, gained

control of the Senate, and caused it to order Caesar to resign his command and disband his army. Caesar's response was quick to follow. Ignoring an ancient law that forbade Roman armies to approach nearer the city than the river Rubicon (in northern Italy) he moved his armies across the river and entered Rome without opposition. Pompey and his senatorial followers immediately withdrew to Greece. Here Caesar met and defeated him at Pharsalus in 48 BC and Pompey fled to Egypt, where he was murdered. Now all-powerful and without rivals, Caesar made himself dictator and consul for life. He became king in all but name.

Caesar planned vast projects and emerged as a great innovator. He founded Rome's first public libraries and reformed the calendar, fixing the months and the numbers of days in the Julian calendar which was to survive his death by more than 1,600 years.

Above left, two of the three coins show the Emperor Justinian II. Christ Himself figures on the obverse side of the third coin with Justinian on the reverse, implying that He, not Justinian, is the true leader of Byzantium. *Above right,* one side of this coin shows Brutus, Caesar's murderer. The other shows a cap given to slaves when set free—indicating that the Roman nation was once again free.

He was without doubt the creator of the Roman Empire.

A modest and retiring man by nature, he toiled conscientiously at the duties of government, but when occasion demanded he acted the role of magnificent ruler of his Empire with pomp and ceremony.

Augustus brought dignity to Rome's public life. He rebuilt and beautified the city, claiming in later life that he had found it a city of brick and left it a city of marble. He encouraged the arts and patronized writers like Virgil, Livy and Horace who glorified the destiny of Rome. Under Augustus, Rome's population grew to more than a million. Its citizens enjoyed a water supply, clean streets, and amenities that were not to be equalled for another 1,500 years.

Augustus left Rome with a vast empire that covered most of the western world. An army of 300,000 men kept peace and order throughout every province, and good roads promoted the prosperity of the Empire. Later, men called the reign of Augustus the *golden age* of the Roman Empire. After his death Augustus was regarded as a god, and later emperors, following the custom of the East, became gods while they still lived.

Caesar proposed to codify the whole of Roman law, to drain the malarial swamps of the Pontine Marshes, and to shorten communications with Asia Minor by cutting a canal through the Isthmus of Corinth in Greece. He planned to conquer Germany beyond the Rhine and to lead an expedition to Persia, but these ambitious plans remained no more than dreams.

He did nothing to bring stability in Roman government beyond perpetuating his own power. He neither evolved a permanent constitution nor made provision for the succession in the event of his death. Men worshipped him almost as a king, and for some of his class this was too much to endure. On the Ides of March in 44 BC, at the height of his power, a band of republicans led by Marcus Brutus, stabbed him to death – accomplishing the most notorious assassination of all time.

The golden age of Augustus

After Caesar's death, power fell mainly into the hands of Octavian (Caesar's 19-year-old grand-nephew and adopted heir) and Mark Antony (Caesar's co-consul). Lepidus, a general who joined them in a triumvirate, had little power and eventually retired. Octavian and Mark Antony trapped and killed Caesar's assassins in Greece in 42 BC, but the victors then struggled for power between themselves. Octavian took Italy and the west, and Antony conquered Egypt and the east.

Infatuated with Queen Cleopatra of Egypt, Antony lost his will to fight. The combined fleets of Antony and Cleopatra were defeated by Octavian's fleet in 31 BC, and in despair the two lovers committed suicide. Octavian returned triumphantly to Rome in 29 BC as unchallenged master of the whole of the Roman territories. Thereafter, Octavian ruled Rome for 44 years. When the Senate gave him the title *Augus-*

The exterior of the Roman Senate House (third century AD). This building was erected on the site of a much older Senate House (second century BC) whose beautiful mosaic floor still remains.

tus (the exalted) the Republic was at an end and Octavian became for practical purposes the first Roman emperor.

The transition from Octavian to Augustus went through several stages before the Senate could bring itself finally to abandon the republican ideal. For a time Octavian was consul, then proconsul and eventually a tribune. He became head of state, and governor of the most important provinces with power to override the Senate. But, shrewder than Caesar, Augustus never admitted that he had swept away the Republic. Ironically, he posed as the restorer of the Republic and the guardian of its constitution and traditions. He never took the title of Emperor, yet was in fact the prototype of the Roman emperors of the three centuries that followed his death.

A horse for consul

For 200 years the Roman Empire continued to be governed in the manner established by Augustus. It survived frequent debilitating attacks on its frontiers and the eccentric and barbarous behaviour of such tyrannical emperors as Caligula – who appointed his horse a consul – and Nero, a cruel neurotic whose misrule ended in suicide. Under the soldier emperors Trajan and Hadrian, and the stoic philosopher-emperor Marcus Aurelius, Rome reached the height of its power early in the second century AD. But the Empire's decline was not far off. Barbarian tribes soon began to make inroads upon its territory, and emperors were increasingly chosen by the army.

Diocletian, a Dalmatian soldier, who became Emperor in AD 284, saved the Empire from disintegration by effecting several necessary reforms. He surrounded himself with a court of oriental splendour and semi-religious ceremonial, and all who

This impressive Roman aqueduct is called the Pont du Gard and is near Nîmes in France. It was constructed during the rule of Julius Caesar (first century BC) as his victorious army moved westwards. There are many such Roman ruins in France and in other European countries and Africa.

approached him had to prostrate themselves in adoration. Like Augustus, Diocletian believed that such an image would raise the prestige of the Empire. Diocletian doubled the size of the army, but broke its power to make and unmake emperors. He completely separated civil and military government, and army commanders ceased to be governors of provinces. Justice, administration and taxation were transferred from the commander to Diocletian's officials. By breaking the army into smaller units, Diocletian ensured that generals commanded fewer men and therefore had less opportunity to attempt insurrections.

To pay for his elaborate court, his enlarged army and his extra officials, Diocletian imposed heavy taxes. A wit of the time said that, 'there were more receivers than contributors'. Finally, in AD 286, as though despairing of the tasks he had set himself, Diocletian set up his court in Asia Minor and appointed Maximian, a peasant from nearby Thrace, to be his co-emperor in the west.

In AD 305 Diocletian and Maximian finally retired, and a struggle for power immediately followed. The outcome of this struggle was that Constantine became Emperor in the very way that Diocletian had tried to prevent. His soldiers proclaimed him Emperor at their headquarters in York, the military capital of the province of Britain. Constantine tri-umphantly led his troops through Britain, across the Channel into Gaul, and then into Italy where he defeated his rivals and marched into Rome.

Constantine was an able organizer, and he completed Diocletian's organization of the Empire, but he made the government of Rome even more autocratic than it was before. To maintain the state and its large defensive armies, Constantine became increasingly despotic. He compelled landowners to recruit men for the army and to collect taxes in their neighbourhoods. Peasants and artisans were bound permanently to their jobs. Merchants had to belong to state-controlled guilds, and their sons had to succeed them. Town councillors found themselves made responsible for the contributions due from their municipality to the government, and they were forbidden to leave the place of their birth. Constantine organized more and more people into guilds and groups, each with definite obligations to the state.

'The emperor never sleeps'

One of the most important changes made by Constantine was to alter the religious policy of the state. Whereas Diocletian persecuted Christians as rebels disruptive to the state, Constantine made Christianity the official religion of the Empire, and put the emblem of Christianity on his coins. The Christian Church and the Roman State came increasingly close together. Constantine began to regulate the Church's affairs and even determine its doctrine.

Constantine also established for himself a new capital, *Constantinople,* on the site of the old Greek town of Byzantium on the Black Sea in AD 330. It was intended to be a replica of the old Rome, even being built upon seven hills. In this city Roman emperors were to carry on an increasingly shadowy rule for another 1,100 years. Constantinople in fact survived for 1,000 years after the Roman Empire in the west had fallen to barbarian conquerors.

For a brief time in the sixth century the decline of Imperial power was halted by the Emperor Justinian. A devout Christian, Justinian built many churches, the most famous being Santa Sophia, the huge domed cathedral of Constantinople. In origin a peasant of Macedonia, he was educated by his uncle, the Emperor Justin (once a private soldier) to be his assistant and then made his successor. Justinian owed much to his wife, Theodora, the daughter of a Cypriot bear-keeper and a well-known actress before her marriage. In moments of crisis her bravery and resolution often steeled him to overcome his habitual indecision.

Justinian had a passion for work. 'The Emperor never sleeps,' a courtier said. He was ambitious and took action to restore the Roman Empire to its ancient boundaries and splendour. His generals recaptured northern Africa, south-eastern Spain, and Italy from the barbarians, but within a few years of his death all these gains were lost. Justinian's most enduring achievement was his codification of the Roman law, planned by Julius Caesar more than 500 years earlier.

One of the great principles of Roman law is laid down in the often-quoted phrase, 'What the ruler has decided has the force of law.' The rise of nation-states in Europe during the sixteenth century was accompanied by a revived study of Roman law, because this principle strongly attracted the rulers of those states. Roman law has had a profound influence over the law of many European countries, including Scotland. But its influence upon English common law has been almost negligible.

Head of Pompey, who formed part of the trium-virate with Julius Caesar and Crassus in 78 BC. He was later defeated and murdered by Caesar.

Triumvirates were often split apart by the ambition of their members. Octavian defeated Mark Antony (above) and Cleopatra in a famous battle.

A bust of Sulla, the aristocratic general who made himself absolute dictator in 83 BC. He did this partly by getting his friends into the Senate.

Head of Octavian Caesar, known as Augustus (the exalted one). He virtually created the Roman Empire and rebuilt and beautified Rome itself.

A mosaic of the Emperor Justinian (sixth century AD). A devout Christian, he built many churches, including Santa Sophia at Constantinople.

'All the Earth is Roman earth'

At the peak of its power, Rome spanned and dominated the civilized world. Here we halt and examine the powerful machine of empire in the days of its greatest glory under Trajan.

DURING THE LONG CENTURIES of anarchy and decline which came afterwards, Romans looked back to the golden age of the five 'good emperors' of the second century – Nerva, Trajan, Hadrian, Antoninus Pius and Marcus Aurelius. And of all these great men, the most revered and honoured after his death was Trajan, who was described even 200 years after his death as *optimus princeps*. 'the most worthy emperor'.

It was under this soldier-emperor that the Roman Empire reached its greatest heights – in both military glory and peaceful enterprise. A standing army of 168,000 regular soldiers, supported by regiments of provincial troops known as auxiliaries, guarded the broad frontiers, which stretched from Britain to the Black Sea, down the Euphrates valley and across the edges of the Sahara south of Tunis, Algeria and Morocco. Within this secure fence, the empire proceeded with its business and saw little of the troops. Some idea of its vast extent and diversity can be gained from our map on pages 882–3.

Trajan was a man of immense capacity: born in 53 AD of an Italian family long resident in Spain, he was the finest example of the new type of emperor, chosen by his predecessor, Nerva, because of his talents and not because of illustrious birth or immense riches. Under Trajan, who ruled as emperor from 98 to 117, the empire flourished in all its many aspects: the army worshipped a man who shared the dangers and tasks of a common soldier, the provinces of the empire were soundly administered, and the economy of the empire prospered.

The peaceful provinces

Under the Republic, the provinces had been incorporated into the Roman state in a fairly haphazard way: some had been conquered for strategic reasons (perhaps to secure a frontier), some as a result of warfare (such as the old domains of Carthage in North Africa), and some merely as a result of the military ambitions of the generals of the later Republic. By about 200 AD, the provinces of the empire were divided between those governed by representatives of the Senate and those governed by nominees of the emperor – and were known respectively as *senatorial* and *imperial* provinces.

The senatorial provinces were those which by Trajan's time were on the whole highly Romanized and peaceful: they formed an inner circle of Mediterranean lands, such as Achaea (Southern Greece), Baetica (Southern Spain) and the old Carthaginian territory in North Africa. These senatorial provinces were without a standing military force (except in Africa)

Perhaps the best of the 'five good emperors' of Rome, Trajan controlled with a sure and skilful hand the magnificent administrative machine which ran the empire.

and relied on local militia in the event of rare local disturbances. Governors for these provinces were selected by lot, from the pool of ex-magistrates who filled the Senate: the emperor made sure that those appointed to govern senatorial provinces were both mature and experienced, by ensuring that a fixed number of years passed between the holding of, say, the consulship (an important senatorial post awarded only to men in their forties well trained in public administration), and the appointment to a governorship. The position of a provincial governor was very like that of a viceroy under the British Raj; ultimately responsible to his sovereign, he controlled all appointments, all the machinery of bureaucracy, and was the final arbiter in matters of justice – except in the case of Roman citizens, who had the right of appeal to the emperor.

The majority of provinces – and all those containing standing military strength – were the personal responsibility of the emperor, who alone appointed men to governorships (again, drawn from the ranks of ex-magistrates). While the governors of senatorial provinces were restricted to a term of office lasting only one year,

imperial governors could be appointed for terms of up to three years, depending usually on their record as administrators and the military situation within the province. Those provinces in which there was a garrison of more than one legion, such as Syria or Pannonia (modern Hungary), invariably went to an ex-consul, being the most senior of ex-magistrates.

New provinces (always by nature 'imperial' since they needed military government) might, if they were small, be assigned to an imperial official known as a *procurator,* who would be a gentleman from outside the Senate: such provinces would need less than a legion to garrison them, and so responsibility was less great. Perhaps the most famous example of these so-called 'procuratorial' provinces was Judea, whose best-known procurator was the ill-starred Pontius Pilate – clearly a man of limited ability. Under Trajan and his immediate successors, the standard of administration was high.

Advice from the emperor

Standards were maintained because all governors received a generous salary, which gave them less reason to 'bleed' their province, and because all had gained much experience during their careers in the imperial armies and as magistrates at Rome. Most important of all was the supervision of the emperor himself; Trajan was prepared to intervene even in the affairs of a senatorial province if there was evidence of corruption and abuse. Governors themselves made use of the empire's communications to consult the emperor on matters of importance: Pliny the Younger, governor of Bithynia (in modern Turkey), for example, found himself in a quandary over how to deal with the early Christians in his province, and consulted the emperor, since 'it is my custom to refer all my difficulties to you, Sir, for no one is better able to resolve my doubts and to inform my ignorance'. Trajan, with his customary blend of humanity and sense, replied that 'these people must not be hunted out; if they are brought before you and the charge against them is proved, they must be punished'. Trajan, as a soldier and man of action, always sought to temper a practical course of action with humane understanding.

While the emperor unobtrusively supervised the administration of the provinces, he was also supreme commander of the army; and during the reign of Trajan this was the more important role. During his reign, Trajan fought three major campaigns: two against the Dacians (who inhabited what is now Romania) and one against the might of Parthia (the Persians), during the last four years of his life. Trajan was first and foremost a soldier,

The Disposition of the Legions in the Roman Empire under Trajan 98–117 AD

Each legion had its own number and title; when Augustus combined three armies into one, he left these intact, hence the same numbers may occur more than once.

A: Hadrian's Wall, Britain

B: Bath, Britain

C: Bingen, Germany

The Danube:
Lower Moesia: I Italica
XI Claudia
V Macedonica.
Upper Moesia: IV Flavia Felix
VII Claudia
Dacia: XIII Gemina
Upper Pannonia: X Gemina
I Adiutrix
XIV Gemina
XV Apollinaris
Lower Pannonia: II Adiutrix
The East:
Cappadocia: XII Fullminata
XVI Flavia
Syria: II Traiana
III Gallica
IV Scythica
Judea: X Fretensis
Arabia: VI Ferrata
Britain: IX Hispana
II Augusta
XX Valeria Victrix
Africa: III Augusta
Spain: VII Gemina
Upper Germany: VIII Augusta
I Minerva
Lower Germany: XXII Primigenia
VI Victrix
XXX Ulpia

This map (on which Latin spellings are used in general) shows the provinces of the empire at its greatest extent, and its guard of legions. From Britain to Syria, Roman towns, aqueducts and theatres were built to an identical pattern, always with superb engineering skill.

and was most at home in the military camp: during his reign, the army was confirmed in its status as one of the most rewarding careers open to citizens and non-citizens alike. While the empire was administered, taxed and engaged in trade, the legions – 28 in all – protected the frontiers and guaranteed the *Pax Romana*, which was the greatest gift of Rome to the peoples of the empire.

The legion was the basic traditional unit of the Roman army; every legion, of 6,000 men, was divided into ten *cohorts* and every cohort into six *centuries*, containing 100 men each. The legionary commander was always from the senatorial class and an ex-magistrate – but one who had decided to pursue a military career rather than go in for administration. Under the legionary commander (known as a *legate*) there served a number of young staff-officers called *military tribunes*: these would be young men either from senatorial families or the sons of rich families outside the Senate, about to embark on their official careers, and gaining experience of army life, and the trials and tribulations of campaigning; Trajan served as a military tribune in Germany while a young man.

H: Leptis Magna, Libya

J: Segovia, Spain

D: Avignon, France

E: Jerash, Jordan

F: Pula, Yugoslavia

G: Sousse, Tunisia

200　300　400　500
miles

AE AND PENNINAE
IAE
TIMAE

BASTARNAE

SCYTHAE

M
UPPER
PANNONIA
LOWER

DACIA

ROXOLANI

Singidunum
Viminacium

UPPER
MOESIA

LOWER
MOESIA

DALMATIA

THRACIA

MACEDONIA

BITHYNIA
et PONTUS

GALATIA

ARMENIA

CAPPADOCIA
L

ASIA

CILICIA

Zeugma

MESOPOTAMIA

ASSYRIA

Euphrates

Tigris

ACHAEA
N

LYCIA et
PAMPHYLIA

SYRIA

CRETA

CYPRUS

PARTHIA

JUDAEA

E

CYRENAICA

Alexandria

ARABIA
PETRAEA

AEGYPTUS

K: Evora, Portugal

L: Nize, Turkey

M: Rome, Italy

N: Athens, Greece

On a huge column in Rome, Trajan perpetuated the story of his wars. Here his army, with its standards and the legion's eagle emblem, crosses the Danube on a bridge of barges.

The non-commissioned officers of the legion were its 60 *centurions*, who commanded the centuries: these men had often been promoted from the ranks, although some came from wealthy families and passed quickly on to a higher rank. In each legion there was a strict order of seniority among the centurions, the most senior of all being named, literally, 'The First Spear' – corresponding roughly with the modern Regimental Sergeant Major. The common soldier, known as a *legionary*, was a volunteer and his only qualification for service in the legions was Roman citizenship: he signed on for a period of 20 years, and when he retired he was given a sizable gratuity, and often a bonus as well. The rewards of looting were also considered an important 'perk' of the serving soldier.

Centurions and legionaries

Under Trajan the legions were spread throughout the empire, based in large permanent camps along the frontiers: the main danger areas – the Rhine, Danube and Euphrates – were naturally those where the legions were most concentrated. During the few years of peace between Trajan's Dacian wars and his invasion of Parthia, the Danube provinces contained a garrison of 11 legions, the

eastern front seven, and the Rhine five: these were the critical frontier provinces, constantly on guard against the Germanic tribes in the north and the cunning Parthians in the east.

Many of the great legionary camps along these frontiers, such as Viminacium, Zeugma and Carnuntun, became virtual cities in their own right. Although the serving soldier was not officially allowed to marry while enlisted, many men 'married' unofficially while in camp (with the blessing of their officers) and, when they were discharged, settled down in the area where they had served.

In addition to the legions, the Roman army also consisted of groups of non-citizen soldiers, known as *auxiliaries*: these men signed on for a term of 25 years, at the end of which they were granted the much-coveted prize of Roman citizenship. Auxiliaries served in units of about 600, both infantry and cavalry, and very often used skills peculiar to their particular tribe or area: the Batavians, for example, from what are now the Low Countries, were excellent slingers and cavalry-men, and were a valuable asset to Roman arms.

The legions and auxiliaries were a solid and dependable bulkhead protecting the empire: but they, and the other features of imperial government, had to be paid for – through the imperial treasury. The emperor gained his revenue through both direct and indirect taxation; and to organize the collection of taxes, officials known as *procurators* acted as the representatives

of the emperor in the imperial provinces, while their senatorial counterparts (known as *quaestors*) supervised taxation in the rest.

The economy of the empire, by the end of Trajan's reign, was in an extremely healthy state. Rome and Alexandria – the second city of the empire – handled an increasing amount of merchant shipping. Trade demands throughout the empire were satisfied by almost every province in its particular way. From the east came spices and perfumes along the caravan trails of Parthia and Arabia; these were carried by ship to Italy, an increasingly voracious consumer of luxury goods. From Spain, Gaul and Asia Minor came metals both precious and utilitarian to decorate the tables and fill the armouries of the empire. From Egypt and Africa came the most important goods of all – grain, to feed Rome and Italy. Marble, dyes, wool, timber and paper were all carried between the provinces, but especially to Italy, where most idle money lay.

The climax of centuries

A thoroughly Romanized Greek of the age of Trajan asked, 'Were there ever so many cities, inland and maritime? Were they ever modernized so thoroughly?' Such a question was more than just formal praise, for the first century and a half of the Roman Empire saw a dramatic increase in the number of towns flourishing within its borders. By 138 AD Spain contained 248 towns of some size, and every province, old and new, could boast a growing urban population. The growth of cities within the empire was a vital part of the process of Romanization: Roman civilization had originated from an urban community and it spread throughout the empire by reproducing similar conditions in each province.

Cities arose as a result of several things: they often developed around legionary camps or settlements of veterans, but just as often they resulted from commercial prosperity. Those cities possessing the titles of *colonia* and *municipia* were most favoured: for they were communities of Roman citizens and were governed by constitutions similar to that of Rome.

The reign of Trajan was by no means unblemished: his Parthian war proved after his death to be just too ambitious. But this was a golden age in the eyes of both contemporaries and later generations. The empire reached its geographical limits during the reign, and the dual system of government based on the partnership of emperor and senate never worked so well again. Trajan's reign was to mark the highest point of Roman endeavour – the climax of centuries of expansion and internal development: all that came after seems very much of an anti-climax in comparison, despite the appearance of men like Marcus Aurelius and Constantine. It was fortunate for Rome that such a man as Trajan should come to the throne at this juncture in her history; it was equally fortunate for Trajan that he should inherit an empire on the point of fulfilling its highest destiny and mission as tutor to her subjects in every aspect of civilization.

Pompeii's grave of ashes

When Vesuvius erupted in 79 A D an entire city was buried in a day. Its beauty and treasures lay hidden for over 1,600 years before the painstaking work of archaeologists brought them to light again.

TOWARDS THE END OF AUGUST, in the year 79 A D, a youth of 18 was staying with his uncle at Misenum on the north shore of the Bay of Naples. The young man was to become one of the two most vivid and accomplished letter-writers in Latin literature. His uncle, a man of 56, an officer and a man of action, was the author of an immensely learned encyclopedia known to us as the *Historia Naturalis,* and was in charge of the Roman fleet then stationed at Misenum. Their names were Gaius Plinius Caecilius Secundus and Gaius Plinius Secundus, known to us respectively as Pliny the Younger and Pliny the Elder. We are inestimably fortunate in having from the pen of the younger Pliny an account of the shattering events of 24 August, written to his friend Cornelius Tacitus, himself destined to become Rome's greatest historian.

'A truly Roman greatness'

At about mid-day, Pliny tells us, his mother said that an extraordinary black cloud was visible over Vesuvius, so his uncle resolved to investigate, but first to continue his routine of sun-bathing followed by a cold dip and a light meal taken lying down. (Throughout this catastrophe one of the most remarkable things is the completely scientific and detached calm and cheerfulness of the elder Pliny – a

1 Despite the damage caused by the earthquake and eruption, the tall columns of the *atrium* (a central, partly roofed courtyard) of the house of Epibus Rufus are still in good condition.
2 A bakery stands as it was abandoned nearly 2,000 years ago. The two flour-grinding pots on the left are fashioned from volcanic stone and were once turned by slaves or donkeys.

truly Roman greatness shines forth from his actions.) The elder Pliny had already decided to go nearer to the mountain to investigate, when a panic request for rescue was brought to him from the wife of a friend of his who lived right at the inner end of the bay and whose only possible way of escape was by sea. Pliny had a quadrireme (a ship with four banks of oars) made ready and was rowed straight towards the dread stream of lava and into the sulphurous murk illumined by tongues of flame and full of hot cinders which rained down death and destruction.

Upon arrival at his friend's house Pliny found that he had loaded all his movable belongings on to a ship. But with what seems to us inexplicable bravado, Pliny reassured his companions by first bathing and then sitting down with apparent gusto

to another meal, after which he lay down and had a sound sleep – he could be heard snoring. Not until the pumice-stones had nearly blocked up the doorway and several neighbouring buildings were beginning to totter did the company decide that it was safer out of doors; then fixing pillows over their heads with towels as a protection against the falling cinders they stumbled down to the shore, only to find that the advancing lava had driven back the sea and that escape was almost impossible. Pliny lay down and twice called for cold water and drank it. Presently the flames and gases forced everyone to flee, and when Pliny sat up he immediately fell back dead; he was, we are told, somewhat asthmatic and his reckless courage had cost him his life.

His nephew, who had not been with him on his last journey, later wrote another letter to Tacitus giving a wider overall picture of the catastrophe. Seventeen years earlier, in February 62 A D, the city had been terrified by a severe earthquake, commemorated in marble bas-reliefs found in the house of a banker named Caelius Iucundus. In this earlier, premonitory disaster most of the casualties were those who did not attempt to flee to the countryside till the rubble of falling buildings had blocked up all ways of escape; so now nearly everyone was desperately jostling towards the gates of the city, which proved a deadly bottle-neck where many were crushed to death. There was besides, the added menace of the cinders and gases which made the countryside at least as dangerous as the town.

Burning mud and ashes

Those who stayed indoors fared no better, though no worse, than those who fled. The vapours and the rain of lava asphyxiated and buried them. One of the most striking features of Pliny's descriptions is that of the lurid inferno which seemed to open up and the weird effects of light. An immense cloud like a pine tree stood up from Vesuvius, whose summit was split by a gigantic crack; darkness fell abruptly, birds fell dead, stones crossed the sky like shooting stars, burning mud poured down the slopes of the mountain and there was a veritable maelstrom as it came into contact with the sea. The darkness soon became like that of a sealed room without lights, shot through with flames like great bolts of lightning, and marked by flickering torches. When after several hours the sun appeared it was pallid as if in eclipse, and by it the city of Pompeii appeared covered with a thick layer of ashes like an abundant snowfall.

It was not till 1748 that archaeologists finally located the site of Pompeii, for it was quite a small city, with no more than

1 The delicate 'Mosaic of Doves'—it is based on a theme from a famous mosaic executed by Sossos of Pergamon.

2 One of the most perfectly designed houses of Pompeii is the House of the Vettii. More than half the total area is made up of the peristyle, which, together with its garden, has been scrupulously restored to its original state.

3 The House of the Great Fountain in the street of Mercury, dedicated to the Nymphs. The steps lead up to the still-functioning fountainhead below a magnificent mosaic portrait. But the water which once gushed from the great heads flanking the arch has long ceased to flow.

4 This carefully restored house is a splendid example of the Samnite style of architecture. The main characteristics are illustrated in the front entrance hall shown here, with its painted balcony and the imitation of marble panels too costly or rare to be easily obtained.

20,000 inhabitants as against the million and a half in Rome at the same period. Pompeii has left no literary record, for even the letters of Pliny scarcely mention it, and there were other towns in the area which have disappeared, Leucopaetra, Oplontis and Taurania to name but three, and all may have been as extensive as Pompeii. Herculaneum, another town of roughly the same size, had been partially excavated some years before work was begun on Pompeii, and the greatest treasure it has yielded is a mass of papyrus rolls, fragmentary and mutilated, containing the works of a famous Epicurean philosopher called Philodemus. Unlike Pompeii, Herculaneum had been covered in a torrent of mud, which had made it far harder to excavate.

Thanks to the incredible patience and skill of Italian archaeologists it has been possible to restore semblances of the corpses found in Pompeii in their original postures at the moment of death. The lava which engulfed them gradually hardened to a shell in which the body decomposed normally, so that by the 'lost wax' process it was possible to obtain casts of the corpses and to discover all sorts of little details about them.

Unable to escape

There is the corpse of a beggar near one of the gates, the Porta di Nuceria, who was wearing sandals of excellent quality, obviously a gift, and who carried a sack for alms. Behind the Great Theatre (almost all Italian towns of any size possessed a theatre, some more than one) was a barracks for gladiators, all of whom seem to

have got away except for two who were locked up with manacled wrists in a small cell. In the same barracks the corpse of a woman wearing magnificent jewels seems to bear out the suggestion that gladiators were permitted visits from courtesans – indeed a graffito records one champion as SVSPIRIVM PVELLARVM, 'the girls' heart-throb'.

Elsewhere we find corpses of young women who had stripped off their clothing so as to run more swiftly; of families with children; and of one pregnant woman and another with her baby clasped to her breast. One girl had lost one of her shoes; a man had been struggling to drag a goat along with him by its halter; and one huge fellow, apparently a slave, had died while struggling to fend off the ashes by brute strength. Animals figure quite prominently: one dog had died in agonized contortions while struggling to get free from a lead which tied it to a wall, and another in terror and hunger had gnawed the bones of its master beside it.

Like most cities in the Roman Empire, Pompeii had shrines of many foreign cults, and it is interesting to see the behaviour of their devotees in this extremity. The priests of the temple of Isis, for instance, were beginning a meal of eggs and fish, most of which has been found intact. Now the worship of Isis was supposed to confer immortality on initiates, and although the priests had in fact left the temple they had obviously stopped to collect the image of the goddess and the temple treasure and carry them away in a sack. The priest carrying the sack fell first, but his comrades picked him up and rallied round him until falling debris crushed several of them. The survivors sheltered in a house where the last of them died while attempting to break down a wall with a hatchet.

Strange cults and customs

The many foreign cults in Pompeii included some which were proscribed even by Roman law. The cult of Isis was found at seaports especially, since she was the patroness of navigation, and her ritual seems to have been a re-enaction of the age-old myth of a sacred marriage and the death and rebirth of the year. Every spring the 'boat of Isis' was carried to the water and formally launched as a sign that sailing could now begin.

Since 186 BC the worship of Dionysus or Bacchus had been forbidden by the Roman senate because of its orgiastic nature, and because secret meetings savoured of sedition. Yet in the famous Villa of the Mysteries outside the walls of Pompeii there has been found a remarkable fresco depicting an initiation scene, obviously devoted to the cult of Dionysus. A naked child recites to the young postulant a list of the initiation rites and phrases; then we see three women round a table, one with her back to the beholder as she conceals some ritual object; then a huge phallus is revealed as the young girl is fiercely lashed by a female figure with dark wings. Finally she breaks out into an orgiastic dance. The whole scene is like something out of a decadent poem by Swinburne.

Although Pompeii has left little literary

1 After the eruption, lava and ash hardened round its victims, forming a solid shell inside which the body decomposed normally. By the lost-wax method it has been possible to obtain plaster casts which tell their own terrible story.

2 From the Villa of the Mysteries – a naked child recites to a postulant the initiation rites for the cult of Dionysus; the following scenes depict their enactment. Because of its secrecy and orgiastic nature, the cult was outlawed.

record, yet from its remains we may gather that it was a settlement of great antiquity going back to the period of Etruscan domination of Italy in the seventh and sixth centuries BC. Scholars have argued that the Pompeians had rather a taste for blood and cruelty and that this was inherited from the Etruscans. At any rate there was a large barracks for gladiators at the back of the amphitheatre, which seated 15,000 people, nearly three-quarters of the city's population. This, together with the wall painting depicting the flagellation of an initiate into the mysteries, is not the only indication that the Pompeians had a remarkable delectation for scenes of violence.

During the seventh and sixth centuries BC the whole of the Bay of Naples came under Greek influence, and Pompeii near the mouth of the River Sarna was of obvious importance as an outlet for the traffic of the hinterland. The beauty of the landscape was another attraction, and so too was the extreme fertility of the volcanic soil, the deposit of long-forgotten primeval eruptions of Vesuvius. Here it seemed that life came very near to the ideal of the Golden Age celebrated by poets and philosophers, when the Earth yielded up its fruits without labour. At all events a life of hedonistic luxury seemed to be the main characteristic of the city, to judge from the sensual paintings which survive and from the innumerable *graffiti*.

Pompeii's wall-scribblings

These *graffiti* deserve a word to themselves. We are quite used to wall-scribblings, but most of those in modern cities sink to a very low level of monotonous obscenity. The obscenity is present at Pompeii, often in extreme form, but although many scribblings are crude and illiterate some illuminate their sensuality with a good deal of wit. Others even infuse a tinge of poetry into their effusions: 'Nothing can endure for ever; when the sun has well shone, it is restored to the ocean; and the moon must wane even from the full. Thus often the wildness of Venus is transformed into thin air.' Others are more epigrammatic: 'Lovers like bees need a life of honey'; and the quality descends by every conceivable step to the directness of 'I am yours for a few coppers' or 'I don't care if you drop dead tomorrow'. With a disgust that finds many a modern echo some passer-by has scribbled, 'I wonder, wall, that you have not yet collapsed under the weight of all the idiocies with which these imbeciles cover you!' Another, possibly a Jew or a Christian, has summed up the attitude of later ages in the simple words 'Sodom: Gomorrah'.

A remarkable feature of the *graffiti* is the large number referring to elections, presumably on to the town council. 'Julius Philippus, vote for him and he'll do the same for you'; 'The neighbours rise up and support Ampliatus'; 'The worshippers of Isis ask you to elect Cnaeus Helvidius as commissioner'; 'Vote for Lucretius'; 'Faber, act, wake up. You're asleep and yet you want to see our man elected.'

Every aspect of the life of Pompeii is illustrated by these scribblings, from the

injunction to passers-by not to commit nuisance to the writing of his name by some foreigner: *Shyroc Habdan.*

After the Greek influence had passed its peak Pompeii came under the dominion of the warlike Samnites, until at the beginning of the first century BC it witnessed the Social War and narrowly escaped being involved in the slave-rising under Spartacus, who actually camped for a time on the slopes of Vesuvius. From then on it gradually became the abode of an increasingly wealthy merchant class who took over the beautiful houses and gardens of the patricians who had migrated there because of the wonderful scenery and climate. We find that these houses are given up to fullers, weavers, merchants of all kinds who have little care for the aesthetic charm of the villas they inhabit.

The famous eruption of 79 AD was not

the only, nor indeed the most devastating, of the eruptions of Vesuvius. On 18 December 1631 more than 4,000 people perished, more than twice as many as in the catastrophe of 79 AD, and as far away as Naples the ash was a foot deep. But the damage was more evenly spread and nowhere else in history has a city come to so sudden and dramatic an end as Pompeii when Vesuvius erupted with such terrible results on that dreadful August day nearly 2,000 years ago.

1 The convulsed corpse of a dog which was unable to break free of its chain. It died of asphyxiation from the choking ash and deadly vapours which came in the wake of the eruption.
2 A view of Pompeii as it stands today. Vesuvius rises in the background; the gentle columns of smoke which still drift from its crater belie the terror it can unleash.

The man from Nazareth

Four brief documents tell us nearly all we know about the life of Jesus. They were written chiefly to explain its meaning. But what actually *happened* during those few years in Palestine?

JESUS OF NAZARETH was not in his lifetime a public figure. He did not move at the centre of affairs. Virtually all that is known about him is to be found in the New Testament, in particular the gospels. Over the last century an immense amount of effort has gone into the study of the documents of the New Testament, and these documents have come to be recognised as genuine products of the age in which they purport to be written.

These four books are not in any sense biographies. The writers were primarily concerned with the religious significance of the events described. This reverses the traditional historical approach, which asked first 'What happened?' and then 'What does it mean?' The writings of the New Testament are concerned to give an account of the *meaning* of the life and teaching of Jesus of Nazareth, and the student of these writings has then to try to deduce, from the interpretations, the actual events behind them.

The New Testament itself is not a unified document; it is an anthology of short works produced by the Christian community in different parts of the Roman empire over a period of almost a century. Of these works, only four deal with the life of Jesus of Nazareth; these are the four gospels.

The missing link called Q

While they contain a great deal of common material, they differ significantly from each other on many matters, and in particular in the ordering of events and their relation to each other, precisely the points in which the historian is interested, but which did not concern the religious purpose of the writers. Three of these gospels – Matthew, Mark and Luke – share a common fund of material, while the fourth, the gospel according to John, the last to be written, is generally held to be more theological and mystical than biographical, although scholars are coming to realize that it is not as unhistorical as was at first thought.

The relation between these first three gospels is, expressed in its simplest form, dependent upon two sources: first the gospel according to Mark, which is generally held to have been written in Rome shortly after the deaths of Peter and Paul in Nero's persecution of AD 64, and which may be to some extent dependent upon the recollections of Peter. Matthew and Luke both expand the gospel according to Mark, blending it with material from another document, the second source, which has since been lost. This document is usually known as Q, and appears not to have been another gospel, but a collection of the sayings and teachings of Jesus. The Sermon on the Mount and many of the famous parables of the Kingdom are from

this source. Matthew and Luke, in addition to using Mark and the Q document, and often changing them in interesting ways, also add special material of their own. The birth stories, which are quite different in the two gospels, come into this category, as do the Luke parables of the Good Samaritan and the Prodigal Son. The story of the last week in Jesus' life appears to have existed in a well-known form before any of the gospels had been written.

Out of all this, what can be said with certainty about Jesus of Nazareth? Most would agree that he was probably born in Bethlehem in the last years of the reign of King Herod the Great. The story of

The traditional site of Jesus' birth, *above,* has been overlaid with marble and illuminated by the lamps of faith in the Grotto of the Nativity in Bethlehem. The Silver Star marks the position of the manger. *Below left,* an ivory Roman Christian panel depicts Jesus ascending into heaven, while Mary mourns in front of the sepulchre, a Roman guard sleeps and an astonished apostle watches.

Herod's attempt to have this potential rival murdered in infancy certainly fits in well with what is known of that king's general character.

Herod was a strong man, who ruled Palestine as the puppet of the Roman empire. After his death, his kingdom was split up. For a time, Archelaus, his son, ruled in Judaea and Samaria but was unable to control or keep on good terms with either the Romans or his Jewish subjects. He was deposed in AD 6 and Judea and Samaria passed under direct Roman rule, exercised not from Jerusalem but from the port of Caesarea. Another of Herod's sons, Herod Antipas, took over the land east of the Jordan and Galilee. These were mixed areas, subject to continual communal trouble, especially the more fertile Galilee. Here there were Jews and Gentiles living together in a state of passive dislike, and at times open hostility. From this point of view, conditions were apparently not dissimilar to those existing in Cyprus in the 1950s, with the imperial power of Rome there in the background to keep the peace.

A prophet by the ford

The Jewish community itself was split into a number of sects. There were the Sadducees, the conservative old guard, who on the whole felt that the community should make the best of things as they were. Opposing them were the Pharisees, more aggressive, more opposed to foreign

The story of the last week of Jesus' life seems to have been well-known and passed by word of mouth long before it was written down. Modern biblical scholars, trying to piece together the events in order, now believe that the New Testament is a collection of short works written over a period of nearly a century, by the scattered Christian community. Of these, only the four gospels – Matthew, Mark, Luke and John – deal directly with the life of Jesus. The first three seem to share a common source of material from a document which has since been lost. The gospel according to John is considered the last to be written. Western artists have treated the story from individual and differing viewpoints. *The Last Supper* by Giambattista Tiepolo, **1**, shows Jesus with his twelve disciples. **2**, *The Agony in the Garden* by El Greco depicts Jesus praying in the Garden of Gethsemane while some apostles sleep and Judas plots with Roman soldiers. **3**, *The Arrest* by Goya; Judas betrays Jesus. **4**, The powerful *Crucifixion* by Mathias Grünewald. **5**, *The Dead Christ* by Andrea Mantegna.

domination, and also theologically at odds with the Sadducees. On the extreme wing of the Pharisee party a movement advocating armed resistance to the enemy grew up during the lifetime of Jesus of Nazareth. This guerrilla movement, known as the Zealot party, eventually became pre-eminent, and in AD 66 the whole country exploded into open rebellion and revolt. After a heroic but vain resistance, the legionary generals Vespasian and Titus destroyed Jerusalem and its temple, and the idea of a Jewish homeland remained a dream until 1948.

Jesus grew to manhood presumably in Galilee, presumably in the Jewish rather than the Gentile communities; his friends were Jewish. Significantly Tiberias, the chief town on the lake of Galilee, is not

mentioned in the gospels – his activities seem to have centred on the predominantly Jewish town of Capernaum.

The ministry of Jesus of Nazareth was a short one, covering only a year, according to the first three gospels – held to be rather more reliable than John on this point. Mark sees this emergence of Jesus on to the public scene as the beginning of the 'good news' of Jesus Christ, the events which were continuing in his own day and of which he was part. Jesus is first seen in connection with John the Baptizer, a preacher in whom the authentic voice of the prophets of Israel was being heard again, crying for social justice and proclaiming the imminent intervention of Yahweh in the history of Israel.

John was operating in the Jordan valley,

at the fords of Jordan opposite Jericho. He attracted a great deal of public attention. Jesus recognized in John the herald of the Messianic Age, and was baptized by him. Shortly afterwards, John was arrested by Herod Antipas and subsequently executed. Not long after John's arrest, Jesus started to preach in the villages and countryside of Galilee, and also to heal the sick. The substance of his proclamation was: 'The time has come; the Kingdom of God is upon you; repent, and believe the good news.'

In proclaiming the Kingdom of God, he was speaking of a subject of great importance to the Jewish people. The Kingdom of God was the event to which all were looking, with a variety of different hopes and expectations. Perhaps for most it

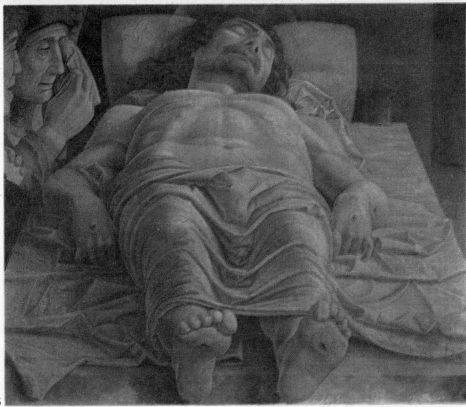

seen the like. He teaches with authority – not like the scribes and the Pharisees.' His manner, penetrating, questioning and cutting through to the heart of the problem, his refusal to fall into any recognizable role – rabbi, healer, Messianic pretender – was too great a challenge to the established prejudices of many people. Some became devoted to him and others became implacably hostile.

Reading the gospels, one gets a vivid impression of the 'springtime in Galilee' being clouded over with growing opposition from the authorities, both the representatives of the religious Establishment and the supporters of Herod's régime, until at last Jesus decides to leave Galilee to think out the implications of this failure, characterized by the complete rejection he experienced in his own village of Nazareth. It may be that he had expected that people would be able to change the direction of their lives and, acknowledging the sovereignty of God, lay hold of the Kingdom.

'You are the Messiah'

Jesus seems to have taken his closest disciples on a journey, possibly two journeys, to the region to the north of the lake of Galilee – Gentile territory ruled by Herod's brother Philip – where he appears to have devoted himself to teaching this small group. It was during this period, near Caesarea Philippi in the far north, that Peter made his great statement of belief. Jesus was apparently discussing with his friends what people thought of him, and asked them, 'Who do you say I am?' Peter replied, on behalf of the disciples, 'You are the Messiah.' (Christ is a Greek translation of the Jewish word Messiah.) This marks a turning-point in the gospel story: it is the first time at which a claim has been made by any of the disciples. In the gospel record Jesus did not refer to himself at all as Messiah, and in Mark's record he does not agree or disagree with Peter, but merely gives the disciples strict orders not to tell anyone about it, and apparently discusses the possibility of his being subject to attack and execution by the authorities. When Peter says that this is not the role of Messiah, Jesus attacks him in the strongest terms: 'Get thee behind me, Satan. You think as men think, not as God thinks.' When it is remembered that the gospels are the product of the *believing* community after the Resurrection, this reticence seems more striking.

It seems quite clear that Jesus of Nazareth thought in terms of a mission from God and not of an office or rank which he held. Immediately after Peter's statement of belief occurs the account of the disciples' vision of Jesus which is normally known as the Transfiguration. During this period he seems to have decided that the Kingdom must be proclaimed in Jerusalem itself, and thereafter he heads south for the Holy City. He would appear to have travelled back through Galilee and, according to Luke, down through Perea on the east bank of the Jordan, crossing over opposite Jericho and taking the steep climbing road up

meant the restoration of sovereignty to the Jewish people, the punishment of foreign invaders and the collaborators within the nation – those who had succumbed to the Hellenizing ways of the Herods or were making big profits out of the crippling taxation imposed on the country by both Romans and Herodians alike.

Much of Jesus' teaching is about the Kingdom. For him the Kingdom is not a political state or a social or economic system; it is a certain quality of living. Unlike, for instance, Plato, Jesus did not present a blueprint of the ideal state, and his characteristic method of description is the parable. For him the nature of the good life can only be expressed in concrete terms. 'Who is my neighbour and what does it mean to love him?' The

parable of the Good Samaritan is the answer.

This method can be seen perhaps most clearly in Matthew 13, where the Kingdom of God is said to be like a sower sowing seed on a variety of ground – in other words, chancy. It invariably involves the acts of discrimination, judging, evaluation – like the farmer who had to cope with the weeds among the wheat. It is unpredictable, mysterious in its action, like the action of yeast in bread, and yet it is worth all other things put together – like the treasure the man found in a field, or the special pearl. In a world full of wandering teachers, miracle workers and men with political aspirations, Jesus of Nazareth stood out. Again and again the people say of him, 'Never before have we

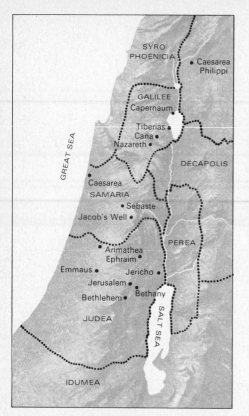

The map of the Holy Land, *above left,* indicates that Jesus travelled widely in his ministry. The river Jordan, *above,* meanders through the barren lands of the Wilderness to the fords of Jordan where John the Baptist preached the imminent intervention of God in the affairs of Israel. The Old City of Jerusalem, *below,* where the climax of Jesus' earthly ministry took place.

were carrying money with the divine image and title of Caesar upon it, and proposed the question to which for centuries the Christian martyrs were to give their answer: 'What, in fact, is owed to Caesar and what to God?' The authorities could not touch him because of the danger of sparking off a riot and bringing down upon themselves the intervention of the Romans.

There could, however, be only one end to all this. The gospels record his last supper with his friends and his institution of the central act of Christian worship. The authorities were able to arrest him during the night, which he was spending, like so many others, on the hillsides around the city. They were led by Judas to the place where he was; one theory is that Judas was a member of the Zealot party and hoped by precipitating a crisis to force Jesus into accepting the role of political Messiah. Some of the Sanhedrin – the ruling council of the Jews – conducted a completely illegal trial, in which they violated their own law by meeting secretly by night and by not following the normal rules of judicial procedure. The charge was blasphemy, but not wishing to incur the wrath of the people, they denounced him to the Governor on a charge of treason against the empire, and eventually forced an apparently rather reluctant Pilate to order his execution.

'This man was a son of God'

Throughout this drama the gospels paint a picture of a man completely self-possessed, the master and not the pawn of circumstances, for while he is completely helpless, yet he continually compels others to expose their true motives and character. The climax of Mark's account is the admiring tribute of the centurion, the uninvolved Gentile, so impressed by the manner in which this Galilean met his death that he says, 'Truly this man was a son of God.'

His followers were, according to the gospel account, bemused and bewildered by his death. It seemed the end of their hopes and dreams. The epitaph for the dead Nazarene was spoken, according to Luke, by a disciple called Cleopas, who said: 'Our chief priests and rulers handed him over to be sentenced to death and crucified him. But we had been hoping that he was the man to liberate Israel.' (Luke 24: 21.) But according to the gospels, he was not to stay dead, and his friends did not mourn a dead Galilean prophet, but hailed a risen Messiah. They proclaimed, incidentally, that his tomb was empty and, primarily, that they met and knew him alive and glorified.

The risen Christ is not, however, the Jesus of history. Whether or not Jesus of Nazareth rose from the dead is a question for which there are insufficient *historical* data to provide a 'Yes or No' answer. What is certain is that his followers believed that he rose from the dead, as do his followers today. The ideas generated by and in opposition to the faith in the resurrection of Jesus of Nazareth have been the principal determinant of Western – and to a large extent world – culture.

from Jericho to Jerusalem. On the way he repeatedly warns his friends that the probable outcome of the adventure will be his death; they, bemused by their preconception of the role of the Messiah, are unable to understand what he is saying to them.

When the party arrives in Jerusalem, it is Passover time. This was the festival which commemorated God's mighty act in delivering the children of Israel from the hands of Pharaoh. All devout Jews who could manage it tried to be there at Passover. The people of Judea flocked to the city. The Jews of Galilee made the journey south, and there would be contingents of the *diaspora,* the colonies of Jews living in practically every major city of the Roman and Hellenic world. Herod had left his fortress palace of Mekeres in Perea and was in the city, and the Roman procurator, Pontius Pilate, had come with an escort of soldiers from Caesarea on the coast. As well as a religious occasion, it was a great market and a time for festivities of all sorts. The countryside round Jerusalem, par-

ticularly the Mount of Olives, would be covered with camps of pilgrims who could not get a lodging in the city. This was clearly an explosive and dangerous atmosphere and the authorities, as always, were worried.

Apparently Jesus' sudden reappearance on the scene was welcomed, presumably in the main by the Galileans who had heard him preach, and he entered the city in a triumphant procession, while the crowd shouted and greeted him with the messianic title of 'Son of David'. He did not behave in a placatory fashion, but during the week before Passover faced the people with the clear challenge: were they in fact obeying the will of the God in whose honour the festival was being held? He physically attacked the commercialization of the Temple, and drew large crowds every day teaching in the Great Court, meeting the trick questions of the authorities with direct answers.

They tried to trap him with such questions as whether it was right to pay the Roman taxes, and he pointed out that they

The Fathers fight for the faith

Passionate and brilliant argument shook the Church throughout its early centuries. The debate hammered out the faith that has held the allegiance of millions of Christians ever since.

OVER TWO CENTURIES of the most terrible persecutions at the hands of Rome had not dimmed the fervour of Christianity, whose zeal was strengthened by an ever-growing procession of martyrs strong in faith and the love of Jesus Christ. The Eastern Emperor Constantine's astounding conversion to Christianity in 313 gave the hated religion a recognized status under the patronage of the emperor, although he did not force it upon the pagans.

Constantine hoped, however, that Christianity would be a unifying force in an empire torn by civil strife. He was greatly alarmed to discover that the Church was bitterly divided within itself. The Christians of the early Church felt an urgent need to define their faith and were now at leisure to do so as a result of the tolerance afforded them. Their arguments revolved around the knotty problems of reconciling Christ's divinity with his humanity, of defining his true relationship to God. The great heresies split the Church across with a passion and a conviction it is hard for us to understand. Nevertheless, the decisions made at the great councils formed to decide these crucial issues are the basis of what Christians believe today.

The New Testament sees Jesus as pre-existent and coming from God. The earliest Christian confession of faith was probably 'Jesus Christ is Lord', and the earliest records show that belief in Jesus as God is deeply embedded in Christian faith and worship. But when this belief is considered in detail, two types of questions are raised. First, what is the relation between Jesus and God who created the world? Could

Top left, cheap jibe from the walls of Pompeii, the drawing of a crucified ass attacks Christian faith. *Top right*, accepted secret symbols of the persecuted faith, fishes and anchor appear on an epitaph that reads 'the living fish'. But out of persecution and secrecy, Christianity developed to thrash out in public the nature of its beliefs, to win the trust of thousands of families like the fourth-century group portrayed on glass, *above*.

Christians worship him as God and remain monotheists (believers in one God)? Secondly, if Jesus had appeared to be a man, how could he also be God? If he was Man, had God suffered on the cross?

The Church eventually answered these questions by the doctrine of the Trinity, agreed at Nicaea (325), and the Definition of the Person of Christ, agreed at Chalcedon (451). In both cases agreement came after a long debate, and not all those who took

part in the debate were satisfied with the conclusion.

The first Christians were Jews and accepted Jesus of Nazareth as the Messiah sent by God to the Jews. They believed that, because of his death and resurrection, a new era had begun in which men could enter a new relationship with God. This was described as redemption or salvation. From their Jewish background they had a firm belief that there was only one God – Yahweh. It happened that, when the Christian mission began to make a real impression on the pagan world, the best pagan philosophy also believed there was only one God. This could have been a point of contact between Christians and pagans, but Christian belief about Jesus seemed to deny monotheism.

Man or God?

Several solutions to this problem were suggested. One was that Jesus was not God but an inspired man given special gifts and powers by God. This was called Adoptionism. Another was that he was not human but divine, and had only seemed to go through human experiences such as hunger, thirst, suffering and death. This was called Docetism from the Greek word 'to seem'. Neither suggestion fitted all the New Testament evidence, or the Church's experience. It was argued, if he was not God he could not forgive; if he was not Man he could not suffer for humanity. So neither suggestion was generally accepted by the Church.

A more profitable line of thought developed the idea of the 'Word' of God from the Old Testament. In Old Testament usage, especially when used of God, the term 'Word' was much more powerful than in modern speech. God's 'word' has a self-fulfilling power of its own. 'My Word', says Yahweh, 'shall accomplish that which I please' (Isaiah 55:11), and 'By the Word of the Lord were the heavens made' (Psalm 33:6). More important, in later Judaism God's 'Word' became synonymous with His 'Wisdom', making it nearer to such English terms as 'idea', 'reason', or 'plan'. It was also personified and given an independent existence. The Greek equivalent, *Logos,* was used in current Greek philosophy for the rational principle that was held to permeate the world.

This background had been used in the fourth gospel and was taken up by the majority of the Fathers, the Christian teachers. Most second- and third-century Christian writers spoke of Jesus as the incarnate 'Logos'. This seemed to save monotheism. It is possible to distinguish between a man's 'Logos' as a thought in his mind and as a word expressed. They are the same 'Logos', but exist in different ways. So, it was suggested, God's 'Logos' had always been with him as his thought, but came into separate existence as his spoken word. Finally the 'Logos' became flesh in Jesus of Nazareth. He was a real man in whom the 'Logos' had become incarnate.

'Son of God'

But this line of thought too had several limitations. It was too intellectual to bear the devotional warmth which the Church's worship was accustomed to give to Jesus under the more human title 'Son' of God. More important it could be understood in a way which either did not imply the full divinity of Jesus or else in a way which destroyed the concept of monotheism.

It could become Adoptionism, seeing Jesus as a man inspired by the 'Logos'. Or the 'Logos' could be understood as an independent being equal to God, thus making two Gods.

One solution was to see the 'Logos' as a different mode of God's being. That is to say that God exists as the Father to create the world, as the Son or 'Logos' during the incarnation, and as the Holy Spirit to inspire Christians and the Church. This form of teaching, called Sabellianism after one of its chief exponents, Sabellius, was rejected by the Church because it involved God in suffering and distorted the human picture of Jesus in the gospels.

In Alexandria in Egypt there lived an old presbyter (officer of the Church) called Arius. His teaching gave rise to one of the best known of the early heresies – Arianism. To understand Arius' teaching we must remember that 'Logos' was used in contemporary philosophy for the rational principle permeating the world. Plato and his followers saw it as a link between God and Man. This idea was widely used by the Alexandrine Christian teacher Origen. Its danger was that the 'Logos' was seen as less than fully God.

Arius developed this idea. He taught that the 'Logos' was divine but less than

God, a sort of demi-god. In the technical language of the debate the 'Logos' was not of the same substance (Greek 'ousia') as the Father.

This teaching kept the distinction between God and creation which Greeks especially thought was important. It was thought that God, by his very nature, could not have a beginning, could not change, and could not suffer. Arius suggested that this remained true of God the Father. It was the 'Logos' or Son who was created by the Father, became Man, and suffered crucifixion.

Such teaching was not acceptable to the Church as a whole. Its chief opponent

was Athanasius, a deacon and secretary to the bishop of Alexandria. He argued that the worship of the Church had always accepted Jesus as God; that Arius' teaching reintroduced the idea of many gods, as in the pagan world and, most important, that only if Jesus was God could he forgive sins and make it possible for men to partake of the divine nature.

Constantine could not make head or tail of these quarrels and began to despair of ever obtaining a united Church, for the situation in Alexandria was tense and everyone, from the highest to the lowest, was taking sides. He wrote to his ecclesiastical adviser, Bishop Hosius of Cordova

How could Christians say they worshipped One God when they believed in Father, Son and Holy Ghost? The illuminated medieval manuscript, *left*, shows the three persons of the Trinity, and thus the key problem that brilliant men in the early Church had had to solve. Those whose theories the Church rejected were branded heretics. One such was Paul of Samosata, who taught that Jesus on Earth differed only in degree from the prophets. Paul, procurator to Zenobia, queen of Palmyra, *above*, was as much a thorn in the side of the Church as his queen was to the Roman empire. Paul's followers outlived him, and had to be rebaptized before being allowed back into the Church. *Right*, Constantine watched the course of such vital but lengthy arguments with alarm, and begged Church leaders not to split hairs.

in Spain, about the contentions, describing them as 'mere words, points difficult to understand, and unprofitable in any case – squabbles, the fruit of a misused leisure'.

But these 'squabbles' were of the utmost importance to people who wanted to be clear once and for all about the essential questions of Man's relationship to Christ and Christ's relationship to God, for on this point, they saw, depended Man's salvation. At last Constantine was forced to summon a council to settle the matter. Bishops from the Eastern and Western Empires met in Nicaea in Asia Minor in 325, at what has come to be called the First Ecumenical (universal) Council.

Unhappily, not everyone could be brought to agree and the Church's inner disputes remained unsolved. Heresy and *schism* (wilful separation from the unity of the Church) were to be features of Christendom for centuries yet. The Arian teaching was discredited, however, for the Council could not support a doctrine which taught that Christ was not fully of the same nature as God. Instead they

produced a creed declaring belief in Jesus as 'The Son of God, begotten from the Father, that is from the substance of the Father, God from God, light from light, true God from true God, begotten not made, of one substance (Greek 'homousios') with the Father'. From this developed the doctrine of the Trinity, that great unifying principle which is the basis of the orthodox Christian faith. Here God, Christ and the Holy Spirit are at one and the same time both one and three.

The Nicene controversy continued, however, and at one time the Athanasian faction was defeated and Arius was reinstated. When Constantine died, his three sons shared the empire. Constantius, who inherited the East, was an Arian and banished the bishops of the Athanasian party. With the rule of Julian from 361 to 363, the empire reverted briefly to pagan rule, but with the succession of Theodosius I the argument was renewed. He it was who summoned the Second Ecumenical Council, this time at Constantinople in 381, where the Nicene Creed, the standard

of orthodoxy, was drawn up in its final form.

There has been much debate about the terms used in the debate. The purpose was clear, to deny Arianism and to assert that, in spite of the intellectual difficulties involved, Jesus was not a creature or a demigod but God. The third person of the Trinity, the Holy Spirit, was the subject of later debates.

With the fall of Rome in 410, Constantinople was then the only capital of the empire. The empire in the East had never been united. There were many reasons for this, one of them being the perpetual rivalry among her cities.

Alexandria and Antioch

Soon after the appointment of Nestorius as bishop of Constantinople in 428, the Church had to face up to the second great conflict which had been threatening her foundations. If Jesus was fully God, how were divinity and humanity combined in one being? Two strands of thought concerning this important issue were present side by side. They were associated with two cities, Alexandria and Antioch.

Alexandrine thinkers generally stressed the divine element in Christ. They emphasized the continuity between the pre-existent 'Logos' and his incarnation in Jesus of Nazareth. God's incarnation in Jesus Christ was to them essentially a divine act, where God was purposely limiting his nature for the purpose of deifying humanity. For them the acts of Jesus are acts of the 'Logos'. The human experiences are additional and relatively unimportant.

The Antiochene school placed more importance on the humanity of Jesus. They did not ignore his divinity but tended to divide him into two. Sometimes they spoke

salvation. To explain the human picture of Jesus in the gospels he suggested that the 'Logos' only took part of humanity. He argued that the seat of sin in Man is his mind (Greek 'nous'), the directive principle, and that if this principle had been present in Jesus it would have been constantly at war with the 'Logos'. Therefore, he suggested, in Jesus the 'Logos' took the place of the human 'nous'. Christ was thus an organic whole, and Apollinarius compares this favourably with what he thinks is the Antiochene tendency to split him into two.

But the Church could not accept this, even on Alexandrine principles. We saw that Alexandrines saw the purpose of the incarnation as 'deifying' humanity. The weakness of Apollinarius' theory was that it only accounted for a truncated humanity.

Mary, mother of Jesus

Apollinarius had been condemned at the Council of Constantinople in 381, but the tendency to undervalue Jesus' humanity, making it merely an outward covering for the 'Logos', continued in the Alexandrine tradition.

Another attempt by the Alexandrine school to solve the problem was made by Eutyches, a monk of Constantinople. Eutyches denied the existence of two natures in Christ, claiming that his humanity was somehow absorbed by his Divinity. His supporters were known as the Monophysites (from the Greek word meaning 'one nature'). This heresy was condemned by the Fourth Ecumenical Council at Chalcedon in 451, but it was adopted by the Copts in Egypt and has never really disappeared.

By that time Bishop Nestorius, a representative of the Antiochene school, had also been accused of heresy. Debate about Nestorius' teaching was complicated by his personal rivalry with his chief opponent Cyril, bishop of Alexandria. Nestorius' heresy was to divide the divine 'Logos' from the human Jesus. Thus he refused to call Mary the mother of God, claiming she was only mother of the human Jesus. One motive for this was to keep the difference between God and Man, avoiding the mixture of divine and human. Another was to keep the full humanity of Jesus so that, being fully human he could redeem the whole man.

Nestorius was condemned at the Third Ecumenical Council at Ephesus in 431. Rivalries between the opposing groups grew to such a pitch that civil disturbances occurred. To settle matters, the emperor Marcian called a Council to meet at Chalcedon in 451. The Church of the empire in the West was also represented.

The council issued a statement of faith combining elements of both traditions. It said that Jesus was '. . . perfect in Godhead . . . perfect in manhood, truly God and truly man . . . acknowledged in two natures, without confusion, without change, without division, without separation. . . .' This is clearly a compromise. It did not settle the debate but defined limits within which the debate might continue. In that role it has been accepted by the Orthodox Churches ever since.

Alexandria in Egypt, famous for its lighthouse, *top*, was also the town from which Christian Fathers shed light on problems of the faith. These men, leaders in Church life and distinguished scholars, formed two main groups – Greek and Latin speaking. *Above*, three of the Greeks, in a twelfth-century mosaic: Basil, John Chrysostom, and Gregory the Theologian of Nazianzus.

of the 'Logos', sometimes of the human Jesus. Behind this lay a way of thinking which stressed the distinction between God and Man. One of this school, Theodore of Mopsuestia, asked: 'What possible relation can exist between One who is eternal and another who at one time was non-existent and came into existence later?' They understood the purpose of the incarnation as a re-direction of Man's will.

Both schools found support for their own arguments in the same passages of scripture. The gospels say Jesus grew in knowledge (Luke 2:52), was ignorant (Mark 13:32) and afraid (Mark 14:35f.). Alexandrine thinkers attributed these things to a voluntary self-limitation by the 'Logos', almost a pretence. Antiochenes argued that they do not refer to the 'Logos' but to the human soul of Jesus.

Both wanted to assert that Christ was both divine and human. The problem was to explain how both elements existed together in the one incarnate Christ. Attempted explanations led extreme representatives of both traditions to propound teaching which the Church as a whole could not accept. They were therefore branded as heretics.

The Alexandrine, Apollinarius, was determined to see Christ's work as wholly the work of the 'Logos'. He would not allow that sinful humanity had a part in Man's

God, Pope and Emperor

The medieval world was shaped in a conflict of secular and religious power. Did Emperors hold their authority from God alone, through favour of Church and Pope, or by right of election?

AFTER THE second century A D, Germanic tribes harried the northern frontiers of the Roman Empire, gradually overrunning its territories until in 410 one tribe, the Visigoths, sacked Rome itself. The political vacuum left by the decay of Rome's secular authority was filled by another unifying force: the ecclesiastical authority of the Christian Church.

The role of the Church was asserted early in the fifth century by a north African bishop, St Augustine of Hippo (354–430). A brilliant and worldly scholar, Augustine had considered various philosophies before turning to Christianity in his thirties. In his most influential book, *The City of God,* he claimed that the Roman emperor received his authority from God and must, for this reason only, be obeyed by his subjects in all matters concerning the State. But questions of faith and morals, said Augustine, were concerns of the Church alone. He thus subtly asserted not only the supremacy of God over the emperor but by implication, the supremacy of God's agent on Earth – the Bishop of Rome. At the same time he initiated a train of reasoning that 1,200 years later culminated in the Stuart theory of the divine right of kings.

The Pope crowns Charlemagne

In 330, the Emperor Constantine had transferred the Empire's capital from Rome to the ancient Black Sea city of Byzantium, renamed Constantinople. By the end of the fourth century the division of the old Empire into a western and an eastern bloc was virtually complete: from Constantinople one emperor ruled the eastern Empire (later called the Byzantine Empire) and from Rome another emperor ruled the western Empire.

Amid the ruins of the western Empire, the Christian Church survived and grew strong. Bishops of Rome sent out missionaries to convert 'heathen' tribes and win over their rulers. By the end of the eighth century almost all the petty kingdoms of the former Roman Empire had been incorporated into the community of the universal Church. The spiritual leadership of the Bishop of Rome was consolidated and he became the Pope.

Relations between the popes in Rome and the emperors in Constantinople were often strained to breaking point. Officially, because no western emperor existed, the eastern emperor was the secular overlord of the Bishop of Rome. But because the eastern emperor did not physically occupy Rome, the popes extended their spiritual authority into the secular field. They came to rule Rome and its surrounding territories (the Papal States) as largely unchallenged masters.

At the end of the eighth century, Pope Leo III (750–816), an astute statesman,

Forehead of a scholar, nose of a libertine, gentle eyes of a saint – Botticelli's imaginary portrait catches the many-faceted character of St Augustine of Hippo, whose fusion of Christian teaching and Classical philosophy profoundly influenced Western thought up to modern times.

The sixth-century Eastern emperor Justinian, who gave this likeness of himself (haloed) to the church of St Vitale, Ravenna, was one of the world's great legislators and a tough enforcer of state Christianity. He persecuted pagans and heretics throughout all his dominions with uncompromising ruthlessness.

took a step designed to free the Papacy from Byzantium's nominal control: he formally created a new Roman Empire. There was in fact a ready-made empire to fill the role, that of Charlemagne, king of the Franks, a Germanic tribe long settled in the old Roman province of Gaul (France). Under Charlemagne (742–814) and his predecessors the Frankish rule had been gradually extended until it reached from northern Germany to central Italy, from the Atlantic coast to western Hungary. Charlemagne, a genial giant of a man, combined skill in war with a passion for learning and wholehearted support for Christianity. He coerced his subjects into observance of the Roman religion and threatened severe penalties against backsliders. His intellectual curiosity led him not only into an enthusiastic support of the Church's scholars, but also into a friendly correspondence with Haroun al-Raschid, the Moslem Caliph of Baghdad. Charlemagne had won the undying support of Leo III by restoring him to the papal throne after an uprising.

Thus assured of Charlemagne's fidelity to the Church, Leo III hoped to create a compliant emperor to replace the recalcitrant in Constantinople. At St Peter's, on Christmas Day in 800, Leo III placed an 'imperial' crown on Charlemagne's head, hailing him as Caesar, the new Augustus. Leo had no doubt that Charlemagne received his emperor's crown because, and only because, he, the Pope, willed it in the name of God. While Charlemagne probably appreciated the significance of the Pope's role, some say that the emperor

later considered himself tricked and that he counselled his son never to receive his own crown in like manner. (A thousand years later, in 1804, Napoleon I was careful to take the crown from the Pope's hands and place it on his own head.)

With the coronation of Charlemagne the Holy Roman Empire of western Europe came into being. The Pope clearly thought of the power of Church and Emperor in Augustinian terms. But did the emperor derive his authority from God, or – since later emperors were elected by seven German princes – from men? And if from God, was it derived directly, or through the Pope? These questions provoked disputes that lasted for centuries.

When emperors were strong enough, they asserted their independence of the Papacy. The iron-willed Frederick I (1123–90), nicknamed Frederick Barbarossa for his red beard, who was chosen as emperor in 1152, informed Pope Anastasius IV: 'We hold this kingdom and empire through the election of the princes from God alone.... Moreover, the Apostle Peter says, "Fear God; honour the king". Therefore, whoever asserts that we hold the imperial crown as a benefice from the Pope, resists the divine institution, contradicts the teaching of Peter, and is a liar.'

The ultimate deterrent

These uncompromising words summed up the viewpoint of the extreme secularists of the Middle Ages. They were to find an echo in Henry VIII's declaration of England's independence from the Papacy in the sixteenth century. But few emperors were as tough as Frederick, and the popes generally retained the upper hand. As for the lesser princes who ruled the various parts of the Empire, their position was clear: they too owed allegiance to the Pope – but only through the emperor. All other Christian rulers in western Europe were more directly 'faithful sons of the Church'. The strong religious element of their daily routines and the religious nature of their coronation ceremonies encouraged subservience to the popes.

The power of the popes was weakest in the lands of the Vikings and their descendants – present-day Scandinavia and England. In England, for example, the leading landowners, meeting in a council called the Witan, often elected their king by choosing the strongest man, ignoring claims of birth and blood. The English attitude to the Church was casual, and so – by Rome's standards – was the conduct of the English Church. But England, too, came firmly into the papal fold in 1066, when William of Normandy (1027–87) seized the throne with the blessing of the Pope, on the understanding that he would hold it as a papal fief.

To enforce compliance with its rulings, the Church possessed an ultimate deter-

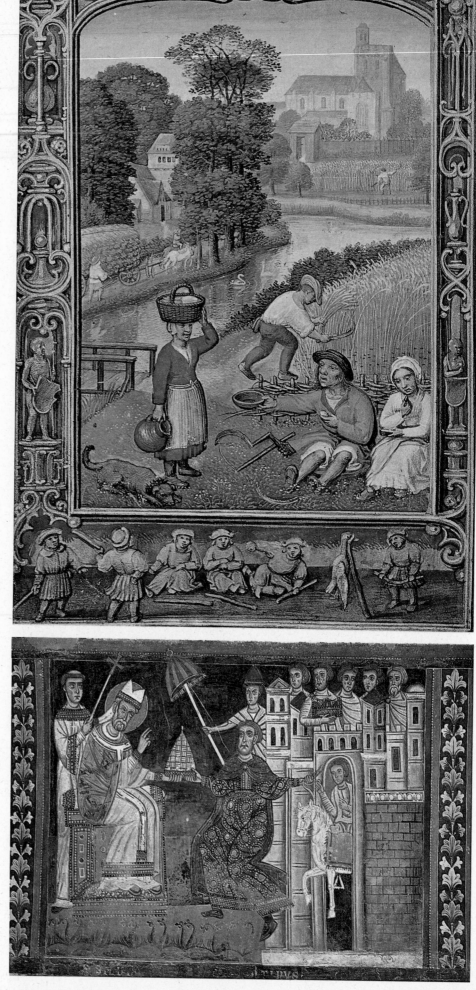

Above, the sense of security in a feudal society is mirrored in this fifteenth-century Flemish miniature of villagers gathering the harvest.

Right, the Donation of Constantine, by which he was alleged to have transferred supreme authority in western Europe to the popes, was a later papal fabrication. This fresco perpetuates the legend.

rent – excommunication. This weapon not only drove victims from the fellowship of the Church – and by implication from the fellowship of fellow men – but also threatened their immortal souls with punishment. This threat no truly devout Christian would face and on two notable occasions popes used this weapon with spectacular success.

In 1075, the Emperor Henry IV (1050–1106), a headstrong young man fresh from triumphing over rebels and rivals in his own lands, refused to obey Pope Gregory VII (1020–85) over the appointment of bishops, and threatened to turn him off the papal throne. Gregory retaliated by excommunicating Henry and telling his subjects that they no longer needed to obey him. Henry held his ground, but his horrified subjects rebelled against the spiritual outcast, and forced him to give way. He fled to plead for the Pope's mercy at the castle of Canossa, in northern Italy. It was the cold winter of 1077, and Gregory decided to make the lesson one that Henry would long remember. Traditional accounts say that Henry waited in the snow-piled courtyard of Canossa for three days before Gregory granted him absolution from excommunication. This humiliation stirred up a deep resentment. A few years later, having regained the loyalty of his subjects, Henry finally deposed Gregory and set up another pope in his stead.

England's churches are closed

Early in the thirteenth century the Papacy reached the height of its power under the domineering Pope Innocent III (1161–1216), elected at the unusually early age of 37. Innocent used the weapon of excommunication against King John of England. John (1167–1216), a wilful and aggressive man with a hasty temper, would not accept Innocent's nominee as Archbishop of Canterbury and in retaliation Innocent not only cut off John, but also put the whole of England under an interdict. Nearly all public religious services ceased, churches were closed, relics and images of the saints locked away, and all but one of the bishops left England. The frightened but angry king defied Innocent for five years, before growing pressure from his subjects forced him to climb down. As a token of submission he had to surrender his crown to the Pope's legate, who kept it for five days before returning it.

No matter how often papal authority was defied, belief in it was accepted as fundamental to the order of life in medieval Europe, even in countries where government derived partly from the old Germanic tribal system of law. This system rested on the principle that authority came from the people rather than from an autocratic monarch. From it grew the concept of common law – that a thing was right if ratified by popular custom. In countries

Above, on his knees, the Emperor Henry IV pleads for absolution before Abbot Hugh of Cluny and his ally Matilda, owner of the castle of Canossa —a humiliation Henry determined never to forget.

Right, tiny, self sufficient in government but dependent on the greater power of Italy, San Marino still has the features of a feudal state.

whose people were of Germanic origin, Germanic tribal law blended with the Church's concept of a downward flow of power and authority from God. In England the interaction of these two ideas was ultimately to bring about the development of a two-chamber Parliament: the Lords – the king's advisers, and generally his nominees; and the Commons – in theory the representatives of the common people.

Concurrently with the development of these ideas of political-religious order, grew the feudal system of political-economic order. The feudal system reached perhaps its fullest realization in England, under the Norman kings.

Feudalism rested on the principle that all land ultimately belonged to the king. His barons and other great lords swore allegiance to him, and in return for their lands raised forces to fight for him in time of war. Lesser nobles, knights and other powerful men in turn held their land from the barons, on similar terms. They, too, had tenants; freemen who could leave their land if they so wished, and serfs who had no freedom of movement and owed their labour to their landlords. As all land was held from the king – either directly or indirectly – he automatically commanded the loyalty and service of all landholders in his kingdom.

The feudal chain of command

In times of trouble the feudal system provided security against the hazard of anarchy, and an efficient system of government. It provided the king – who, whatever his faults, could be expected to defend the realm against attacks – with a quickly mustered army. Moreover, it worked two ways: while lesser men owed service to their lords, the lords in turn were bound, both by duty and necessity, to protect those under them. Thus, although the medieval serf had hardly any freedom, he enjoyed considerable security.

Just as the king was owner of all land, so, under the feudal system, he was the source of justice. To decide important issues between disputants he held court. His barons to decide lesser cases held lesser courts, and so on down the hierarchy. The Church also had its courts, but these dealt with spiritual matters, the general administration of the large Church estates and issues not falling within the king's jurisdiction.

Not surprisingly it was the Church that produced Europe's leading political thinkers during the Middle Ages. Foremost among them was St Thomas Aquinas (1225–74), a kindly Dominican theologian who reintroduced the ideas of the Greek philosopher Aristotle into western political thought. According to Aquinas, there are two kinds of truth: the truth of reason, found by the application of Aristotle's logic; and the truth revealed in the Bible and in Church doctrines. Since both reason and revelation are the means by which God makes Himself known to Man, Aquinas held that neither kind of truth could ever contradict the other.

The 'need' for secular power

Aquinas tried to show that the feudal system was not only in accordance with the will of God, but also rational because it laid down and guaranteed the rights and duties of both rulers and subjects, and promoted the stable conditions necessary to a virtuous life. Aquinas insisted that not only must God's purpose always prevail, but also that the Pope must ensure this by deposing rulers who defied the Church or disobeyed God's laws.

The last important political thinker of the medieval period was a poet, Dante Alighieri (1265–1321), a brilliant, unhappy Italian who spent much of his life in exile. Dante supported the cause of the emperor rather than that of the Church, because he believed the Church had failed in its task of maintaining a just and stable political order and that a reinvigorated, restored empire should replace it in the secular sphere. Early in the fourteenth century he wrote a treatise, *On Monarchy*, revealing his vision of a universal empire possessing all secular power, working independently of, yet in harmony with, the Papacy. In his mind the two powers did not overlap – one looked after man's material needs, the other guarded his spiritual well-being and led him to that Paradise which Dante was later to describe in the *Divine Comedy*.

But Dante's vision was no more than a dream: the Empire, like the Church, was no longer capable of the task he planned for it. By the end of the fourteenth century the emperors were largely ineffectual, owing their election to princes who were often subordinate only in theory. More powerful than the emperors were the firmly established hereditary rulers of rising powers like England and France.

Yet Dante drew attention to the *need* for secular power. He revived thoughts of the great days of the Roman Empire and paved the way for the next stage in the history of government: the rise of strong nation-states.

Above, Dante is today known almost exclusively as the author of the *Divine Comedy,* an account of his journey through the worlds beyond death – as shown in this fresco, where he is standing with the gateway of the Inferno to his right, the Mount of Purgatory at his back, and over his head the ten heavens of Paradise. But the poem also embodies his philosophy of government set out in the treatise *On Monarchy* – that the emperor was needed to guide man's earthly happiness, the pope to chart a path to happiness hereafter. Readers of the *Comedy* were meant to see in it the solution for contemporary ills: a strong empire to restrain man's selfish greed, a Church once more embracing poverty and purity.

Right, flanked by Aristotle and Plato, with the Arabian philosopher Averroes at his feet, St Thomas Aquinas, 'the Angelic Doctor', sits throned in triumph in this fresco from the church of St Catherine, Pisa. Aquinas did for the later Middle Ages what Augustine had done for the early years of the Church: he produced a brilliant reconciliation of Aristotelian philosophy – which scholars at that time thought of as a rational system that could be used without appeal to Christianity – and the revealed and reasoned truths of the Christian faith.

The Hammer of Thor

'From the wrath of the Northmen deliver us' ran the prayer hastily composed by monks in northern England. These fierce warriors were called 'the barbarians' – but what were they really like?

THE QUIET FARMS slept beside the sea. The cattle were stalled, the lanterns out, the little Lares and Penates, the Roman household gods, watching over the family from their niche beside the hearth. Suddenly keels grated on the pebbles. Torches flared; there was a brief panic, girls screamed, the hay-ricks streamed flame into the dark, and the yellow-haired barbarians were away, carrying what they could seize and leaving behind destruction and fear.

They came in waves

Their raids on the little island of Britain, one of the outposts of the Roman Empire, had grown more frequent since the beginning of the fifth century. The Roman army was withdrawn to Gaul in 407 to safeguard the more important provinces of an empire harried from without and disintegrating within. Then it was that the pirates saw their chance. Not only gold and loot lay waiting for them, but land, too. They came in waves. Two Roman-British commanders, Ambrosius Aurelianus and the legendary Arthur, held them at bay for a time, but they came again and again. The settlements of the West Saxons became Wessex, those of the Angles East Anglia, while the Northern raiders called their territory Northumberland.

Gradually the land absorbed them. They intermarried, built settlements, raised

1 A model of a Viking ship floats in a Norway fjord. In such ships, invaders from the north glided silently to the attack, striking terror into the hearts of Englishmen along the coast.

2 The Vikings, like other ancient peoples, buried their dead in *barrows,* burial mounds, where their spirits were believed to linger on. The barrows above are in North Zealand in Denmark.

crops. Historians still dispute how much they destroyed of Roman Britain and how much they assimilated, but certainly very little of it survived, either its building, its customs or its language. Bede, an eighth-century historian whose work is substantiated to a great extent by modern research, said that the home-country of the Angles (South Denmark) was depopulated; the whole of the people had migrated to Britain, women, children and all. The Roman 'Britannia' hitherto inhabited by the Celts, had become 'Eng-

land', land of the Angles and Saxons.

It was 400 years after those first raids that these Englishmen in their turn knew the terror of ships in the night, of plunder and burning and tall men with bearskin cloaks and huge gold rings on their arms, fierce men who roared the names of gods very like their own as they slew. In 400 years, memories of a threat from the sea had long been forgotten. The English were as astonished and terrified as the Roman Britons had been, when for the second time the cry of 'The Northmen! The

Northmen!' was raised round the coast.

These new raiders were from further north than the Saxons, whose lands had been the flat plains round the Elbe and the Weser in Germany. The home of the 'long-hairs' was Scandinavia. Their swift, narrow ships lurked in the *viks,* the creeks and fjords cleft between the mountains, waiting to waylay passing merchant-ships. Frequently they would glide out to go raiding overseas – *viking.*

They had a great deal in common, these two peoples who overran Britain, and together they shaped the whole character of what we now mean by the English people. They were something new. They had not known the all-pervasive Hellenizing influence of the Greeks, nor to any great extent the civilizing rule of Rome. They were 'the barbarians'.

It is true that the Germanic peoples – though not the Norse – had come within the bounds of the empire; but the Roman genius had always been to impose order rather than thought. There had never existed a colloquial Latin to correspond with the *koine,* the Greek which was spoken all over the Hellenized world. Classical Latin was a literary form based rigidly on the great writers, while there was not the lively interest in education which might have ensured some unity of language or of loyalty to the image of the empire. Those Saxons who came to Britain brought with them only a few Latin-based words, all to do with war or trade – wall, street, mile, wine, butter, cheese; this was the only impact which Rome had made upon their own culture.

And what was their culture? What beliefs had they shaped, in their huts on the moors and fens of North Germany and Denmark? Their chief god was Woden, god of battle and of death. Men and beasts were offered to him for sacrifice. His favoured symbols were the horse, a male fertility symbol, and the wolf and raven, the battlefield scavengers. The farmers' god was Thunor, who maintained order in the Universe and subdued the elements with his magical hammer.

A war-god, Tiw, and a goddess, Frig, were also worshipped, but the old religion was superceded by christianity before much written record of it had developed, and much of it has been lost to us. What remains are the ghosts and demons who haunted their land. They lurk in innumerable British place-names, often unrecognizable except to scholars. Shucknall, in Herefordshire, 'the goblin-haunted hill'; Worminster, near Glastonbury, 'the dragon's tor'; Marshaw, in the West Riding of Yorkshire, 'the demon's copse'. The spirits of the dead lived in burial mounds called barrows and in the miasma rising from the fens; monsters lived in lonely tarns, dragons in the mountain caves.

These myths reached a far more sophisticated stage in the far North, where Christianity took longer to penetrate. (Augustine had landed in Kent in 597, but the first Christian king of Norway, the Viking hero Olaf Tryggvason, died only in 1000.) They stem from the same source, for the Norsemen were of the same race as the Saxons; they had crossed from Germany to Finland to colonize Scandinavia.

Icelandic authors

Our knowledge of them, however, comes from material written in Iceland. This country was colonized just before 900 by Norse chieftains wishing to preserve the traditional way of life which at that time seemed in danger, through an attempt to introduce a centralized form of government. Their sense of tradition was thus particularly strong, and fortunately Icelandic poets and historians in the next 300 years recorded almost all we know of the myths and religion of the Norsemen.

We have to rely on these Icelandic authors, not because the Vikings could not write – they had an alphabet made up of letters in angular strokes, called runes – but because to them writing was not a means of communicating facts. The runes were holy things. Therefore, they were not used as letters on parchment, but were always carved, and were sacred to their master Odin, the god of poetry and wisdom. The enormous tradition of poetry by which their myths were transmitted was thus entirely vocal – to be spoken or sung by the court poet or harper, or by the young lords themselves, as the ale-horns passed round the king's great hall.

The language of their poems reveals a strain of great beauty and sensitivity in these fierce sea-raiders. They loved to use 'kennings' – allusive, descriptive phrases instead of an ordinary noun. A famous one is 'swan's-road' for the sea. *Beowulf,* the great Anglo-Saxon poem which recounts a myth from the common Germanic homeland, calls a sword *beadoleoma,* 'ray of light in battle' – for the sun glints on the

British artist Arthur Rackham depicted Woden raging across the sky on his sacred steed. God of battles and death, he rides to vent his anger on his enemies.

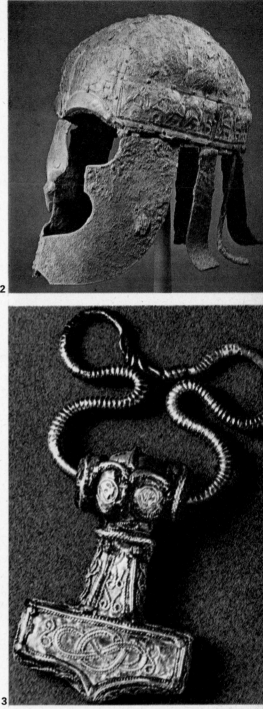

1 The huge, red-bearded figure of the god Thor, hero of warriors, strides through the sky brandishing his fearsome hammer Mjöllnir, defending gods and men from the depredations of giants.

2 Viking blacksmiths were marvellously skilled in making weapons, a warrior's most precious possession. The bronze Vendel helmet is an example of their art.

3 An amulet in the shape of a hammer, symbol of Thor, was thought to provide divine protection. These and other golden jewels were given to the warriors by their lord.

naked blade; a man's body is his 'garment of flesh', his 'heart-prison' – the cage which confines his eager soul. Men were 'trees of gold' – but as corpses on the battlefield they were 'the raven's feast', and the raven itself was 'the osprey of the spear-storm'.

Odin's ravens were called Huginn and Muninn (Thought and Memory). They were believed to bring victory, and the *Anglo-Saxon Chronicle* tells us that in the year 878 King Alfred captured from the Vikings in Devonshire a magical banner woven by the three daughters of Ragnar Lothbrok, a Scandinavian ruler of the eighth or ninth century. The raven upon it was said to flap its wings or droop them to prophesy success or defeat. Odin was also accompanied by two wolves, Geri and

Freki, and travelled on his grey horse, Sleipnir – who was sometimes pictured with eight legs, to indicate that he galloped with unusual speed through the air and over the sea.

Odin, the lord of magic, gained his mastery over the runes only at a price. An extraordinary story is recorded in the *Poetic Edda,* an Icelandic collection of mythical and heroic poetry written in about 1270. Odin himself describes how he hung on 'a windswept tree' for 'nine full nights, wounded with a spear . . . on that tree of which none knows from what roots it rises'. He continues: 'I peered downwards, I grasped the runes, screaming I grasped them. . . . Then I began to be fruitful, to grow and to prosper; one word

sought another word from me. . . .' The Christian similarities in this have deeply exercised scholars but the whole is woven from many strands of myths surrounding Odin, who was called 'lord of the spear' and 'god of the hanged', and was the chief recipient of human sacrifices.

This terrible old man, who had passed beyond death to master the secrets of other worlds, loved strife, and used to wander around the world in disguise, stirring up hatred and war. Every warrior who fell in battle went to Odin, to his palace Valhöll – Valhalla. This was modelled on the halls of the Norse chiefs, huge rooms with a vast central fire; there the lord showed his liberality by making gifts of rings and ornaments to his followers, by the great feasts which he held and the quantities of ale and mead which flowed at his table. So it was in Valhalla, with the additional bonus that the warriors could spend the day in fighting each other, but rise up whole again in the evening to drink and sing.

They followed their leader

This picture embodies a good deal of the particular character of the 'barbarian' society. They brought to the world a concept of loyalty to a leader rather than to a city or an idea. They were not a race of city-builders; they were destroyers of what they did not understand, and wanderers rather than settlers. They followed their leader. His position was one of clearly defined responsibility. He had to feed them, supply them (liberally) with drink and give generously of gold rings, brooches and ornaments which they loved. (Like peacocks, the male was the dressier of the sexes; male jewellery far outweighs female in archaeologists' finds.) In return, they were bound to him with the closest ties, pledged to fight for him and not to survive him if he was killed in battle.

This close comradeship brought about a great respect for custom. As in any society in which men eat, drink, sleep and undergo strain together, rules evolved, unwritten yet binding. They were not imposed from above for the sake of discipline —with the exception that a man's *wergild*, the money payable to his family if he was killed, was a fixed sum which rigidly defined his social class. It was this law of custom which operated after the Norman Conquest, when the manorial court used to meet in a village to settle local disputes. It may be seen as the source of the interest in local government which is still characteristic of 'Anglo-Saxon' peoples. Their sometimes undue respect for tradition and for long-established methods of pro-

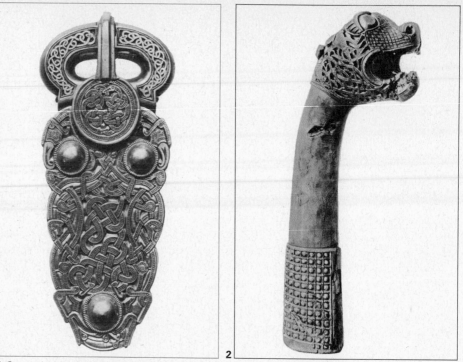

1 Serpentine forms coil over a gold buckle, part of the treasure found on the ship unearthed at Sutton Hoo in Suffolk – the complete burial ship of an unknown Saxon king.

2 Ships of the dead carried souls far away into the ocean, the Vikings believed. This slender, delicately carved head-post tapering to a lion's head is from the Oseberg ship.

cedure may also be attributed to this cause.

While they respected Odin, the hero of these warriors was Thor, the old Thunor of the Saxons. This huge, red-bearded figure, with his hammer Mjöllnir, strode from Asgard, the home of the gods, to Midgard, the home of men, defending both from the attacks of the giants who lived in the east, in Jötunheim. He was an enormous eater and drinker and performed Herculean feats of strength. On occasions he was involved in low-comedy situations: once a giant demanded the goddess Freyja as his bride and Thor was sent instead, wearing Freyja's dress (and his own red beard). His appetite at the wedding-feast was unseemly (an ox and eight salmon) and he concluded by splitting his bridegroom's head open.

This boisterous sense of humour reappears in the names which the Vikings bestowed on their notabilities – Ragnar Shaggytrousers, Eirik Bloodaxe, Harald Blue-tooth – and even in the occasional place-name in England. Brocklesby, for instance, is the farm of the man who lost his trousers.

'Beauty and mortality'

And yet it does not do to underrate these men because they liked serious drinking and schoolboy jokes. They were brave with a savage's disregard of pain – their *berserkers* fought in the skins of bears, without armour, in a trance of battle-rage. But they were not savages. They could endure because they understood pain, of the heart as well as of the body.

The poems *Deor* and *The Wanderer* are bitter remembrances of happier days – yet in *Deor* the refrain runs: 'That grief passed; this also will.' Women are not mentioned in their poems; there is no word of love. Yet the language and the thought are full of what the great Anglo-Saxon scholar Professor Tolkien calls 'the beauty and mortality of the world'.

They honour the hero above all; but he does not have to be on the winning side. One of the greatest poems is *The Battle of Maldon*, the story of an over-confident Saxon leader whose magnanimous gesture to a Viking band brought his death and that of his followers. The spirit of Dunkirk speaks through the old Saxon warrior who looks his death straight in the eye and says only, 'Courage the more resolute, heart the keener, pride the greater as our might lessens.'

1 The Vikings were master ship-builders. Long, slim vessels like the Gokstad ship were built to battle with the savage waves—and to steal noiselessly along foreign coasts.

2 The Jelling stone in Jutland was raised by King Harald Blue-tooth who, the runes say, 'won for himself all Denmark and Norway and converted Denmark to Christianity'.

Monks, friars and scholars

Out of the religious orders of Europe, with their preoccupation with theology and law, grew the idea of the university, the 'home of universal knowledge', liberalism and inquiry.

INVADING TRIBES broke up the Western Roman Empire, replacing it by barbarian kingdoms. Rome fell in 410 AD. The old organization did not disappear at once, and former Roman officials remained in the employ of the new rulers. But in the centuries which followed, much of the imperial framework withered away, especially the system of education which had flourished in Hellenistic and Roman times.

By the time of the empire there had developed a type of grammar school which was based largely on the educational theory of Plato's last dialogue, *The Laws*. These institutions provided a kind of instruction not dissimilar from that of the grammar schools of later ages. They were secular in character and imparted the basic literacy required in administration and the conduct of affairs.

The immediate heir to the Roman imperial organization was the Christian Church. The bishop of Rome, in his capacity of pope, was its recognized leader. Secular education declined, and by the time of the emperor Charlemagne (742–814) it had disappeared. In its stead a new system had gradually developed within the power of the Church. This consisted of the cathedral schools, where teaching was controlled and carried out by the clergy.

The power of the Church

The period following the fall of Rome was too troubled for learning to flourish widely. However, it *did* continue within the Church, for several reasons. To begin with, there was the need for men who could read and write in order to carry on the affairs of the Church itself. In this way the Church assumed power in state matters as well, since the only competent administrators of that period were clerics. Moreover, there was continued interest in the history of the Church and in theological problems, which led to the keeping of archives and the study of documents. Insofar as the literary culture of the ancient Greek and Roman authors survived in the West, it was largely the Church which preserved its memory.

The monasteries exercised a powerful influence in this regard. The origins of the monastic movement are various. The idea of groups living together under a strict rule was, of course, not new. The Essenes, at the time of Christ, had been such a body. Amongst the forerunners of Christian monasticism were the hermits, individuals who lived alone and away from the throng, in order to be closer to God. Later, in the fourth century AD in Egypt, there developed groups who lived this kind of life. In the West, the movement gained strength in the sixth century, especially with the foundation of the monastery on Mount Cassino by Benedict. Here he perfected his plans

Monasteries were centres of learning in the Middle Ages. Monks, among the few who could read and write, thus exercised great power.

for monastic reform and composed his Rule to regulate the life of his monks, who were originally intended to be laymen.

The monastic way of life was based on three principles: obedience, chastity and poverty. The extreme asceticism of some of the hermits was on the whole not encouraged. Furthermore, in the course of time, many of the monasteries became quite rich. This was inevitable, for they became centres not only of literary learning, but also of the practical arts. In particular, if anything resembling scientific agriculture was pursued in those days, it was the work of the monks.

Until the tenth century, most of the religious houses of Western Europe simply obeyed the Benedictine rule. The monastery of Cluny, founded in 910, became a

At the age of 25, St Francis of Assisi, founder of the order of Franciscan friars, renounced his comfortable life in order to help the poor.

centre for the reform of the whole movement. One new element was the formal grouping of houses into religious orders, with a head directly responsible to the pope. After this, many other orders arose, obeying modified rules. Particularly important were the Mendicant orders of friars (who lived on alms), which were formed in the thirteenth century: the Franciscans, Dominicans, Augustinians and Carmelites.

Unlike the monks, the friars were brotherhoods not as closely tied to their institutions, and in the main they worked directly in the outside world. The aspect of poverty implied in these orders could not always be strictly observed. Their influence has been enormous. In education especially, the Franciscans and Dominicans played a leading role in the life of the universities.

Medieval universities

Just as the grammar schools of ancient times had disappeared, so had institutions of higher learning. Justinian had abolished the Academy at Athens in 529, Alexandria had been overrun by the Arabs in 642. It is not until the eleventh century that we hear of new efforts in this field. About that time, new schools began to rise in Italy. In Salerno, there was a famous school of medicine, and at Bologna a law school. These were secular institutions. At the same time, in France the cathedral schools became centres of theological study, especially in Paris. Out of these beginnings arose the medieval universities.

The term 'university' in those days simply meant a corporation. In Italy it was the learners who came together in scholastic guilds, in Paris it was the teachers. The community itself was known as a *studium* (study) and later as a *studium generale*. In due course, scholars and masters came to be associated in the one organization, which later was simply called a university. The students were organized into 'nations', where men from one country belonged to only one guild.

In Bologna, at first it was the students who hired and paid their teachers. When the institution became more firmly established, professors were paid by the city authorities. In the early years, when the school taught only law, students were mainly grown-up men. A teacher who did not suit them might well find himself dismissed.

The University of Paris grew out of the cathedral school. Here it was the study of logic, by way of preparation for theology, which was most famous. To begin with, it was the teachers who were organised. The school became established as a *studium generale* not long after 1150, about the same time as Bologna.

Oxford, which had long been the site for various schools, became a university as a result of an exodus of English scholars from Paris in 1167. The organization of Oxford is based on the pattern of Paris. The colleges were founded to give assistance to poor scholars. Cambridge, also a school town, achieved university status towards the end of the twelfth century, and gained strength from a migration of Oxford students in 1209.

Four faculties

The early universities were soon followed by many others. These later institutions were, however, all established by charter, either from the pope or from the secular ruler.

The medieval universities generally had four faculties: theology, law, medicine and the liberal arts. Of these, the first three trained men for a profession, while the last did not. It produced men who, in their turn, would become teachers. In many cases, a study of arts was taken as a preliminary to the other faculties. Indeed, without logic, which belonged to the arts, it was not possible to cope with theology or law.

The liberal arts were so called because they pertained to the free man and were not primarily directed at the pursuit of a career. They were seven in number, divided into one group of three and one of four. The *trivium* consisted of grammar, logic and rhetoric, the *quadrivium* of arithmetic, geometry, astronomy and music. These were the traditional studies which had formed the curriculum of grammar schools in Roman imperial times, and continued to be taught throughout the Middle Ages.

The trivium is concerned with the study of language. The word itself means the 'three ways', and the subjects were considered to be necessary for any other study. It is from this that we derive our modern

1 Amaury de Bène, a twelfth-century theologian, lectures to four clerics in a classroom at the University of Paris, famous for its study of logic as a preparation for theology.
2 The medical school at Salerno in Italy, founded in the eleventh century, was an early secular university. The study of medicine was based on the writings of Greek and Arab scholars.

word 'trivial' which originally suggested, not something unimportant, but rather what is to be taken for granted. Grammar is the science of correct use of language. Logic, or dialectic as it is sometimes called, shows how to reason correctly. Rhetoric, or oratory, teaches how to use language effectively; it is essential for the advocate.

In the quadrivium ('four ways') students are first introduced to the mathematical studies of number and figure, and then proceed to science. All four subjects go back to the tradition of Pythagoras.

For each of the seven subjects there were prescribed texts and exercises. Since books were scarce and expensive, the method of transmitting information was the lecture, in which the teacher dictated from a prepared manuscript, so that each scholar had his own copy.

The Dominican order

Since the invention of printing, the merely mechanical part of the lecture has become outdated. However, with an inspired teacher, a lecture can also be an occasion for the student to see a mature mind coming to grips with a subject, and this aspect remains valuable.

At the end of his course, the student, by passing certain tests, could himself become a master licensed to teach. This was the original significance of a degree. In France it is to this day called a licence.

The theological and liberal arts faculties were closely linked with the Church; anyone teaching in them had to be a cleric. The universities as a whole grew out of the monastic movement, and this aspect certainly survived in some places until the nineteenth century. In particular the Dominican and Franciscan orders became deeply involved in university education.

The Dominican order, named after its founder, was first established in Toulouse in 1215. Dominicans soon founded houses in all the great university towns, and became active as teachers within the universities. Amongst them were Albert the Great at Cologne, and above all Thomas Aquinas (1225–74), who studied at Naples and Cologne, and taught at Paris and in Italy. To Aquinas is due the adaptation of Aristotelian doctrine to Christian theology, which has become the official theological theory of the Church of Rome. In the later fifteenth century, the Dominicans ceased to be Mendicants, and were from then on allowed to have property. This did not seem to conflict with their work as missionaries, preachers and university teachers. A more sinister aspect of their history is the important role they played in the running of the Inquisition.

The order of the Franciscans was founded by Francis of Assisi (1181–1225). At 25,

1 Friars, like the Dominican Vincent de Beauvais, were not tied to their institutions like monks but worked in the outside world. Their influence, especially in university-teaching, has been great.
2 Many medieval colleges extended charity to the poor people living nearby. Students of the College of Ave Maria in Paris are here delivering food and clothing.

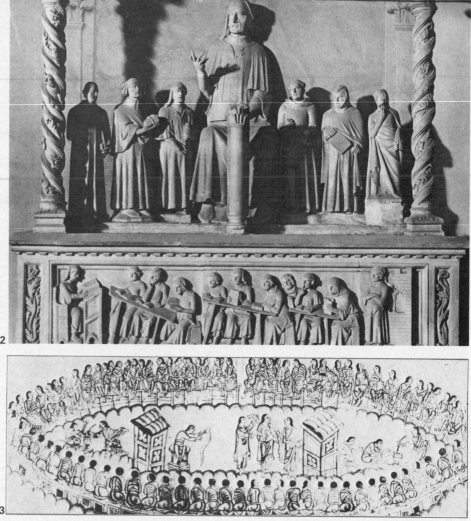

1 A manuscript illustration shows the students of New College, Oxford, with their founder, William of Wykeham. The university came into being in 1167.
2 The Tomb of Guittone Sinibaldi (1272–1337), one of the leading professors of law at Europe's leading law school in Bologna. A classroom scene appears underneath in low-relief.
3 Scholars in a ring listen attentively to their teachers at Trinity College, Cambridge, in an illustration from a Canterbury Psalter.

he renounced his comfortable life and began to serve the poor, existing himself in poverty. In 1209 he sought and obtained papal permission to establish his new rule. By 1223 this had developed into the Mendicant order of Franciscan friars.

As with the Dominicans, the practical problem of property arose, but in this case there were long-drawn-out quarrels and divisions that lasted three centuries. They led to an ultimate split between the Observants, who kept the old vow of poverty, and the Conventuals, who did not. Despite these quarrels, the tradition of helping the poor was always observed. The Franciscans were prominent amongst the early missionaries in all parts of the world.

Franciscan schoolmen

In the universities of Europe, the Franciscan order furnished a long line of distinguished thinkers in all fields. Those of the English province were perhaps the most outstanding. Roger Bacon (1214–94) studied and taught at Oxford and Paris. He insisted that discovery involves not only logical deduction but also experimental testing, a doctrine for which he was twice condemned and once locked up for 14 years. Duns Scotus (1270–1308) studied at Oxford and taught both there and later at Paris and Cologne. William of Ockham (c. 1295–1349) was the greatest of the Franciscan scholars. He studied and taught at Oxford and Paris. He was important not only as a philosopher but also in the struggle between papacy and empire, coming out strongly against the pope.

In general, these Franciscan philosophers were opposed to Thomism, the theology of Thomas Aquinas. He had argued that reason and faith overlap: some religious truths could be known by reason alone, for instance that God exists; whereas others, like the Holy Trinity, require revelation. Against this, the Franciscans held that God was not knowable by reason: the religious sphere depends on faith. In this, they contributed to the decline of Church power and paved the way for the Reformation of the sixteenth century.

Although travel in the Middle Ages was both slow and dangerous, the scholars of medieval universities were often more mobile than their modern counterparts. A famous teacher would attract an audience from far afield, and scholars would wander from place to place, visiting various schools before taking their degrees. In central Europe this tradition continued until the twentieth century. The student body, divided into the various 'nations', was thus largely international. This was possible because there were no language barriers: the international language of learning was Latin, a tradition inherited from the Church. The modern world has not yet achieved the freedom and mobility which accompanied the existence of a universal tongue.

On the whole, the scholars who entered the medieval universities were younger than students today. Fourteen and even younger was not an unusual age of entry. The reason is that, in terms of today's

system, the liberal arts course would cover the later grades of school and the first year at university. It was then still possible for one man to become master of a whole field of knowledge. The immense growth of knowledge since then, and the resulting division into ever more specialized departments, has made this impossible. The old tradition of the unity of knowledge becomes more difficult to preserve.

Humble scholars

Although the medieval universities came to take the place of the schools of ancient times, their social role was somewhat different. In the Roman Empire it was the sons of the ruling classes who were sent to school. The medieval scholar was on the whole of humbler origin. The ruling nobles were largely a military caste, not interested in learning, even if there were occasional exceptions such as the Emperor Frederick II, who founded the university of Naples in 1224. It was not until the time of the Renaissance that education once more became the mark of the ruler and gentleman: a change due precisely to the spread of education by the early universities.

As Europe revived after the Dark Ages, professional men, administrators and teachers were needed in numbers greater than the old cathedral schools could supply. Except for specifically religious foundations, universities have since become secular, but in their organization and tradition they retain to this day vestiges of their clerical past.

them, more than from the secular Church, men sought moral guidance, emotional reassurance, and, on occasion, effective protest. In the complex relationship between Church and State, they had an important part to play.

As there was but one God and one Church, so there could be only one emperor. The Byzantine Empire in theory represented the whole Christian world. Other states were temporary and regrettable aberrations, or they were part of a divine plan to chastise the Byzantines – who often called themselves the New Israel – for their sins and heresies. An emperor who met with frequent defeat or opposition was no true emperor. He could be deposed by a successful rival, who evidently was more favoured by God. Emperors came and went – sometimes with bewildering rapidity – but the Empire, and the divine plan whose instrument it was, were indestructible.

The Iconoclasts

This view of the world gave to the Byzantines great confidence. It strengthened their technological and economic superiority and their often brutal military power when things went well, and gave them a resilience and toughness in the face of adversity and defeat. And it meant that political conflicts were seen in religious terms.

In the dark days of the mid eighth century, Leo III and his patriarch declared that the adoration paid to images of saints was idolatrous. Supported by the armies of Asia Minor the Iconoclast emperors began to smash icons, to hack the mosaics from the walls of churches, to close monasteries and confiscate their property, and to denounce and persecute the supporters of the old religious practices. For a century, with a brief respite, the Iconoclasts held power.

The theologians of Iconoclasm were sincere enough in their views. The long years of defeat and humiliation at the hands of Arabs and Bulgars were a token of divine displeasure, they believed, and the cause had to be found. The subtle philosophical arguments about the relation of image and reality, inherited from Greek philosophy, seemed suspect in a rougher age. But behind the theological dispute lay the puritanical attitude of the tough peasant soldiers of Asia Minor, on whom the Empire's fate now depended. They resented the sophisticated culture of the capital, and were hostile to the growing wealth and power of the monasteries.

Byzantium was not only Christian, it was Greek, and especially so since the loss of its Egyptian and Syrian provinces in the seventh century. In Byzantium, as in the Hellenistic world whose heir it was, being Greek had nothing to do with race. It was a matter of language and culture. Many leading figures in the Byzantine world, including some emperors, were of Armenian origin: John Axuch, the friend and chief minister of Emperor John II, was a Seljuk Turk; Romanos, known as the greatest hymnographer of the Orthodox Church, was a Syrian; Gregory Pakurianos, commander-in-chief of the Byzantine army in the eleventh century, was a Georgian. The absorptive power of Christian Greek culture was as great as that of pagan Greek culture had been.

Yet the Byzantines did not call themselves Hellenes (Greeks) – not until their last days anyway; they were known as Romans – for the Roman Empire had never come to an end in the East. For them there was no Dark Age cutting them off from the ancient world, no sense of being the survivors of a cataclysm, such as was often found in the West. This sense of continuity made it easy and tempting for them to try to re-create the ancient world, although this was of course a Christian version of it.

The Byzantine political and military recovery after the century of Iconoclasm was accompanied by a cultural renaissance. Men sought out, copied, studied and imitated works of classical Greek literature, philosophy and science. They learned anew from Thucydides, Polybius and Plutarch how to analyse men's individual character and their political behaviour. They used the rhetoricians of Greece as models for speaking and writing with elegance and persuasion. From Galen and his successors they learned the secrets of medicine. From Archimedes, Euclid and Ptolemy they gained the austere insight of mathematics. They even studied the Greek

The Byzantines used their secret weapon – Greek fire – with great success against the Arabs. A mixture of quicklime, petrol and sulphur, it burst into flame when the quicklime came into contact with water.

novelists and learned from them the art of fiction. Their heritage rather overwhelmed them. One sometimes wishes they had been less concerned with conservation and more with self-expression. Yet originality is there, though it often masquerades as imitation of classical models. Occasionally, in following up Plato's thought, men challenged the fundamentals of Christian revelation, even if unwittingly.

Literacy and culture were not the monopoly of the clergy. Laymen were men of letters, and a scholarly layman might even find himself appointed patriarch, and rushed through the canonical orders in a few days. Such a one was Photios in the ninth century, the most learned man of his age, who became an ecclesiastical statesman of the highest order. Surprisingly, many emperors were themselves men of letters: Byzantine society was immensely more enlightened than that of Western Europe, at any rate until the

Hagia Sophia in Istanbul (Byzantium) was built in the sixth century. Its many domes greatly enhanced the effect of the sung liturgy of the Eastern Orthodox Church. It is now a museum.

latter's emergence from the Dark Ages.

It is significant of the weight of inherited tradition that all serious literature was written in what was virtually ancient Greek. The spoken tongue never made the creative breakthrough into literature that it made in Western Europe. But classical Greek was never a dead language in Byzantium as Latin was in the West, especially in the lands of Germanic speech. Even the half-educated understood it – or thought they did. There is some poetry in the vernacular from the twelfth century onwards; but for all serious purposes men spoke and wrote in the tongue, if not of Plato, at least of the fourth-century patriarch John Chrysostom.

In the visual arts we find Greek, Roman

and Eastern elements fused and blended into something new. Many of the exquisite reliefs in ivory and alabaster are classical in feeling and inspiration. In the mosaics, paintings and icons with which Byzantine churches were adorned, the human figure loses its classical proportions; the eyes are emphasized, as in Egyptian mummy portraits and the figures become flat and detached from real, three-dimensional space. Seen against their brilliant gold or blue backgrounds, they are magnificent symbols of a transcendent world, into which they lead the eye and soul of the beholder.

Byzantine churches had an exterior of plain, or very simply decorated, brickwork. But the interior depicted in gorgeous colour the pattern of the universe and the plan of salvation, from the prophets in the porch, through the procession of the saints and the events of the life of Christ to the Virgin resplendent in the apse. The whole was surmounted by Christ the Pantokrator – the Ruler of All – in the cupola. The worshipper was drawn into the timeless world which surrounded him on all sides.

Confidence and strength

The abstract, ascetic figures of the ninth century (the Iconoclasts destroyed most earlier ecclesiastical figured art and produced none themselves) are replaced by austere and powerful figures in the tenth and eleventh centuries. They can still be seen today in Greece at the church in Daphni, at Hosios Loukas and at the Nea Moni in Chios. These are the expression of the confidence and strength of Byzantine society of the age. As in literature, so in art the twelfth century sees a return to more dynamic and classical representations. The great mosaics of Norman Sicily, Palermo, Monreale and Cefalù, the work of Byzantine artists, show this art at its best.

After the Byzantine restoration of 1261, a new, tenderly humanist style appears, based upon the classical art of the previous century. The magnificent, warm frescoes and mosaics of the Karie Cami in Istanbul, only recently published in full, are the finest monuments of this closing period of Byzantine art, which certainly contributed to the flowering of the Italian pre-Renaissance art of Giotto and his contemporaries. And Byzantine artistic tradition lived on after the fall of Constantinople in Crete, where Domenikos Theotokopulos, whom we know as El Greco, was born and educated.

Secular art is less well known, though it seems to have passed through the same stages as ecclesiastical art. It has come down to us through book illustrations, since the great palaces with their frescoes and mosaics are all destroyed.

Seen from the perspective of today, the chief role of Byzantium was in the conservation of ideas from the classical world to the Renaissance when elsewhere they were lost. But it was never a passive, disinterested conservation. Like all societies, the Byzantines adapted and transformed and added to their heritage and they have passed it on to us, their heirs.

The mosaics inside the church at Daphni are ablaze with gold, yet exhibit the restrained style of a mature and accomplished civilization. Solomon is one of the biblical characters shown.

A tenth-century ivory panel depicts Christ blessing Romanus II and his wife, Eudocia. The emperor launched a successful expedition which captured Crete from the Saracens.

The view from the East

The lands of the East have always been the birthplace of religions. Searching for Enlightenment, meditating on the complex laws of Fate have been central preoccupations in millions of human lives.

THE EAST is called the land of the rising sun. This has long been taken not only literally, but also in a figurative sense, for the Orient has been considered as the source of wisdom and illumination. However this may be, it is remarkable that all the great religions alive today are of Eastern origin – if we allow that the Near East is part of the East. Nevertheless, we shall here exclude the three religions which belong to the 'people of the Book' – namely Judaism, Christianity and Islam. We are concerned with the religious systems of the farther East: India, China and Japan.

Early in the second millennium BC, Aryan peoples from Central Asia drifted into northern India and settled there. They brought with them a religion of many deities dominated by a male sky god, a system related to that of the northern invaders who brought the Olympian deities into Greece round about the same time. The beliefs and practices of these tribes became mixed with a variety of native religious cults, and over the centuries absorbed a great many other influences. As a result, Hindu religion as it exists today contains a whole range of religious cults and a vast number of gods each with his devotees, and there are some conflicting practices.

Three main gods

The original sacred texts are those of the *Veda,* mostly written in Sanskrit, the language of the Aryan invaders. These texts sum up the early religious knowledge of Hinduism and contain the practical details of the various sacrifices and rites. The *Upanishads,* somewhat later writings usually called *Vedanta* (that is, the end of the *Veda*), are more philosophic in character and contain the central theoretical ideas of Hinduism. One can hardly call these principles doctrines, because Hindu religion on the whole does not enjoin particular beliefs on its followers. Depending on the special historical circumstances, it developed in many different ways and is therefore fundamentally tolerant of every variant. Moreover, each main group tends to regard its own special god as superior to the others, so that there is no uniquely recognized order of importance.

The three main god figures are Brahma the creator, Vishnu the preserver and Siva the destroyer. Of these Brahma later tends to become regarded more as a kind of life-giving force or 'first cause', as is seen from the fact that the concept of Brahman is explained in the *Upanishads* as a ritual formula embodying the world soul. In contrast to this stands the individual soul or Atman. According to this theory, it is possible for the individual to attain salvation through recognizing his essential

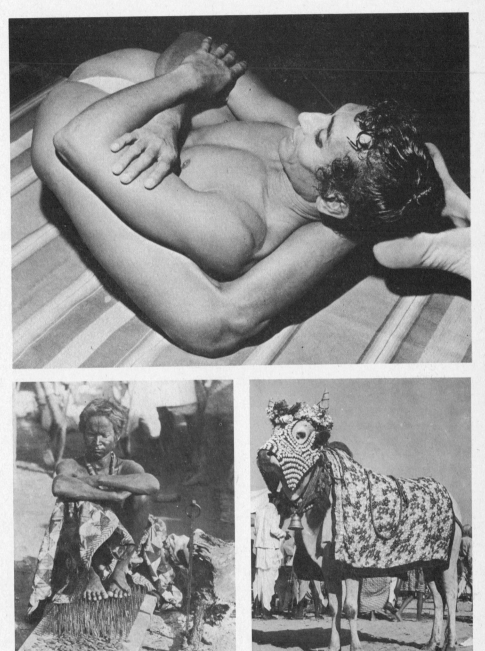

Ankles crossed behind his head, a Yogi, *top,* demonstrates an amazing feat of physical contortion, achieved by adherents of the Indian Yoga philosophy who believe that control of the mind over the body leads men to salvation. *Above left,* an Indian fakir sits on a bed of nails, miraculously without pain. Originally Moslems, there are now many such holy men of all creeds who still wield influence in country districts. *Above right,* cows and bulls are sacred animals to Hindus, possessed of mystical powers. This gaily clad animal entertains crowds in Delhi.

unity with the world, so that Brahman and Atman are ultimately one, as recorded in the Sanskrit phrase *tat tvam asi,* which means 'that thou art'.

The god Vishnu is held to have appeared in various incarnations, the most important being Krishna and Rama, so that here there is some link with actual history. Siva the god of destruction is also a god of fertility, so that we find opposite notions combined in one godhead. Besides these, there are many other gods and goddesses, each symbolizing one or several forces in the world. Each god has his female consort who may be worshipped in her own right.

A central notion of Hinduism is that of Karma, or fate, which stands for the moral quality of any human existence, and shapes it according to the individual's merits.

Existence is infinite in past and future, and good or bad fortune are the result of good or bad deeds in the past. However, Man is regarded as free to choose good or evil in his future action. A good life leads to rebirth into a better life, and a bad life to reincarnation in a lower form.

Closely linked with this view is the caste system, which is explained in mythical terms in one of the hymns of the *Rigveda*. According to this, when the Gods created the world order, they sacrificed a primeval being to Brahma (Lord of Creatures). This operation gave rise to the four social castes: the Brahmans, or priestly class, who guard and exercise the ritual practices, issued from the victim's mouth; from his breast came the soldiers; his legs the peasants; and his feet the traders. Not mentioned here is the fifth and lowest order, which consists of the 'untouchables', who perform menial tasks considered to be defiling. Each caste in turn is subdivided into many layers, so that the total structure of Hinduism consists of well over 2,000 castes, or stations, each with its own specific tasks and functions, and each largely isolated from the rest. Transition from one caste to another is impossible in one lifetime, although a meritorious life can lead to rebirth in a higher caste, just as a bad life can mean reappearance in a lower caste or even in the form of an animal.

Officially abolished

The three upper castes occupy a privileged position. They are called 'pure' or 'twice-born', in that they are subject to ritual purification and to a consecration which symbolizes a second birth, somewhat in the way of baptism. The other orders exist to minister to the needs of those above them. Each caste lives according to its own regulations and customs. Anyone who fails to observe the rules of his caste may find himself expelled. One restriction which applies to all Hindus regards the eating of beef. The cow is a sacred animal, the representative of Mother Earth, and to kill or eat it is a fearful crime. Some Hindu sects forbid the eating of all meat, because killing an animal transgresses the principle of non-violence.

In present-day India the caste system has been officially abolished, but its effects still remain: people with different caste origins tend not to mix socially. The old caste system somewhat resembled the social structure of feudal Europe, without the refuge of free towns.

While originally Hinduism did not possess any theory of salvation, we saw that there developed a view that escape from the cycle of birth and rebirth was possible through the union of the soul with the world spirit. Another, less abstract form of salvation came to be seen in devotion to a more personal god figure regarded as the manifestation of benevolence. Nevertheless, there is no question of a salvation of the world as a whole.

At a popular level, the practice of Hindu religions is, of course, not linked with these more philosophical concepts, and its practices are often centred more on the images of the gods which are kept in

The Hindu caste system is officially abolished in India, yet its influence still lingers on. *Above,* members of the fifth and lowest caste, the 'untouchables' worship Hindu gods in their village; they are so called because they perform tasks which are considered by other castes to be defiling. *Right,* one of the most important Hindu gods — Siva, destroyer and fertility god.

shrines and temples. As to these houses of God, it is interesting to note that they are not built on high places, as are the temples of the Greeks.

Insofar as Hindu religion is tied to the caste system, it cannot be taken up by anyone who is not born into a caste. At a philosophic level, however, the religious speculations of the *Vedanta* have had considerable influence on thinkers elsewhere. One curious circumstance is that we find the cycle of birth theory in the religious thought of the Greek philosopher Pythagoras in the sixth century B C. Whether this is merely a coincidence we shall probably never know. On the other hand, the notion of the individual soul striving for oneness with the divine soul is found in a number of Western philosophers (Spinoza, for example) and seems likely in part to be due to Eastern influence.

Separate creeds

Hinduism, then, is really a combination of religious and social practices. Because of its tolerant nature, it has developed many sects, some of which have become separate creeds. One of these is Jainism, based on a principle of extreme asceticism, or self-discipline. The religion of the Sikhs is an amalgam of Hindu and Moslem influence.

Most influential of all, though not now extant in India, was the religious movement of Buddhism which arose in the second half of the sixth century B C, about the same time as the beginnings of Greek philosophy.

In its origin, Buddhism may be regarded as a critical comment on the Hindu way of life. According to legend, a rich and hand- some young Indian prince, Siddhartha Gautama, was out driving in his chariot. On the way, he met an infirm old man, and realized that all men were eventually brought to this state. On other excursions he met people disfigured with disease and finally came across a corpse. Disillusionment was complete. He was forced to the conclusion that the joys of life were fleeting, while fundamentally all life was suffering and must end in death. The more men clung to life, the more they suffered. Given that Man is subject to the cycle of rebirths, the only way of salvation from suffering is through an escape from that cycle. This is achieved by suspending desire and thus achieving a state of nothingness, or *Nirvana*.

At the age of 29, then, he left his family and home to become a preacher, living the life of an ascetic and begging for his food. The spirit of evil tried to entice him away from the self-appointed task of teaching men the vanity of their desires, but Gautama was steadfast. In the course of his wanderings he settled down for some years with a group of five monks and lived

Magnificently clad in their brilliant robes, young Buddhist monks, *top left*, study for their exams in the courtyard of their college in Bangkok, Thailand, where Buddhism tends to be very orthodox in character. Buddhism originated in India in the sixth century BC but no longer exists there. Hinduism is the predominant faith of India and contains a great variety of beliefs and practices. *Above left*, a funeral pyre at a crematory *ghat* (Hindu word for landing stairs from a river) on the Ganges at Benares. *Top right*, a Hindu holy man from Malaya. *Above right*, a wandering hermit shows his indifference to material things by pouring boiling water from a hot spring over his feet.

a hermit's life seeking the way of release into Nirvana by a régime of ascetic exercises and meditation. In the end he concluded that asceticism was not the right way, unlike the teaching of the Jainist movement which arose at the same period. Having recognized that the proper path lay in a middle course, avoiding excess both in attachment and in detachment, Gautama resumed his wanderings.

One day, some time later, he rested under a tree and fell into a deep state of unconscious detachment; and so gained the enlightenment of the vanity of all things. He had at last come to the threshold of the state of nothingness, or Nirvana. From that time on he was Buddha, that is the Enlightened One. Once more resisting temptation, he decided not to enter Nirvana immediately but to preach the doctrine to help men to escape from the suffering of life. He founded a monastic order and went on spreading the doctrine as an itinerant teacher. He died at the age of 80.

This account of the life of Buddha virtually tells the nature of the original Buddhist doctrine. According to tradition he preached it to his five hermit companions at Benares when he had become enlightened. This sermon is for the guidance of those who have turned away from the world. It enjoins the middle course, avoiding the extremes of worldly pleasures and asceticism alike. Buddha refers to himself as the guide, or *tathagata*. Enlightenment, which leads to Nirvana, consists in knowing the four Truths.

The first of these is to recognize that life is essentially painful. The second is that pain is caused by the thirst for life which keeps Man tied to the cycle of rebirth. To escape from pain we must abandon this craving for life, which is caused by an attachment to being and to sensual pleasure as much as by error and ignorance. By suspending the will and the emotions we become liberated from the cycle of rebirth. The third Truth, then, is that having thus been freed, we enter the state of Nirvana, a condition in which the soul dissolves into nothingness, being perfectly at peace and unmoved by the senses. It is a state of absolute indifference to everything, it lies beyond all contrasts, even that of good and evil. It cannot really be described except by saying that it is undifferentiated nothingness in which all feeling is drowned, a state of neutral non-existence. The fourth of the holy Truths is the Eight-fold Path which leads to the attaining of Nirvana. It lays down the following principles as constituting the

middle path: right views, right aims, right speech, right conduct, right livelihood, right effort, right memory, right meditation.

Those who follow the path of the Buddha renounce worldly possessions. They join a monastic community, donning the typical yellow robe, and abide by the *dhamma*, or law of the Buddha.

The Buddhist doctrine rejects the Atman theory of Hinduism and instead regards Man as a bundle of volitions and instinctive reactions. These are in a ceaseless course of change – one Buddhist illustration is that of a constant flame, which is the same yet not the same, and ceases only when the fuel is stopped. A very similar picture of change is given by Heraclitus, one of the early Greek philosophers, who lived a little after Buddha's time.

Hinayana, Mahayana and Zen

The central notions of Buddhist philosophy considerably influenced the German philosopher Schopenhauer, who adopted the view that the will was the source of pain and evil. The original teachings of the founder are the basis of *Hinayana* ('small vehicle', that is, conveyance, to salvation), while the *Mahayana* ('great vehicle') is a more liberal variety that became fixed in pomp and pageantry, travelling mainly to Tibet, China and Japan. One Japanese variant is Zen (literally 'meditation'), which emphasizes self-control and meditation as a way towards achieving harmony. Once this has been attained through *satori* ('enlightenment'), even difficult tasks become seemingly effortless.

The main Chinese contribution to religious thought is due to Lao-tse ('the old

philosopher') in the sixth century BC. It is dominated by the principle of Tao, 'the way', a notion originally derived from the paths of the stars. It is to be understood as the universal ground of being. The path of right conduct is in some respects like the middle course of Buddhist teaching, and leads to a similarly low esteem for action. Out of this somewhat mystical doctrine Kung-tse (Confucius) a generation later evolved a code of practical ethics for good administration and civilized living, through an orderly framework of traditions and observances. The well-trained official, imbued with Tao, will of himself command respect without having to enforce it. Tao is here seen as a balancing of opposing tensions. Indeed, the principle of Tao as harmonious balance is a basic notion in the popular religious

The Hindu god Vishnu is said to have made contact with mankind through a number of incarnations, of which Krishna is widely worshipped. There are many legends about him and he appears in many forms. *Above*, men and beasts watch in gratitude as Krishna swallows the menacing forest fire. *Left*, a turn of a Tibetan prayer wheel is equivalent to repeating the prayers inside.

tradition of China to the present day.

In this overview we have left out the old Persian religion of the Parsees, the Japanese state religion of Shinto and various other developments. We have emphasized the two great systems of religious thought that began in India as most characteristic of the genius of Eastern religion. The outline, though incomplete, brings out a vital difference between East and West. Where we are used to an ethic which seeks improvement or salvation through action, even if this may involve the curbing of the individual, the East aims at attaining the good through extinction of the self. The Christian may lose himself in mystical union with the Church, but that is not the same as the annihilation of self involved in Nirvana.

The negative strain of Eastern religious thought reflects Man's resignation in the face of the extremely harsh and precarious condition of his life, which in turn tends to undermine efforts at change. In this respect, Japan can no longer count as being imbued with a predominantly Eastern outlook, for Christianity is growing fast, especially through the schools related to the churches. The fatalism of Eastern religious thought is perhaps best compared with the similar element in the ethical theories of the Stoic philosophers of Hellenistic times in Greece.

India's cultural conquest

No armies, no colonizers were sent to South East Asia by India but right across the region her faiths and arts took root. It was a peaceful revolution, the work of traders, monks and scholars.

1

2

3

TRAVEL 1,500 MILES eastwards from India into the lands of South East Asia. These are the countries and islands which India never took by force but which show evidence of how vigorously her arts and religious faiths took root. In Thailand, the *Khon*, a classic dance accompanied by a recitation of the *Ramakien*, the Thai version of the story of the Indian god-hero Rama, is still performed. In the Buddhist temples the fairy-like walls are carved with gilded eagles with human bodies, representing Garuda, messenger of the Indian god Vishnu. In Cambodia the walls of the vast ruins of Angkor are covered with sculptures of Indian myths and legends. In Java the massive temple of Borobudur is carved with scenes from the Indian *Jataka Tales* – stories of the Buddha's many lives on Earth. On the island of Bali, 10,000 temples are dedicated to a localized form of Hinduism. How this vast area was so influenced by India is a mystery which historians are still at work on. Only dimly is the pattern of this important but neglected episode in history now beginning to emerge.

'Lands of gold'

The *Ramayana*, which is more than 2,000 years old, refers to a 'gold land with water on both sides', and both this epic and India's sacred *Puranas* mention a 'barley land with water on both sides'. It is now thought likely that the 'land of gold' to which India's traders were sailing about 2,300 years ago were Burma and Malaya. Apart from gold, the Indians sought tin and offered trinkets in exchange. Indian trade in the area was part of a much larger trading system which operated between the Mediterranean and Indonesia. Although Indian seamen dominated this trade, Malay-Indonesian sailors were also

1 The Borobudur, a huge Buddhist temple near Jogjakata in Java, was built by Sailendra kings at the end of the eighth century. Basically Indian in design, the Javanese builders stamped it with their own distinctive style.
2 The bas-reliefs on the terraces, which extend for three miles, on the Borobudur illustrate scenes from the lives of the Buddha.
3 A demon in human form sits astride the prow of a royal Thai barge. The barge is used once a year during an autumn religious procession on the Chao Phya river in Bangkok.

very active at this time, and almost certainly had an important share in the trade. Beads and glassware made in the Mediterranean area became fairly common in what is now Vietnam as early as the third century BC, and in the first and second centuries AD Roman beads found their way to Johore in Malaya and elsewhere in the area.

A geographical work compiled by the cartographer, Ptolemy of Alexandria in about 165 AD and subsequently translated and revised by a Byzantine scholar, located several ports in South-East Asia. The information given in this work corresponded fairly closely with descriptions

found in Indian literature. The *Jataka Tales* and other legends, for example, tell of journeyings to *Suvarnabhumi* (probably Burina), indicating that this place was a South-East Asian 'Eldorado'.

Why did the Indian traders sail eastwards? Some scholars suggest that in the last two or three centuries BC, India lost its traditional sources of supply of precious metals when nomadic tribes cut the trade route northwards from India through Bactria to Siberia. They think that Indian merchants looked to South East Asia as an alternative source of supply. But is it likely that sailors could have disseminated the complex culture of India so thoroughly? Most experts now believe that the Indianization of South East Asia was accomplished by Indian Brahmans (Hindu priests), invited to South East Asian courts by rulers whose interest was aroused by the accounts of Indian civilization given by Indian and Indonesian sailors.

Much of the scanty information available comes from Chinese records. According to these an Indianized kingdom, Funan, was founded in Cambodia in the first century AD by Kaundinya, a Brahman called *King of the Mountain*. Chinese records refer to several Brahmans by name. Some of these appear to have founded royal lines between about the second and fourth centuries, as in Champa, a state near Funan. The likenesses of Hindu gods, particularly Siva and Vishnu, together with the Buddha, began to appear in scattered places throughout the area, fused or modified in form by local religious ideas.

I-tsing, a Chinese Buddhist pilgrim *en route* for India, called at Sumatra in 671 and mentioned two states: Malayu (near present-day Jambi) and Srivijaya. He spent six months at Srivijaya – already a centre of learning for Mahayana Buddhism – and there studied Sanskrit grammar. I-tsing recorded that more than 1,000 Buddhist monks lived at Srivijaya, observing the same rules and ceremonies as were practised in India. In 685 he returned to Sumatra from India to do further research and recorded the information that Srivijaya had absorbed Malayu. Srivijaya, a maritime power, was already expanding into nearby peninsulas and islands and sending armed forces to attack the kingdoms of Java.

Trade and honours

Unlike the Chinese, whose scholars meticulously recorded all that they saw and heard, the Indians and Indonesians of the period kept few reliable written records. Consequently little is known about Srivijaya during the century following I-tsing's visit, except from diplomatic records kept by the Chinese. These describe how the king of Srivijaya sent dwarfs, musicians and brightly coloured parrots as gifts to the Chinese emperor, who was pleased to confer honours and titles on the king.

By 775, Srivijaya, under a king of the Sailendra dynasty, apparently held much of the Malay peninsula which, under Srivijaya's influence, had been won for Mahayana Buddhism. Several kingdoms

rose, flourished and passed away on the island of Java, and parts of the island were under Srivijaya's control from time to time.

Towards the end of the eighth century a huge Buddhist temple, the Borobudur, was built in central Java, near the present-day city of Jogjakarta. This vast temple, built in the form of a *stupa* (Buddhist burial mound), stands 150 feet high. Its highly sculptured galleries, terrace by terrace, extend for three miles, circling the

On the island of Bali, Hindu beliefs moulded by native practices survive to the present day. At a cremation, bones of the long-dead are borne on paper towers which are then burned.

mound nine times. It has no interior. Thousands of bas-reliefs illustrate the Mahayana Buddhist scriptures, particularly the lives of the Buddha. The three top terraces contain about 400 statues of the Buddha beneath bell-shaped coverings. Borobudur was built by the Sailendra kings of Java who, like the Khmer kings of Cambodia, covered their country with temples and shrines containing miles of stone carvings. The vastness and architectural grandeur of these monuments bear witness to the advanced civilization which must have existed in Java about 1,200 years ago. Although the monuments were basically Indian, the Javanese builders stamped their own unique style on them.

The bas-reliefs around the base of the Borobudur were – mysteriously – covered by stone walls. The Japanese, who occupied Java between 1942 and 1945, uncovered part of these bas-reliefs and found that they illustrated the results of good and evil deeds in life, which determine *karma* (fate). Why were the fine carvings executed only to be covered up? One scholar gives a possible explanation. He suggests that the complete name of Borobudur was *Bhumisambarabhudhara*, meaning 'the Mountain of Accumulation of Virtue on the Ten Stages of the Bodhisattva', and that the base of the temple represented the first stage. The aim of the Sailendra King Indra was to become

This immense smiling Buddha reclines at the old capital of Thailand, Ayudhya. It was built of cement on bricks and has the marks and signs by which a true Buddha is recognized.

a *bodhisattva* (a near-Buddha who elects to remain on Earth), and the 'first stage' was reserved for him; it would be uncovered when the king reached the desired spiritual condition. The ideas behind this are probably very old, stemming from ancestor worship rather than Buddhism.

Siva replaces Buddha

To the north of Java's Buddhist Sailendra kingdom lay the Sanjaya kingdom, whose smaller, less spectacular temples were dedicated to the Hindu cult of Siva. The Sanjaya kings, who were to some extent under the suzerainty of the Sailendras, gained their freedom by 856. Not only were the Sailendras finally overwhelmed by the Sanjayas, but Buddhism in central Java was replaced by the cult of Siva, the event being marked by the construction of *lingas* (stylized phallic symbols) in the Hindu fashion. The last Sailendra king of central Java, Balaputradeva, when defeated and driven off the island, crossed to Sumatra. By means now quite unknown, he became king of Srivijaya – possibly he had a claim through blood relationship.

In 988 the ambassador of Srivijaya in China began his journey homewards, but on reaching Canton heard that Sumatra was under attack from Java. When, after some delay, he arrived in Champa (now

1 Wat Benchamabopitr, or Marble Temple, in Bangkok was built in 1899 of white Italian marble with glazed roof tiles. On the gables are *Negas*, demi-gods of rain.
2 Garuda, messenger of the Indian god Vishnu, is portrayed as a gilded eagle with a human body. It stands in front of the Temple of the Emerald Buddha in Bangkok, Thailand.
3 Two girls wear the elaborate costumes and traditional head-dresses of Thailand's classical dances. The graceful poses and hand movements show the influence of India.

Vietnam), so depressing was the news from Sumatra that the ambassador returned to the imperial court of China in 992 and requested that Srivijaya should be placed under Chinese protection. He was followed soon after by envoys from King Dharmavamsa of East Java, who complained to the Chinese of Srivijaya's aggression against their kingdom. The Chinese recorded all these events in their *History of the Sung,* and seem to have regarded it as only right and proper that the southern 'barbarians' should lay their petitions before the imperial emperor. As always, the Chinese saw themselves as the policemen of the area – the civilized arbiters between irresponsible vassals.

Appeasing India

Little is known about the war between the two island powers except that Srivijaya, supported by its subordinate states in Malaya, eventually won. The Srivijayans burned down Dharmavamsa's palace, killed him and destroyed his empire. Srivijaya's victory was partly due to good diplomacy; the Sumatran kingdom managing to keep on good terms with both the Sung dynasty of China and the Chola dynasty of India, China and India being the Great Powers of the period. In 1003 King Chulamanivarmadeva of Srivijaya piously declared that he had built a Buddhist temple so that prayers might be

chanted for the longevity of the Sung emperor. Two years later the same king built another temple, which was generously endowed by the Chola King Rajaraja, thus cementing Indo-Sumatran trading relations.

The niceties of Indo-Sumatran relations were, however, rudely exploded only four years later, when Indian vessels began extensive attacks eastwards across the Indian Ocean, determined to wrest commercial power from the sailors and merchants of Srivijaya. King Rajaraja claimed, somewhat improbably, that in 1007 he captured 12,000 islands. His son and successor actually attacked Srivijaya's possessions in Malaya.

All this was duly reported to the Sung emperors by the outraged envoys of Srivijaya. The Chinese could hardly have welcomed this demonstration of Indian power, and in 1028 indicated their feelings by conferring special honours upon Srivijaya's ambassador. It is also interesting to note that accounts of events in Srivijaya made their way to Baghdad, capital of the Arab-Persian dynasty of the Abbasids; to the Arabs, Srivijaya was the empire of Zabag.

In 1030, Sumatra and Java struck a

The *Wayang Orang,* a drama set to music, based on ancient Indian Hindu legends, is performed in classical costumes in Java.

bargain, sealed by a royal marriage, and combined to defend themselves against encroachment by marauding forces of Chola Indians. Of the next 34 years, nothing at all is known. From 1068 the old pattern began to repeat itself: the Indonesian states alternately co-operated and warred among themselves; sometimes Srivijaya was on friendly terms with India, at other times it defended its territories against Indian pressure. Always China appeared as the elder brother, expecting to be officially informed of what went on, acting as umpire, expressing approval or disapproval. Probably the Chinese interest was commercial rather than political.

Century after century the Chinese diligently recorded their information and impressions. Srivijaya continued to flourish but not quite as well as before. In 1178 it dropped from first to third position in China's league table of wealthy barbarian states; Arabia and Java having supplanted it. In 1225 the Chinese *Record of Foreign Nations* listed Srivijaya as only one of 15 vassal states in Malaya and western Indonesia. The Chinese Inspector of Foreign Trade described the Srivijaya capital, Palembang, as a city built around creeks and waterways which teemed with people living in boats, houses on rafts, or in huts on the banks. The picture which emerges is not dissimilar from present-day Bangkok or the Chinese cities of the Yangtse Kiang. In 1292 Marco Polo visited Sumatra and referred to the leading state as *Malayu.* After 600 years the very name of Srivijaya had disappeared.

Islam and Mongolian invasions

Already, before Polo's visit, the king of Ligor, an emergent state of the eastern Malayan Peninsula, was interfering in the affairs of Ceylon, so weakening his realm that by about 1290 it succumbed to attack and possible annexation by the T'ai, a people who, over several centuries, crept slowly southwards from China into present-day Thailand and neighbouring states. The tangled relations between Ceylon, the T'ai and the Indonesian kingdoms were probably governed in part by religious rivalries between the Mahayana and Theravada Buddhist sects. Ligor, a Mahayanan state, possibly intervened in Theravada Ceylon because of a dispute involving the possession of relics of the Buddha, particularly his begging bowl and the famous tooth kept at Kandy in northern Ceylon.

While the states of South East Asia quarrelled and destroyed one another, the Sung empire reeled under Mongol attack, and in 1279 disappeared completely to be replaced by the Mongol Yüan dynasty. The Mongol grip on South-East Asia proved to be tighter than the Sung's. Meanwhile a new and powerful influence had arrived from across the Indian Ocean – Islam. Already by 1300 the harbours of Malaya and Indonesia were filled with Arab ships, manned by Moslems anxious to spread the message of the Prophet Mohammed. Slowly at first, and then decisively, Islam chased Buddhism and Hinduism out of Malaya and Indonesia; only Bali resisted the new faith, retaining its own form of Hinduism.

Holy wars of Islam

The Prophet Mohammed inspired his armies of followers to sweep across Egypt, Persia, across North Africa and the shores of the Mediterranean to found a huge empire, united by a common belief.

AT DEAD OF NIGHT in the summer of 622 A D soldiers burst into the house of Mohammed. They were sent by the rulers of Mecca to arrest him as an enemy of the people and a danger to the security of the city, trading centre of the Quraysh clansmen of Arabia. Pulling Mohammed's relations and servants from their beds, the soldiers thrust torches into their faces, peering from one silhouetted figure to another to find the man who called himself the Prophet of God, and who secretly conspired with the enemies of the Quraysh in the rival trading city of Yathrib (now Medina). In the confusion, Mohammed, accompanied by Abu Bakr, his disciple and fellow merchant, slipped away into the night, fleeing to the desert hills where they hid in a cave.

Messenger of God

By morning the Quraysh had posted notices putting the price of 100 camels on Mohammed's head and many of his former neighbours sought to earn the reward. One band of pursuers actually peered into the cave where the fugitives hid, without seeing them. Mohammed's supporters made secret trips from Mecca to bring the fugitives food and fast camels, and after several days' journey they came within sight of Yathrib, 200 miles to the north. To the people of Yathrib, Mohammed was no traitor, but the messenger of God. They welcomed him to their city and he entered in triumph with an escort of 70 soldiers. The flight to Medina, called the *Hegira*, 'the breaking of bonds', was so important to Moslems – those who 'submitted to God'

1 Moslems believed they had divine support in battle. The Angel Gabriel encourages Mohammed during the siege of Bam Nadir.
2 After the Umayyad dynasty fell, minor dynasties

– that they dated the beginning of their era from the event.

During the next ten years most of the Medinans adopted the new faith, but Mohammed's success brought him little peace. Practically the whole of this period was spent in bitter, merciless warfare, often against the Quraysh. The character of inter-tribal warfare in Arabia at that time may be judged from a passage in the

and the Berbers ruled Spain until the Nasrids (1232–1492) unified the country. At Granada they built the Alhambra Palace where the Court of the Lions was reserved for the king's harem.

Koran, the Holy Book which Moslems claim to be the words of God revealed to Mohammed and committed to writing after his death: 'The Messenger of God may take no captives until there has been slaughter in the land.' An example of this philosophy in practice occurred when Mohammed was faced with the problem of what to do with the Bani Quraiza, a Jewish tribe allied to the Moslems, who were discovered to be secretly negotiating with the Quraysh. When the Bani Quraiza had been taken prisoner, Mohammed, undecided what to do with them, passed the task of judgment to the chief of another allied Jewish tribe, a man who under stress of wounds in battle had become a fanatical Moslem. This chief decreed: 'I condemn the men to death, their property should be divided among the victors, their women and children should become slaves.' On the following morning the sentence was carried out exactly as decreed. Thus the early days of Islam were bathed in blood.

By 632, when Mohammed died, most of Arabia had fallen to Islam. At his death the gentle, faithful, and prematurely old Abu Bakr, was appointed *caliph* (successor). Unaffected in character by his elevation to what was virtually a kingship, Abu Bakr continued to sell his cloth in the market place. Meanwhile, his commanders, with his blessing, embarked on a *jihad* (holy war) against Syria, then a province of the Byzantine Empire. In a terrific burst of energy, the Moslem armies cut clean through the enfeebled Byzantine and Persian Empires. Syria fell by 635, Palestine and Mesopotamia by 640, Egypt by 642, Persia by 643, Tripolitania by 647, and Cyprus by 649. Abu Bakr had died after reigning only two years, and this vast empire was won under the leadership of the peppery-tempered Omar (reigned 634–644) and the aged, incompetent Othman (reigned 644–656). Both these men, the second and third caliphs, were assassinated.

Reign of warfare

Reluctantly, fearful that he might suffer the same fate, Ali, son of Abu Bakr and son-in-law of Mohammed, became the fourth caliph (reigned 656–661), elected, like his predecessors, in Medina. Ali's reign was haunted by the ghost of Othman, whose bloodstained shirt, clasped by the hacked-off fingers of his wife, hung in a place of honour in the mosque at Damascus, reminding the faithful of a barbarous murder. Although Ali had tried to prevent Othman's murder, the fact that he had accepted the caliphate with the support of the assassins made him suspect, and many Moslems took up arms against him, including Ayesha, whose considerable influence in Moslem affairs derived from the fact that she was the widow of Mohammed. In 656, the forces of Ali and Ayesha clashed at Basra. Ayesha led her forces into a ferocious fight that ended only when she was taken prisoner on a battlefield strewn with 13,000 corpses. Ali, always merciful, sent her back to Medina, where, under guard, she could meddle no more in his affairs. But beyond Ayesha lay other enemies, and Ali spent his entire five years' reign in warfare. In 661 he too fell to an assassin's blade. Typically, before he died, painfully gasping out the last hours of his short, tragic reign, this merciful and self-denying man forbade the torture of his murderer.

Ali proved more powerful in death than in life; more influential as a martyr than as a conqueror. In him the Persians found

1 The arched portal leads to the Masjid-i-Shah, or royal mosque, in Isfahan, Iran. Built by Shah Abbas I, it is completely covered with tiles.
2 Shah Jehan, ruler of the Kara-Kyunlu Turkomen who took over most of western and southern Iran, rides with his son, Dara Shukoh.

a posthumous saviour, a champion against their Arab co-religionists. By 679 the mainly Persian *Shi'ite* sects ('partisans' of Ali) were divided from the majority Sunnite sects, followers of the *Sunni* (traditional record of the sayings and doings of Mohammed) by a basic schism.

Following the death of Ali and the bitter disputes that arose from the event, power passed to the Umayyad family. Ali's enemy, Muawiya, who at 60 was in fact old enough to once have acted as clerk to Mohammed, became the fifth caliph, setting up his capital in the fertile and bustling trading city of Damascus.

The pleasant climate and Byzantine

culture of Damascus began to mellow the flinty, desert-born character of Islam. The easy-going Muawiya married a Christian, appointed infidels to posts of high responsibility and gave honours to poets, a class of people banned and detested by Mohammed. He turned desert-dwellers into sailors, building ships and sending the faithful to make naval war against Byzantium itself. The Umayyad dynasty ruled from Damascus for nearly a century. They built grand, decorated mosques like the Dome of the Rock in Jerusalem and the Great Mosque of Damascus and lived almost as grandly as the Byzantine emperors. The Umayyads advanced their territories beyond Bukkara and Kabul in the east, consolidated their grip on northern Africa, took Spain, and advanced across the Pyrenees into France.

In 732, a hundred years after Mohammed's death, an Arab army pushing northward through France was halted by the Franks, with whom it fought an indecisive battle between Poitiers and Tours. Unnerved by this first check to their power, the Arabs wavered. They were ill-dressed to face the icy-cold weather, the terrain was unsuited to their usual methods of fighting, they believed themselves to be outnumbered and – worst of all – they had quarrelled among themselves over the booty they had captured. Abandoning town after town, the Moslems withdrew from France. Following this first check to Moslem power the Umayyad dynasty began to totter: Africa, Persia, and Central Asia rose in perpetual revolt. When the horse-racing caliph Hisham died, to be succeeded by the proud, profligate and atheistic Walid, the doom of the Umayyads was set. Revolt after revolt broke out. After Walid was assassinated in 744, the Umayyad Empire experienced another six years of anarchy.

Terrible vengeance

The murder of Ali had cast a shadow over the whole period of Umayyad rule, and it was to prove the final undoing. In 747, Abu Muslim, a Persian slave once bought in the market at Mecca by the head of the Quraysh clan, raised a revolt to destroy the Umayyads and replace them by the Abbasids, a family descended from Mohammed's uncle Al-Abbas. In 750 the armies of the two rival families clashed near the Tigris river in northern Iraq. The Abbasids flew black banners and (although not Shi'ite) draped their soldiers, horses and camels in black as a symbol of mourning for the martyrdom of Ali and of his many descendants killed by the Umayyads. After nine days the Umayyads broke ranks and fled; shortly afterwards Damascus itself fell.

The Abbasids wreaked a terrible vengeance for Ali. By a trick they murdered almost the entire Umayyad family; they dug up the rotting bodies of the dead caliphs, thrashed them, and flung their remnants on to fires. From 750 to 1258, the main leadership of Islam passed to the Abbasid dynasty. Its main capital was Baghdad, and its culture predominantly Persian. Only Spain was left to the Umayyads, and in 756 they established an

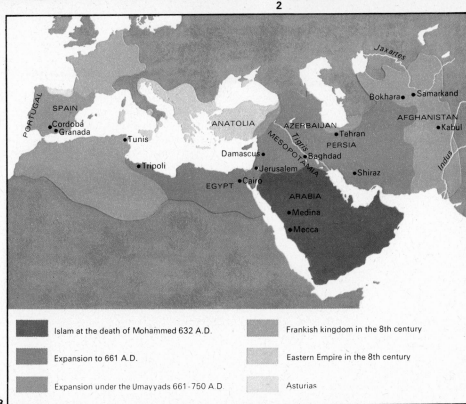

1 At Badr in 624, Mohammed and his followers fought and defeated the Quraysh. An armistice secured Mohammed's return to Mecca in 630.

2 Mohammed, on the left, gives the two-pointed Sword of Islam to Ali, his son-in-law. Ali ruled from 656 until his murder in 661.

3 The map shows that Islam extended into Persia, across southern Europe and northern Africa.

Map legend:

- Islam at the death of Mohammed 632 A.D.
- Expansion to 661 A.D.
- Expansion under the Umayyads 661-750 A.D.
- Frankish kingdom in the 8th century
- Eastern Empire in the 8th century
- Asturias

independent emirate with Cordoba as the capital of its thriving civilization. Baghdad quickly developed into a centre of great culture, its wine-bibbing caliphs permitting a degree of gaiety that would have outraged the stern piety of the early Arabian Moslems. Great literature and art stemmed from Baghdad, and the painting of living creatures – abhorred by Mohammed – was practised freely. The Golden Age of Baghdad (762–1055) is symbolized by the colourful reign of Harun al-Rashid (reigned 786–809) – the Caliph of the *Arabian Nights*.

Very little expansion of Islam occurred under the Abbasids, and they could not prevent the disintegration of the Islamic world into rival caliphates. After the reign of Harun al-Rashid, the Baghdad caliphs lost much of their power, and local rulers became quasi-independent,

127

issuing coins in their own right. Spain was Umayyad, and Morocco fell to Idris Ibn-Abdallah, a grandson of Ali, who founded the Idrisid dynasty. Egypt broke away in 970 to become an independent caliphate with its capital at Cairo, under the Fatimids – a family that claimed direct descent from Fatima, the daughter of Mohammed. The Fatimids established a flourishing culture that in many ways rivalled that of the Abbasids.

The province of Khorasan, with its centre in present-day Afghanistan, ruled in 1000 by Mahmud of Ghazni (the capital city about 100 miles south of Kabul) became a powerful state in its own right. Mahmud's territory lay at the eastern outpost of the Abbasid Empire at a time when the great westward movement of the Mongol-Tartar peoples was under way. One branch of these peoples, the Turks, were absorbed by Khorasan. Turk soldiers fought Mahmud's wars and Turk governors ruled the districts of his domains. Mahmud came to dominate the Abbasid Empire and his soldiers beat off later waves of Turks from the east. The enfeebled Baghdad caliphate effectively held only a wedge of territory along the Tigris and Euphrates north of Baghdad, to the Persian Gulf south of Shiraz. The vast territory under Mahmud's suzerainty stretched from the Caspian Sea to the Ganges.

After Mahmud's time, the Seljuks, another wave of Turks, led by Toghrul Beg, overran Khorasan and in 1055 seized Baghdad. Toghrul Beg allowed the weak Abbasid caliph to remain in Baghdad, but assumed the office of *sultan* (sovereign). The Seljuks, becoming Moslems, went on to seize Jerusalem, and clashed with the Christian Crusaders. Yet another wave of Turks, the Osmanli or Ottoman (followers of Osman), came westward. In the fourteenth century they seized Anatolia from the Seljuks and set up the Ottoman dynasty, which lasted until 1922.

Mongol-Tartar invasions

Meanwhile, Mongol-Tartar invasions continued and gathered pace. In 1258 the armies of Hulagu, grandson of Genghiz Khan, turned their flame-throwers on Baghdad, then a city of perhaps two million inhabitants. The caliph was beaten to death, and dreadful days of rape, pillage and destruction followed. The stench from a million decaying corpses drove the invaders away in fear of the plague that they had brought about. Thus, after 500 years, the Abbasid caliphate disappeared. Nothing, it seemed, could stem the Mongol-Tartar tide; it threatened to sweep away not only Islam, but Christendom too.

Egypt too, was threatened, but its rulers were of sterner stuff than the Abbasids. They were Turk and Circassian slaves who had seized control of Egypt in 1250 and established the Mamluk (slave) dynasty, which lasted until 1517. The Mamluk armies met the dreaded Tartars near Jerusalem in 1260 and gave them their first, and decisive defeat. In so doing they saved Islam and possibly Christendom in three continents.

But the Mongol power was by no means

Abd al-Rahman I founded the great mosque of Cordoba in 785. During the 300-year rule of the Umayyads, Cordoba in Spain became a centre of the Moslem world, rivalling even Baghdad.

exhausted; rather it was diverted. In the fourteenth century a mighty new conqueror, Timur the Lame (Tamerlane), took northern India, Afghanistan, Persia and Syria, and for a time held Moscow and Delhi. Timur's power was virtually unchecked, and those who resisted him met grim fates. Yet Timur was no savage, but a patron of the arts and a devout Moslem. His capital at Samarkand was a bustling centre of trade and culture.

In 1258 the invading Mongol armies of Hulagu, the grandson of Genghiz Khan, sacked Baghdad and threatened to sweep away Islam. Here Hulagu is entertained by his brother, Mangu.

While Islam expanded in Central Asia it withered away in Spain, and was finally expelled in 1492. In 1526, while the Moslem Turk armies of Sultan Suliman the Magnificent defeated the Hungarians in Central Europe and stood ready to march on Vienna, the Mongols struck at India. Baber, a Moslem descended from both Genghiz Khan and Timur, took Delhi and founded the Mughal Empire. Thus the formidable Mongol-Tartar-Turkish hordes spread the faith not only in India, but in south-eastern Europe, Russia, and China.

Islam in Asia

The Moslems had begun as peoples of the desert, but within half a century of Mohammed's death they emerged as competent sailors. By the tenth century, they were regularly sailing the sea routes eastward to Indonesia. During the time of the T'ang dynasty (ended 907), Persian and Arab ships regularly traded with China; they even sacked Canton. By the thirteenth century, tiny Moslem states had been established in Sumatra. From Sumatra, Islam spread peacefully through Malacca to Java, and thence to most of Indonesia. From the eighth century onwards, Arab influence began to creep southwards along the coasts of Africa and beyond the Sahara.

But by 1600 the great days of the Moslems were already over in both the political and cultural fields. By 1900, outside China and the decaying Turkish Empire, almost all Moslems were under British, French or Dutch (and therefore Christian) rule. Yet the Islamic religion continues to expand, particularly now in Africa. Like Christianity its fanatical days are over, but it is still the faith of more than 400 million people in the warm belt of land between Mauritania, on the western edge of the Sahara, and Indonesia.

Mohammed and the impact of a vision

The word Islam means 'total resignation to God'. Today it is the faith of millions and has helped to shape the course of world art and science. Its story begins in the vision of a camel driver.

ISLAM IS the religion of Mohammed the Prophet, called in a vision to convert the pagans to the worship of Allah, the one God. In the past it shaped an empire; today, hundreds of years after the event, it is one of the major religions of the world, claiming over 400 million followers. Who was the man and what is the strength of a religion and a civilization which inspired such allegiance?

Mohammed was born in Mecca into the Quraysh tribe in AD 570, when the Arab tribes were still predominantly pagan. An orphan, he was brought up by his grand-father and an uncle and was soon em-ployed as a shepherd and camel driver. After such humble beginnings, his mar-riage to a wealthy widow at the age of 25 established his status in Meccan society. Mohammed is said to have experienced supernatural visitations during periods spent in meditation in the nearby moun-tains. It was not until he was 40 years old, however, that he received his call to prophesy as the mouthpiece of Allah and set out to convert Arabia.

The country was beset by a bewildering number of cults and religions, including the worship of astral gods, fertility god-desses, genii and sacred stones. Allah, the name for God, was probably already known to the Quraysh tribe as a High God. *Islam* means 'total resignation to God' and Mohammed's faith can be sum-med up in the words. 'There is no god but God and Mohammed is the prophet of God.' It is an austere faith, with the central belief being the submission to the absolute power of Allah.

Allah, the one God

Islam claims to be a divinely revealed religion given to the world by Mohammed, the last and greatest of a succession of prophets. The doctrines of Islam, its pre-cepts and practices, are enshrined in the Book of God – the Koran – which is re-garded as divinely inspired, a message dictated to the Prophet Mohammed in Arabic.

Throughout the Koran the belief in Allah as one and universal is emphasized, as distinct from the Christian concept of the Trinity. God sits on his throne in the seventh heaven, surrounded by angels – sexless beings who hold the throne high and praise him eternally.

According to the Koran, Allah created the world in six days and each new life is created by Allah breathing into a soul. Man is soul and body and in Man is good and evil – the evil is inherited from Adam who was tempted by Satan. Between man-kind and the spirits are genii, male and female, inhabitants of the desert and created by fire.

On the day of judgement, known as 'the

Facing Mecca, Moslems prostrate themselves in unison before Allah on a bridge spanning the Nile. Wherever they are, whatever they are doing, five times a day Moslems must stop to worship.

hour', an angel will sound a trumpet, the Earth will be broken up, and the souls will rejoin their bodies. Allah will appear on his throne, the great Book will be opened, and a list of his deeds will be given to every man: a balance will be used to weigh good and evil. The genii will give evidence against those who have worshipped idols. The righteous will then enter into the pleasures of heaven – feasting, brilliant garments, sweet scents, music and the enjoyment of the delights of the black-eyed daughters of paradise – and the wicked will be cast into the fiery ditch, where pains of body and soul will be united.

The great attraction of Islam is that it is a practical religion for practical people, living everyday lives. No Moslem is in any doubt as to how he should carry out his religious duties, of which there are five:
1, Once in his life the Moslem must say with absolute conviction, 'There is no God but Allah and Mohammed is his prophet.'
2, Prayer, preceded by ablutions, must be five times daily – on rising, at noon, in mid-afternoon, after sunset and before retiring.

The face of the worshipper must be turned towards Mecca.
3, The Moslems must give alms generously and provide for the poor.
4, If possible every Moslem must make the pilgrimage to Mecca once in his life.
5, He must keep the feast of *Ramadan,* the holy month, during which believers in good health may neither eat nor drink nor indulge in worldly pleasures between sunrise and sunset.

In addition, alcohol, gambling and the eating of pork are forbidden and male Moslems are circumcised. Polygamy is permitted, sexual relationships outside marriage are discouraged and marriage can only be contracted with the wife's consent. A man may divorce his wife easily in many Moslem countries, but she cannot divorce him. Changing social con-ditions, however, are bringing changes in custom and law.

When Mohammed was a child, the Arabs were divided into warring tribes, a few of them Christian, but mainly pagan. By giving them a strong, simple faith he overthrew idolatry and welded the tribes together. Under his leadership they recaptured the holy city Mecca, where the Prophet had been scorned. Mohammed died in Medina soon after this victory, in 632. His followers, under various leaders, took Damascus, Antioch, Jerusalem, Persia and Egypt. At the end of the seventh century they began to add the provinces of North Africa; Gibraltar fell to their zeal in 711 and soon afterwards they took Spain. Sicily was captured in 827.

Unified for the first time in a common belief, the Arabs made an astonishing intellectual expansion, filling a cultural vacuum. The Greek and Roman civilizations were only a memory; Christian Europe was at a low ebb. Into this void came the new, major force of Islam, which was to exert an enormous influence on Europe for centuries.

For Islam was not just a system of beliefs: Mohammed's religion created a system of statesmanship, a system of society, law, philosophy, science and art – a whole new civilization with religion as a unifying and dominating feature.

This situation followed naturally from Mohammed's basic beliefs. Between Allah and the believer there is no mediator. Islam has no priests, no sacraments, no formal ritual. Why, Moslems argue, should there be mediators between Man and his maker, who has known him before his birth and is 'nearer to him than his jugular vein'? In life and in death Man stands alone with Allah.

The empire of Islam

Thus Islam is the direct government of Allah, the rule of God. The state of Islam is personified by Allah; Allah is the name of the supreme power, acting in the common interest. For example, the Public Treasury was 'the Treasury of Allah', the Army was the 'Army of Allah' and civil servants were 'the employees of Allah'. Islamic law is essentially a doctrine of duties; it is legally obligatory to fulfil agreements, but it is also a moral duty. All laws have a moral or religious foundation.

The new unity of the Arabs under Islam, their early evangelical zeal, an increase of population about the time of Mohammed's death, and the low morale of the countries about them – all these factors contributed to the Arabs' success in conquering such a large part of the known world. But they did much more than conquer; they brought to Europe a new culture. They introduced the Western nations to Greek philosophy, science and medicine, and gave to them the intellectual fruits of the Islamic mind, sharpened and enriched by the impetus of a new faith.

Unlike the barbaric tribes which swarmed over Europe after the break-up of the Roman empire, throughout their occupation the Arabs preserved intact both their language and their religion. They did not persecute Christians, believing the Christian faith to be good but incomplete, and by their comparative

Above, a staircase leads from the Kaaba to the seven tiers of the Moslem Paradise. The Angel Gabriel appears with Mohammed in the first, together with the Prophet's human-headed horse Buraq, which transported him to heaven in a dream. Key episodes in the Prophet's life: *right,* Mohammed, conscious of a religious vocation, is visited by the Angel Gabriel, who reveals his mission: to lead the Arabs to a new faith. Beset by persecution in his home town of Mecca, Mohammed flees to Medina under the protection of Allah in 622, *top right.* In 630, the Prophet marched on Mecca with 10,000 men and took the trembling city with ease. He seized the Kaaba, denuding it of all idols except the black stone, *centre right,* henceforth the holy symbol of Islam.

tolerance won many converts to Islam. Moslem and 'unbeliever' alike felt themselves to be citizens of a vast empire of which Mecca was the religious, and Baghdad the cultural and political centre.

Of this immense cultural dynamic which Mohammed released the philosopher Ernest Renan wrote: 'Of the features presented by this unexpected appearance of a new consciousness in mankind, the strangest and most inexplicable is perhaps the Arab language itself. This language, unknown before, suddenly develops itself to us in all its perfection, with its flexibility and its infinite richness so completely developed that from that time to our own it has undergone no important change.'

The revelation of the Koran, the oldest authentic example of Arabic literature, sowed the seeds for this growth. The Koran could not be imitated, but it was a pattern. Accomplishment begets accomplishment. But not only must something be accomplished; to inspire to greater effort it must be *seen* to be accomplished,

and the poets and the writers kept alive the inspiration of the Koran, sang the praises of Islam's accomplishments, inspired its armies to battle and scorned Islam's enemies.

One of the greatest services of the Islamic world was to simplify and explain Greek thought, saving it from extinction, and bequeathing it to the West. One of the most famous of the Moslem philosophers was Avicenna (980–1037). His philosophical system is mainly a clarification of Aristotle's thought. Throughout his life Avicenna was particularly concerned to give rational explanations of Moslem theological dogma, particularly prophetic rule, miracles, divine providence and immortality.

The Moslems in Spain

In Spain, in the tenth century, Islamic philosophical development probably reached its height. Philosophic and scientific studies were promoted by numerous universities and schools. Knowledge and culture generally were more widely diffused in Moslem Spain than in any other part of Europe. Intellectual activity was fostered by the fusion of the peoples and the greatest intellects of Spain found inspiration in Damascus and Baghdad. Later Islamic philosophy spread to Italy and to the remainder of Europe and undoubtedly influenced Thomas Aquinas, Eckhart, Dante and other Christian thinkers.

Just as the development of the Arabic

language, inspired by the Koran, made possible the spread of Islamic culture, so the development of a practical system of mathematics facilitated many other studies and simplified and increased trade.

So-called 'Arabic' numerals are probably Indian in origin but the Arabs either adapted or rediscovered them. The zero, all important in our numerical system since it enables us to keep the figures in a series of 'powers' of units, tens, hundreds and so on, was known to the Arabs at least 250 years before it was introduced to the West. Algebra, geometry and trigonometry were all largely Islamic developments.

From about 750 to 1055 Islam enjoyed a golden age, translating many of the Greek scientific and medical works so that this knowledge was eventually incorporated into the heritage of the West. Many original scientific, biological, medical and chemical treatises were also written by the Arabs. Rhazes, for example, produced many works on anatomy and on various diseases. His work on smallpox and measles was widely translated and was still in use by doctors in the second half of the nineteenth century. On the practical side, laboratories and hospitals were set up which were models for those of the West many centuries later.

Islamic-inspired art also explored new forms and patterns. As a result of the discouragement against portraying the human form, Islamic artists became extremely clever in creating intricate patterns based on abstract, geometrical designs or on natural shapes such as the leaves and stems of plants. Thus our name for this type of patterning is 'arabesque'.

When the Arabs conquered a score of countries and the Islamic empire became larger than that of the Romans, they adapted a host of varying styles of architecture into a recognizable Islamic style. Like all the intellectual developments discussed, this could be traced directly to the faith of Islam: most of the early buildings were mosques or other religious houses and when the Moslems came to build palaces and castles they adapted the religious style.

Arches and stained glass

The Western world owes a considerable architectural debt to Islam: the pointed, ogee, Tudor and multifoil arches are Moslem in origin, and some scholars attribute the invention of stained glass to Islam. Ornamental and pierced battlements also came from Cairo to Italy and Spain. The Arab lattice of woodwork, used to conceal the women's apartments of a house,

or as a screen in the mosque, was copied in English metal grilles. Islamic architecture culminated in great works such as the Alhambra, the palace and fortress of the Moorish monarchs of Granada. Buildings such as these, beautiful (a Moorish poet described the Alhambra as 'a pearl set in emeralds'), exquisitely planned, painstakingly executed, are an expression of the dynamic ideology which is part of the faith of Islam.

Philosophy, science, medicine, art and architecture – the same dynamic is always there – the basic faith inspiring artistic and intellectual achievement. And it is significant that the leaders of Islamic thought were not only Arabs and Moors. The faith of Islam inspired the peoples they conquered so that many important contributions were made by Egyptians, Spaniards and Sicilians.

For centuries, Islam and Christianity interacted one with the other. At first Christianity was overshadowed by Islam and then Islam entered into the Christian system and enriched its culture. Islamic superiority lasted until the fourteenth century. Then Christendom discarded the fetters of medievalism and developed its own intellectual strength. As this happened, Islam began to stagnate, weighed down by an orthodoxy that had become cumbersome.

In the seventeenth, eighteenth and nineteenth centuries the Islamic power slowly declined. Politically many Moslems passed under European rule although Arabia, Turkey, Persia and Afghanistan remained Moslem, not only in religion but in government. However, even these countries were soon opened up to European influences. But although as a temporal and cultural power Islam has declined, it has certainly not been submerged. The Islamic religion is currently expanding fast. To adapt to changing times, Islam is rapidly modifying its traditions, especially in the social sphere, particularly its attitude to women.

In the centuries gone by, the contribution which Islam made to Western civilization was immense. Its influence on our culture today lives on in a thousand everyday things, as part of our heritage.

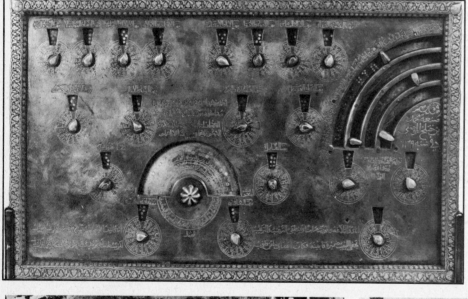

The development of practical mathematics was one of the many aspects of Islamic civilization. *Top,* an astronomical table in brass inlaid with silver from thirteenth-century Mesopotamia testifies to the ingenuity of the Arabs. In the field of science they were also active, producing many original works on anatomy and disease: *left,* a clinical consultation. Underlying all these achievements is the faith of Islam, a living force which welded an empire and reverberated down the ages. *Right,* today millions of pilgrims journey to Mecca to worship before the Kaaba.

The Moors in Europe

Spain's Islamic conquerors set up a civilization that recharged a stagnating Europe. But in an inglorious finish, the Christians threw out the people who had so enriched their lives.

EUROPE IN THE TENTH CENTURY was going through one of its darker ages. The glorious Roman Empire had long since fallen to the Germanic barbarians; in the place of the mighty empire were many smaller, fragmented states enjoying none of the security, prosperity or culture of the past. But in the southwest corner of Europe there had emerged a brilliant contrast to this bleak picture, a civilization outshining by far anything Europe could offer.

Here was the Spanish city of Cordoba, the largest, wealthiest, most civilized city in Western Europe. Visitors marvelled at its main streets, lit and paved, a state of luxury unheard of elsewhere. With its beautiful architecture, its large houses and population of half a million, the city was also noted for its 300 public baths, its 70 libraries and its numerous bookshops. Scholars from all over Europe recognized its advanced standards of art and learning. As a city or a centre of culture only Constantinople, the Byzantine capital, could compare.

Quarrels among Goths

Perhaps the most striking feature of the city was its 700 mosques. For unlike Constantinople, heart of Eastern Christendom, Cordoba was a Moslem city, the capital of Islamic Spain in the tenth century. The Iberian peninsula had changed greatly since its days as a province of the Roman Empire. First it had been conquered by a tribe of barbarians, the Visigoths. Then, in the early years of the eighth century, an army of Moslem Arabs from North Africa had sailed across what are now called the Straits of Gibraltar, to invade the Visigoth's kingdom.

Chroniclers at the time wrote that the Moslems were encouraged to invade by one Count Julian, a Gothic lieutenant in North Africa who was incensed that King Roderick had seduced his daughter, studying at Toledo, the Visigoths' capital. This is the legend; at any rate the Moslems profited by the Goths' decadence, and their quarrels amongst themselves. Gothic strongholds like Seville and Toledo soon fell to the Moslem armies and within the short space of seven years (711–718) most of the peninsula lay in their hands. These Moslem conquerors, who came to be known as Moors, were to rule in Spain for more than seven centuries. Although their Christian enemies grew strong enough to drive back the Moors from the thirteenth century onwards, it was not until the fifteenth century, and the joint forces of Ferdinand and Isabella, that the Moors were overrun and the Christian re-conquest of Spain completed.

The Moslem invasion of Spain, al-

1 A mosque at Cordoba, showing the ornate Moorish architecture. Mohammed, Islam's founder, ordered his followers to conquer unbelievers though not necessarily to convert them.

2 Twelfth-century Cistercian abbey church built in the much more simple Gothic style. It was said that Christian rulers, when they wanted an architect, applied to Cordoba.

though sudden and unexpected, was a quite natural extension of the Islamic Empire, a continuation of the mighty Arab onslaught against infidel unbelievers. Since the death of the prophet Mohammed in 632, the Arabian peoples, exalted by their new faith, had expanded their domains enormously. Attacking their neighbours on all sides, they had eaten into the Byzantine Empire and crippled that of the Persians. Within a century they had taken Iraq, Syria and Egypt and progressed right along the coastlands of North Africa. Driven on as much by the desire for plunder as Islam's command to subject the infidel, it was only a matter of time or opportunity before they attacked the weak Visigoths in Spain.

Nor did they intend to stop at Spain. In 720 Moorish armies crossed the Pyrenees into the land of the Franks, taking Narbonne and sacking the greatest monasteries of southern France. But in 732, near Tours, the Moors were defeated in a pitched battle with Charles Martel, prince of the Franks. Historians once regarded this battle as the saving of Christendom from the Moslem menace. This is certainly an exaggeration. Fighting continued in Provence for several decades afterwards. It was only gradually after several more such defeats that the Moors accepted they were achieving little and abandoned their raids and ambitions north of the Pyrenees. Far more important for Christian Europe was the failure of the Moslems in the East. In 717–718 they had attacked Constantinople. Had the Byzantine Emperor, Leo the Isaurian, not successfully repulsed them, it seems probable that the whole of Eastern Europe would have been overrun, as was to happen seven centuries later with the Ottoman Turks. But for the moment Islam had to be content with

Another example of the intricacies of Moorish architecture. Their lead in other fields, such as medicine, agriculture and commerce, made Spain one of the wealthiest areas in Europe.

ized state out of such turbulent chaos were aggravated by divisions amongst themselves. Fierce rivalry developed between the Arabs and the Berbers, the North African tribesmen who had been converted to Islam and provided most of the men for the invasion of Spain.

It was not until the rule of Abd-al-Rahman III (912–961) that the Moorish state was set on a secure footing. Abd-al-Rahman inherited a formidable task. Such had been the success of provincial revolts and Christian raids that the Moslem conquest had shrunk to Cordoba and its environs. Gradually, however, Abd-al-Rahman recovered the lost provinces and began to forage northwards into the Christian kingdoms of Leon and Navarre. Under his successors, until the end of the tenth century, Moslem rule in Spain became more complete than at any other time.

Much of the quality of the Moorish civilization which flourished in the tenth century around Cordoba stemmed from the Moors' tolerance towards their subject peoples. Although there was a bitter power struggle with the Christian kingdoms, the Christians living under Moorish rule were allowed to practise their own religion freely. Islam dictated only that non-Moslems be subjected to Moslem rule, not necessarily converted to the Moslem faith. Many Jews in Spain, who had been viciously persecuted under the Visigoths, were allowed to live in peace under the Moors; in fact Jewish merchants were responsible for much of Islamic Spain's prosperous trade. But both Jews and Christians, as non-Moslems, had to pay

Spain as its only foothold in Europe.

Unlike the Romans, or even the Visigoths, the Moors were unable to create a strong, centralized rule over the people of Spain. They were never able to subdue parts of the northwest, the area where Christian kingdoms were to emerge in strong resistance to the Moorish invaders. The Moors' new land, which they called Al-Andalus, had no fixed northern frontier, and there was a shifting no-man's-land between Al-Andalus and Charlemagne's territory. Here there was continuous raiding – Charlemagne, King of the Franks, himself hoped to subdue the Moors, but failed badly in his attempt to capture Saragossa, in 778. After this Charlemagne left Spain alone. But the Moors were also up against independent-minded rulers in outlying provinces, and restless subjects in the cities. There were

several notorious bloodbaths in dealing with such insurrections. In 797 the governor of Toledo, believing his people restless, arranged a banquet for selected guests at his newly built castle. As each entered the courtyard a sword fell upon his neck. The corpses were then thrown into a long ditch freshly dug for building purposes; this incident came to be known as the 'day of the ditch'. Not long afterwards a whole section of Cordoba's populace – 300 people – were massacred and their dwellings ploughed into the ground.

Much of the fighting in the early years of the Moorish conquest resulted not so much from religious conflict between Moslem and Christian as from power struggles between local rulers. Religion was of little account; indeed men readily changed their religion to swear allegiance to a new lord. The famed Spanish hero, El Cid, was a nobleman from the Christian kingdom of Castile who first changed sides to fight for the Moors, then later broke away to lead his own, independent, army. The Moors' difficulties in creating an organ-

Details from a pillar in the beautiful Alhambra palace, Granada. The Moors spared nothing to make it as magnificent as possible, even diverting a river to provide flushing toilets.

tribute taxes. They also suffered some inequality before the law and were generally regarded as inferiors by their Moorish masters.

The Christians' attitude to the Moors was somewhat contradictory. On the one hand they could not help appreciating that the Moors had created a civilization superior to their own. Spanish towns, in decline under the Visigoths, revived under the Moors. There was order, with officials and regulations; and organization, with guilds and corporations. The Moors were better tradesmen, better architects, better engineers and better farmers than the Christians. They were better read and more cultured. The Christians realized all this, even the Christian rulers of the kingdoms in the north. One writer has commented that whenever the Christian rulers needed a surgeon, an architect, a master-singer or a dressmaker, it was to Cordoba they applied. When the Christians finally recaptured Seville in the thirteenth century, the soldiers entering the city could not repress their amazement at its splendour.

On the other hand the Christians were determined to overcome their own inferiority and to recapture their lands from the invader. But this spirit was strongest in the Christian kingdoms emerging in the north, outside Moorish territory. For many Christians under Moorish rule the lure of Arab superiority was strong enough for them to become converts to Islam. They were known as Muwallahs. Gradually it became increasingly difficult to distinguish between these Spanish Moslems and the Arab Moslem population, particularly with the high degree of intermarriage between the Arabs and the native people. Most of the Moors arrived in Spain without women and took Spanish wives. Intermarriage extended to the highest level; Christian noblemen, even kings, offered their daughters in marriage to their Moslem overlords. Many Christians while not fully embracing the Moslem faith did adopt Arab manners and customs.

Boom in trade

Far from being a clash between the religions, here was a very fruitful partnership. With Jews, Christians and Moslems living and working together, Moorish Spain became one of the wealthiest and most thickly populated areas of Europe. Agriculture flourished, with the Moors bringing to Spain new methods of irrigation as well as numerous new crops and fruits such as rice, cotton, oranges, apricots and peaches. Industry thrived, Al-Andalus being particularly noted for its magnificent textiles, furs and pottery. Trade boomed as far afield as India and Central Asia. Scholarship and learning were stimulated by the Moors' access, through Moslem culture in the East, to the best of Greek and Roman thought and Byzantine and Persian art. Standards in medicine and science were well in advance of other states. Education was so widely spread that a high proportion of Spanish Moslems could read and write, a situation unknown in the rest of Europe.

From the beginning of the eleventh century, however, the Moorish state began to fall apart. Petty disputes between rival leaders weakened the central authority, giving the Christian kingdoms precisely the opportunity they wanted. Instead of paying tribute to the Moors, the Christian kingdoms began to demand tribute from the various Moorish factions. The Christian King Alfonso VI even managed to extract tribute from Seville, now the strongest Moorish city after the decline of Cordoba. In 1085 the Christians captured Toledo. It was never again to be in Moorish hands.

Such was the shock of this defeat to the Moors that they decided to invite a tribe

1 Wood carving in Toledo Cathedral showing the surrender of Granada, the last Moorish stronghold in Spain, in 1492. A wave of persecution and destruction followed the Christian victory.

2 A scene from a series of parchments, called *Songs of the Virgin Mary*, commissioned by Alfonso the Wise. It shows Christian knights giving thanks after victory over the Moors.

of Berbers, the Almoravides, from North Africa to help in what had become a desperate struggle against the Christians. But these crude and war-like Berbers were unable to restore the civilized rule of their Moorish predecessors. A policy of savage intolerance against non-Moslem subjects drove thousands of Christians and Jews out of Al-Andalus into the Christian kingdoms. As Moorish fortunes declined further another horde of Berbers, the Almohades, were summoned from North Africa in 1146.

Although the Almohades established a brilliant capital at Seville – to become renowned as a vigorous intellectual centre – they were unable to hold back the Christian advance. In 1212 the Christian King Alfonso VIII inflicted a decisive defeat on the Moors at Tolosa. After this all hopes of reviving Moorish dominion over Spain collapsed. Al-Andalus was to be carved up between the Christian sovereigns and local Moslem rulers.

The Christians' strength had always suffered from the separate Christian kingdoms quarrelling amongst themselves. But by 1230, with the union of Leon and Castile (on the edge of Al-Andalus and so called for its defensive castles), the Christians really took the offensive. In quick succession Ferdinand III recaptured Cordoba (1236), Valencia (1238), and after an arduous siege, Seville (1248).

Only one Moorish centre now remained, that of the Nasrids at Granada. Although it was only able to survive by paying a heavy tribute to Ferdinand III, the Nasrid court, at the magnificent Alhambra Palace, saw the revival of earlier Moorish glories. Nothing was spared in making the Alhambra as splendid as possible – there was even a system of flushing toilets in some bedrooms, ingeniously created by means of a river diverted to flow through the palace. Like Cordoba and Seville before it, Granada too became a centre of both commerce and learning, attracting scholars from Europe and the East.

But the Christian leaders were impatient to reclaim all Spain for themselves. Under the combined forces of Ferdinand of Aragon and Isabella of Castile, Granada was taken in 1492, the year Columbus discovered America. Christian rule was not to prove so tolerant as that of the Moors. Ferdinand and Isabella not only expelled the Jews (1493), but they tried to force the Moors to convert to Christianity. Some did, becoming known as Moriscos, but a vicious Inquisition was set up to harry those thought to be insincere. The Christians now turned against everything Moslem. Ferdinand and Isabella had Arabic manuscripts burned in the streets. Later Philip II ordered the destruction of all Moorish baths. Finally in 1609 any remaining Moriscos, perhaps half a million, were forcibly deported en masse. It is estimated that between 1492 and 1609 about three million Moors had been banished or executed. Christian Spain could find no role for them.

Arab discoveries

It was an inglorious ending to the history of the Moors. Spain, indeed all Europe, was greatly in their debt. It was through Moorish Spain that Europe's stagnating mind became acquainted not only with the advanced art and scholarship of the East but with Greek philosophy. Spanish thinkers such as Maimonides and Averroës not only interpreted and translated the learning of the ancients, but passed it on to European scholars attracted to Toledo or Seville.

It was through the Moors that many Arab discoveries were introduced to Europe. Knowledge of how to make paper passed into Spain from Morocco in the mid-twelfth century, and from there into France. It is probable that Arabic numerals and the concept of zero were introduced to Europe through Moorish Spain, although Italy is another possibility. Above all the Moors had established in Spain a civilization all of its own, much of which lives on to this day. Great efforts had been made to create beauty of all kinds. Poetry, especially love-poetry, seemed to flow in the Moors' veins. Music was another passion – Europe owes the lute, as well as the oval guitar to the Moors. Many of their superb buildings, their mosques and palaces, remain for all to visit and admire, witness to a past Christian Spain could ill afford to reject.

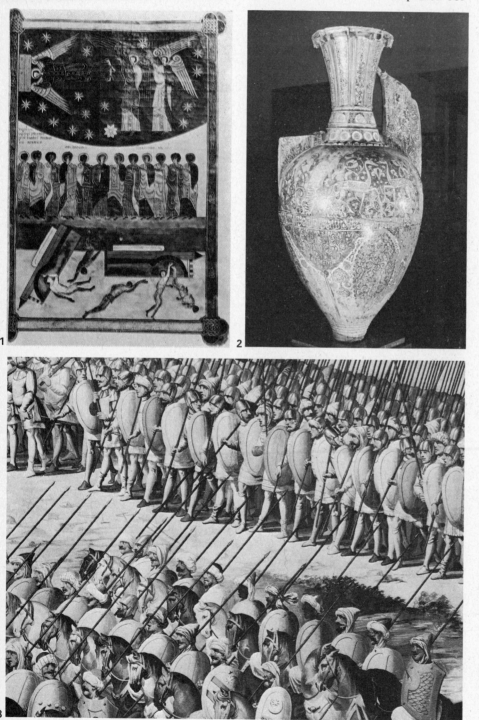

1 The 'occupation' saw a new art style called Mozarabic evolve. This example, from the eighth-century *Commentary on the Apocalypse,* shows how it combined Islamic miniatures and the primitive idioms of Visigoth folk-art.
2 One of the famous series of vases in lustre and blue made for the Alhambra palace. The Moors brought to Europe all that was best in Byzantine and Persian art.
3 Moorish troops drawn up for battle. Many Christians, including at one time El Cid, the great Spanish hero, fought for the invaders.

The Norsemen are coming!

Fearless, wild and savage, the Vikings in their long-ships were the scourge of the European coasts. Centuries before Columbus set sail, they discovered America and established a colony.

IN THE BLEAK, HARD LANDS of the Scandinavian and Danish peninsulas lived one branch of the Teutonic peoples that took no part in the assault on and break up of the Roman empire. They were known variously as Northmen, Norsemen, Danes and, later, *Vikings* (inhabitants of the *viks* – bays and inlets). Up to the eighth century, the rest of Europe had almost no contact with them and knew very little about them.

Like the other Teutonic peoples, the Vikings were mainly flaxen-haired, blue-eyed, tall and strong. One of their sagas describes the typical Norseman as 'the fiercest of all in anger and terrible in the punishment he inflicted on his foes. These he destroyed by fire, by the cruel fangs of his wild hounds, by serpents, by stoning to death or by casting them headlong from the sheerest of cliffs.' We are told too that, in spite of his fierce wrath, 'he was the bravest of all in battle, scorning to flee from three adversaries, he was the gladdest and gamesomest of men, kind, generous and gloriously attired.' But few Europeans between 750 and 950 AD would agree that the Norsemen were notable for their kindness, generosity, gaiety or love of sport.

Liberty and unwritten laws

The Norsemen were not one politically united people, but consisted of several diverse tribes, each with its own leader. Each tribe was intensely jealous of its liberty, determined to oppose any attempt to set up a strong, super-tribal government. 'We have no kings,' they claimed, although they observed generally agreed social rules. The bonds that bound the tribes together were common customs and religion, and unwritten laws which laid down procedures for the division of spoils, and for punishment for treachery, theft and other crimes.

The Norsemen were hunters and farmers who, when times were hard in their inhospitable land, marauded southwards overland from the Danish peninsula, attacking other Teutonic peoples. These sporadic, laborious and often fruitless raids ended in the eighth century, when the Viking Age, which lasted about two centuries, began.

The Norsemen of Norway turned to the sea largely because of the geographical nature of their homeland. Their mountainous country was thickly forested, the soil poor, and communication difficult. The sea offered an additional source of food, and the long Atlantic coastline, with its countless fjords, offered good sheltered harbours. The Norsemen developed a type of boat capable of sailing the stormy waters of the northern ocean, and became expert sailors and navigators, men more

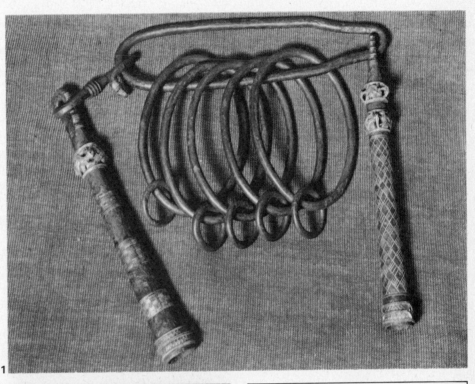

1 This iron rattle, with decorated handles, was found in the ninth-century Oseberg burial ship. It was probably used while travelling to frighten away animals and evil spirits.
2 One of the strongly carved wooden heads which decorates a cart from the Oseberg ship.

3 Christianity spread to Denmark in 823 but was not firmly established for another 200 years. This crucifix, one of Denmark's earliest, is made of gilded copper plates mounted on a wooden base. Christ is depicted as a stern and victorious Viking king.

at home on sea than on land. They laughed at the tempest. 'The blast,' they said, 'aids our oars, the storm is our servant and drives us whither we wish to go.' The hunting, fishing and crude farming of the Norsemen were, in time, unable to support their rapidly expanding population. Quarrels and feuds between tribes became incessant. The barrenness of their own land contrasted with the comparative richness of others. Once the disparity became apparent, the Norsemen began

to employ their skills as sailors and warriors to seize what they lacked from other peoples. From the end of the eighth century, the Norsemen ravished and plundered the shores of every land from the Baltic to the Mediterranean.

The Vikings raided sometimes in small parties, sometimes in fleets that numbered hundreds of ships. Their sturdy boats, long and open, with high prows and sterns and square sails, were driven by oarsmen. They were narrow enough to travel up

1 This colourful twelfth-century Norwegian tapestry, known as the Baldishol Tapestry, represents the months of April and May.

2 The pagan Viking warriors, in their long-ships and on foot, exploded into Christian Europe and ventured across the North Atlantic.

3 Many cooking and storage utensils were found in the Oseberg ship. This finely made butt is evidence of Viking craftsmanship.

4 The cart from the Oseberg ship, made of beech and oak, is carved with scenes illustrating the violent Viking sagas.

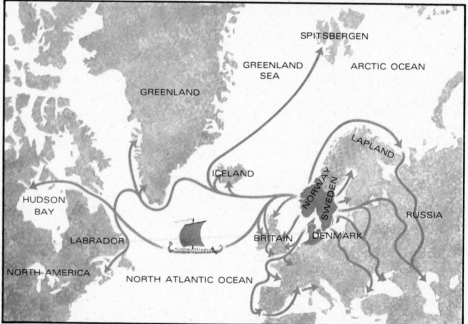

rivers and, when necessary, light enough to transport overland. A typical Viking vessel carried 40 to 60 warriors, each clad in a suit of mail with steel helmet, armed with a lance, a sword, a dagger and an enormous battle-axe. Some were also expert bowmen. The Vikings ranged their shields along the sides of the boats as they rode the waves.

One of the first Viking attacks recorded was against a port on the coast of Dorset in 789. The port-master and some of the villagers hurried down to the harbour to stare at three Viking ships; never before had they seen anything like them or like the men who sailed in them. These unfortunate onlookers soon paid the price of their curiosity, for the Vikings slaughtered them. The raiders then quickly filled their boats with booty and when the plunder had ceased, put back to sea with all haste. An unceasing series of surprise attacks on coastal Europe then began. Elsewhere in England, the Vikings swooped down on the abbeys of Lindisfarne, Jarrow and Iona, and the coast of Northumbria, burning priceless manuscripts and putting the monks to the sword.

They harassed the coastal settlements of Ireland, beginning with an attack on Lambat Island, near Dublin. Here too, they carried off the treasures of the monastery and slaughtered all the monks there. Again and again they returned to plunder and ravage, to seize everything of value. They came and went so unexpectedly, and with such speed, that the inhabitants (who had no regular military forces) were almost completely defenceless. The terror the Vikings aroused is voiced in a verse written by a Gaelic poet. He is glad that a storm rages, because it will prevent the Vikings from coming ashore:

Sharp is the wind tonight,
It ruffles the ocean's white hair;
Tonight I fear not the cruel Norwegians
Coursing on the Irish Sea.

By the ninth century the coasts not only of western, but even of southern, Europe were under constant attack by the Vikings. Even the territories of the powerful Charlemagne were not immune from their harrying, but in time he succeeded in containing their attacks by maintaining fleets to patrol the coastline and river mouths. Charlemagne then turned the tables on the Vikings, striking at one of their main bases in Frisia (now Holland) and driving them back into Denmark. His successors, however, were too weak to contain the Vikings. The raiders then sailed their

ships up the rivers at will, striking far inland on foot or on horseback, and pillaging far and wide. Six hundred Viking boats attacked Hamburg, which was set on fire. The Vikings also attacked Rouen, Nantes, Toulouse and Bordeaux, and laid siege to Paris. As a final insult they stabled their horses by the tomb of Charlemagne – dead only a few years – in the cathedral of Aachen. A commentator of the 860s in France complained: 'The number of ships grows and the endless stream of Vikings never ceases to increase. Everywhere Christians are victims of massacres, burnings, plunderings . . . countless ships sail up the Seine and evil grows in the whole region.'

Plundering the Mediterranean

Other Vikings steered their dreaded ships southwards. Not satisfied with plundering and despoiling Cadiz, Seville and Lisbon, they sailed through the straits of Gibraltar and raided the Mediterranean coasts as far as the Gulf of Genoa. In all these expeditions the Vikings kept to their hit-and-run tactics; only later did they begin to settle in any of the lands that they attacked. Their first permanent settlement was in the island of Walcheren near the mouth of the Scheldt, where they settled

in the mid-ninth century. Later, they annexed other islands or occupied lower reaches of rivers, setting up bases from which to attack the mainland. When they had worn down the resistance of the natives, the Vikings moved inland, forced the further cession of territory and founded new settlements. In this way they attempted to take over England, at that time divided into seven petty kingdoms. They occupied the Isle of Sheppey in 836 and Thanet Island in 850. By 878 they had so extended their control over the mainland that they seemed destined to become its rulers.

In that year Alfred the Great, king of Wessex, who had been reduced to the point of conducting guerilla warfare with a small band of followers from his hiding-place in the Somerset marshes, suddenly rallied his forces and won a great victory over the Danish Vikings at Ethandune (Edington) in Wiltshire. But even after this defeat, the Danes were still strong enough to enforce their claim over north-eastern England. Under the terms of the Peace of Wedmore, Guthrum, the Danish leader, became a Christian and divided England with Alfred: the area north of a line from the Thames to the Lea, called the *Danelaw*, went to Guthrum; the south,

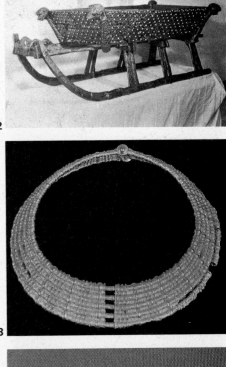

1 The beautiful Gokstad ship, found near Oslo-Fjord, is one of the best relics of the Viking age. Over 72 feet long, its solid construction and slim lines suit it to rough seas.
2 The three sleighs found in the Oseberg ship show signs of wear on their wooden runners. This one is decorated with elaborate carvings and the heads of strange monsters.

3 Scandinavian goldsmiths showed great artistry in precious metals. This filigree gold collar of the fifth century was found in Sweden.
4 The ninth-century ornament is known as the Alfred Jewel. Two and a half inches long, the outer ring is inscribed 'Alfred ordered me to be made'. In the centre is an enamel portrait of a king holding two sceptres.

together with London, to Alfred. During the next half-century successive Saxon kings employed their wiles and arms in whittling away Danish power. But the Danes struck again in the reign of King Ethelred the 'Unready' (*unraed* meant 'bad counsel'); weak leadership and disloyal nobles laid the country open to the enemy, and King Sven Forked-Beard finally forced the English to accept him as king in 1013. In 1017, the *Witan,* the governing council of England, elected Sven's son, Knut (Canute) king, and he absorbed Britain into his Scandinavian empire.

Simultaneously with these events in England, an attempt was made to seize Ireland. Turgesius, a Viking chief, took a large fleet there and made expeditions inland. The Vikings overran Ulster, central Ireland and the areas bordering the Shannon. Finally, Turgesius was defeated and drowned by Malachy, Irish king of Meath. Malachy's successor inflicted several defeats on the invaders, who began to quarrel among themselves. Although the Vikings failed to conquer the whole of Ireland, they succeeded in establishing permanent settlements along its eastern and southern shores, at Dublin, Howth, Wicklow, Arklow, Wexford, Limerick, Cork and Waterford.

Pagan raiders settle down

In 911 Charles III of France (Charles the Simple) concluded a treaty with Rollo, a Danish leader, ceding the coastal part of northern France to the Vikings. Here they organized a strong state later called *Normandy,* 'the Northmen's state', destined to play an important part in later European history. From here, in 1066, William (the Conqueror), a descendant of the Norse raiders, was to annex England and place it finally under Norman rule. Wherever the raiders settled they integrated with the native people. They intermarried with them, accepted the Christian faith and, through a process of assimilation, abandoned their old ways and habits.

Rollo, for example, was baptized in 912.

The establishment of overseas settlements was connected with events taking place in the Viking home territories. In 890 Harald Fairhair subdued his turbulent fellow-chiefs in Norway and made himself king of the whole country. Harald Blue-tooth united Denmark in about 950, while Eirik extended his rule over Sweden. These new national kings demanded obedience and taxes from the subjects. Some of the hitherto free and independent chiefs, to whom kings were anathema, could not bring themselves to accept their new masters or to pay tribute and taxes. A great exodus began from Scandinavia to the Orkneys, Shetlands, Hebrides and Faroes, to Ireland and to Britain, places where they could settle free from the rule of royal overlords.

Some of the Norwegians resented the actions of Harald so bitterly that they actually set out in raiding parties from their new colonies to attack his territory. Harald, in turn, was determined to punish them for their expeditions against him. He fitted out a powerful fleet and sailed west to wreak vengeance on his former fellow-chiefs. He punished them so severely and wrought such destruction that some decided to sail to new lands.

They sailed to Iceland, a land of whose existence they had been aware for some time. There they founded a colony which attracted their most turbulent and defiant warriors. Greenland was known to the Icelanders by about 900, but was not colonized for another three generations.

The Swedish Vikings, called *Varangians,* expanded eastwards. A Varangian tribe, the *Rus,* probably gave its name to Russia. The Swedes travelled via the Neva and Volkhof rivers as far inland as Lake Ilmen. Viking ships made their way down the Dnieper and crossed the Black Sea.

Denmark's largest Viking burial ground is at Lindholm Hills in North Jutland. Here the 682 graves, of which 200 are barrows with stones, form the outlines of a ship.

Following the example of the Vikings in western Europe, they began to plunder and pillage Byzantine towns, churches and monasteries. They attacked Constantinople itself, and agreed to abandon the siege only after payment of a large sum of money.

The Swedish Vikings continued to extend their influence over the many Slavic principalities of Russia. These petty states were often at war with each other, and their quarrels hindered the developing trade with the Black Sea merchants. Eventually Rurik, a Swedish chieftain, took the district of Novgorod, and in 862 made himself its prince. His principality later absorbed that of Kiev, and later still Moscow.

Lost colonies of North America

The founder of the Greenland colony was Eirik the Red, a daring man banished from Iceland in the 980s for murder. According to the Icelandic sagas, Bjarni Herjulfsson, a Viking fisherman from Greenland, was blown off course by a storm which drove him south until eventually he reached a point off the coast of Labrador, or perhaps Newfoundland. When he returned home he related his adventures and described the forested shores he had seen. Leif the Lucky, Eirik's son, sailed off in search of those new lands. He and his companions reached the coast of what is now New England in about 1003. There they landed, and called the territory *Vinland,* after the wild vines that grew there. Other Viking expeditions to American waters followed. Life in America seems to have become more and more difficult, and the Vikings eventually abandoned Vinland, probably in the early twelfth century.

Tremendous as the achievements of the Vikings were in their conquest of land and sea, they must not be dismissed as mere barbarians. Their vitality and force also went into the production of a distinctive art and a great literature – through which run always images of the sea, the 'swan's road', which was their second home.

The Norman Conquest

In 1064 Harold Godwin gave his pledge that William, Duke of Normandy, should succeed to the English throne. Two years later the pledge was broken; the outcome was the Norman invasion.

1

2

1 A map of England and France at the time of the Norman Conquest in 1066. Also shown are the sites of Harold's previous engagements which contributed so much to his defeat by the Normans.

2 After the Conquest, William retained only a small group of alien nobles who replaced the Anglo-Saxon aristocracy. Here William grants land to his nephew, the Earl of Brittany.

ANGLO-SAXON ENGLAND ended with the Norman Conquest in 1066, when William, Duke of Normandy, led the last successful invasion on English soil. He found a country of mixed characteristics. Previous invaders – Romans, Saxons, Norsemen and Danes – had all left their mark, and although her own traditions were always a barrier to a complete political unity, the struggles against the Danes in the ninth and tenth centuries had given England a greater semblance of unity than she had ever experienced before. The Anglo-Saxon achievement had, therefore, been a very great one. England was the only central-ized state in Europe, with divisions into shires and hundreds, a powerful and elec-tive monarchy, a uniform law and a national system of finance, a thriving trade and accelerating growth of towns.

The reign of Edward the Confessor (1042–January 1066) formed a direct prelude to the Conquest: therein lay the causes of the event. Edward had no children and it was his avowed wish that he be succeeded by his cousin, William, Duke of Normandy. In 1051 he declared William as heir to the English throne and William is alleged to have visited England where he probably received some promise of recognition as Edward's successor.

As his reign drew to a close Edward turned more and more from matters of state to his own deep religious interests, and his preoccupation aided the rise in power of the House of Godwin. Harold Godwin, as Earl of Wessex from 1053, was no less concerned than William with securing recognition as king when Edward died, and, from the English point of view his claim was very much stronger than that of either William or the other rival claimant, Harold Hardrada, King of Norway. This immense and wealthy king, soon to impress his size and strength on

England's soil, had inherited a claim to England's throne from a deal settled many years before by an English king, Harth-acnut, and Magnus, King of Norway.

The source of much of the history of the Conquest is the famous piece of em-broidery known as the Bayeux Tapestry, probably made in England for Odo, Bishop of Bayeux, within 20 years of the battle of Hastings. The Norman-biased tapestry relates in picture form, and as a tragedy, how Earl Harold went on a mission to France, probably in 1064. Despite the con-fusion of the records, which leave the purpose of the visit an open question, Harold was very probably sent to confirm Edward's alleged promise that William should succeed him. The tapestry further records how he took an oath of allegiance to William at Bayeux. When Harold

accepted the English crown in 1066, the Normans bitterly resented the broken pledge.

The last days of Edward the Confessor were marred by a rebellion in Northumbria, and confused even more by his whimsical change of heart over who should succeed him; Edward now recommended Harold as his successor, and in January 1066, he died.

Harold was hastily crowned king. A strong and intelligent leader, he seemed the best man to deal with unrest at home and the double threat from Norway and Normandy.

Forebodings of evil

Harold governed England, justly but harshly, for nine months, keeping the loyalty of his magnates for the whole of his reign. But the appearance of Halley's Comet in July 1066 seemed to many men to bode evil, and events were to justify their fears. Early in May 1066 Tostig, exiled Earl of Northumbria, landed in England from Norway with an army. Meanwhile William, determined to establish his claims on the English throne, had prepared for an invasion. King Harold called up his militia and fleet and arranged for defence against the Normans. Then in September 1066 Harold Hardrada and his fleet joined Tostig; together they sailed up the River Ouse as far as the small town of Riccall in Yorkshire.

The Norwegian forces advanced on York, and at the village of Gate Fulford, two miles south of York, Hardrada crushed the English resistance led by Earl Edwin (of Mercia) and Earl Morca (of Northumbria) on 20 September. The town of York surrendered and the invaders withdrew to Stamford Bridge.

Day after day Harold's army waited for the Norman forces to arrive. But eventually the strain of William's delay forced Harold to disband his militia and to 'standdown' his fleet. Then news of the Norwegian invasion sent him to the North at full speed. Four days after the battle of Fulford he fought and won the battle of Stamford Bridge: Harold Hardrada and Tostig were both killed. Then on 27 September, the wind which had kept the Norman fleet in the Somme changed direction and William made an easy crossing to England, landing at Pevensey in Sussex. The Norman invasion had begun.

Harold probably did not hear of the Norman landing until 1 October: he hastily collected what levies he could and made a forced march south on the long journey on 11 October. William moved from Pevensey to Hastings and then to the hill later known as Battle. Over two weeks of marching and fighting had begun to tell on the English forces; exhausted now, they found themselves facing, for the first

The Bayeux Tapestry: 231 feet long and 20 inches wide, it represents in 72 scenes the Norman conquest of England.

1 In 1064 Harold visits William with a message from Edward the Confessor that William is to succeed him.

2 Edward the Confessor dies, having just recommended Harold as his successor. His body is taken to be buried in Westminster Abbey.

3 Harold breaks his oath to William and is crowned king instead. On hearing the news, William calls his men to prepare for war.

4 With men and horses on board, the Norman vessels set sail for England.

5 The Norman army lands at Pevensey. Meanwhile, Harold is fighting the Norwegians in the North; he does not hear of William's landing until four days later, and, collecting what levies he can, makes a forced march south.

6 The Battle of Hastings; with their bows and arrows and heavy war-horses, the Normans have a decisive advantage over the defenders. Here their cavalry charge the tattered and exhausted English ranks.

7 Harold plucks the fatal arrow from his eye (although he was more likely killed by a sword). The English turn and flee, while below, dead soldiers are stripped of their armour.

time in battle, William's monopoly of well-equipped archers and cavalry. The unwieldy battle-axe of the English was no match against them. Harold therefore took up a defensive position on Battle Hill, along a half-mile front, with his infantry forming a 'shield-wall' at the front and on a gentle slope. The English had a slight numerical advantage, but the actual size of the two armies was very small by modern standards, only 5–6,000 men were involved on each side.

William ordered his allied forces into three divisions: Bretons to the left,

Normans in the centre, the French king's forces to the right, with his archers at the front and cavalry at the rear. He therefore had the additional advantage of mobility over Harold. The first attack by the Norman archers was, however, ineffectual and the Bretons on the left were forced back. But the English who pursued them were cut down by William's knights; twice more the English left their high positions, losing many men in the process. The battle raged all day and the exhausted English started to flag. Then disaster struck. Harold's two brothers fell in the afternoon, and in the final attack, late in the day, Harold himself was killed. Tradition tells that he was fatally wounded by an arrow in the eye, but it was more likely by a blow from a Norman knight. Their king dead, the remnants of the English army broke and fled: Harold's death marked the end of the battle and the end of Anglo-Saxon England.

The Norman Conquest was not merely a military conquest: although contemporaries (like William of Malmesbury) would say that England was won in this single battle the real victory was to take five years. William had first to be recognized as king: divided councils ensured his success, and responsible English opinion, anxious for peace after a decade of continuous wars, turned to him. William promised to rule as Edward's legal successor and on Christmas Day he was crowned in Westminster Abbey.

William's subsequent career in England (1066–87) was highly successful but never easy: risings in the North and West had to be put down and supporting raids from Denmark and Norway beaten off. He maintained the English frontiers with Wales and Scotland; the Scottish king recognized his overlordship and most of the Welsh princes did likewise. But William had to be harsh to bring about the desired changes in England and he still had to rule in Normandy. In the winter of 1069–70 when the rising unrest briefly erupted, he devastated whole areas of country: new castles and the scorched-earth policy broke the resistance and made the countryside unprofitable to Danish invaders.

Legality and continuity

William already had a sound knowledge of the country and its customs and he found a thriving administrative system which he was wise enough not to alter dramatically. His immediate aim was to maintain a sense of legality and continuity with the Anglo-Saxon past, and his policy of Normanization did not begin until after 1070.

The Norman invasion, unlike the earlier Saxon and Danish invasions, was not a national immigration. William did not bring a great following to England; many of his army were dismissed after 1070, and he used only a small alien group of Normans as his advisers who proved sensitive to English opinion.

Yet society itself underwent a profound change in William's reign. Although there was already present in Anglo-Saxon England a type of feudalism, the concept of Norman feudalism was unknown. Until 1066 society was a fluid class system; after 1066 it was a fixed and permanent caste system, for Anglo-Saxon inequalities were expressed in terms of birth and different services to the king, while Norman social differences were expressed in terms of various land tenures.

The Norman regime was aristocratic, and it established the concept that all land belonged to the king, to be distributed as gifts to his followers, in return for specific services. This gave a new uniformity to English social and political life.

The Domesday Book. It was compiled in 1086 to find out how England was 'peopled and with what sort of men' and so-named because it was felt there could be no appeal against it.

Vassals, or landholders, were expected to provide, as part of the contract, and in return for their 'fiefs', an 'aid' of a fixed number of properly equipped knights to serve for 40 days in each year. Allegiance of vassal to lord was built up on a pyramid structure, stretching through society.

The effect of feudalism on the upper ranks of society was revolutionary. The new Norman aristocracy replaced the English nobility of the court of the Anglo-Saxon kings. By the time the Domesday Book was compiled in 1086 only two of the king's tenants were of English family. The English landowners had either fallen in battle, emigrated or were exiled.

The peasant classes were socially depressed by the introduction of feudalism. Before the Conquest peasants were legally free and able to abandon their land if they wished: under the feudal system the class deteriorated into serfdom because land now had to be paid for in labour services. On the other hand, slaves as a class disappeared. Yet in effect, the peasants simply exchanged their Saxon for a Norman lord. The village was still the main unit of the English countryside: villages sent juries to the shire and hundred court and participated in the militia: the new manorial court dealt with the day to day affairs of the village under the jurisdiction of the lord. Although these feudal courts were still below the shire courts, they were important in general not only because they were beneficial to the peasants but because they settled, for the military tenants, the differences between the old and new order.

William replaced the Anglo-Saxon 'Witan' (meetings of earls and bishops), with a feudal assembly called the 'curia regis' in which his major tenants-in-chief sat as a right and an obligation, in order to advise their king and to seek justice. Although the king had absolute power, as God's 'thegn', or deputy, he could not govern unless he had the good will of his chief vassals. The assemblies met at Christmas, Easter and Whitsun, in a different part of the country each time, and their decisions had the force of law.

A good example of the thoroughness of the Normans is the Domesday Book, ordered by William at Christmas 1085 to find out how the whole of England was 'peopled, and with what sort of men'. The impetus for the investigation was probably military and it carries unique information on every facet of medieval life: it shows, for example, how the English thegns had been replaced by the Norman barons, and how the number of boroughs had increased from 65 in 1066 to 90 in 1086, due to the stimulus given to urban life by the Conquest. The detail and lay-out of the survey presupposes a high degree of administrative efficiency and gives typical views of England at three periods: Edward, the Conquest, and from 1066. It was named 'Domesday' because it was felt that there could be no appeal against the verdict of the inquest.

Besides the introduction of feudalism into English society the Conquest also had important effects on the Church, the towns and the countryside of England. The military obligations of the Church were extended after 1066 since eleventh-century bishops and abbots owned land on a large scale, and were subject to the same obligations and duties as the laity.

William had sworn to protect the Church and although he had the blessing of the Pope he was careful not to allow the latter too much control of English ecclesiastical affairs.

An expanding society

The Conquest did not suddenly change the rural Saxons into urban Normans, for Saxon towns had been developing from the reign of Alfred. But the growth of town life was greatly accelerated after 1066. The demands of the new aristocracy increased trade internally and with the Continent. The military needed roads and walled towns, and the Norman administrators demanded safe meeting places in which to work: all this aided the establishment of new centres of population. As the towns grew, so the inhabitants began to demand special privileges: the towns were granted borough charters, which allowed men to impose rules of industry and trade and to solve their special problems in their own courts and by their own customs. Continuity, from Anglo-Saxon to Norman, was a prominent feature in the countryside at this period, while development of the manorial system provided the machinery for Norman discipline and organization.

As the Norman period of English history advanced, changes in social and political life became more marked: Norman influence slowly began to be felt in literary, cultural and architectural fields. That the English king was a ruler on both sides of the Channel was to affect English history for centuries to come. The sons of the Conqueror, William Rufus and Henry, completed the work of William, and later monarchs built on the synthesis of Anglo-Saxon and Norman England.

Crusaders to the Holy Land

Fighting to keep the Holy Places open for pilgrims, the crusaders achieved little of lasting religious value. But they were instrumental in developing trade and spreading Arab culture in the West.

THE BURNING SUN of Syria had not yet reached its highest point in the sky as a knight of the Red Cross paced slowly along the sandy desert near the Dead Sea. He had left his distant northern home to join a cause by which Christians might regain possession of the Holy Land, Palestine, which had been captured by the Turks in the eleventh century.

The dress of the rider, and the accoutrements of his horse, were peculiarly unsuitable for a traveller in such a country. As though his coat of linked mail, with long sleeves and plated gauntlets, were not enough weight of armour, he also carried a heavy triangular shield suspended round his neck. To protect his head he wore a barred helmet of steel, covered by a hood and collar of mail drawn around his shoulders and throat. His legs were sheathed, like his body, in flexible mail. A long, broad, double-edged sword, on his right, shaped like a cross, matched a dagger on the other side. The knight also bore a long steel-headed lance secured to his saddle, with one end resting on his stirrup. Over his armour the knight wore a coat of embroidered cloth, frayed and worn. The knight's coat bore, in several places, the arms of his family, although much defaced. Many a blow had almost effaced the motto on his shield.

This description of the crusader knight portrays one of the thousands of soldiers who journeyed south and east to fight in

the religious wars. He stood as a symbol of the clash between two expanding civilizations: Arab Islam and European Christianity.

From the third century onwards, Christians from western Europe and Byzantium went on pilgrimages, either singly or in groups, to the shrines and sacred places of Palestine – the Holy Land. When Islam developed and expanded into Palestine in the seventh century, the Christians were, for the most part, well treated and unhindered in their devotions. Occasionally, however, they suffered insults and ill-treatment from the Moslems. The situation improved during the reign of Charlemagne, crowned Holy Roman emperor in 800, who corresponded with the Caliph Harun al-Rashid of Baghdad. Charlemagne arranged with the Caliph that Christian pilgrims and residents would not be molested by the Arabs so long as they paid their taxes and conformed to agreed rules of behaviour.

Appeal to the pope

Moslem tolerance declined in the eleventh century, when the Seljuk Turks, recent and militant converts to Islam, occupied most of the land which forms present-day Turkey, Syria and Palestine. The Seljuks inflicted severe defeats on the armies of the Byzantine empire and threatened its capital, Constantinople. Alexius, the Byzantine emperor, sought military aid from

The crusaders tried to control their territories in the Middle East from castles built in Moslem style. The huge Hospitallers' Crak des Chevaliers was captured by Saladin in 1188.

all western Christians and addressed a special appeal to Pope Gregory VII. But Gregory, although sympathetic, could give little practical aid, for he was locked in a struggle for power with the Holy Roman Emperor.

Gregory's successor, Urban II, spurred by reports that Christian pilgrims to the Holy Land were being enslaved and murdered, gave the aid which Gregory had refused. Urban was motivated by much more than the wish to free Palestine. He hoped that western aid would bring the Eastern Orthodox Church (which had split from Rome in 1054) firmly back into the fold. At the same time, he saw a way to rid Europe of the warring feudal lords whose rebellious attitudes frequently threatened the authority of the Church.

In the autumn of 1095 he summoned the bishops, lords and knights of western Europe to a meeting at Clermont-Ferrand in southern central France. In an impassioned speech, Urban implored them to cease their sterile feuds with each other and to unite into a Christian army to drive the Seljuks from Syria and Palestine. Such a force, he declared, would be God's army fighting God's war against the heathen. His address stirred his listeners:

enthusiastically they cried, 'God wills it!' and pledged their swords to the holy cause.

Preparations began immediately for the first and most successful crusade – a word derived from the cross (Latin *crux*) which the knights and their followers wore on their breasts when advancing east, and on their backs when returning home. The First Crusade consisted of two forces. One, badly organized, set off early in 1096 under the leadership of Peter the Hermit, a French monk. Hordes of undisciplined enthusiasts followed the banner of the cross through Europe, taking various routes to Constantinople and over the Bosphorus to Asia. Thousands perished on the march, and those who survived were massacred by the Turks.

The Holy City is saved

A powerfully equipped, more experienced, fighting force set off in the autumn of 1096 under the leadership of Godfrey of Bouillon, Duke of Lower Lorraine and his brother Baldwin; Raymond, Count of Toulouse; and Robert, Duke of Normandy. These men, like most of the crusaders, were French or Flemish. Assembling at Constantinople in 1097, this tougher band of crusaders advanced into Asia Minor, took Edessa and Antioch, and in 1099, after savage fighting, Jerusalem.

The bloodstained knights then set up a Roman Catholic kingdom of Jerusalem, with Godfrey of Bouillon as its ruler. They also founded smaller, Roman Catholic states, dependencies of Jerusalem, at Edessa, Antioch and Tripoli. The defence of the conquered territories was entrusted largely to the Knights Templars and the Knights Hospitallers, bands of priestly

1 An illuminated capital from a handbook for crusaders, compiled in 1321, depicts Saladin waving a sword at cowering Christians.
2 King Louis of France, who was later canonized as a saint, led his Second Crusade to Tunis in 1270 where he died of the plague. In this manuscript, he is leaving Paris with his knights and a procession of devout monks.

soldiers whose energies and skills were dedicated to 'holy war' and the protection and care of pilgrims.

Godfrey and his fellow rulers faced a difficult task. They found themselves rulers of states with few subjects to rule, because the inhabitants had been almost wiped out by the crusaders, and they in turn, having fulfilled their vows to regain the Holy Land, went home. Later, many immigrants from western Europe were persuaded to settle in the new states.

Christian rule lasted nearly half a century before Zangi, a Moslem governor, uniting several Moslem rulers, began a drive of reconquest, continued after his death by his son, Nureddin. Edessa was the first of the crusader cities to be taken. When news of its fall reached Europe, Saint Bernard of Clairvaux, the most influential figure in the Church at that time, called for another crusade. His preaching aroused great fervour in the west and even Louis VII of France and Conrad III of Germany were persuaded to go crusading. But the Second Crusade was badly organized; the Byzantine emperor, who distrusted the westerners, treacherously betrayed their positions to

Nureddin, and this resulted in a crushing defeat by the Turks. When the crusaders failed to take the strategically important city of Damascus, the Second Crusade petered out without having accomplished anything.

The Third Crusade was sparked off by the actions of Saladin, a Kurdish warrior, whom Nureddin proclaimed sultan of Egypt in 1171, thus for the first time uniting the Moslems of Egypt, Iraq and Syria against the Christian threat. Saladin, a cultured man of great courage and integrity, advanced his empire from the Libyan desert to the river Tigris. His recapture of Jerusalem, one of the three crusader states, for the Moslems in 1187 followed by his capture of most of the cities and castles in the other states of Tripoli and Antioch, led to the Third Crusade (1189–92).

Richard 'Lion-heart' sails alone

In 1189, three European monarchs – the Holy Roman Emperor Frederick Barbarossa ('Red-beard'), Richard I of England, and Philip Augustus of France – each set out with an army, to recover the Holy Land. The French and English kings went

by sea, setting sail from Marseilles. Frederick Barbarossa led his forces by land, following the route taken by earlier crusading armies. The enemy leader whom Saladin most feared, Frederick Barbarossa, failed to reach Palestine. Most of his army perished on the march, and he himself was drowned while crossing a swollen stream in Asia Minor. The king of France also played only a small part in the crusade. He quarrelled bitterly with Richard, whose arrogance made him many enemies, and soon returned home, leaving the English king to bear the brunt of the fighting.

Although the English conquered Cyprus en route and captured Acre after a siege, they failed to take Jerusalem. Richard did, however, recover the ports of Haifa, Caesarea and Joppa, and persuaded Sala-

1 The principal points of attack by the first six crusader armies who travelled overland by sea from France, Germany, Italy and England to wrest the Holy Land from the Moslems.
2 The triumphant entry of the crusaders into Constantinople, painted by Delacroix, shows the savagery and ruthless massacre by knights and their followers in the name of Christ.

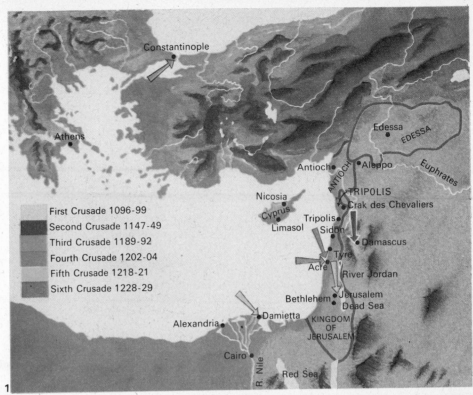

First Crusade 1096-99
Second Crusade 1147-49
Third Crusade 1189-92
Fourth Crusade 1202-04
Fifth Crusade 1218-21
Sixth Crusade 1228-29

din to guarantee Christians unmolested access to the Holy Places. Richard, whose feats of arms had earned him the nickname 'Lion-heart', then returned to Europe. Travelling overland, he was caught and imprisoned by the Duke of Austria, with whom he had also quarrelled during the siege of Acre; it was two years before he was ransomed and allowed to return to England, in 1194. After the departure of Richard, Christian power in Palestine steadily declined. The Holy Land was soon under Moslem rule again.

The Fourth Crusade (1202–04) was launched largely at the instigation of the ambitious Pope Innocent III. It was at this time that the crusaders, led by French barons, struck a bargain with the Venetians, who agreed to transport them by sea from Venice to Palestine. But, being unable to pay the Venetians' fee, the crusaders gave them military assistance in an attack on the Byzantine empire to promote the commercial interests of the Venetians. Outraged at this turn of events, which destroyed all his hopes of a unified Church, Innocent III excommunicated the entire crusader army. Undeterred, the crusaders deposed Alexius, and appointed Baldwin of Flanders as Byzantine emperor in his place. Thus the Fourth Crusade changed the history of the Byzantine empire, but was irrelevant to Palestine. It was an affair between Christians, in which the Moslems were not involved.

The Children's Crusade

The most futile of the expeditions was the Children's Crusade, which took place in 1212. Thirty thousand French boys and girls, led by a shepherd boy named Stephen, and 20,000 German children under the leadership of a lad called Nicholas, set out to accomplish what the military forces had failed to achieve. With touching faith, they believed that the waters of the Mediterranean would divide to let them pass, as they believed that the Red Sea had done for the ancient Jews in their flight from Egypt. They thought that, having crossed to Palestine, another miracle would oust the Moslems from Jerusalem and restore it through them to the Christian faith. Some of the children lost heart

Crusaders disembarking at Damietta which they besieged during the Fifth Crusade. They hoped to exchange the city for Jerusalem but were forced to retreat by the flooding Nile.

and returned home before going very far. Those who continued on the crusade died from hunger or exposure, were drowned at sea, or were seized and sold as slaves. So ended the most tragic of these heroic but sordid adventures.

The Fifth Crusade sailed for Egypt in 1218, and besieged Damietta, hoping to exchange it for Jerusalem. After a siege of 17 months, the sultan of Egypt, Al-Kamil, did indeed offer the return of the whole kingdom of Jerusalem if the crusaders would leave Egyptian soil. But their leader, the papal legate, refused this reasonable offer; the war dragged on and he was finally forced to abandon the siege and return home – a total failure instead of a possible success.

The Sixth Crusade (1228–29) was led by Frederick II, the Holy Roman Emperor. Frederick II was an odd man to lead a

In 1189 Richard I sailed from England to join Emperor Frederick Barbarossa and Philip Augustus of France in the Third Crusade. Here Richard enters Acre in triumph after a long siege.

crusade – a free-thinker and heretic who, having driven two popes to despair, was excommunicated by a third, Gregory IX. In the court of Sicily, excommunication mattered little and Frederick could afford to regard it with humorous cynicism. Frederick hit back at Gregory IX by addressing a document to all the crowned rulers of Europe, suggesting that they enter into a union to rid themselves of papal interference in their affairs. Having launched this deadly idea, which was to eat into the basis of papal power, Frederick departed on his 'crusade'.

Arriving in Egypt, Frederick met the sultan, a fellow sceptic in religious questions. The two men concluded a commercial agreement and the sultan transferred Jerusalem to Frederick, who became its king. Returning to Lombardy, Frederick drove out the papal armies which had invaded his territories, and forced the pope to end his excommunication.

Crusades of a kind continued into the fifteenth century. They achieved little; most were directed against the growing might of the Ottoman Turks rather than towards recovery of the Holy Places.

The crusades were essentially the product of their time, bound up with the medieval way of life, especially with feudalism. One part of the feudal contract bound vassals to give military aid to their superior lords in return for guaranteed protection. As a result the great feudal lords throughout Europe formed militias, ever ready to engage in private warfare with each other. Only when the opportunity came to fight a powerful common foe did the feudal lords sink their petty disputes and make common cause. The crusaders were professional soldiers for whom war was a most honourable occupation. When lesser lords were not assisting their superiors in military exploits, they found entertainment in plundering a rival's villages, sacking his castles, or holding him to ransom. Appalled at their savagery, the Church introduced in the eleventh century the *Truce of God,* which forbade fighting during Lent and Advent, and between Wednesday night and Monday morning of each week. This curb on the warlike nature of the lords at home, was a powerful factor in sending them off to fight and plunder elsewhere.

Influenced by the enemy

In the long run the most important results of the crusades were economic, social and cultural, rather than political or religious. Paradoxically, they speeded the end of feudalism, because in order to find the money to finance their expeditions, kings and lords took money from their serfs instead of services. East-west trade was given an extraordinary impetus. The products of India, China and Persia came to Syrian seaports to be exchanged for the wares of Europe.

The crusades enriched and broadened the intellectual outlook of medieval Europe by bringing large numbers of Christians into close contact with Islamic culture. Moslem art, geography and science contributed largely to Europe's 'great leap forward' – the Renaissance.

John's clash with the barons

In 1215, King John put his seal to 'Magna Carta', the great charter of English liberties. Civil war was averted and the legal relations between crown and people defined for centuries to come.

THE NORMAN PERIOD of English history was well into its second century when King John added his seal to the Great Charter in 1215 and acknowledged the claims of his barons. Until that moment no king of medieval England could claim more power than John and there was no group of people so jealous of their inherited rights and privileges as the barons; 'Magna Carta' was the product of a blazing clash of interests and personalities; it was to set the tone of king-subject relations for centuries to come.

The defeat of King Harold at the battle of Hastings in 1066 meant not only the beginning of the rule of the Norman kings but the start of the gradually increasing tension between the Crown and its leading subjects which was eventually to produce the Charter of 1215. The barons saw the growing strength and efficiency of the central government as dangerous to their positions as leaders of the realm.

The new law and order

Contemporaries remarked upon the security of citizens under the rule of William (1066–87), when a man and his gold were well protected, and this iron rule, well illustrated by the great increase in the number of castles which soon studded the countryside, enabled the smooth introduction of continental feudalism into English society. A man now owed allegiance both to his immediate lord and to the king, and England was given a unity she had never experienced before. The Domesday Book, in itself an indication of the growing royal interference in the lives of men, showed how completely society had changed by 1086.

Law and order continued to be maintained by William's successors (apart from during Stephen's troubled reign) and were greatly extended under Henry II. The violent and carefree William Rufus (1087–1100), accidentally killed while hunting in the New Forest, was succeeded by the wiser and less boisterous Henry I. Henry recognized that the anxieties of his barons were growing; state interference had to

1 An effigy of Richard I, king of England from 1189 to 1199. Despite his continuous absences and huge demands on England's resources, he was regarded as a hero by his subjects.
2 John flourishes his crown before the bishops to emphasize his royal authority in the dispute over a successor for the Archbishop.
3 The seal of Stephen Langton. When John defied Langton's papal appointment, he was excommunicated and England placed under an Interdict.

be relieved if their fears were to be allayed. He therefore reassured them by issuing a Coronation Charter, and later, a Charter of Liberties, in which he promised to abide by the law of Edward the Confessor. The Charters set out what were considered the legal relations between Crown and barons, but, even more important, they established a precedent which the barons were not willing to forget, and the Charter of 1135 is the direct forerunner of 'Magna Carta'. King Stephen likewise had to reassure his barons by issuing two charters and Henry II by issuing one. The barons of 1215 saw themselves as defenders of what Henry I had promised.

During the reign of Stephen, when 'God and His angels slept', the feudal system lapsed into 'feudal anarchy' and this riotous interlude showed how easily such complicated machinery as the feudal system could break down. Henry II (1154–89), grandson of Henry I, found election after Stephen's death an easy manoeuvre and he steered through such changes as were necessary to give England something like an official system of government for the first time.

Henry's system was severely tested in the short reign of Richard I (1189–99), the 'Yea and Nay' king, when his continual absence in the Holy Land necessitated the maintenance of government by civil servants: Richard I was to pay only two brief visits to England during his ten years of rule and it is in his reign that the scene was set for the playing of the almost

The remains of the Abbey Presbytery at Bury St Edmunds. On this site the barons swore to compel the king to accept their demands.

administrator; he reformed the currency and established Liverpool as a port; he was successful in his policy towards England's neighbours; and he was responsible for the development of English law. Yet he was not a suitable king for his time: he was too wild and emotional, he was irresponsible, cruel and suspicious – well named as 'nature's enemy'. He could be called an unlucky king.

In the 25 years between the death of Henry II and the death of John, England's power and prestige were seriously reduced. By 1216 it faced a series of disasters: Normandy had been lost to the French King; England had become a Papal fief; there was a civil war and the threat of foreign invasion. However, not all this was due to the shortcomings of John himself. Richard Cœur de Lion had seen England merely as a reservoir of cash from which to finance his crusade – he said he would have sold London itself if he could have found a buyer – and the effects of this rape of England's resources were still felt in 1215.

John takes the throne

Since John was Henry II's youngest son, he was not given any lands to rule and was jestingly nicknamed John Lackland. But before King Richard set out on the Third Crusade in 1190 he gave John six counties to administer, virtually as a country within a country, the rest of England being left in the care of William Longchamp. John therefore had an excellent basis from which to plot the downfall of his brother. It is at this stage that the legendary figure of Robin Hood appears and he is a fine indication of what was thought of John at the time—the cruel brother exploiting the poor people during the king's absence in the Holy Land.

John was soon to have his full share of power, however, for on the death of Richard in 1199 he was chosen as king by the barons in preference to the grandson of Henry II, Arthur of Brittany: rumour suggested that John himself had murdered his nephew in 1203 in a fit of drunken rage. At his accession John faced serious problems: the straggling Angevin Empire, legacy of Henry II, was at best difficult to hold together, and since Philip II of France was already planning to attack England's French possessions the loss of Normandy became only a matter of time. John gave Philip his excuse by breaking feudal law when he married Isabel of Angoulême, already promised to a vassal of Philip, and war broke out in the spring of 1202. John had little military skill and even less enthusiasm; when the Château Gaillard fortress fell in 1204 all of England's Norman possessions, except the Channel Islands, were lost to the French. These disasters drastically cut the spending power of the Crown, and since the barons

The field of Runnymede, believed to be the place where John set his seal to 'Magna Carta'. Had he refused, civil war would have followed.

tragi-comedy events of the reign of John.

Historians have never been able to make up their minds whether John was a 'good' or a 'bad' king: medieval England had a different set of standards for judging its kings than we have today. A 'good' king was successful in war, guaranteed the well-being of his leading subjects, and maintained good relations with the Church, but John could claim none of this. We would call him a good king for working hard and for being an efficient administrator but his barons disliked any developments which reduced their power. Thus Richard I, who spent most of his reign out of England and who demanded huge sums of money, received a good press from the chroniclers because he embarked on a Holy War and because he did not interfere directly with his barons. John, on the other hand, received nothing but scorn from his biographers.

John was a man of inconsistencies and paradox. He was an able judge and

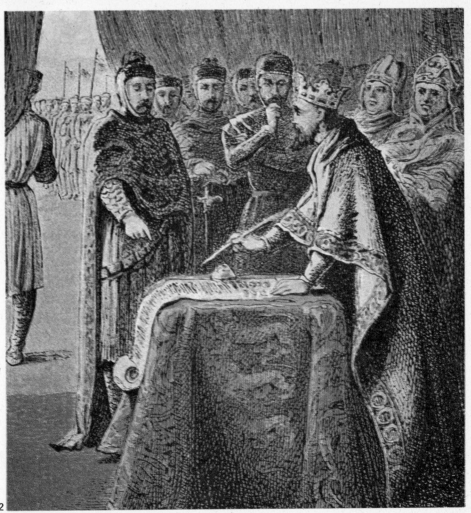

1 'Magna Carta': signed in 1215 and containing 63 clauses in all, it is one of the most momentous documents in English history.

2 Quill in hand, King John signs the great charter which set out in legal form the contract between the sovereign and the people.

themselves had lost their Norman lands they began to think again about their king.

John 'Softsword', as he was now called, became even more unpopular when he quarrelled with the Church. After a disputed election for the position of Archbishop of Canterbury, Pope Innocent III ignored John's candidate and chose instead Stephen Langton. John refused to accept Langton and retaliated by illegally seizing areas of Church property. For her sins, England was placed under an Interdict in 1208 which virtually halted all public worship throughout the land. The Pope followed this up by excommunicating John in 1209. Excommunication was probably the worst thing that could happen to any king, and John was forced to make peace with the Pope only because of the serious situation it created at home. In 1213, as a final insult to the Crown and to England, John surrendered England and Ireland to the Pope and received them back as a vassal. Added together these events kindled the smouldering pile of grievances which was soon to break out into the baronial revolt.

Defeat in war and Papal humiliation could only serve to enrage the barons who now distrusted more than ever the 'evil customs' of John and his predecessors.

new Archbishop of Canterbury, saved the country from civil war; but even this could not alter the battle of Bouvines in July 1214 when John made a last desperate attempt to regain Normandy. The crushing defeat he suffered proved to be more than the barons could stand. The use of force became inevitable and while John prepared for imminent civil war the more extreme barons captured the City of London during Easter 1215, calling for the restoration of their ancient rights and privileges. After two weeks of bargaining between the king at Windsor and the barons in London the two sides decided on a great meeting to be held on 15 June 1215 in the meadow called Runnymede, near to Staines. After much haggling, here by the River Thames, the terms of the 'Magna Carta' were finally agreed upon; both sides added their seals and copies were distributed throughout the land.

Rights and liberties

In the Charter John promised most of what the barons demanded: the 63 clauses specified among other things, freedom of the Church, protection for foreign merchants, freedom from increased taxes without consent of the barons, free justice for all, and most important for the future, the right of a man to be 'judged by his equals under the law of the land'. Weights and measures were to be regulated and law and justice reformed; from now on no man could be tried without a reliable witness to testify against him. Welsh grievances were to be considered, all foreign mercenaries dismissed and 25 barons elected to guard the Charter. A special charter of the Forest was added in 1217 to protect men from the Crown's severe forest laws.

It is astonishing that John was persuaded to sign such a document. The final clauses in effect gave authority to his subjects to declare war on the sovereign. His submission to its humiliating demands was witness to his genuine desire to avoid civil war and to govern well. The charter was to become a symbol against oppression. Whenever freedom was threatened in the centuries which followed men were to speak of it in their defence. Justifiably, 'Magna Carta' has been called the foundation of the rights and liberties of Man.

1 An early manuscript showing baronial life in John's reign. The barons' prime purpose was to protect their position as leaders of the realm.
2 John I, successively nicknamed John 'Lackland' and 'Softsword'. But whether good or bad, historians have never been able to judge.
3 Henry II, father of John and the first English king to give England some semblance of an official system of government.
4 Henry I; realizing baronial anxiety must be allayed, he issued the first Coronation Charter and a Charter of Liberties.

These 'evil customs' were simply the Crown's attempts at raising more money by extending royal power, and to the barons of John's day any form of change was suspect, even though the Crown's fortunes were seriously reduced due to the cost of foreign wars and rising prices. John therefore made full use of existing sources of revenue, such as feudal benefits and fines for breaking the forest laws, and modified them where necessary to produce money. To help in the collection of money John himself travelled about the kingdom more than any king had ever done before – his visit to Newcastle in 1201 was probably the first by an English king for 50 years – and the barons soon associated these visits with interference and more taxes. The delicate balance between the Crown and its subjects was upset; the only way to restore it was to tie John down with the demands of 'Magna Carta'.

John quarrelled with his barons constantly from as early as 1206; a treasonable plot had been discovered in 1209, and in 1213, when a group of barons called the Northerners refused to join John's expedition to retrieve his lost continental lands, an open breach seemed imminent. Only the intervention of Stephen Langton, the

Mongols: the scourge of Christendom

From the obscurity of their barren homeland the Mongol hordes, led by Genghiz Khan, mounted their attack on the world. Wave after wave of them overran Asia and Europe, from Hungary to Korea.

THE ARID, now barely inhabited, Mongolian Plateau of eastern central Asia was for hundreds of years a centre of dynamic human activity. From this vast region of the cold Gobi desert, for reasons still largely unknown, emerged wave upon wave of energetic nomads, against whose remorseless attacks no state within 4,000 miles of Mongolia, however strong or civilized, could consider itself immune. Long before the Ch'in emperor constructed his Great Wall to defend China in the third century BC, lesser Chinese rulers had been compelled to build defences against the Hsiung Nu. These Mongolian people, later called *Huns,* struck terror into the heart of Europe in the fourth and fifth centuries AD, plundering as far westwards as present-day France and Italy. By about 1300 AD the Mongol empire was the largest the world has ever known. The rise and fall of the Mongol empire is one of the great wonders of history.

From earliest-known times the Mongols' whole way of life has depended on animals and their products. Sheep, goats and cattle provided their food, clothing, tents and riding equipment; small, stocky horses and two-humped camels carried the Mongols and their equipment from one patch of pasture land to the next.

Trained to fight from boyhood

Mongol children, nourished by fermented mares' milk called *koumiss,* quickly learned to ride and like their parents became more at home on horseback than on foot. Large savage dogs accompanied the nomads on their wanderings, driving their domesticated animals and guarding their encampments. Among the few non-animal products which the Mongols carried were the wooden frames of their portable felt tents (called *gers,* or *yurts*) and a chest armour of wood or iron which they developed for organized warfare. Their principal weapon was the bow, and Mongol boys learned to shoot arrows from small bows with great skill. As they grew to manhood, they increased the size of their bows and the length of their arrows, which they shot at enemies with deadly accuracy.

For well over a thousand years various Chinese dynasties claimed suzerainty over the Mongol tribes, as they did over most other peoples who lived within about 1,500 miles of the emperor's palace. But the Mongols, being tough and mobile, were not an easy people from whom to exact tribute, and more often than not the Chinese preferred to forgo the tribute rather than try to exact it.

The Mongols burst out of their obscurity into history in the early thirteenth century when Temujin ('Ironsmith'), a tribal leader, united a number of loosely organized tribes into a single, disciplined force.

1 Genghiz Khan, the fierce leader who united the Mongolian tribes into a fighting force and set out in 1206 to conquer the world.
2 Mongolian boys learned the art of war while still young. Genghiz Khan, followed by his white-robed mother, fights at the age of 12.
3 The map shows the vast spread of the Mongol empire. Begun by Genghiz Khan, it was extended by his ambitious sons and descendants.

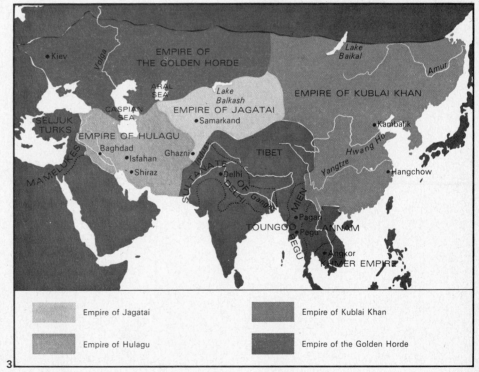

Empire of Jagatai	Empire of Kublai Khan
Empire of Hulagu	Empire of the Golden Horde

With this force he subdued the remaining tribes, and hammered the Mongols into an efficient fighting force. In 1206 Temujin assumed the title of *Genghiz Khan* (King of the Earth) – a hint that he intended to conquer the world.

Genghiz Khan's first target was close at hand – the rich civilized lands of northern China, where the once powerful Sung dynasty had ceased to have any influence. These northern lands had fallen under the control of the Kin (or Chin), an agricultural, hunting and fishing people of the area later called Manchuria. Under the spur of oppression, the Kin had developed into a warrior people in the early twelfth century, defeating the northern Sung dynasty, and bringing northern China

Tamerlane, a brilliant Mongol warrior, was notorious for his terrible cruelty and merciless slaughter of his enemies.

under their rule. Theirs was a brutal régime and they made slaves of many of the Han people who lived in northern China.

Genghiz began his offensive against the Kin in the classical Mongol way by withholding tribute. At the same time, he made a secret pact with the Sung in the southern part of China. He began his attack on the province of Hsi-Hsia, in what is now north-central China, in 1211. The Kin empire was protected by the Great Wall of China, built more than a thousand years earlier, but by that time somewhat in a state of disrepair. The Mongols, experts at sieges, soon overran the Wall and the fortresses, where the Kin soldiers sought refuge, slaughtering the garrisons and the civilian inhabitants. Killing, plundering and burning, the Mongol hordes swept all before them, driving across the northern provinces to Yenching (now Peking), the Kin capital. By 1215 Yenching had fallen and the Mongols controlled the whole of China north of the Hwang Ho, the Yellow River. They stripped the Chinese cities of their

wealth, and conscripted the ablest of the Chinese soldiers to instruct the Mongol armies in strategy and the use of new weapons, including explosives. The northern Chinese welcomed the Mongols as liberators from the hated Kin, rather than as oppressors. Many of the Kin took service under the Mongols; others returned to Manchuria and obscurity, from which their descendants later emerged as the Manchus.

Genghiz Khan decided to leave southern China alone and swing westwards, through central Asia, towards the rich Moslem kingdom of Persia. His well-trained and highly mobile troops swept through the difficult country of what is now southern Siberia, overcoming the hazards of snow and heat, floods and desert sands. They captured and looted many famous cities, including Samarkand, Tashkent, Bokhara and Herat. It was Genghiz Khan's rule to spare cities which surrendered but pyramids of skulls bore mute witness to the Mongol ferocity where people resisted. Northwest India and Afghanistan fell to the invaders. In 1222 they entered Europe, defeating Russian and Bulgarian armies. By the time he died Genghiz Khan ruled from the Yellow Sea in the east to the banks of the Dnieper in southern Russia.

He foresaw that this vast, loosely organized empire could not survive intact for long. He decreed that at his death it should be split into four parts ruled by his three surviving sons, Ogdai, Jagatai and Tule, and the descendants of his eldest son Juji, who had died earlier. When, therefore, he died in 1227, after a hunting fall, the title of khan passed to Ogdai, and he and Tule began a fresh campaign of conquest and pillage in China, which was to last until 1279.

In the west, a Mongol army invaded eastern Europe. It was led by Batu, Juji's son, and Subotai, one of Genghiz Khan's *orkhons* (marshals). They crossed the Volga and attacked Ryazan, 100 miles southeast of Moscow, took the city by assault and killed the citizens. Moscow (then of minor importance) and Kiev, a far greater city, in the Ukraine, were also quickly captured; Kiev was razed to the ground. The Mongols then swept into Poland, and Hungary, whose people were the only ones of Mongol race still outside the control of Genghiz Khan's successors. There they won a resounding victory at Pest, killing over 70,000 of the Hungarian army, crossing the Danube on the ice and laying waste a great deal of the countryside. The campaign was abandoned when news came of the death of Ogdai; Batu had to return to the Mongolian capital, Karakorum, where the *kuriltai* (great council) met to decide on Ogdai's successor. Batu later went back to Europe, where he founded and ruled a new Mongol state on the lower Volga, known as the Golden Horde.

Thousands massacred

The new khan was Ogdai's son Kuyuk, whose seven-year rule was relatively uneventful. The khanate then passed to Tule's sons, the eldest of whom, Mangu, became Great Khan in the 1250s. In 1258 Mangu's younger brother, Hulagu, crushed a revolt which had broken out in Persia, and captured the city of Baghdad, then the centre of Islam. The Caliph of Baghdad, who proved unco-operative, was beaten to death and hundreds of thousands of his people were massacred. Hulagu then advanced into Syria, capturing Damascus and Antioch. Mesopotamia, the fertile land between the rivers Tigris and Euphrates, was laid waste, and remained so for more than 600 years. Hulagu was contemplating taking Jerusalem when once again the death of a khagan (Great Khan) halted a Mongol campaign: Hulagu returned to Mongolia in 1259 to attend the kuriltai. His keenness to return was probably influenced by a severe defeat at the hands of an Egyptian army led by the Mameluke Sultan Kutuz, at Ain Jelat.

The successor as Khagan, chosen by his own troops, was Kublai, a younger brother of Mangu and Hulagu. Kublai and Mangu had together been conquering southern China and Tibet. Hulagu established his own dynasty in Persia, acknowledging his brother's supremacy as Great Khan.

Kublai Khan ruled as emperor of China for 35 years. He adopted the dynastic title of emperor in 1271, some 11 years

1 Babar, who invaded India and founded the Mogul empire in the sixteenth century, at a banquet with one of his advisers.

2 In this mausoleum in Gur-Amir, Samarkand, is the tomb of Tamerlane, who died in 1405 on his way to attack China.

3 This lamasery now stands where Ogdai, son of Genghiz Khan, built the Mongol empire's capital of Karakorum in the thirteenth century.

4 During Kublai Khan's rule of China, art and international trade flourished. This decorated celadon vase dates from the Yuan dynasty.

after he came to power, founding a dynasty known as the Yuan dynasty, which lasted for more than a century. He loved Chinese culture, and ruled according to traditional Chinese ways. But he mistrusted the Chinese politically (minor rebellions flared throughout his reign), and drew his counsellors, governors, and officials from other territories under Mongol rule. He abhorred unnecessary bloodshed, and had won territory from the Sung with only a few deaths, compared with the wholesale slaughter of his ancestors. His court at Peking was rich and brilliant. He encouraged artists, writers and musicians, and developed trade with other countries. Shipping thronged the busy ports of Fuchow,

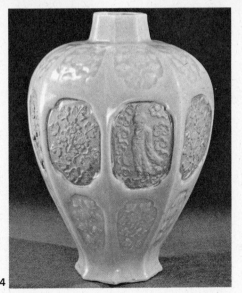

Hangchow and Canton. He built better roads and sign-posted them, and also established a simple postal service. Himself a Buddhist, he adopted a tolerant attitude to other religions: Christians, Buddhists, Taoists and Moslems were equally welcome at his court.

Kublai Khan became famous in Europe through the writings of a Venetian ex-

plorer and trader, Marco Polo, who lived at the court from 1275 to 1292. Marco Polo has left us a vivid description of Kublai and of Khanbalik, as Peking was then known. The Great Khan, he wrote, was of moderate height, his complexion 'fair and ruddy like a rose'. By his four wives he had 22 sons.

Kublai's palace aroused the special admiration of Marco Polo. He told of its huge size – the great hall alone could hold several thousand people, he said – and of its shining roof. Ceilings and walls were adorned with gold and silver. In the grounds was an artificial lake, stocked with a great variety of fish.

Too large an empire

Despite Marco Polo's tales of peace and prosperity, all was not quite so quiet as it appeared. At a time of slow communications, it was impossible for one emperor to rule an area stretching from Hungary to the China Sea. Even in southern China Kublai's authority was never really acknowledged, and in Russia, Persia and other distant territories little heed was paid to the dictates of an emperor who, Chinese at heart, had little real interest in his other provinces. But an attempt to overthrow him by his cousin, Kaida, and

Nayan, the greatest Mongol general of the time, was swiftly crushed in 1288 by Kublai who, despite advancing age, retained all his old military skill.

After the golden age of Kublai, who died in 1294, at the age of 78, the Mongol empire swiftly began to break up. The rulers of the outlying provinces went their own ways and Kublai's successors, able and benevolent rulers though they were, could not hold the empire together. The principal breakaway states were the Golden Horde, and the Persian kingdom under the descendants of Hulagu.

In China itself storms, floods and earthquakes brought pestilence and suffering. So wretched and unhappy was the lot of the Chinese that a Buddhist monk, Chu Yuan-chang, attributing the misfortunes of his countrymen to rule by foreigners, determined to end their reign. He formed the Red Turbans, a secret band of armed peasants, who rose in revolt. Despite his religious vocation, Chu was a man of rare military ability. From 1355 to 1368 he fought a series of battles, winning over more and more of the wealthy landowners to his side and gradually pushing the armies of the Mongols further north. The last of the Mongol emperors fled to Mongolia, and in 1368 Chu proclaimed himself as Emperor Tai-tsu, first of the Ming Dynasty. Not content with bringing the rule of the Mongols in China to an end, Chu dispatched a huge army and in a series of successful campaigns broke the power of the eastern Mongols.

In the west, the Russians tried to drive out the Golden Horde, and broke its power after two victories in 1378 and 1380. Another group, the White Horde, under their leader Toktamish, then reunited the tribes of the Golden Horde and ravaged Moscow and other cities in a series of attacks. But Toktamish overreached himself when he tried to demand the cession of territories ruled by another Mongol chief, Timur (1336–1405), whose capital was Samarkand. In many hard battles

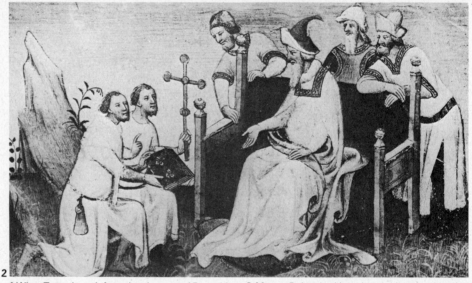

1 When Tamerlane defeated and captured Bayazid, he imprisoned the Turkish sultan in a cage and had him carried about until he died.

2 Marco Polo, the Venetian explorer and trader, kneeling before Kublai Khan who ruled China for 35 years until he died in 1294.

Timur broke the power of Toktamish, finally defeating him in 1391. His victory scattered the tribes of the Golden Horde and allowed the Russians to regain control of the territory.

Timur was called Timur the Lame – Tamerlane – from a wound which left him with a permanent limp. He was a military genius, but fortunately for the Russians his ambitions lay south and not north. After crushing the Golden Horde, Tamerlane swept down into Persia, capturing Baghdad and pressing on through the Khyber Pass into India. There he stormed Multan and Meerut and sacked Delhi. He returned to Persia to find that the Mamelukes of Egypt and the Ottoman Turks had united against him and recaptured Baghdad. He stormed the city, defeated the Mamelukes at Aleppo, and then attacked the Turks. He defeated the Turkish Sultan, Bayazid the Thunderbolt, at Angora in 1402, and took him prisoner. Once again Mongol armies threatened

Europe. But Tamerlane's ambitions lay elsewhere. He returned to Samarkand, the capital of the new Mongol empire he had created. Three years later, in 1405, he died on his way to attack China, and the new empire collapsed.

A century later one of his descendants, Babar, raised an army and invaded India. There he established a fresh Mongol state called the Kingdom of the Great Mughals. His grandson, Akbar, who succeeded to the throne of the new state in 1556, set out to end the distrust and dislike which existed between Moslems and Hindus. Himself a Moslem, he married a Hindu girl and appointed Hindus to government posts. Under his absolute but benevolent rule justice was administered impartially, better standards of weights and measures were introduced, and many beautiful buildings were erected. The rule of the last great Mongol leader was a complete contrast to the destruction and massacres carried out by his forebears.

Life with the lords of the manor

For an English villager under the Normans, the world ended with the bounds of his village. His king depended on its doing so, knowing change would come as the serfs' horizons widened.

A CROW, flying over England on any one day of the 300 years between the reigns of William I and Richard II, would see, repeated hundreds of times, much the same scene below: a manor-house, tucked within its sheltering wall; a small church shaded by yews; one or two streets, deeply rutted in winter, white dust in summer, between a cluster of thatched huts; a water-mill beside the stream; everywhere the reek of the dung-heaps outside every door, everywhere alive with straying children, barking dogs and a few wandering hens – the whole a little island set in a pattern of striped fields and surrounded on all sides by miles of dark forest or thorny wasteland.

These were the English villages, the strength of the country, base of a strictly organized pyramid whose top was the king. This pyramidal structure of society had developed in Saxon times. When the Vikings threatened, villagers looked for protection to the *thane,* the man responsible for raising a local band of fighting-men for the king of his part of England. Gradually his function became defined: he must guard the village and provide shelter for families and beasts within the palisade round his house when the Northmen struck. In return, the villagers would work for him or provide payment in food or crops.

The essence of the system, as it developed under the Normans, was that the only man in England who actually *owned* land was the king. He allowed his great lords to hold large parts of the country as tenants-in-chief, provided that they gave him soldiers in time of war. Each baron had to supply a stipulated number of trained, equipped men-at-arms. The great lords in turn leased some of their properties to lesser lords. These would hold one or several villages for their overlords, supply-

Protestantism first stirred in England 150 years before the ideas of Luther startled Europe. John Wycliffe sent 'simple priests' all over the country to preach the need for Church reform.

ing a proportion of the soldiers whom the great lord had promised to the king, administering local justice and running the estates. The villages were called *manors* and the lord's house, the central feature, was the *manor-house.* The lord of the manor kept for himself part of the land, called his *demesne,* and leased the rest to his smaller tenants.

In his frequent absences, the lord was represented on the manor by his steward, who acted for him. If the steward had several manors under his care, the day-to-day administration of each manor would be carried on by a bailiff. Below the bailiff came a reeve, elected by the tenants, who acted as a kind of farm foreman. Many manors were under the control of bishops or abbots, who acted as 'lords' on behalf of the Church. Barking Abbey, for example, controlled nearly

1,000 acres of land in Essex and large estates in four other counties at the time of the Domesday Survey (1086).

Almost all the tenants had to perform certain customary services as payment for the land that the lord gave them. Each manor also had its specialized tradesmen. But the blacksmith, the miller, the shepherd, the swineherd each had his own plot of land. The parish priest, himself usually a peasant's son, lived by farming his 'glebe' side by side with his people.

Bound to the land

Tenants with the highest status, the *freemen,* often paid money rents, but some gave service, working on the lord's demesne. Part of a freeman's rent might be paid in corn, poultry or some similar produce. Freemen could usually marry whom they pleased, leave the manor if they wanted to, and sell their produce as they wished. Other tenants were legally serfs, tied directly to the land on which they lived. They came under the jurisdiction of the manor court, or *moot,* held once a fortnight by the lord or his steward, open to the whole village and basing its judgements on customs handed down from times past, which even the lord could not change with impunity. Freemen had the theoretical right of appeal to the king's justices who travelled on circuit. There were many kinds of serfs, and their descriptions and status varied from one part of the country to another. They included *socmen* (tenants by *soc,* a fixed service); *villeins* (inhabitants of the *vill,* or *village*); *cottars,* who owed labour as rent for their cottages; and *bordars,* whose status was similar to that of cottars.

Villeins were the most numerous and well-to-do serfs. The service they gave, and the payments they made were of great importance to the overall prosperity of the

A pattern stamped by centuries upon English fields can still be seen today, *left,* near the village of Laxton, Nottinghamshire. Each farmer leased a number of acre or half-acre strips — called 'ridges' or 'lands' — usually 30. These were not all in one place between hedges, but were spread among those of his neighbours in the big open fields. Furrows made by the plough, *right,* served to divide and to drain the strips.

manor and of the country as a whole.

What were called *praedial services* were connected directly with the land. The villein was bound to give 'week work' on the demesne for about three days each week. Some lords exacted four or five days' work from villeins, while in continental Europe six days' labour was not unknown. Ploughing was the main work required. Villeins holding the full *virgate* of land (anything from 15 to 80 strips in the arable fields) had also each to provide a yoke of oxen; it took eight beasts to pull a large plough, which might be shared by four villeins. Other services owed to their lord by villeins included carting produce and materials either on the manor or between manors, harrowing, hoeing, mowing, reaping and dipping and shearing sheep.

Boon work was extra work required by the lord at seed time and harvest. From the villein's point of view this was probably his most irksome obligation, for he had to work for the lord at the very time when his own crops had to be sown or harvested. Many lords tried to make boon work less unpopular by turning it into a social occasion, rewarding the forced labourers with food and drink.

The normal pattern of agriculture was the open-field system. The land was normally divided into three great fields (in some cases only two), and one field was left fallow each year to recover its fertility. Of the other two fields, one was sown with wheat, the other generally with barley and oats. Each field was divided into strips, usually of an acre or half an acre, the acre being reckoned as the amount of land that a plough drawn by eight oxen could plough in one day. Each strip was one 'furrow-long' (furlong), the distance an ox-team could go before pausing to turn round and draw breath. The usual width was four poles, the pole being the wooden shafts attached to the yoke of the oxen. Each farmer's strips were scattered over the arable fields, so that each man had a just proportion of good land and poor land.

An ox for an inheritance

The medieval farmer was better at growing crops than he was at breeding cattle. Because of the difficulty in feeding animals in winter, since root crops were unknown, all but a few animals were slaughtered in late autumn. Medieval cattle, sheep and pigs were small and poor; only in later centuries was good stock selectively bred. In general, however, food seems to have been plentiful on most manors. Famine was comparatively rare; the worst famine recorded lasted from 1315 to 1321. Then, as now, wheat was the staple food in England.

Apart from the duty to give work to the lord, various obligations were exacted from the villein's family. A villein's son had to pay *heriot*, the best beast he possessed, in order to inherit his father's land. The villein paid *merchet* to the lord when his daughter (in some cases his son) married. The lord took a keen interest in the marriage of a village girl. If she married a man from outside the manor, her children would belong to the manor where their father lived, with a consequent

1

loss to the lord of potential labour. Lords exacted a fine called *leyrwite* in cases of adultery or incontinency, on the grounds that a girl's misbehaviour cost the lord his right to merchet. The lord also had to give permission before a villein's son could take an apprenticeship, or enter the Church. The right rested on the idea that the lord had first claim on the boy's services.

The medieval farmers also had to pay the lords for specific rights. *Pannage,* the right to let his pigs root for acorns and other food in the woodlands, cost a penny for a grown pig, or a halfpenny for a young pig. The right to gather firewood from the wasteland was secured by the payment of 'wood-penny'. Villages were forbidden to own millstones or possess an oven. They ground their corn at the lord's mill and baked their bread in his oven, giving him part of their flour and bread in payment. Probably the reason for having a communal bakehouse lay in the desire to prevent fires, for the huts of farmers in early medieval times were built mostly of wood or wattle and daub, and had thatched roofs. In later medieval times, communal ovens became rare, because cottages were built of stone or brick.

By present-day standards, even these improved cottages were very poor. Most of them contained only one or two rooms. In *The Nonnes Preestes Tale* Geoffrey Chaucer, writing in the late fourteenth century, drew a vivid picture of a 'narrow cottage' belonging to a widow, in which 'full sooty was her bower, and eke her hall'. The 'bower' was the sleeping quarters of the family; the hall was the living room, which the family often shared in winter with their animals. The widow's fire blazed away in the middle of the floor, the smoke finding its way out through gaps in the roof. A few of the more substantial medieval cottages still survive. One of these, a wooden-framed cottage at Didbrook, in Gloucestershire, has walls filled in with laths, plastered and built up with clunch (a kind of tough clay mixed with straw

and dung). Most homes were of this type.

Better cottages were built of stone. One of these cottages, still standing in the Gower Peninsula of South Wales, was built in 1415 – the year of Agincourt. It consists of one room, 14 feet square, floored with tightly trodden earth. Above this room is a loft floored with timber, and reached by a ladder. A large chimney with a crude open grate and an oven is set into one wall. When the farm animals crowded in with the family for shelter, or for safety from thieves, such a home must have been more than cosy. The widow in Chaucer's story had three large sows, three 'kine' (cows), a sheep and chickens. The widow, says Chaucer, 'in patience lived a full simple life'.

Medieval farmers had little furniture. Their main possessions might consist of a few chests standing against the walls, a bacon rack swinging from the rafters, farm implements hanging on the walls, and a great metal pot for stewing food over the fire. In addition, a farmer might possess home-made wooden platters and spoons. His clothes would probably be of leather from his own animals, or spun and woven from wool, hemp and nettles. The farmer's family made these treasured possessions themselves during the long winter evenings, by the flickering glow of foul-smelling rush-lights dipped in animal fat.

Alehouses and archery

Life was not entirely grey and wretched for the medieval farmer. When the lord visited his manor, or others came to visit him, there would be processions to see. Dancing was a common recreation, and every village had its alehouse. His round was broken by the many Church festivals, which gave him 30 or 40 days of holiday every year, full of rituals, ceremonies and processions. Archery was encouraged by the lords, but football (which was more popular) was not, because it distracted men from the archery which was useful practice for war.

As early as 1200, the feudal-manorial

The fall of Constantinople

In the year 1453 the Turkish army under Mehmet II thundered into Constantinople, capital of Byzantium. A valiant, two-month siege had been broken, and an empire had come to an end.

1 In 1339 the Byzantine emperor, Manuel II, visited the capitals of Europe to appeal for help to save Constantinople from the Turks. He failed, and the city fell.
2 An engraving of the Turks sweeping into Constantinople illustrates the Christian tales of atrocity and bloodshed. Yet quarters which voluntarily submitted appear to have been spared.

IN THE YEARS following 1066, when England was held fast in the grip of William the Conqueror, certain Anglo-Saxons fled from their homeland to the far-off city of Constantinople. There they took refuge, and many went on to serve in the Byzantine emperor's special bodyguard.

The emperor lived at that time in a magnificence unparalleled amongst Christian rulers. Yet 300 years later, in 1400, the Byzantine emperor Manuel II was himself a supplicant in England before King Henry IV. He had set out the previous year to visit the Christian capitals of Europe in a desperate bid for help to save Constantinople from capture by the Moslem Ottoman Turks. Even then, they were fast closing in upon 'the Queen of cities' as the Byzantines called their capital.

This contrast between earlier splendour and later humiliating poverty came about partly because of weaknesses within the Byzantine Empire itself and partly because of the strength of its enemies and the greed of its Christian neighbours.

From the seventh century onwards the Byzantine Empire had set up military centres in its provinces, manned by officers and soldier-farmers. The system was meant to provide a defence against Arabs, Slavs and Central Asian Turkic tribes. It ended by becoming a network of great military landed families whom even the most powerful emperors failed to control. From the eleventh century onwards the crown even had to grant many of its own rights, such as collecting taxes, to individual landowners in return for military service. Thus the grip of the central authority

over the provinces grew continually less effective.

This weakness was increased by intermittent struggles for control of the central government and by the class conflicts in big cities such as Thessalonica, when for a time the poorer people gained control and wreaked their terrible vengeance on the governing class.

Another trouble for the Byzantine government came with the growing power of foreign capitalists within the Empire. It began when the maritime republic of Venice was given special trading privileges in return for naval help against the Normans invading Greece in the eleventh century. The great trading city of Venice hung on tenaciously to these privileges which give it exemption from paying customs dues in the Byzantine Empire, through which so much lucrative trade passed. As Venice grew in strength so did her Italian rivals Genoa and Pisa, and they too tried to make advantageous trade treaties with Constantinople.

The threatening Turks

While neighbouring Latin powers grew more aggressive from the eleventh century onwards, the difficulties of the Byzantine government were increased by fresh outside attacks directed against all parts of the Empire. From the mid-eleventh century Turkic tribes from Central Asia were hammering on the eastern frontier and by the end of the century Seljuk and other Turks had conquered much of the rich territory of Asia Minor, where they set up their own Moslem principalities. Nomad Turkic tribes raided across the River

Danube penetrating far into the Balkans. Norman adventurers reached Italy and took possession of the last remaining Byzantine provinces in the south. To add to Byzantium's troubles, the Crusaders arrived from the Latin West, upsetting Byzantine diplomacy and foreign policy. They set up troublesome, inadequately-defended little Christian states in what had once been the Byzantine provinces of Syria and Palestine.

Little more than 100 years after the First Crusade had set out came the dramatic prelude to the final downfall of Constantinople. In 1203 the West organized the Fourth Crusade which was intended to attack the Moslems, but a year later it turned against the Byzantine capital. Venice was the leading light and profited most from the destruction of the old Byzantine Empire, which safeguarded its trade. Other westerners set up little principalities on Byzantine soil. But the so-called Latin 'Empire' of Constantinople was short-lived. In 1261 the Byzantine emperor recaptured the capital and returned from his exile in Nicaea in northern Asia Minor. But he ruled over a greatly diminished empire and had to tolerate some of the Latin principalities, such as the Duchy of Athens. The Venetians still held their strategic lands and valuable trading posts. Italian families controlled most of the islands of the Aegean Sea. Certain Greek kingdoms such as Epirus in northwest Greece or Trebizond on the southern shore of the Black Sea were never controlled by the Byzantine emperor, now re-established in Constantinople. To all intents and purposes the

Byzantine Empire had been effectively broken up by the Fourth Crusade.

For Byzantium the period from 1204 to 1453 was little more than a long-drawn-out death-agony. Constantinople, once 'the city of the world's desire', was worn-out and shabby after its Latin looters had departed; its Byzantine rulers were too poor to rebuild the once-splendid imperial palaces. And although they had turned out the Latins, other and more potent dangers arose. In the mid-thirteenth century the political shape of the Middle East had been changed by the arrival of the Mongols from Central Asia. Although they never actually took possession of Asia Minor, their expeditions in this area caused great upheaval and destruction. Out of the confusion which they left behind there arose a number of small new Moslem Turkish principalities. In the fourteenth century the Byzantines were left with only a bare foothold in Asia Minor, while the Turkish principality of Osman grew in power. These Ottoman Turks were situated almost opposite to Constantinople and frequently served as mercenaries in the armies of the rival Byzantine factions. Then they gained a foothold in Byzantine European territory. Weakened by its long struggle with the Balkans and its other Christian enemies, Byzantium was unable to prevent the Turks from steadily increasing their stranglehold on the tiny remnant of the Byzantine Empire left in Europe.

The rift between the Churches

It was in this desperate situation that the Emperor Manuel sought help from Western Christian states in 1399. Emperors before and after him had tried to get western military aid in return for the reunion of the Churches of Rome and Constantinople. These two great branches of Christendom had grown steadily apart, particularly since the eleventh century, and the sack of Christian Constantinople in 1204 by fellow Christians had aggravated the rift. Although Greek rulers and Constantinople's high officials and churchmen might be willing to agree to reunion with Rome in return for military help, this was never the wish of the Byzantine rank and file. Whether laymen or clergy, they preferred to be under Ottoman rule rather than recognize the hated Roman Church.

There were, too, other factors which made it difficult for Byzantium to get effective aid from the West. Certain influential Western parties such as Venice, Genoa and Aragon probably did not want a revitalized and restored Byzantium: they were only concerned to protect their economic interests in the eastern Mediterranean and in the Black Sea, their monopoly of minerals, their control of the grain trade with South Russia and their lucrative customs dues.

The fifteenth-century Byzantine emperors must have realized that the fall of the city was almost inevitable. There is a spirit of resignation in Byzantine writings of the late Middle Ages: the Byzantines accepted their fate as God's punishment for their sins. And yet there is the

Inside Santa Sophia, the Cathedral of the Holy Wisdom. Shortly before the fall of the city, strange lights full of ill-omen flickered above; days later it was a Turkish mosque.

constant hope that some miracle would occur; that the Virgin, the special protectress of the city, would come to its help. In 1402 the Ottoman Turks were badly defeated at the battle of Ankara in Asia Minor by Tamerlane, the Mongol Timur from the Middle East. To the Byzantine this seemed like divine intervention. But the respite was not for long. When in 1451 the Byzantine ambassador and historian Sphrantzes learnt of the accession of Mehmet II to the Ottoman throne, he said: 'This is the worst news that I could possibly hear.' The new young sultan was ruthless and determined and had announced that as soon as he controlled the reins of authority he would 'destroy the Empire of the Romans and bring all the Christian Empires to nought'.

Mehmet, 'cunning as a fox', soon showed his hand. Constantinople was built on a triangle of land with the sea on two sides and on the west, a land-wall. The long narrow sea inlet on the northern side formed the harbour known as the Golden Horn. Both land and sea boundaries were fortified. Once the capital had commanded the entrance to the sea of Marmora and the passage through the Bosphorus straits to the Black Sea. But now the Asia Minor shore was in Ottoman hands, with a fort called Anadolu Hisar standing on the Asian bank of the Bosphorus.

During the spring of 1452 Mehmet built another fort called Rumeli Hisar on the European slopes of the Bosphorus (where it still stands). The Ottomans thus commanded the Bosphorus. Beyond the massive fortified walls on the western land side of the city, Mehmet was known to be massing his troops in Thrace. He was said to have at least 150,000 men between the sea of Marmora and the Golden Horn, including the famous regular soldiers, the Janissaries, as well as many irregulars called Bashi-Bazouks and innumerable hangers-on out for plunder. His artillery included enormous cannons. The largest needed 60 oxen to drag it up to the walls of Constantinople and 200 men to keep it in place on its wagon. By early April 1453 the Turkish army was outside the land-walls.

Constantinople's defences

The Byzantines had refused an offer to spare their city if it surrendered. They shut their land gates on 2 April and broke down the bridges over the 60-foot-wide *foss* or ditch. The fortifications were arranged in three lines: the inner wall was approximately 40 feet high with lofty towers at intervals; a second or outer wall with towers ran parallel to it; the third wall was a kind of crenellated breastwork which formed the inner wall of the foss. These fortifications were entered through gates placed at intervals. Halfway along the wall the ground dipped forming the little valley of the River Lycus. It was here in this valley that the Ottomans concentrated their attack. The besieged were estimated by Sphrantzes, the emperor's secretary, as numbering 6,983 men including 2,000 foreigners, mainly Venetians and Genoese. Among them was the famous Genoese soldier Giustiniani, who took charge of the defence of the land-walls, concentrating on the second or outer wall since the inner wall was in a bad state of repair. A great chain or boom had been placed across the entrance to the Golden Horn and ships were stationed across the boom to protect it. On the north shore of the Golden Horn was the suburb Galata, the walled city of the Genoese trading colony, which was playing a waiting game of uneasy neutrality.

Turkish troops took up their place before the land-walls with their heavy artillery; the sultan's brilliantly coloured

1 Variously described as ruthless, determined and cunning as a fox, Mehmet II made it his avowed ambition to 'bring all the Christian Empires to nought'.
2 Rumeli Hisar, built as a fort by Mehmet in 1452, gave him direct command of the Bosphorus, the narrow sea passage which Constantinople depended on for access to the Black Sea.
3 Sultan Murad II. From 1421 to 1451 he widely extended Ottoman power in southeast Europe. But he was a lover of culture first and it was left to his successor to crush Constantinople.

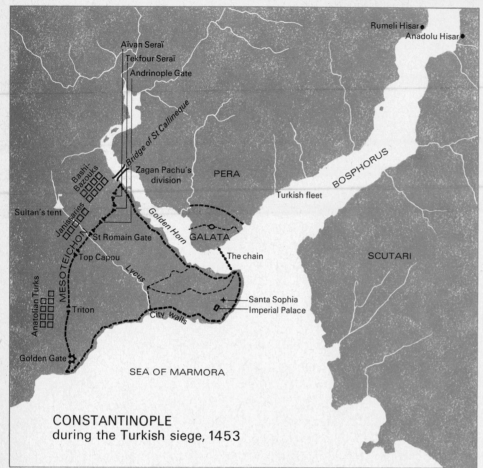

CONSTANTINOPLE
during the Turkish siege, 1453

Map labels:
Rumeli Hisar
Anadolu Hisar
Aïvan Seraï
Tekfour Seraï
Andrinople Gate
Bridge of St Callineque
Zagan Pachu's division
PERA
BOSPHORUS
Turkish fleet
Bashi-Bazouks
Sultan's tent
Janissaries
St Romain Gate
GALATA
Golden Horn
The chain
SCUTARI
MESOTEICHON
Top Capou
Lycus
Anatolian Turks
Triton
City walls
Santa Sophia
Imperial Palace
Golden Gate
SEA OF MARMORA

the ground as it was being carried in procession round the city; this was followed by a thunderstorm and a cloudburst and a dark fog; strange lights were seen playing over Santa Sophia, the cathedral of the Holy Wisdom. The emperor was advised to leave the city which God had abandoned, but he refused. On the evening before the attack all, Greek and Latin alike, went to the cathedral and there they celebrated the last Christian Liturgy to be held in the Great Church. Then each man went to his post on the outer wall. About an hour after midnight the attack began: first the Bashi-Bazouks, then the Anatolian Turks and finally the Janissaries. At the crucial moment the Genoese leader, Giustiniani, was wounded and carried through the inner wall into the city to a Genoese ship in the harbour. Amidst the dismay this caused, Mehmet spurred on his Janissaries, who succeeded at last in breaking the stockade at the outer wall and gaining access to the city through the inner wall. Other Turks had made their way through a small postern gate to the north and had raised the Turkish standard. The cry went up: 'The city is taken.'

'The spider is now the watchman'

The Turkish entry was followed by panic amongst the Christians. Barbaro, a Venetian who was present, tells how everybody who could do so escaped by ship, but so many were killed that their heads in the Golden Horn and the sea of Marmora reminded him of melons floating in the canals of Venice. Certain quarters of the city seem to have been spared, probably because they voluntarily submitted to the Turks. Mehmet himself rode first to the church of the Holy Wisdom which was at once converted into a mosque; then he went to the imperial Great Palace, never fully repaired after the sack of 1204. He is said to have quoted two lines from a Persian poem, 'The spider is now the watchman of the imperial palace and has woven the hangings before the doorway. The mournful song of the owl echoes through the imperial tombs of Afrasaib.'

The city was rapidly rebuilt, refortified and repopulated. Mehmet allowed his Greek subjects to keep their religion and he encouraged the election of a new Patriarch, Gennadius, who repudiated all union with Rome and was given control of the once independent Orthodox Churches of Serbia and Bulgaria. Many Greek magnates served the Ottoman state, which by the end of the fifteenth century controlled Greece, the Balkans and Asia Minor. It was a humiliating fate for an empire convinced of its universal mission. But Byzantium had served Christendom well: it had kept the Arabs out of much of Europe; it had taught the young Slav nations their statecraft and had brought them Christianity; it had given the world its own creative medieval art and its Greek heritage of literature and science. And even under Ottoman domination its people were still able to keep alive their Church, their Greek language and their Hellenic national spirit, all of which were to flower again after independence had been gained in the nineteenth century.

tent was pitched opposite the Lycus valley sector of the front, while the Turkish fleet in the Bosphorus and the sea of Marmora tried to cut off supplies and to force their way across the boom into the Golden Horn. From 12 April onwards the Turkish guns bombarded the city walls and the Turkish soldiers tried to fill in the foss. Great gaps were made in the outer wall which the Christians were defending. On 20 April four Genoese ships dodged through the Turkish fleet and reached the Golden Horn behind the boom. This defeat stirred up Mehmet to renew his attempts to gain possession of the Golden Horn. His engineers now contrived to bring ships overland from the Bosphorus into the Golden Horn. They were fixed on wheeled cradles and dragged over rollers by oxen – to the dismay of the Christians, on 22 April about 70 Turkish ships made their appearance in the Golden Horn.

Dark omens and defeat

The struggle dragged on for another month. Within the city Greeks, Genoese and Venetians quarrelled. Food and ammunition were short. A ship which got through on 23 May reported that no Venetian rescue fleet could be seen in the Aegean. Meanwhile Mehmet keyed up his forces for a final general assault planned for 29 May, promising three days' unrestricted looting. Then on 28 May there was silence in the Turkish camp and its soldiers rested and fasted before the assault.

Inside the city Mehmet's intentions were realized. During the days of 25–27 May there had been bad omens. The picture of the Mother of God had fallen to

A map of Constantinople in 1453 shows the three city walls, the positioning of the Turkish divisions and the defences of the besieged garrison before the final attack was launched.

Constantinople's Golden Gate: placed at the seaside end of the outer wall, it was one of seven gates which studded the defence. They were closed shortly before the Turkish army arrived.

`The most serene republic'

Medieval Venice, dominating the cross-ways which linked the trade routes of Europe and Asia, was the greatest maritime power of the age. How did her citizens achieve their unique way of life?

FOR A HUSBAND she took 'the everlasting sea'. She was rich, proud, civilized, prodigal with gold, the delight of the world's greatest painters. She was the *'Serenissima'* – Venice, most powerful maritime city in medieval Europe, queen of the Adriatic, the Black Sea, the Mediterranean.

The beginnings of this greatness were humble enough. In the fifth century the barbarian Lombards and Goths invaded the collapsing Roman empire and swept down the Italian peninsula. A group of refugees, fleeing from the conquerors, left the mainland and sought shelter in a compact group of small, barren islands in lagoons off the northwest Adriatic coast.

The Venetian republic was built there, physically on foundations of mud, with canals serving as streets, as in the old part of Venice they still do. But in the economic and political sense, Venice had foundations based on rock – the rock of commerce. The city-state provides a supreme medieval example not only of a government, but of a whole way of life, based on trade and sea traffic.

The form of government which was to be the chief feature of Venetian society was established early. In A D 466 the members of the new community entrusted the management of their affairs to 12 tribunes, one chosen from each island settlement; but two centuries later, when local rivalries threatened to destroy their unity, they appointed a chief magistrate, the Doge. The first Doge took office in 697. The Doges held office for life, but there was no hereditary principle; each Doge was chosen afresh. In the course of the next 1,100 years there were to be 120 Doges in

In a tumult of flying arrows and breaking oars, over 200 galleys of Venice and Spain defeated the Turks at Lepanto in 1571. Some 15,000 Christian slaves were freed from the Turkish ships.

all. The republican governmental system of Venice assured its freedom from family quarrels and disputes over succession, which bedevilled its less fortunate neighbours.

At first the Venetians acknowledged the authority of the Byzantine emperors, ruling from Constantinople, but after they had resisted an attack made upon their islands early in the ninth century by the Franks under Pepin, King of Italy, son of the Emperor Charlemagne, they organized themselves into an independent republic. In 828 some Venetian traders stole the body of St Mark from Alexandria and took it back with them. Henceforward St Mark became the patron saint of Venice, and the lion of St Mark its emblem. To receive the saint's body a chapel adjoining the Doge's palace was built. In the eleventh century this was rebuilt as the magnificent basilica of St Mark.

Ships for the Crusaders

Placed as they were astride the Mediterranean highway linking east and west in the ancient and medieval world, their whole outlook being away from the Italian mainland and towards the sea, the Venetians increasingly became a maritime people. They built themselves a fleet of merchant ships, and made their city a centre of commerce. By the end of the tenth century they had established control over the Adriatic and suppressed all the pirates there.

Their opportunity to extend their activities further came a century later with the successive Crusades which were organized in Christian Europe to fight the Moslems who held the Holy Land. The great armies which marched eastward against the Saracens, as the Moslems were called, required fleets of hitherto unprecedented size to transport men and supplies to Palestine. Expeditions from the crusading countries assembled in the large Mediterranean seaport towns, which became the supply depots and transit camps of the armies. Here most of the ships needed were built. The riches earned from the first three Crusades alone enabled Venice, by the end of the twelfth century, to obtain commercial bases in Tyre and other leading Syrian ports, and to build up a large carrying trade.

The superiority of Venice was made clear in 1177, when Pope Alexander III and the Emperor Frederick I, who had been at loggerheads for nearly 20 years, met in the city to effect a reconciliation. The Pope presented the Doge with a consecrated ring, saying: 'Receive this as a pledge of the sovereignty which you and your successors shall have over the sea.' Every Ascension Day the Doge performed a ceremony known as the *Sposalizio del Mar*. In the superbly decorated Venetian state galley, the *Bucintoro*, the Doge was rowed out, escorted by councillors and notabilities in their gondolas, to the Adriatic, where he cast a gold ring into the waters to symbolize and celebrate the marriage of Venice and the sea.

Of all the Crusades, the most advantageous to Venice was the notorious Fourth Crusade. When the crusading

177

armies mustered in Venice in 1202, they were unable to raise the 85,000 silver marks which they had agreed to pay Venice for provisions and the hire of ships. The republic interned them until they agreed to discharge their debt by conquering the Dalmatian port of Zara for the Venetians. It was then agreed that the Crusade should be diverted further against Constantinople, which the Crusaders captured in 1204. For three days this Christian city was wildly looted, and Venice and the Crusaders shared the booty equally.

At the height of its power in the fifteenth century, Venice possessed an extensive empire. It held Crete, Corfu and many islands in the Aegean, a strip of coast-land in the Morea, and the Dalmatian coast from Trieste to Albania. It also had treaty rights in Constantinople, Trebizond, Alexandria and other ports which made the Black Sea and the Mediterranean free to her ships.

Soldiers of fortune

Such a powerful position was only achieved as the result of an almost continuous struggle during the fourteenth century with Genoa, Venice's most serious Italian trade rival. Both republics were half-ruined in their long-drawn-out contest. Genoa never really recovered from its defeat, and ceased to be an important maritime power. Venice, on the other hand, soon made good its great losses and went on to fresh achievements and expansion.

·Much of the fighting in Italy in those days was carried on by mercenary armies, led by *condottieri*, soldiers of fortune skilled in warfare, who sold their services to the patron whose fees or cause they preferred. Fighting thus being contracted out, the merchants of Venice were free to devote themselves to trade. The power of Venice rested upon commercial prosperity. Its sea routes provided vital arteries for the circulation of European trade, linking the land-routes of Asia with the Mediter-

1 'He hath an argosy bound to Tripolis, another to the Indies; I understand moreover he hath a third at Mexico, a fourth for England. . . .' Ships of the merchants of Venice, ranging over the world like those of Shakespeare's hero, brought greatness to their city. The Doge's sumptuous marble palace is seen in this picture by Canaletto, who captured the lively charm of the Venetian scene, where even today funerals and merchandise alike must travel by water, 2 — perhaps beneath the famous 'Bridge of Sighs', 5. In the 1720s Canaletto portrayed another lively aspect of contemporary Venetian life in *The Stone Mason's Yard,* 3, which bordered on the Grand Canal. Her artists were Venice's pride. Giovanni Bellini's cool tranquil picture of the Doge Leonardo Loredan, 4, itself almost embodies the ideal of the 'most serene republic'.

ranean, and the Mediterranean with the Channel ports. From the start of the fourteenth century, six convoys set out each year from Venice for the Black Sea, Greece and Constantinople, the Syrian ports, Egypt, the Barbary coast, England and Flanders. They brought back to Venice, Indian spices, carpets, damasks and jewels, Scandinavian wood and furs, English wool, Flemish cloth and French wine.

Among the cargoes was maple wood from Bosnia and Dalmatia, imported into Venice by Turkish merchants. This beautiful wood was eagerly bought by the lute and violin makers of northern Italy. Using it, they achieved the lovely appearance and tone of the great Brescian and Cremonese fiddles. The dyes and resins which made the famous Cremona varnish also came in through Venice: gamboge from southeast Asia, copal from Africa, turpentine, shellac and amber.

Venice thrived on trade. The square at the Rialto and the streets near it were lined with shops and warehouses. Hundreds of goldsmiths and money-changers, the bankers of those days, carried on their business there.

Pilgrims and slaves

Human cargoes also brought profits for Venetian ships. Important among these were Christian pilgrims bound for the shrines in the Holy Land. In 1399, Venice obtained from the Turkish government a guarantee of protection for all such pilgrims carried in its ships, and thereby gained a virtual monopoly of the business. Important also for Venice was the slave trade. The chief market was Egypt. The Mameluke Sultans, who governed Egypt from the middle of the thirteenth century, required choice girls for their harems, and male slaves for their armies. These the Venetian shipowners supplied, obtaining them usually from the Moslem settlements bordering the Black Sea. Venetians also bought slaves, taking mostly girls for domestic service. By the end of the fifteenth century, when the Turkish government at last forbade Venetians to transport Moslem slaves, there were about 3,000 slaves in Venice.

Though trade brought the greatest wealth, Venice had thriving industries. One of these was shipbuilding. Italian ships in the Middle Ages had short lives.

4

5

They could not withstand the Atlantic seas, and even in the Mediterranean did not last for more than five or six years. Consequently there was a constant demand for new vessels, and the Venetian state-owned *Arsenal* (the name comes from the Arabic *dar sana,* 'house of work') was a flourishing shipyard, where thousands of workmen toiled incessantly. Other state-owned industries in Venice were banking and the salt-trade. A distinctive Venetian speciality was the manufacture of ornamental glass vessels, of such unrivalled quality that Venetian glassware became renowned throughout the medieval world. To keep the technique of manufacture secret, workmen were forbidden to leave the city. Those who did were pursued and killed.

Second only to the commercial foundation of Venice's power was her stable constitution, which gave her an important advantage over faction-ridden Genoa. Venetians claimed that the constitution avoided both despotism and anarchy. In 1172 the elected Great Council was set up as the main law-making body, and the growing power of the established merchant class was shown by the law of the *Serrata* (closing) which in 1297 restricted the Council's composition to families descended from its original members, whose names were written in the *Libro d'Oro,* the Golden Book.

The Council of Ten

The Council elected members of the Senate (which was concerned with policy), the *Collegio* (executive), which consisted of the heads of government departments, and the six *Savii Grandi,* each of whom acted as chief minister for a week in turn. At the summit of the constitution was the Doge, elected for life, and his six Councillors, who had the right of entry into every council.

In 1310 the notorious Council of Ten was first set up 'to preserve the liberty and peace of the subjects of the Republic and to protect them from the abuses of personal power'. It consisted of 17 members, 10 elected annually and not immediately re-eligible, plus the Doge and his six Councillors. It had overriding and secret powers which it used to save Venetian independence in times of war and other national emergencies. Fearsome stories of secret arrests and perpetual imprisonment have become attached to its name. But these belong to the last years of the Republic, when frequent plots and terrorism threatened the state's existence, and ruthless action seemed to be the only defence. In Venice's great days there was universal loyalty to the Republic, because the rule and the prosperity of the merchant oligarchy were identical with the interests of the people as a whole.

Although the rule of the Council of Ten was despotic, there was another side to the coin. The state provided hospitals for the sick, pensions for those who had retired, and care for the orphans and widows. Taxes were low, the courts dispensed justice efficiently, and the laws, though imposed by an oligarchy, were often progressive. One, for example, barred chil-

Top, Gentile Bellini, elder brother of the more famous painter, incidentally celebrated his city's fine buildings and rich inhabitants as he painted a local miracle: a relic of the Cross, falling into a canal, upholds its rescuer in the water. *Above,* Venice's wealth depended on her ships. This view of part of the city, made in 1480, shows their importance in the islands' life.

dren from working in dangerous trades. Another compelled merchants to comply with a 'Plimsoll line' so that ships should not be loaded beyond the safety margin.

After the defeat of Genoa, the Venetians began to look inland, and by the middle of the fifteenth century had established an empire on the Italian mainland which stretched almost to Milan. But Venice's territorial greed contributed to its downfall. To gain an empire, Venice engaged in frequent wars with its Italian neighbours. These contests seriously strained its power. The Turks captured Constantinople in 1453 and began to restrict the Levant trade. Almost immediately the nations on the Atlantic seaboard sought new routes to the east. In 1486 Bartholomew Diaz rounded the Cape of Good Hope, and in 1498 Vasco da Gama voyaged to India. The discoveries of these new routes enabled the Portuguese to break Venice's commercial monopoly, and undercut the city-state's prices for eastern goods. The importance of the Mediterranean trade routes declined, causing the end of Venetian prosperity and its importance as a centre of ship-building.

Venice, however, continued to resist the Turks in a series of courageous wars. Its ships fought in 1571 in the great Battle of Lepanto, which shattered Turkish naval power. In the seventeenth century Venice struggled for more than 20 years to defend Crete, inflicting serious damage on the attackers. Yet despite these efforts, the Venetian empire disintegrated. Venice lost much of its Aegean territory in 1479, Cyprus in 1573, and Crete in 1669. By 1718 it retained only Corfu and a few Dalmatian ports.

In the eighteenth century, many travellers were attracted by the city's lagoons, fine buildings, artistic treasures, theatres and pageants, but Venice no longer counted in the affairs of Europe. When Napoleon finally extinguished the Republic of Venice in 1797, it was never revived.

Milan's soldier princes

Under the Sforzas fifteenth-century Milan became a leading centre of Renaissance Italy. Their rise from mercenary soldiers to ruling princes makes them uniquely representative of their age.

ONE EVENING in 1384, according to legend, a band of mercenary soldiers out seeking recruits approached young Muzio Attendolo as he was working on the small family farm. Taking up an axe, the boy declared that he would throw it at a nearby oak: if it stayed there, he would join them. The axe stuck and Muzio embarked on a military career that was to elevate the family from obscurity to fame as one of the pre-eminent dynasties of Renaissance Italy.

The Attendoli were a substantial family in their locality, Cotignola, in the Romagna district of Italy. War-like and clannish, they lived a life of harsh austerity and whether or not the story of the axe is discounted, their upbringing admirably suited Muzio and his brothers for careers as soldiers.

Soldiers of fortune

Instead of maintaining standing armies to fight the almost perpetual wars they waged against each other, the Italian states of the fifteenth century hired freelance soldiers called *condottieri*. The system provided unlimited opportunities for advancement to successful condottieri and most of them sought to set themselves up as independent lords over a state or district, either by direct conquest or in payment for their services. Muzio's career, and those of his two sons, Francesco and Alessandro, followed the pattern of many of these soldiers of fortune.

For some 15 years Muzio served under the famous condottieri leader, Alberico da Barbiano, who was so impressed by the boy's enormous strength that he dubbed him 'Sforza' (strength). Muzio then moved on to command his own mercenaries, contracting his services independently to many masters, and he soon became the foremost general in Italy. But his territorial acquisitions were limited to some lands in the Romagna (including his native Cotignola) and Naples, and it was left to his two sons Francesco and Alessandro to achieve the status of princes.

Francesco, when his father was drowned in 1424, succeeded to his command and to his lands, and together he and Alessandro directed their energies to carving out territories from the Papal States. In 1433 Francesco secured the lordship of the March of Ancona in the service of the Duke of Milan, and in 1445 he financed the purchase of Pesaro for Alessandro, whose successors retained it until 1512.

Francesco's rule in the March was conscientious but the territory was under constant attacks, sponsored by Pope Eugenius IV whom Sforza had alienated by his conquests. After 16 years of tenuous control Francesco was forced to concede its loss.

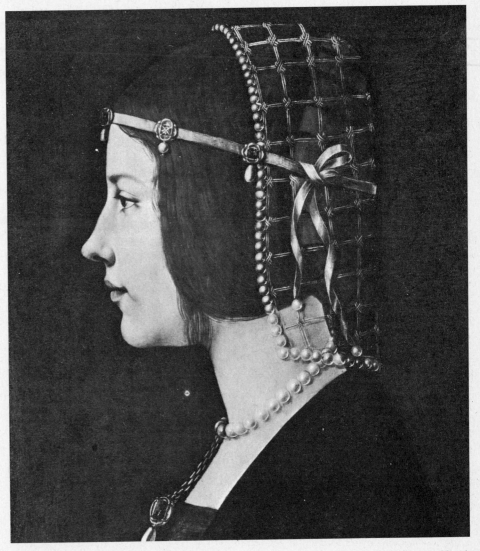

His ambitions had, however, already been diverted to the Duchy of Milan. He had been employed alternately for and against its Duke, Filippo Maria Visconti, in Milan's incessant wars with Venice. During a period of reconciliation in 1433, he became betrothed to Visconti's daughter, Bianca Maria. The proposed dowry included Sforza's succession to the duchy, and eight years later the wedding was celebrated.

In 1447 the direct male line of the Visconti was extinguished with the death of Filippo Maria, but Sforza's chance of succession was denied by the proclamation of a Milanese republic by the citizens. Although continuing war with Venice rendered Sforza's services indispensable, as commander of the Milanese forces his hold on the state was limited to three towns. Unable to achieve his ultimate ambition in the service of the republic, he reversed his allegiance and laid siege to Milan. With a duplicity typical of Renaissance politics, Milan and Venice made peace behind Sforza's back, but the siege

Beatrice d'Este, wife of Ludovico 'il Moro'. Energetic, vivacious and intelligent, under her direction the court at Milan reached the height of its brilliance.

was upheld and in February 1450 the inhabitants overthrew the republic and invited Sforza to become their duke.

Francesco now occupied the highest position ever won by a condottiere. As the acknowledged peer among them he had undoubtedly inherited his father's military talents and he allied those with a statesmanship his father had never possessed. In his external policy, he recognized that the constant feuding among the Italian states was inviting intervention from the great European powers and he successfully fostered alliances of the five principal states to maintain a balance of power in the country. He enjoyed close personal friendships with Cosimo de Médicis of Florence and Louis XI of France. In his domestic policy his rule, although despotic, did much to promote the prosperity of the duchy and the welfare of its inhabitants. Waterways were constructed, financial abuses removed and many building projects undertaken, notably a hospital and the castle. Despite his success Francesco was always ready to listen personally to the complaints of his subjects.

Contemporaries describe him as a typical fighting man, tall and majestic, and serious in expression. The court of Milan reflected his simplicity and love of domestic life. On one occasion, he wrote to delay the arrival of a visitor to Milan until after a Saturday 'for on that day the ladies will be washing their hair and the troops have their work to do'. Though no scholar, he had a great admiration for learning and both he and Bianca took a keen interest in the education of their eight children. Many of the prominent teachers of the new humanist education were employed, notably Francesco Filelfo, who organized the education of the children, stressing the balanced development of mind and body and, on Francesco's insistence, fitting them for princes.

On his death in 1466 Francesco left several sons. Ascanio (1455–1505) became a cardinal and influential diplomat in the affairs of the papacy and Milan. Two other sons, Galeazzo Maria and Ludovico Il Moro, in turn succeeded to the duchy.

Assured of external security by Francesco's foreign policy, the ten-year reign of Galeazzo Maria was an oppressive period for the Milanese. The new duke differed totally in character from his father. He was vain – neurotically proud of the whiteness of his hands – wilful, dissolute and extravagant. He imposed a cruel, arbitrary despotism, and such senseless injunctions as that to the people of Pavia forbidding them 'to dance after one o'clock at night on pain of death' were frequent.

Costs of patronage

His harsh rule was, however, mitigated by two factors. Firstly, he continued and expanded his father's foreign and economic policies, introducing new agricultural products such as rice, and promoting trade, the principal source of Milan's wealth. Secondly, it was during Galeazzo's rule that the Milanese court became famous for its splendour and artistry, and the exotic diversions organized there became the wonder of all Italy.

The cost of this patronage and extravagance fell, of course, upon the people, who were heavily taxed. But in spite of the oppressiveness of Galeazzo's rule, his murder in 1476 failed to ignite the popular rising his assassins had anticipated and the succession of his seven-year-old son, Gian Galeazzo, was peaceful. The murder ushered in the uncertainties and divisions of a regency, however, and these were ultimately to prove fatal to the continued rule of the Sforzas.

The regency was headed by Gian Galeazzo's mother, Bona of Savoy, but effective power belonged to Francesco's former secretary, Cicco Simonetta. Not unnaturally he was horrified when he discovered that Bona had reached an agreement with the most ambitious of Galeazzo Maria's brothers, Ludovico. 'Most Illustrious Duchess, I shall lose my head and you, in due course, your state' was his prophecy and it was shortly realized. Simonetta was executed and Bona induced to sign over the guardianship of the boy to Ludovico who soon developed a pathetic domination over the nominal duke.

Ludovico had been born in 1451, the fourth son of Francesco and Bianca Maria. He was christened Ludovico Maurus and although the second name was later changed it survived in the designation 'Il Moro'.

It is with the court of Milan under

1 The supreme example of the successful condottieri, Francesco I. An enlightened despot and statesman, he was able to foster an alliance of the five principal Italian states.

2 Bianca Maria, daughter of Filippo Maria Visconti and wife of Francesco. An admirer of the new learning, she engaged foremost teachers to educate her children along humanist lines.

1 Under Francesco and Ludovico Milan became a famous cultural centre. This painting shows Bernadino of Treviso presenting Ludovico with his commentary on Aristotle's *Meteorologica*.

2 The young duke, Gian Galeazzo, reading from Cicero. Trustful and simple-minded, his death in 1495 paved the way for the proclamation of Ludovico as duke in his stead.

Il Moro that the Sforzas are most closely associated. The dominant figure was his wife, Beatrice d'Este, whom he had married in 1491. She was energetic and vivacious, and court life under her direction was the height of grace and wit, constituting a constant round of exotic balls, masquerades and hunting-parties. She shared her husband's interest in literature and art and many artists were employed – though not always paid – to undertake a variety of projects. Leonardo da Vinci and Bramante executed some of their greatest work under Il Moro's patronage, and it was during this period that Leonardo painted his famous mural, *The Last Supper*.

Il Moro's reforms

Il Moro had a genius for administration and a concern for the social welfare of his subjects. He introduced anti-plague measures, managed a model farm along scientific and economic lines, encouraged learning and took a keen interest in Leonardo's plans for a new city designed to let in air and light. Milan was then one of the richest states in Europe, with an income equivalent almost to that of England. But the extravagance of the court and the cost of the wars in which Il Moro became involved seriously inhibited many of his schemes and their benefit to the population was nullified by the

The upshot was that Ludovico was proclaimed duke by the Milanese and duly invested with the duchy by Maximilian in 1495. At last a Sforza duke could claim a legal title to his state in addition to popular acceptance and the recognition of the other Italian states.

The contrived legality of Sforza's rule, however, did not deter the new King of France, Louis XII, from enforcing his claim to Milan. In 1498 the duchy was invaded by a combination of France, Venice and the pope, and Ludovico was forced to flee to Germany. There he succeeded in raising a force of Swiss and returned to regain the duchy. He re-entered Milan in triumph, but was deserted by his Swiss soldiers in the ensuing Battle of Novaro and taken as a prisoner to France. He died in 1508.

The end of the Sforzas

Despite Ludovico's defeat, such was the appeal of the name to the Milanese that two Sforzas were yet to rule as dukes. Both were sons of Ludovico and Beatrice and both were maintained as puppets by foreign powers. The Swiss, who were vitally interested in Milan as a trade outlet and source of food supplies, expelled the French in 1512 and installed Massimiliano as duke. But three years later they were driven out by the new King of France, Francis I.

Massimiliano renounced his claim and the Holy Roman Emperor, Charles V, and the other enemies of French power now turned to his brother, Francesco, as the figurehead for their designs in Italy. All told, Francesco was restored to the duchy three times. He died without heirs in 1535 and Milan finally lost its vestigial independence to become part of the Holy Roman Empire.

The Sforzas had represented in their various personalities the essential qualities of the Renaissance. Francesco I provided the supreme example of the successful condottieri of the early Renaissance, of the triumph of natural talent and the power of the sword, unaided by legal title or high birth; he personified the spirit of individualism. Ludovico and Ascanio were the cultured patrons of the arts, diplomatists and theoreticians of the arts of ruling states; Galeazzo Maria, the macabre tyrant, was no less typical of his age.

If a single thread is to be traced through the 85 years of Sforza rule, it is the desire to legitimize and perpetuate the dukedom they had grasped. Until 1495 only popular will sustained them, but that this was sufficient title in fifteenth-century Italy is seen by the ineffectualness of the imperial bestowal of the titles of duke in 1495. The maintenance of the Sforza rule was in practice determined by foreign policy. Francesco I and Galeazzo Maria preserved a stability in Italy, aiming at all times to keep the foreigner out and to protect their strategically vulnerable duchy. How misplaced was Ludovico's confidence in his own ability to maintain himself as duke by the shifty arts of diplomacy is revealed in the aftermath of the French alliance.

1 Filippo Maria Visconti, ruler of the Duchy of Milan until 1447. His daughter's marriage dowry included a promise that Francesco Sforza should succeed him as duke.
2 In 1482 Leonardo da Vinci came to Milan at Ludovico's invitation. His sketch for a monument to Francesco Sforza introduced a new boldness of technique but the statue was never cast. (Royal Collection, Windsor Castle.)

taxation which followed.

The most notorious deed in the career of Il Moro was his compact with Charles VIII of France in 1494, for in the long period of foreign intervention it began, the Italian states were reduced to mere pawns in the rivalries of the great powers. Ironically the fateful alliance was the product of Ludovico's overriding political objective – the maintenance of the authority he had so doubtfully established.

His niece, Caterina, had warned him before that states were defended by deeds not words, and the history of the Sforzas had so far testified to the truth of this maxim. But Ludovico was no soldier, he was hesitant and superstitious in his actions, and he genuinely believed that he could manipulate by a cynical diplomacy the powers of Europe and Italy to fulfil his purpose of retaining control of the duchy. The alliance with France sprang from his fear of an imminent invasion by Naples. Gian Galeazzo had married, in 1489, Isabella of Aragon, the grand-daughter of the king of Naples, who was now preparing to enforce her rights. By supporting a French claim to Naples, Ludovico sought to embroil Naples in a diversionary war. In doing so, he set a fatal precedent, for France possessed an equally solid claim to Milan in the person of the Dauphin, the future Louis XII, who was the grandchild of a Visconti.

Meanwhile, two more events seemed to set Ludovico even more firmly in control. He came to a secret agreement with the heir to the Holy Roman Empire, Maximilian, providing for the latter's marriage to a Sforza in return for investing Ludovico as Duke of Milan. Then in 1495 Gian Galeazzo died, and although Ludovico is generally held to have poisoned his nephew this seems unlikely, for he was a physical coward and shrank from inflicting pain on others if he could possibly avoid it.

Alexander, the secular pope

Alexander VI has gone down in history as vicious, self-seeking and depraved. Yet he was also a brilliant statesman and organizer whose greatest ambition was to gain control of Italy.

RENNAISSANCE ITALY has produced some of the most spectacular men in history; but of them all, perhaps none has achieved greater notoriety than Pope Alexander VI, Rodrigo Borgia.

Alexander VI was a man of enormous stature. He had a brilliant mind, he was one of the great patrons of Renaissance art, he was an excellent organizer and diplomat, and he had a unique gift for restoring order in time of trouble. Above all he was a man who understood and was able to deal with many of the problems which faced the fifteenth-century Papal States, but he was not a spiritual leader.

Ever since the sixth century, the pope had traditionally been not only the spiritual head of the Western Church, but a secular ruler as well. The two roles were fundamentally irreconcilable and by the fifteenth century, the Church had lost much of its original fervour and purity; not only had the position of the pope become largely a political one, but we find Alexander far from alone as a pope who openly acknowledged that he had children in defiance of the clerical vows of celibacy. The Borgia children have, however, become a legend. Historians differ widely as to their number, but the three most famous were Juan, Duke of Gandia, Cesare, who carried out the scourges of the nobility on the pope's orders, and Lucrezia.

1 Alexander VI, Rodrigo Borgia, pope from 1492 to 1503. His career drew much attention to the materialism and corruption of the Church, and directly contributed to the Reformation.
2 St Peter's in Rome, as it appeared at the time of Alexander. His most hated rival, Cardinal della Rovere, had it rebuilt when he became Pope Julius II.

Juan, the eldest, figures the least while Lucrezia's reputation as a satanic murderess at her father's court bears no examination in the light of contemporary accounts; that she was married three times was largely in the interest of her father's plans. Of them all, Cesare has most reason to bear his reputation. He was ambitious and ruthless; in carrying out his father's commands he made enemies of some of the most powerful families in Italy. Nevertheless, it was his efforts, at Alexander's instigation, which unified the Papal States and consolidated the Vatican's position in Italy.

Perhaps Alexander's greatest crime in the eyes of fifteenth-century Rome lay in the fact that he was of Spanish birth and origin. Few of the stories which have made him so notorious are proven, but Julius II,

who followed Alexander as pope and who as the Cardinal della Rovere schemed continuously to bring about the Borgias' downfall, hated everything Spanish and in this might lie the clue as to where the foundations for the Borgia reputation lie.

Like Louis XIV of France 200 years later, Alexander soon realized that until the ruling nobles were crushed they would always represent a threat to the papacy, and like Napoleon, he realized that the instruments best suited to carrying out his policies were his own family. In such a time and place as Renaissance Italy there was no one else to be trusted and to this end he used his children, whom he openly and passionately adored. He was accused of trying to establish a Borgia heritage, if not a hereditary papacy, and of using his position to advance Borgia interests. Whilst the charges are understandable, so, in the circumstances, are the actions defendable. Yet because of its spectacular nature and because of its significance as a turning-point in the history both of Europe and of the Church, the reign of Alexander VI, which did not differ so greatly from any other Renaissance pope, has an importance unique in its century.

A benevolent uncle

Rodrigo Borgia was born in Spain in 1432 and at the age of 17 went to Italy where he soon became the favourite of his uncle Cardinal Alfonso de Borgia. In 1445, the cardinal was elected Pope Calixtus III and, by the time he died three years later, he had created Rodrigo (then 24) a cardinal and made him vice chancellor of the Church. It was a position Rodrigo held under subsequent popes for nearly 40 years, growing in wealth and esteem and eventually becoming not only one of the richest, but one of the most powerful members of the College of Cardinals.

By 1492 Italy was in a state of growing civil unrest; to the south lay Naples, ruled by King Ferrante, an aged despot, whose throne was tottering on the verge of collapse. As the illegitimate son of the Spanish king, Alfonso V of Aragon, his claim to Naples was challenged both by his cousin Ferdinand of Aragon and by an even older claim through the House of Anjou by Charles VIII of France. In the north was the mighty Lodovico Sforza, who ruled the Duchy of Milan as the regent of his nephew Gian Galeazzo. It was no secret that he planned to become the Duke of Milan himself and to further this end he made an agreement with Charles VIII to support the latter's pretensions to the Neapolitan throne. As the dispute flared open, the claimants turned to Rome, for the Kingdom of Naples was a papal fief and thus the pope had authority to hand the Crown to whomsoever he wished.

1 *The Borgia Family,* by Rossetti, shows Alexander with Lucrezia on his knee, while Cesare looks over her shoulder. The identity of the children in the foreground is not certain.
2 Lodovico Sforza (1451–1508), the powerful Duke of Milan. His cunning and political skill almost equalled Alexander's and he represented a constant threat to the papacy.
3 In 1498 Cesare Borgia forsook his cardinal's robe to command his father's troops. He was the principal instrument by which Alexander carried out his scourges of the nobility.

But that same year, Pope Innocent VIII had died and the papal chair was vacant. At the Conclave held to elect his successor the two rival kings, Charles and Ferrante, were equally hoping for a pope who would sanction their respective claims. Thus Charles VIII supported Cardinal Ascanio, brother of Lodovico Sforza against Cardinal della Rovere, the chosen candidate of King Ferrante. Eventually deadlock was reached between the two rival factions and as time was beginning to run out they chose the one man who had remained aloof from the argument save for the discreet jingle of his gold—Rodrigo Borgia. He took the name of Alexander VI.

One of the first actions of the new Spanish pope was also one of his most momentous. Ferdinand and Isabella of Spain, anxious to avoid rivalry on their home ground with their neighbour Portugal over the New World possessions being claimed by mariners from both countries asked him to negotiate a settlement. The result was five Papal Bulls which were promulgated in the Treaty of Tordesillas (1494). This arbitrarily divided 'the lands and islands in the West' with a line drawn across the Atlantic at a point 370 miles west of the Cape Verde Islands. Everything east of the line went to Portugal; everything west of it to Spain. France,

Holland and England all protested furiously at this arbitrary move; but by his action – which only a pope could have taken in the virtual certainty of obedience – Alexander had prevented vast civil conflict and laid foundations for the peaceful development of two huge empires.

The major threat to Alexander at the beginning of his reign was the powerful Sforza of Milan. To try to allay this Alexander engineered the marriage in 1493 of his daughter Lucrezia to Giovanni Sforza, a cousin of both Cardinal Ascanio and Lodovico. Little did he anticipate the difficulties the union was to involve when, a few years later, it became apparent that the wretched boy was impotent and that the marriage had never been consummated.

Upon the death of Ferrante in 1494 the French king renewed his claims to the Neapolitan throne but Alexander stood firmly on the side of Ferrante's son and in May he crowned him Alfonso II. Della Rovere now did a complete switch; siding with Ascanio and the other cardinals who favoured the French, he fled to France, where Charles was preparing to invade Italy. Charles's eventual arrival in Italy was welcomed by Lodovico Sforza who was now the Duke of Milan (his nephew had died, probably at Lodovico's own hand) and he urged Charles to advance south and march on Rome.

Plans for reform

To Alexander this represented a serious threat. He knew that the king had as advisers not only della Rovere and Sforza but many cardinals who were pressing for a general council at which they intended to reform the Church and depose the pope. Charles VIII, a young hunchback of dissolute habits and doubtful sanity, who was fired by visions of conquest, not only of Naples but of all Italy – with perhaps the Imperial Crown at the end of his glorious road – entered the Papal States late in 1494. One by one the pope's representatives went over to his side. When Charles finally entered the city the pope and his guards shut themselves up in the Castle Saint Angelo, while the cardinals pressed the French king to organize the Council. But since Charles was only interested in reaching Naples he had lost all interest in reforming the Church and instead went on his way. Before him all was in panic. Alfonso II, rather than stand and fight, abdicated and fled to Sicily taking his treasure with him. He was succeeded briefly by Ferrante II who soon followed him. When Charles arrived there was no one left to defend the house of Aragon and the population at first greeted him as a hero.

But behind Charles's back the Spanish monarchs of Aragon and Castile, Ferdinand and Isabella, decided to intervene. Together with most of Charles's former supporters who felt he had betrayed their plans for reform, they formed the Holy League in alliance against him with Venice, the German Emperor Maximilian, the Duke of Milan and Alexander. Charles, alarmed and concerned, hastily retreated north on 20 May 1495 and only just

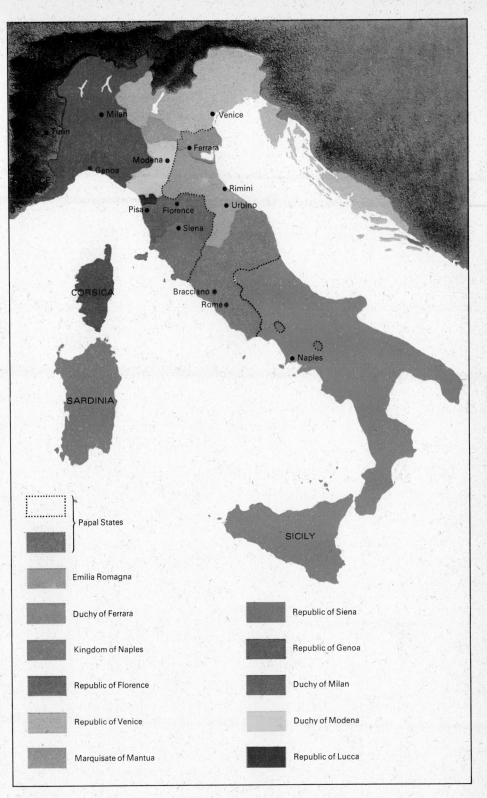

A map of Italy in the time of Alexander showing the extent of the Papal States, and the area of Alexander and Cesare's political and military operations.

Papal States

Emilia Romagna

Duchy of Ferrara

Kingdom of Naples

Republic of Florence

Republic of Venice

Marquisate of Mantua

Republic of Siena

Republic of Genoa

Duchy of Milan

Duchy of Modena

Republic of Lucca

managed to escape across the Alps at the end of July.

Ferrante regained his throne with the help of Spain, and Alexander, realizing that the ambitious nobility of Italy would have to be crushed if his own position was to be assured, proceeded to put his plans against the nobles into operation.

To carry these out he first recalled from Spain his eldest son, the Duke of Gandia, whom he intended to turn into a great Italian prince and the figurehead of his operations.

But before anything could be achieved, on 14 June 1497, the Duke of Gandia was murdered. There is no evidence as to who was the assassin but theories abound. Gandia stood as the enemy of the powerful family of Orsini, who had so recently lent their support to Charles VIII and feared their property might at any moment be confiscated. Should that happen he was bound to be the recipient. Moreover, the pope's marked favouritism of the boy, who showed little to deserve it, had aroused both public and private jealousies. The Sforza family too could well have ordered the assassination, for they were at that time smarting under the accusations of impotence which Lucrezia was bringing against her husband Giovanni, and the pope was preparing to annul the marriage. And not least of those who stood to gain by Gandia's death was his brother Cesare. though at the time he was not suspected.

Stricken with grief the pope turned to plans for reforming the Church. He approved a Reform Commission composed of some of the ablest and most respected minds in Rome for a programme of far-reaching and radical reforms. But before the end of the year the idea had been dropped. Cesare's influence over the pope began to become increasingly noticeable. Immediately after Gandia's assassination he was sent as legate to crown the new King of Naples, Frederick. The following year he left the Church to take up the sword at the head of his father's troops and so fill the place vacated by his brother's death.

In August 1498 Lucrezia, freed from her disastrous marriage, was married to Alfonso of Aragon, Duke of Bisceglia, the natural son of Alfonso II of Naples. In the same year Charles VIII of France died and relations with France eased considerably.

The year 1500 saw the Jubilee of Christ's birth with thousands of pilgrims flocking to Rome: it must have been a magnificent sight, but beneath the glories many of the devout saw the materialism and corruption which were to drive men like Martin Luther to make his revolt in the years to come. The first indications of the growing disillusionment with the Church as it stood had in fact been felt three years earlier at the time of Charles VIII's invasion. Florence had always been pro-French and one Florentine in particular had looked on Charles as a new redeemer – until his burning and looting armies proved themselves all too human. His name was Fra Girolamo Savonarola and his calls for strict moral reform and the suppression of classical art coupled with his attacks on the Medici (the ruling family of Florence) fired the enthusiasm of the populace whose mood he had caught.

Savonarola's denunciation

At the time, Alexander, who had been walking a political tight-rope, was anxious to break the alliance between the French and Florence and he feared that any suppression of the friar would only serve to unite the two parties against him. At first he merely tried to restrain the priest through his superiors, and even invited Savonarola to Rome, but finally he had him excommunicated. Savonarola's popularity began to wane and when an ordeal by fire which the monk undertook to prove his spiritual strength failed there was an outcry against him. Arrest quickly followed; Savonarola was brought to trial and executed on 23 May 1498. He was a brave man who had seen the corruption of the Church and sought to remedy it, but he had been born before his time.

Meanwhile, in 1500 Alexander began his campaigns against the nobility with Cesare at their head. Cesare first turned to central Italy where he intended to carve a state of his own and subdued Catherine Sforza, the tyrannical Governor of the towns of Imola and Forli. Then in July 1500, Alfonso of Aragon, Lucrezia's second

1 Pope Julius II; as Cardinal Giuliano della Rovere he schemed continuously to bring about the downfall of the Borgias, and his avowed hatred for them may be a clue to their reputation.
2 A statue of Fra Girolamo Savonarola, the Florentine monk who sought to expose the materialism and corruption of the Church; Alexander VI had him burned at the stake in 1498.

husband, was attacked in a Rome street. Wounded, he was carried back to the Vatican where despite constant care he died. Apart from freeing Lucrezia for another political marriage, it was an open secret that the Borgias had designs on Naples and again Cesare has been accused of the crime.

Resuming his campaign in central Italy, Cesare and his army with the full support of the new King of France, Louis XII, advanced on the Romagna. Rimini expelled its ruler and welcomed the liberator. Only when he came before Florence was Cesare forced to withdraw in the face of French opposition, the old alliance still holding strong. Louis XII now declared he wished to have the Kingdom of Naples. Alexander had consistently played off France against Spain, and at the head of the French troops, Cesare marched on Naples to fight for Louis's claim. The short campaign was successfully concluded and he was richly rewarded.

Alexander then turned on the Colonna family, two of whose leaders had recently lost their lives defending the Neapolitan king, and whom Alexander accused of being enemies of the Church. From their lands he created two new Borgia titles, and shortly afterwards, captured Riombino.

A wolf in the wolf-pack

Between 1501 and 1503, with the help of Louis, Alexander and Cesare brought about the downfall of nearly all their most powerful enemies. At last Alexander's dreams of securing the Papal States and the Holy See were beginning to be realized. Then suddenly, in 1503, Alexander died after a brief illness. An epidemic of fever was raging in the city; nevertheless, the state of his body after death gave rise to speculations that he had been the victim of poison.

Why was the influence of this brilliant, cruel, scheming pope so great? In Italy he succeeded because he was a match for the rulers of rival states – a wolf in the wolf-pack. The record of his philosophy is preserved by Niccolò Machiavelli; it is bitter, ruthless and has little in common with the teachings of the Church he led.

His incapacity as head of the Church was not unique to Rodrigo Borgia, but it came at a time when the new spirit of rationalism was springing to life in northern Europe. Savonarola's denunciations were echoed far beyond Italy; men like Erasmus in the Netherlands and Dean Colet in England tried to bring about reforms within the framework of the Church itself, but Rome had a reputation for vice and corruption worse than most kings' courts. Had Alexander VI effected the reforms which he planned, he might have been able to contain the Reformation as the Treaty of Tordesillas had contained the exploitation of the New World. But his policy was above all that of an earthly ruler, and in reducing the spiritual stature of the papacy to perhaps its lowest he was instrumental in bringing about the decline of its earthly power – an irony of fortune very much in the medieval tradition which he had so ruthlessly set aside.

Spain's Catholic kings

Isabella of Castile and Ferdinand II of Aragon: together they united fifteenth-century Spain and led their country from internal chaos to become one of the foremost European powers.

A PRINCE in disguise was riding through Spain. Dressed as a mule-driver, with dirty clothes, a few companions and a bunch of unco-operative mules, he was threading his way through country full of enemy soldiers to the castle where a princess with red-gold hair waited for him to rescue her from the wiles of her wicked brother.

It sounds utterly improbable – but this was the fairy-tale start to a real marriage, one which lasted like a rock for 35 years and which was the means of uniting three corrupt, faction-ridden countries into the greatest power in Europe.

He was Ferdinand, Prince of Aragon – short, dark, swarthy, 17 years old. She was his cousin, the 18-year-old Isabella, half-sister and currently heir to the vicious, perverted King of Castile, Henry IV. After the death of her father, John II of Castile, when she was three, Isabella had been brought up in virtual banishment, her only companion a mother gradually sinking into insanity – until the new King Henry realized her possibilities as a negotiable property and summoned her to court. For six years she had been avoiding matches which he sought to arrange for her with a succession of elderly invalids or debauchees: the tubercular heir of Navarre, the fat old King of Portugal, the treacherous Master of Calatrava, and finally, the effeminate brother and heir of Louis XI of France. Isabella had extricated herself from these proposals with extraordinary skill; like Elizabeth Tudor, her natural gifts were developed in a hard school.

Her position was, however, perilous. The power of the Crown had never been lower in Castile; Henry was hated by his people and despised by the nobles who 3

1 Isabella the Catholic: dedicated, thorough, statesmanlike, and joint sovereign of Spain with her husband Ferdinand from 1479 to 1504.
2 Ferdinand's astuteness, cunning and martial talents were the perfect complement to Isabella: together they presented a magnificently united front to the nation.
3 A map of fifteenth-century Spain showing the provincial boundaries, and with special reference to the places mentioned in the article.

were the real rulers of this intransigent country. He had two possible heirs: Isabella herself and a six-year-old girl, Joanna, who was certainly the child of his queen, but less certainly Henry's (his impotence being a tavern joke throughout Spain). The luckless little girl was always known as La Beltraneja, after her most likely father, one Beltran de Cueva. Henry had signed an agreement in favour of Isabella, but as La Beltraneja grew older he saw in her a better prospect, and tried to goad Isabella into open defiance in order to disinherit her. When, by great tact and diplomacy, she avoided his traps, he reopened the question of marriage to the King of Portugal. Isabella took refuge in flight to the castle where she was born, Madrigal de las Altas Torres, near Avila, and appealed to the man she had always intended to marry and for whom she had defied her brother: Ferdinand, heir to the throne of Aragon.

Henry's empty rage

He set out to her rescue, mules and all. But the king's troops were on their way to arrest her; desperately she sought help from the martial Archbishop of Toledo. With a force of 300 men he galloped to her aid, escorting her safely from Madrigal to the city of Valladolid. It was in the castle there that Ferdinand found her. They met on 13 October 1469; on 19 October they married.

Henry showed his rage by immediately proclaiming La Beltraneja as heir to Castile, but it was an empty gesture. Daily the young, energetic couple grew more popular. She was dedicated, thorough, statesmanlike; he astute, ingenious, a true soldier: their complementary talents held a promise of stability and good government for two kingdoms which must inevitably soon be joined. The major force in Castile was not the king but the *Cortes*, a council of two deputies from each of 18 cities, which guarded ancient privileges and acted as a check on overbearing royalty. It had already sworn to recognise Isabella as heir; now many of the great lords, too, declared themselves in her favour. So did one walled citadel after another: Seville, Jaen, Avila.

But Henry, dying in 1474 in agony from a perforated ulcer, left no will. He died on a winter morning in Madrid; by nightfall Isabella, 45 miles away in Segovia, had the news. She acted with characteristic speed. Ferdinand was helping his father to ward off a French threat to Aragon; she dared not wait for his return – La Beltraneja had her supporters too. By the following morning Isabella had mounted a coronation. (Fortunately the crown jewels were kept in Segovia.) Heralds raised the shout of 'Castile for the King don Ferdinand and the Queen dona Isabella.' Ferdinand, when he returned, was furious at her unfeminine decisiveness, and needed to be placated by a document making it clear that his name would henceforth precede hers on all official papers. They took as their motto *tanto monta,* of equal importance.

Ferdinand's first victory

They needed that unity. The King of Portugal, from whose marital designs Isabella had twice escaped, now announced that he considered his niece, the 13-year-old La Beltraneja, to be the rightful Queen of Castile, and intended to marry her and defend her title. Backed by France, he invaded, and the inexperienced sovereigns' undisciplined army disintegrated before the prospect of a siege. Truly devout though Isabella was, in this crisis she did not hesitate to requisition half the Church's silver, with a promise of repayment in three years (which she kept) and to use the vast sum thus acquired to buy cannon, pay mercenaries and train troops. When Ferdinand attacked the Portuguese forces for a second time at the Battle of Toro (1477), he was ruthless and successful. The threat of foreign invasions had united the warring factions in Spain; this crisply achieved victory increased the respect of Europe for the new rulers. Together they went joyfully to Toledo and founded the huge monastery of St John of the Kings. Already they were living up to their proud title of 'los reyes Catolicos' – the Catholic kings; by 1479 Ferdinand's father was dead and he was King of Aragon in his own right.

It was in Toledo, too, in 1480, that the Cortes met for the session which laid the foundations of modern Spain. Isabella, by then already mother of a daughter and son, had just given birth to her third child, the tragic Joanna 'the mad'. Yet at a time when most women would have rested, Isabella was meeting and supervising the representatives and the five royal Councils every day during the first six months of 1480. During those meetings laws were promulgated which brought huge sums of money back to the Crown from the pockets of nobles who had received them from Isabella's corrupt predecessors. Hundreds of castles were ordered to be demolished, so that private armies were no longer a danger. The country's legal system was codified and its administration improved; one remarkably advanced move was the provision of legal counsel for poor men from public funds. Taxes were regularized, tariffs lifted, private mints abolished and the debased currency restored.

The Catholic kings had put their house in order; but they still had to make Spain entirely Catholic – and, for that matter, entirely Spanish. Seven hundred years earlier, Moorish hordes of Moslems from North Africa had swept through the land, driving the inhabitants into hiding in the mountains of Galicia and the Asturias. Only over centuries of bitter fighting had they regained part of their kingdom but the Moorish kingdom of Granada – roughly the eastern part of

The Madonna of the Catholic Kings shows Ferdinand and Isabella with their children in adoration before the Virgin Mary. In 1480 Isabella established the Inquisition to purify the Church.

present-day Andalusia – held out. It was the dream of Isabella's life to expel them for ever.

Before she would embark on a holy war, however, she had to purify her own Church. Many Spanish cities had large Jewish populations, and a great number of these Jews, who tended to be rich, able men, had reaped the advantages to be gained from joining the established Church. But were they genuine converts? Isabella wanted the nation's spiritual life to be as free from dubiety as its legal system. She was not concerned with Jews practising their own faith, and gave specific orders that these were not to come under the rule of the Holy Office – the Inquisition – which, in response to the pleas of the Papal Nuncio, was established in Seville in 1480. Her target was solely the *marranos,* 'converts' who were suspected of still practising their 'heathen rites' under the cloak of Catholic piety. In their context, her intentions were good; but the horrors which they ultimately let loose have for centuries blackened the name of that Church which she sought to exalt.

It was certainly in a mood of exultation that the 'reyes Catolicos' set about the reconquest of Granada. The prize was rich; the great ports of Almeria and Malaga, 100 fortified towns – and over it all, Granada itself. The kingdom was ruled by Mulai Hasan and his formidable senior wife Ayesha, who was urging the claims of

1 *The Triumph of Columbus* by Robert Fleury. The great navigator and explorer kneels to kiss the sovereigns' hands on his return from the New World in 1493.
2 Today, Toledo is little changed from the time when it was capital of all Spain. In 1480 the Cortes met there with Isabella for the session which laid the foundations of modern Spain.

his weak, unpopular eldest son, Boabdil. (She had quarrelled with Mulai Hasan, a half-senile old man, obsessed by the charms of one of his Christian slaves.) He could forget the girl for long enough to fight, however, and at first the war went ill for the Spaniards. He massacred the inhabitants of Zahara, and at Lija the Moors inflicted on Ferdinand the worst defeat of his career as a soldier. Boabdil, always unlucky, was taken prisoner, but the Catholic kings realized that he was far more useful making trouble in Granada than as a Spanish prisoner. They let him return to the city, where he chose this unlikely time to begin a civil war against his father for the crown. Isabella left this situation to rage, and scoured the country for troops, cannon, money, supplies. Equipped with an army, thanks to the efforts of his indefatigable wife, Ferdinand marched on the apparently impregnable city of Ronda, which is perched on a mountain beside a 600-foot gorge. He feinted on the way to draw off the Moorish army, flung his troops round the city, cut off its water-supply and bombarded it with huge cannon and balls of flaming pitch. Within ten days Ronda surrendered. After a much more painful siege, lasting three months, Malaga fell too. Isabella went back north to pawn the crown itself for cash; Ferdinand moved

to Baza, north-east of Granada. But there, everything went wrong. He built vast barracks and siege-towers, only to have them washed away by the rains; there was plague in the camp, and floods destroyed the mountain roads over which came the supplies. Isabella had them rebuilt – she found supplies, she found mules; then she came herself in armour to Baza. A few days later, to the astonishment of everyone the city suddenly surrendered, and with it the rest of the Moorish kingdom –

except for Granada.

In the spring of 1491, the Spanish army moved into the great flat plain which lies before the city and, after endless secret negotiations, Boabdil was finally brought to realize the hopelessness of his situation.

On 2 January 1492 he rode out of his lovely Alhambra palace for the last time. Upon the tallest tower was hoisted a vast white flag with a silver cross; the choirs burst into the *Te Deum,* and the heralds raised a new cry for their masters:

be allowed to remain. The edict which she signed for their expulsion may have had some political justification: it would have been unwise to allow the many Moors still in the kingdom to band together with their old allies. But to order them to leave the country within four months – leaving their money and possessions behind – was an act of cruelty from which Spanish trade and culture never recovered. The departure of some 200,000 weeping exiles on 2 August 1492 must have totally obscured the sailing next day from Huelva of Columbus, bound 'westward to the Orient'. But if his departure went unnoticed, his return was triumphant: a procession through Barcelona with the sovereigns, crowds staring at his feathered 'Indians', and the presentation of a lump of gold from the New World to Isabella as proof of the wealth to come.

Perhaps that period marks the height of the reign of the 'reyes Catolicos'. Isabella's last years were scarred by the deaths of her son, her eldest daughter, and her grandson, which left as heir to Spain the unstable Joanna and her greedy, callous husband, Philip the Fair of the House of Hapsburg.

Dark plots and treachery

Worried and ill, the great queen did not rest. The last codicil to her will, dated three days before her death, was concerned with plans for new codification of the laws and a request that the Indians in her new colonies should be treated with justice. She died in Medina near her birthplace of Madrigal, in the north of Spain, in November 1504.

After the removal of her stabilizing influence, Ferdinand (who did not wish to be reduced to being merely the King of Aragon, after having ruled all Spain), Philip and Joanna fought for the throne of Castile in a bizarre sequence of plots and treachery. In 1505 Ferdinand remarried, to Germaine de Foix, niece of the King of France, in a vain effort to produce an heir of his own. When he died in 1516 he named as heir to both Aragon and Castile Joanna's 15-year-old son Charles (later the Emperor Charles V), who had been brought up in Flanders and spoke no Spanish; but the condition was made by the Cortes that if Joanna – who had been 'restrained' in the grim castle of Tordesillas – were to recover her sanity, the throne must revert to her. It was in Charles's interests to see that she did not.

Joanna lived on – withered, lice-ridden, raving – until the age of 76. In the world outside Tordesillas, her grandson Philip II married her sister Catherine of Aragon's only child, Mary Tudor; fleets laden with the gold Columbus had discovered enriched the Spanish treasury; the nation which Ferdinand and Isabella had forged was enjoying its proudest days.

From the darkest beginnings, the extraordinary abilities and unity of purpose shown by 'los reyes Catolicos' had led them on to create this nation; just how dark were those beginnings, and how near to the surface they lay, Joanna still provided tragic evidence long after Isabella's bones were dust in her tomb.

1 Isabella's daughter, the tragic Joanna 'the mad' and her husband Philip. On Ferdinand's death Joanna was imprisoned by her son Charles in order that he might succeed to the throne instead.

2 A panel from the cathedral in Granada, showing the Moors being forcibly baptized into the Catholic faith after the city had been reconquered by Ferdinand in 1492.

'Granada for the King don Ferdinand and the Queen dona Isabella!'

Later that year the king and queen interviewed in the cool courts of the Alhambra, a sailor who had been clamouring for their attention since 1486. A visionary, an explorer, a man of unknown origins, an avaricious title-hunting snob, Christopher Columbus was a truly remarkable character. Ferdinand would grant him neither money nor ships, having no patience with his demands for a tenth of the profits, for the ancient royal title of Admiral and for the post of Viceroy. But Isabella listened to his proposals. She had interviewed Columbus before – and refused him money on his terms. Now a counsellor whom she trusted urged her to give him another hearing.

They had an uncomfortable interview. Ferdinand lost his temper yet again on hearing the man's demands. Columbus remounted his mule and headed for the mountains, his plans rejected, his terms denied. Within the next four hours Isabella took a decision which probably changed the history of the world – certainly of Spain: she changed her mind. Her messenger caught Columbus outside Granada and escorted him back to the palace.

In that spring of 1492 Isabella had relished the joys of being hailed as a Christian heroine, victor over the infidel. Once again her fervour got the better of her essential humanity. She decided that her realm needed further purification; it was not enough to test the faith of converted Jews. Practising Jews could not

To India by way of America

With five little ships, Ferdinand Magellan set out to sail round the world. Although he was killed after two years of storms and starvation, one of his fleet completed the voyage.

IN THE FIFTEENTH CENTURY many people in western Europe began to develop an almost insatiable curiosity about unknown places and peoples. For the first time in 400 years European sailors dared to lose sight of land – no seamen had willingly done this since the Vikings had abandoned their raiding and colonizing expeditions in the eleventh century.

There was an economic, as well as intellectual, basis to exploration. The treasures of the East included spices, highly prized in Europe where the shortage of winter feeding stuffs compelled farmers to kill off most of their stocks in late autumn and store the meat in salt through the winter. Rich people craved for spices to make their often strong-smelling meat more palatable. Spices came mainly from the East Indies (the Moluccas), called by the Europeans the *Spice Islands*. Goods from the Spice Islands were borne in ships by way of Malaya and India to Egypt and Arabia, and from there they were taken overland to Mediterranean ports and shipped to Venice. Losses on the journey, taxes and the profits taken by many traders, middlemen and carriers, multiplied the price of spices as much as a hundred times between the Moluccas and western Europe.

Spice from the East

In 1453, when the Turks took Constantinople, capital of the Eastern Roman Empire, they cut the overland caravan routes which were vital to east–west commerce. Shrewd merchants of the times realized that a fortune could be made by those who could bring spices and other luxuries from the East Indies by sea. They therefore encouraged bold seamen to search for such a route. One route, it was thought, was to be found by sailing round the southern tip of Africa (then believed to extend only a short distance past the Equator) and then due east. Even more imaginative men were to be found who believed it possible to reach the East by sailing westwards across the Atlantic. The practical implications of the idea that the Earth was a sphere, put forward by the Greek geographer Ptolemy during the second century AD, was revived and became a topic of intellectual argument.

Portugal led other European nations in the exploration of the world's seaways. Its sailors followed the African coastline and discovered a new route to India and the East. The great burst of activity among the Portuguese was sparked off by Prince Henry the Navigator (1394–1460), the aesthetic, scholarly son of King John I of Portugal. For 42 years, from 1418 onwards, Henry devoted his energies and wealth to preparing the way for his country's

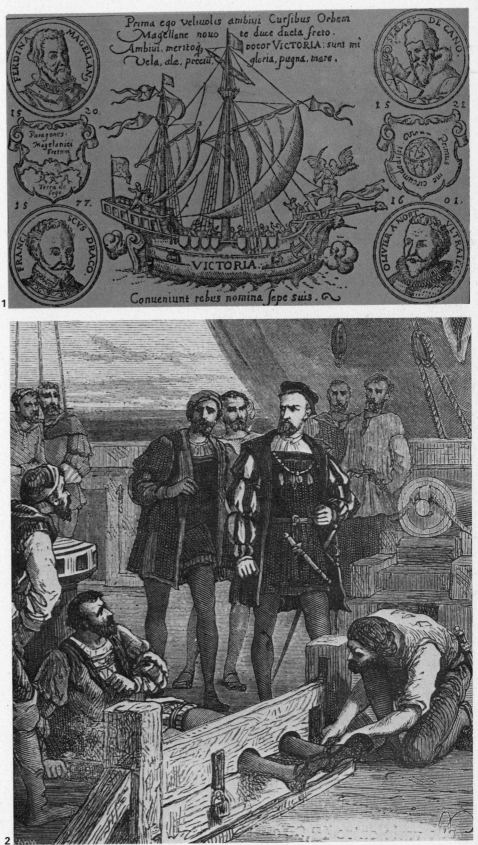

1 This ship, of only 85 tons, was the first to sail round the world. One of Ferdinand Magellan's fleet of five, it set sail in September 1519 and returned to Spain three years later.

2 Throughout his voyage Magellan had to deal with frequent mutinies. When Juan de Cartegena disputed his authority, Magellan ordered him to be put in the stocks.

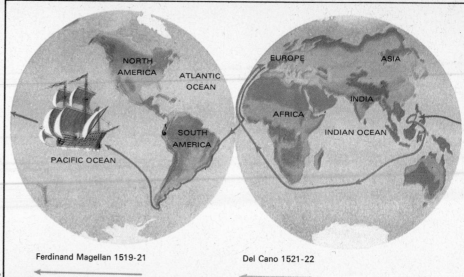

Ferdinand Magellan 1519-21   Del Cano 1521-22

NOVA ACVRATA TOTVS AMERICÆ TABVLA

1 This early quadrant was used for navigation at sea. By measuring the altitude of a star it was possible for a pilot to fix the latitudinal position of his ship.

2 The map shows Magellan's exploration in search of a western route to the Indies.
3 Ferdinand Magellan, a Portuguese, was financed by Spain to sail round the world.

4 This map, engraved in 1562, shows the extent of Spanish exploration of America. On the shores of South America Magellan found giants, and named the country Patagão – Land of the Big Feet.

predominance at sea. He founded a school for navigators and employed cartographers to produce practical maps and charts for them to use. Curiously, he never ventured on the voyages that he planned, but before he died his seamen had discovered the Madeiras, the Azores, the Cape Verde Islands and had mapped the coast of Africa as far south as present-day Sierra Leone.

Building on Henry the Navigator's work, his great-nephew John II of Portugal, who became king of Portugal in 1481, determined to find a sea route to the rich markets of India. In 1487 his sea-captain Bartholomew Diaz rounded the southern tip of Africa in a storm and reached the Indian Ocean. Diaz had to turn back because his crew mutinied, but another Portuguese mariner, Vasco da Gama (c. 1469–1524), reached India 11 years later.

Portugal's main rival in the struggle to open up a sea trade with the Indies was Spain. But Spain's efforts to find a route to the Indies were directed westwards across the Atlantic. Spanish interest in

exploration owed much to the insistence of Christopher Columbus (1451–1506), a navigator, under the patronage of Queen Isabella of Spain, who believed that there was a way round the Earth. He accepted Ptolemy's estimate of the size of the Earth, and calculated that China lay only about 3,550 miles west of Europe, an error of about 8,000 miles.

Islands of the Atlantic

When Columbus made his first voyage across the Atlantic in 1492, he thought that the first islands he came to lay immediately east of the Spice Islands. Not until after Columbus was dead did other explorers find that he had discovered a new continent, later called *America* after an Italian navigator, Amerigo Vespucci. Many navigators tried to find a passage through the American continent to the ocean which was known to lie on the other side: all failed.

Another Portuguese, a navigator in the service of Spain, eventually found a way

around the new continent. He was Ferdinand Magellan (Fernão de Magalhais) (c. 1480–1521), son of a Portuguese nobleman. As a boy page at the court of John II, Magellan had incurred the enmity of the queen's brother, Manuel, who had charge of the pages and of astronomical and navigational studies at the court. Magellan was a keen student of navigation, but his hopes for an early chance to go to sea were dashed when in 1495 John died and Manuel became king. During the next ten years Magellan spent his time as a civil servant at the Lisbon headquarters of the Portuguese maritime service. His chance came in 1505, when he sailed with a fleet sent to establish trading stations in Africa and India. Magellan spent the next eight years in eastern waters and was able to explore on his own account.

On his return to Portugal King Manuel not only refused to allow him to make a further voyage to India, but dismissed him from the royal household. Four years

later, Magellan offered his services to Charles V who had become king of Spain in 1516.

In Spain, fortune smiled on Magellan. Friends arranged his marriage to an heiress and secured him an audience with Charles. To the king Magellan put forward his plan to seek a westward route to the Indies through a strait which he believed existed at the southern end of the American land mass. He demonstrated his ideas on a globe stolen from the Portuguese royal palace.

Dividing up the new lands

With the pope's blessing, Spain and Portugal had divided the non-Christian world between them and, in 1494, established a demarcation line about 1,100 miles west of the Azores. Portugal claimed exclusive rights to all new lands discovered 180° eastward of this line, and Spain to all lands 180° to the west. Magellan planned to approach the Indies from the Spanish side, to prove that the highly prized Spice Islands lay in Spain's half of the newly discovered world.

The Spaniards provided Magellan with a fleet of five small ships – the *Trinidad*, flagship of 110 tons; *Victoria*, 85 tons; *Concepcion*, 90 tons; *Santiago*, 75 tons; and *San Antonio*, 120 tons – with a total complement of 268 men of nine different nationalities. It was agreed that the fleet should carry provisions to last for two years. But many of the provisions were never loaded because Magellan was defrauded by the merchants. Consequently, his ships set sail from Sanlucar on 20 September 1519 with only about half the food which was needed for the voyage.

A very full account of the voyage is preserved in the diaries of Antonio Pigafetta, a Venetian, who sailed with Magellan because, as he wrote, Magellan was 'desirous of seeing the wonderful things of the ocean'. By December the ships sighted the coast of Brazil, which was in the half of the world claimed by Portugal. In order to avoid the Portuguese, Magellan headed south until he came to a deserted harbour, which he called the Bay of Santa Lucia, now known as Rio de Janeiro Bay. There his sailors repaired storm damage to the ships and took on supplies of fresh fruit and vegetables. Magellan got his reluctant men back to sea, but only after quelling a revolt against his discipline. After two weeks' delay he set sail southwards in search of the passage through to the west. A huge inlet many miles to the

An early map of South America shows the passage Magellan found to the Pacific. He called it Todos los Santos but it now bears his own name. On the southern shore lies Tierra del Fuego.

south seemed to be the promised strait but it turned out to be the mouth of a mighty river, now called the Rio de la Plata. Disappointed, Magellan led the fleet south again – further south than any previous explorer had been.

The winter closed in and the weather grew colder and rougher. At the end of March 1520, he put into another bay, which he named Port St Julian. This lay only 200 miles from the southernmost point of South America. Here the voyagers spent the winter. They explored the land and made friends with the American Indians who lived in the area. These were tall people – 'so tall we came only to the head of his waistband', said Pigafetta of one – with large feet wrapped in skins which made them look ever larger, so the sailors named the country Patagão (now Patagonia) – Land of the Big Feet.

At the beginning of their stay at Port St Julian, Magellan quelled a serious mutiny by some of his Spanish captains who resented their Portuguese leader.

195

the remainder of his fleet sailed out into the smooth ocean which washes the western coast of the Americas. He named it the Pacific, because its waters were so peaceful after the stormy seas of the Atlantic. The air was cold, although it was summertime, so Magellan headed west by northwest into the unexplored oceans, into warm, spring-like conditions. For three months the seamen sighted no land except a few desolate, uninhabited islands. Their hardships were appalling and many died of disease and malnutrition. Pigafetta's diary records: 'We only ate old biscuits reduced to powder, and full of grubs and stinking ... and we drank water that was yellow and stinking. We also ate the ox-hides which were under the main-yard, also sawdust and rats.' At last, in March 1521, the three ships reached the Mariana Islands, which lie midway between Japan and Australia. There they obtained fresh food and water, but the inhabitants of the first island they called at, Guam, were so unfriendly and stole so much property from the ships, that Magellan called the islands Islas de Los Ladrones – the Islands of Robbers. As soon as he had sufficient provisions, he sailed on to the Philippines.

Magellan is killed

In April, the little fleet anchored in the harbour of the island of Cebu, where Magellan and his men soon made friends with the chief, whom they converted to Christianity.

Magellan, in addition to converting the chief, persuaded him to swear loyalty to the king of Spain, and in return proclaimed him ruler of all the islands. The chief of the small neighbouring island of Mactan refused to submit to this chief and Magellan led a raiding party on his village to subdue him. But as they fired the houses, native warriors rushed out with clubs, bows and spears and in hand-to-hand fighting on the beach Magellan was killed.

Hurriedly, the remainder of the expedition returned to their ships and sailed away to the west. There were now too few of them to sail three ships, so they abandoned the *Concepcion,* the least seaworthy, and burned it. Of the 108 men left, none had sufficient skill to navigate a direct course to the Spice Islands. Not until November 1521, after seven months of piracy and wandering, did they eventually reach the islands. There they loaded cargoes of the precious spices they had come so far to seek. Despite their grim experiences, the sailors decided to sail for home in opposite directions. The *Trinidad* followed the route back across the Pacific, but was either wrecked or captured by the Portuguese. The *Victoria,* commanded by Sebastian del Cano (one of the former rebels whom Magellan had kept in chains at St Julian), sailed by way of the known route round the Cape of Good Hope. The ship reached Seville in September 1522, about 12 days under three years after the fleet set sail. With del Cano were a handful of emaciated men – all who had survived the first voyage round the world.

The rebels seized control of the *Victoria, San Antonio, Santiago* and *Concepcion,* and plotted to take the flagship, *Trinidad,* and kill Magellan. But Magellan sent disguised raiding parties aboard the *Victoria* and the *Santiago* and recaptured them. With the three ships he then controlled, he blocked the entrance to the bay. Outmanoeuvred, the mutineers surrendered. Magellan hanged one of the ringleaders, and hung his body, and that of a rebel killed in the skirmishing, from gibbets erected on the beach. Magellan also put more than 30 other mutineers, including several noblemen, in chains, working hard labour.

Not until then did Magellan discover the shortage of supplies. He realized that his planned leisurely exploration of Patagonia was no longer possible and he sent the *Santiago* southwards to reconnoitre alone. After fighting its way 60 miles along the coast against severe gales, the ship was wrecked. All but one of the crew escaped, and one of the survivors stumbled back along the coastal strip to fetch help from the fleet. When their comrades had been rescued, Magellan took the remaining ships to a bay near where the *Santiago* was wrecked, which offered a good harbour for the rest of the winter. He released the rebels from their chains, but marooned on the desolate coast one of the captains and a priest who had tried to start another mutiny.

When spring came in mid-October 1520, Magellan led his ships south once more. They ran into a terrible storm which scattered them. Magellan thought he had lost all the fleet except his flagship, but when the storm died out after a week a look-out spotted the *Victoria* on the horizon. The two ships then set out to search for the *San Antonio* and the *Concepcion.* Soon afterwards the two missing vessels came in sight, flying all the flags and bunting they had aboard because they had found the channel to the west. Eagerly, Magellan led his fleet into the strait which

1 Magellan, in a small boat, leads his depleted fleet through the tortuous strait to the Pacific, while a sailor takes soundings with a line.
2 In 1521 Magellan raided the island of Mactan. He was killed in the fighting on the beach, but his expedition went on round the world.

he called the Strait of All Saints (Todos los Santos) but which now bears his own name. But only two ships followed him. Under cover of darkness the *San Antonio,* which carried a large part of the supplies, slipped away to the east and sailed back to Spain. On the southern shores of the strait, fires lit by the Indians burned so brightly at night that the Spaniards called it Tierra del Fuego – the Land of Fire – the name it still bears. Finding a way through the maze of channels of the strait was a brilliant piece of navigation and evidence of Magellan's genius.

Late in November 1520 Magellan with

The Crescent over Europe

Few nations have ever expanded their boundaries so ruthlessly and swiftly as the Ottoman Turks. But eventually the very size of their empire defeated them and they sank into political eclipse.

ON 29 MAY 1453 the great city of Constantinople, capital of eastern Christendom and once the dazzling centre of Byzantine learning and civilization, fell to the Turks, a race of Moslem warriors advancing west from the Asian steppes. After years of preparation and a final siege lasting two months, the mighty army and navy of Sultan Mehmet II had captured the walled city to fulfil a long-standing Turkish ambition. As was customary in cities captured by storm, the sultan's troops ravaged Constantinople in a wild hunt for plunder and loot, and men, women and children were slaughtered mercilessly until blood ran in rivers down the streets.

As streams of refugees fled across the Bosphorus into Europe, news of the city's fall sent tremors of fear, despair and shock throughout Christendom. Yet the fall of the city cannot have been altogether unexpected for the Turks' victory was the climax of more than a century of Turkish expansion into southeastern Europe. What perhaps explains the profound shock felt in the West is that Europe had chosen largely to ignore what had been happening in its southeastern corner.

To the banks of the Danube

By 1340 the Turks had seized as much as possible of the Byzantine Empire in Asia Minor. Then, crossing the Bosphorus into Europe, within ten years they proceeded to secure nearly all the Byzantine possessions in Europe, pushing on into the Balkans, through Thrace and Macedonia to Bulgaria and Serbia. Eight years later the Turkish armies had advanced as far as the banks of the Danube.

What provoked this driving expansion? The earliest Ottomans, named from Sultan Osman, whose father had founded their state in Anatolia in the mid-thirteenth century, were *ghazis*, Moslem warriors dedicated to fighting to the death religious wars against the infidel Christians, and to extending the Moslem frontier. Another powerful motive for doing battle was the desire for plunder; indeed the supremacy of the Ottomans over other communities of Turkish ghazis came about largely because the Ottoman state, which bordered on Byzantium, offered greater opportunities for expansion and booty than any other state, and thus attracted the most able Turkish fighters.

As Ottoman territory grew, religious zeal against the enemy became less important. What had begun as a holy war against the Christians turned into a more materialistic struggle for land, slaves and plunder. The capture of Constantinople gave these free-booting hordes a natural capital, particularly well sited for an empire with provinces in both Europe and

A sixteenth-century European portrait by Hans Eworth, probably of Suliman the Magnificent, illustrates all the severity and majesty of the Ottoman ruling class.

Asia Minor. From then on the Ottoman Empire had something of a structure – with a settled centre at Constantinople, able to expand on the edges wherever possible.

As the Ottomans advanced their frontiers, they found that Europe offered little resistance. For one thing the Christian powers were divided amongst themselves and the earlier crusading spirit of the eleventh to thirteenth centuries, when the Christian states joined in sending vast collective armies in holy wars against the Moslems, had almost entirely vanished. The rise of Byzantium itself had split Christendom, and the continuing disputes between the Papacy and the Greek Orthodox Church, whose leader, or patriarch, sat at Constantinople, were one reason for the failure of any combined Christian attempt to save the city.

Even the alarming fall of Constantinople failed to warn Europe that the Ottoman

menace could be met only by a united front. In the following centuries the rivalry between the French king and the Habsburg emperor, between the old Catholicism and the new Protestantism, reduced the possibility of effective opposition still further. No one came to the aid of Hungary at the crucial battle of Mohacs in 1526, and even when the Ottomans penetrated as far as Vienna three years later, they found it defended by the Habsburgs only. Had the Ottomans not had their own problems during the great chaos in Europe caused by the disastrous Thirty Years' War (1618–48), they could have made even more spectacular advances. It was not until the late seventeenth century that Europe smoothed over its divisions to present anything like its full strength against them.

Perhaps the most obvious aspect of the Turkish advance was the might of the Ottoman armies. The Ottomans' extraordinary fighting strength was based on two elements: the first being the *spahis*—light and mobile cavalry who easily outmanoeuvred the ponderous and undisciplined heavy cavalry of European armies. Enticed onwards by the continual promise of fresh plunder, they were constantly on the move fighting new campaigns.

The second element, the *janissaries*, a corps of infantry archers later equipped with hand guns, were the sultan's own crack troops. Forbidden to marry or to take up civilian trades, they were renowned for their discipline and bravery, and for their unquestioned loyalty to the sultan. They were all slaves, taken from the conquered lands in the Balkans, through the *devsirme* system. At irregular intervals every three or five years, levies were taken of all Christian boys between eight and 20 who were then given special training. After becoming converts to Islam they were destined not only for the janissaries but – the best of them – for the highest offices of state, both in the army and in the administration. Indeed they could look forward to far greater power than any Moslem subjects, whose careers were limited to the religious hierarchy.

With all important state posts filled by slaves, competing on their merits alone, the way was open for outstandingly able men to reach the top. This made for a far more efficient bureaucratic and military machine than most European states could offer, hindered as they were by corruption, nepotism and inherited feudalism. At the hub of this machine was the sultan, who personally led his armies into battle. In theory his power was virtually absolute.

Perhaps the greatest of the sultans was Suliman the Magnificent, and it was under his rule (1520–66) that the Ottoman Empire rose to its zenith. Within a year of becoming sultan, Suliman marched against Hungary and took Belgrade. A few years later, at Mohacs in 1526, he won the greatest of his victories when his janissaries routed the heavy cavalry of the Hungarian magnates, killing the Hungarian king in the battle. From there he advanced to plunder Buda, but by this time a claim to the vacant Hungarian

1 Sultan Mehmet IV: his mania for hunting frustrated the attempts of his ministers to restore the waning Ottoman power and he was eventually deposed in 1687.
2 Successor to Suliman was the notorious Selim the Sot, an incompetent, dissolute drunkard. His one noteworthy contribution was to initiate the conquest of Cyprus in 1571.
3 In 1453, Sultan Mehmet II rode triumphantly into the Hippodrome at Constantinople. After a two-month siege the Byzantine capital had finally fallen to his army.

1 The year 1529 saw the Ottomans, under Suliman, laying siege to the Austrian capital of Vienna. But their attempt to take the city was successfully foiled.

2 Suliman's greatest victory was won at the Battle of Mohacs, where his troops totally routed the Hungarian heavy cavalry. This miniature shows the Turkish army on the battlefield.

throne had come from Archduke Ferdinand of Austria, brother of the Habsburg emperor, Charles V, and in 1529 Suliman's attempt to take Ferdinand's capital city, Vienna, was successfully repulsed. Thereafter, although the Ottomans remained in control of most of Hungary, they never managed to break down Vienna's defences.

Suliman did not confine himself to land battles, however. With the capture of Constantinople, the Ottomans were able to join in the struggle of the Mediterranean powers for control of the lucrative trade routes to the Orient and he began to make the Ottoman presence felt in earnest, allying with a fleet of pirate admirals to extend his power along the North African coast. After capturing Rhodes in 1522, just a year after his conquest of Belgrade, he was in the ideal position to strike at Spain and southern Italy. But the Ottomans were not really a sea-faring race. They were very much more successful on land and most of their naval victories were won by their pirate allies. Soon after Suliman's death, the Ottoman fleet was decisively beaten at Lepanto in 1571, and although the Ottomans quickly recovered, they never succeeded in upsetting Spain's hold on the Mediterranean; they failed to capture Malta and they were unable to invade Italy.

After Suliman, Europe and the Ottomans reached a state of deadlock. It seemed that the great Turkish movement into Europe had exhausted its impetus and could advance no further. A revival of Turkish aggression in the mid-seventeenth century, with attacks on Crete, on the Habsburgs, and invasions into the Ukraine only served to expose the latent weakness in the Ottoman machine. Not only did a Habsburg army beat the Ottomans at St Gotthard in 1664, but the Turks again found themselves having to withdraw from an attack on Vienna, this time after a 60-day siege in 1683. Eventually, under the pressure of more Austrian victories, the Ottomans were forced to make peace. It was the first time they had admitted defeat and yielded territory. By the Treaty of Karlowitz in 1699, Austria gained most of Hungary, and Poland, Russia and Venice all shared in the spoils of the Ottomans' waning power.

Fortunately for the Ottomans, within their empire, relations between Turk and European were far more agreeable. The Ottomans, after all, had to keep in order a huge polyglot empire – in the seventeenth century between 25 and 30 millions – of many diverse races and creeds; and for the most part, the rulers were content to let their subject peoples live as they wished. The Ottoman Empire was an artificial mixture of widely different institutions and cultures. Its capital, Constantinople, which had remained an important centre of communications and administration, thrived on the jostling together of different communities. After the early ghazi period, non-Moslems were not only allowed to practise their own religion, but were also put to good use within the empire. And, of course, Christian slaves provided the backbone of the army and the administration.

By the end of the seventeenth century, with the Treaty of Karlowitz, it seemed that Europe had, in effect, turned the tables on the Ottomans; by contrast to the preceding centuries it was now Europe who was gaining strength as the Ottomans grew weaker. On the Ottoman side, several factors were making for decline. One trouble was that the limits of expansion seemed to have been reached. The Ottoman armies only campaigned in the spring and summer. Marching from Constantinople, it was as much as they could do to reach Vienna and central Europe, let alone mount a series of drawn-out sieges. Feeding and supplying the vast army over such a distance was a tremendous problem.

Seeds of dissolution

On the other hand, once the empire stopped expanding there were disastrous results. Without the enticement of constant booty and new lands, the sipahis either became restless and discontented, or settled down lazily on what lands they had, which they then wished to pass on to their families. Similarly with the janissaries, prone to revolt if kept idle too long at home in Constantinople. When they began to marry and to take up civilian trades to make up for their lack of booty, their *élite* structure broke down.

Nor was the Ottoman Empire geared to defending or consolidating frontiers it already had. It remained essentially nomadic; it had to keep expanding its frontiers. With the limit reached, it went into decline.

If Suliman had been followed by leaders of similar stature, the decline might have been arrested. But most of his successors were hopelessly incompetent and unfitted

Crack troops in the Turkish army were the janissaries, a corps of infantry archers renowned for their discipline, courage, and for their unquestioned loyalty to the sultan.

for the task. His son, Selim the Sot (1566–74), was a notorious drunkard. In the next century, Ibrahim (1640–8) was deposed after spending most of his time in pursuit of his passions. Even Mehmet IV (1648–87), sultan at a time when his able ministers were staging a comeback, showed little interest in the art of government, indulging instead a mania for hunting. He, too, had to be deposed. Because the sultan was so central a figure in the Ottoman system, these deficient personalities had disastrous effects.

Generally, the Ottoman Empire had failed to advance its ideas. While western Europe was experiencing the ferment of the Renaissance and Reformation, the Ottomans stagnated, taking little interest. Even militarily they lost ground, stubbornly clinging on to the unwieldy siege artillery they had once found useful in taking enemy cities. And Ottoman outdated methods in farming and industry provided no basis for an expanding money economy.

Paradoxically, by 1815, as the Ottomans grew weaker and weaker, the European powers saw that the break-up of the Turkish Empire would endanger European peace. What became known as 'the eastern question' arose, with the major powers hovering anxiously over the territories once effectively controlled by the Turks, but now bubbling with discontent.

Russia had a particularly strong interest; by the late eighteenth century it had decisively beaten Turkey in war and established itself on the Black Sea. Like Austria, Russia had a natural concern with obtaining an outlet to the Mediterranean, and its 1774 treaty with Turkey provided it with a special claim to intervene in the Ottoman Empire's internal affairs, on behalf of the Christian minorities.

By 1853 Tsar Nicholas was describing Turkey as the 'sick man of Europe', and suggesting ways of partitioning its empire. Conflicts and quarrels were inevitable, particularly between Russia and England. England wished not only to ensure that Russia did not become too powerful, but was anxious to safeguard communications with its own empire in India and the Far East. The direct outcome was the Crimean War, a victory for Britain and France over Russia, and the Congress of Berlin, a settlement imposed on Russia by the other European powers. In the background lay the desire of many groups of non-Moslem Turkish subjects, like the Greeks and Slavs, for their independence, their freedom from the now decadent Ottoman rule. The wretched eastern question was only finally settled with the founding of Kemal Atatürk's new Republic of Turkey in 1923. The Ottomans in Europe were no more.

For nearly six centuries the Ottomans had waged an almost constant war against the Christian West. Over the last two centuries the struggle had been a defensive one, the Ottomans fighting a rearguard action to counter the challenge of the West. The challenge was effectively met only by absorbing it – from the nineteenth century, the Turks began to undergo a successful, if often tortuous, process of westernization. Naval and military schools were re-organized, students sent to European countries, and educational reforms carried through. The old Ottoman system of feudalism was abolished. Western ideas particularly on political matters, received more and more attention.

The incursions of a nomadic empire were over; in its place, and under the impact of the West, rose the modern Turkish state.

Despite all the Ottoman conquests, in Turkey the most menial jobs were still performed by Moslem subjects. These workmen were painted building a castle for Murad II.

The protest which split Christianity

Moved by high moral principle, Martin Luther started a movement which divided the Christian Church. Political forces combined with religious ones in widening the breach with Rome.

1 A woodcut shows the laity receiving both the bread and the wine at Communion as Luther preaches, while on his left members of the clergy, including the pope, are dragged into hell by demons. Such visual propaganda was popular.
2 Raphael depicts Leo X as a typical worldly Renaissance pope, flanked by two cardinals.
3 Brandishing pitchforks and flails, German peasants loot and rob churches. In the centre, Luther tries to keep order. Though not in its origin a religious struggle, the Peasants' War gained impetus from the general controversy.

ON 31 OCTOBER 1517, the rector of the castle church at Wittenberg in Germany posted a notice on his church door inviting discussion on certain points of theology. This simple incident had far-reaching results. The man was Martin Luther and his action is generally regarded as the beginning of the Reformation. In the next generation the spiritual and secular power of the pope was broken; the medieval concept of Christendom – a united Christian Europe – was lost forever; and the Middle Ages came to an end.

But long before, movements had appeared in European thought which made something like the Reformation almost inevitable. Nationalism was growing and with it the desire to separate the state from the Church. In theory the pope was the supreme ruler in secular matters as well as spiritual. As recently as 1493, Pope Alexander VI had used this authority to divide the newly discovered world of America and the Indies between Spain and Portugal. In practice, though, fifteenth-century rulers in Spain, France and England had limited papal power by claiming some control over the Church in their own lands. The pope was becoming one ruler among others.

The Renaissance, with its rediscovery of classical learning, its stress on the dignity of Man and its appeal to fearless scholarship, was often hostile to the medieval Church. Erasmus, who produced the first modern edition of the Greek New Testament in 1516, mocked the ignorance of the clergy and criticized theologians for useless word-chopping. He and others exposed the superstition of much religious practice.

There was also a desire for reform within the Church itself. Councils at Constance (1414–18) and Basel (1431–9) had suggested administrative reforms, though little had been done. From 1512–17, a council sat in the Lateran Church at Rome, where reform was discussed. There was certainly need for it. Pluralism – holding and being paid for several offices at once – was common. Church appointments were given as rewards to men who had no intention of fulfilling the duties (Antoine du Prat, Archbishop of Sens, entered his cathedral for the first time in his funeral procession). Many clergy and monks were ignorant and immoral. Lots of people before Luther wanted to reform such abuses.

Alongside the classical revival of the Renaissance, the fifteenth century saw a revival of religious concern. There was a longing for the supposed simplicity and earnestness of the primitive Church. This was expressed in different ways by Wycliffe in England, Huss in Bohemia and Savonarola in Italy. A number of religious communities were established. Some men, troubled about their souls, practised their religion with great fervour.

Such movements influenced the Reformation. But Luther was not merely a mouthpiece for them. His dissatisfaction with the Church was different and deeper. He was above all a religious man. He had an overwhelming sense of the holiness and majesty of God, and of Man's insignificance beside him. His imagination fed on medieval pictures of Christ the terrible judge, demanding perfect obedience and threatening eternal damnation.

Luther's search for salvation

Against this background he sought spiritual peace with God. He became an Augustinian monk and practised such asceticism that his health was impaired. He used the sacraments and venerated the saints. But peace eluded him. He believed that God demanded perfect obedience from a pure heart and could not be sure that his obedience was perfect, his motives pure.

There was a further possibility. It was taught that Christ and some of the saints had achieved more than perfect obedience. The extra goodness which they had not needed for their own salvation was stored in a treasury of merit. This could be made available by the pope through indulgences, by which the soul was 'let-off' a certain period in purgatory. Indulgences were normally conditional on venerating a relic, performing some religious practice, or making a gift. Luther tried this method. He was even able to visit Rome, which had more relics than any other city. He was disillusioned and returned unsatisfied.

In 1511 he was moved to Wittenberg and began serious study of the Bible. In 1513 he began to lecture on it in the new university there. He had no dramatic conversion, but his lectures show a gradual change in his thought which was completed by his reflections on St Paul's Epistle to the Romans. By 1517 his basic position was worked out.

Previously he had wondered how God could remain just and yet allow sinful men into fellowship with himself. Now, led by St Paul, his thoughts dwelt more on Christ. He came to believe that Christ had felt the alienation Luther felt, and endured the judgement Luther feared. In Christ then, God had put himself on the side of Man and made it possible for Man to approach him. The decisive move had come from God's side, not Man's.

Luther's attitude to this was sheer wonder. It never ceased to amaze him, and he never attempted to explain it. The essential point was that God was not to be thought of simply as holy and just, removed from Man. The Biblical emphasis was on God's love and mercy. His justice

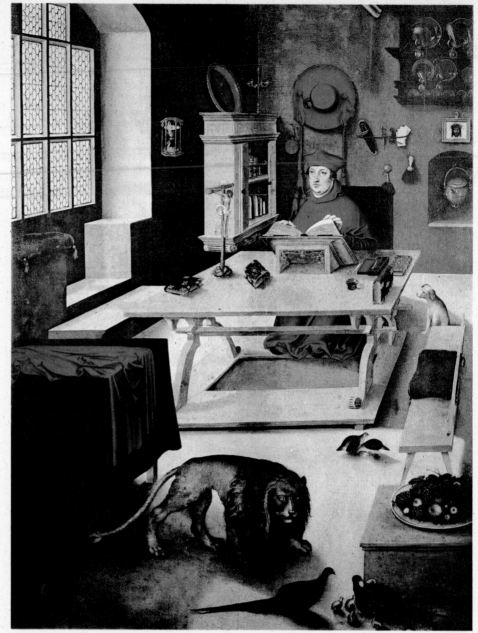

was not expressed in strict legality, but in making men just through Christ. Man was not to seek merit to be worthy of God, but to accept by faith what God had done for him. This is the doctrine of Justification by Faith. In Luther's words, 'I grasped that the justice of God is that righteousness by which through grace and sheer mercy God justifies us through faith. Thereupon I felt myself to be reborn and to have gone through open doors into paradise.'

Luther was also a pastor. It was his pastoral concern which led to his attack on Rome. In 1517 Albert of Brandenberg, already Bishop of Magdeburg and Halberstadt, became Archbishop of Mainz. To pay the pope, Leo X, for the irregularity of holding three offices at once, he was obliged to borrow money. To help Albert reimburse himself, Leo allowed him to proclaim a plenary indulgence throughout Germany. The faithful were asked to make gifts for the rebuilding of St Peter's in Rome (though Albert was to keep part of the money). For this pious act they could obtain remission of all sins, for themselves or their relatives in purgatory. It was not exactly buying forgiveness, but

Albert of Brandenberg had to borrow heavily to pay Leo X for allowing him to become Archbishop of Mainz. Abuses arising from the sale of indulgences to repay his debts roused Luther to protest.

was easily understood in that way. The Dominican monk, Tetzel, who was in charge of the proclamation, encouraged that belief. He seems to have used the jingle 'as soon as the coin in the coffer rings, the soul from purgatory springs'.

The elector of Saxony, Frederick the Wise, refused permission for the indulgence to be proclaimed in his territory, including Wittenberg. But some of Luther's parishioners crossed the border to buy pardons. Luther had already criticized the relics which Frederick kept at Wittenberg. It was the indulgence proclaimed by Tetzel which led to the notice on the church door inviting theologians to debate indulgences.

The notice consisted of 95 theses. They criticized indulgences for taking German money to Rome, and attacked the doctrine of merit which lay beneath them. The second of these points was the most important. Complaints of financial exactions had often been made before with no result.

1 In 1520 the pope issued a Bull declaring some of Luther's teachings heretical and giving him 60 days to recant. Instead, when the 60 days were up, Luther burned the Bull publicly.
2 Luther's uncompromising search for truth led him to question basic points of doctrine, providing a focus for dissatisfaction with the Church.
3 Indulgences remitting years in purgatory are being sold at such a rate that new coins have to be minted on the spot. The papal authorization hangs from a pole on the right.
4 Luther appeared before Charles V at the Diet of Worms in April 1521. He refused to recant 'unless convinced by the testimony of Scripture or by an evident reason . . . seeing that it is not safe or right to act against conscience'.

It was the theological attack which led to the break with Rome. This distinguishes Luther from others who wanted reform. He saw the political, financial, administrative and moral abuses which others complained about. But his complaints were more basic. They went deeper, to the heart of medieval Christianity. That is why Christian humanists such as Erasmus could not join him.

Growth of a movement

Suddenly Luther found himself a leader for all who opposed Rome. Many who neither understood nor greatly cared for theology rallied to him. His theses, translated into German, were printed and circulated freely. Sermons and pamphlets soon followed. During the next four years he engaged in debate in print and in person, at various assemblies, with the theological experts of Rome.

He hoped at first to reform the Church from within. He claimed that if the pope knew what was being done in his name he would forbid it. But it became clear that a break was inevitable. Denial of the validity of an indulgence was in effect to deny the authority of the pope. Luther appealed first to a council of the Church. But he would not allow that even a council could contradict Scripture.

Biblical and historical studies led him to deny the accepted doctrine of the sacraments, and thus undermine the special position of the clergy as purveyors of the sacraments. He argued that according to the New Testament every Christian was a priest, called to serve God in his own occupation.

In 1520 came three of his most famous works. *The Babylonian Captivity of the Church* argued that the Church had been enslaved by the clergy through a false doctrine of sacraments. He reduced the number of sacraments to two, Baptism and the Eucharist (Holy Communion). He denied that the elements of the Eucharist actually became the flesh and blood of Christ through the action of the priest (Transubstantiation), as the Church stated. The efficacy of the sacrament depended on the faith of the recipient. *The Address to the German Nobility* called on Christian Princes to take reform of the Church into their own hands and abolish tribute to Rome, celibacy of the clergy, masses for the dead, pilgrimages and religious orders. *The Freedom of the Christian Man,* addressed to Leo X, set out Man's relation to God on the basis of faith in Christ rather than merit.

Quick action from Rome was needed. An early restatement of some doctrines might have satisfied Luther. Prompt political action might have silenced him. Pope Leo X underestimated the seriousness of the situation. He tried to control Luther through the authorities of the Augustinian order, and failed. He tried diplomatic approaches to Frederick the Wise, but Frederick was pleased to have an eminent theologian at his university and in any case he was becoming sympathetic to Luther's views.

Burning the Papal Bull

Not until 1520 was a Papal Bull issued. This declared some of Luther's teaching heretical and gave him two months to recant. Its publication throughout Germany was treated with derision. When it reached Luther he burned it, together with some books of Canon Law. In April 1521 Luther appeared before the Emperor Charles V at the famous conference, the Diet of Worms, and again refused to recant. He was now excommunicated by the Church and outlawed by the state.

On leaving Worms, Luther was 'kidnapped' by order of Frederick and taken to Wartburg Castle for safety. Meanwhile, in some places, his ideas were translated into practice. Priests celebrated Mass in lay clothes and gave both bread and wine to the laity. (Previously only bread had been given in case the blood of Christ was spilled.) Services were simplified and translated into German. Monks and nuns left monasteries and convents. Money intended for monasteries was devoted to other uses. Priests married. Fasts and Masses for the dead were discontinued.

Unfortunately, reform was often an excuse for rioting, destruction and looting. Some preachers argued that all material elements in religion were wrong, since matter could not convey spirit. Many claimed special revelations from God independent of the Church, Christian tradition or even Scripture. Luther's innate conservatism was offended. He re-

1 After the Diet of Worms Luther was removed for safety to Wartburg Castle by order of Frederick the Wise. He remained there for ten months, writing and translating the New Testament.
2 The doorway of the castle church at Wittenberg. Here, on 31 October 1517, the rector posted 95

theses for debate, in accordance with current practice. The Reformation was under way.
3 A colleague of Luther's at the University of Wittenberg, Philipp Melanchton, became one of the leaders of the Reformation. He provided the official doctrinal statement of the new sect.

turned to Wittenberg.

He was too late. The violence which had begun as religious protest led to the Peasants' War (1524–5). Some preachers, notably Müntzer, supported the rebels. Luther supported the landowners in vicious counter-measures, which lost him much sympathy.

Reform became bound up with politics. Now that Rome had been defied, states and independent cities could choose to remain loyal or to reform. Those that reformed did so in different ways. The influence of different leaders was apparent at different places – Zwingli at Zurich, Bucer at Strassburg, Oecalampadius at Basel, and in the next generation Calvin at Geneva.

At the Diet of Speyer (1529), princes who wanted reform protested in favour of toleration of reformed worship in Catholic lands. Hence the title Protestant. Toleration of Catholics in reformed lands was, in theory, accepted. In fact, neither side was ready for religious toleration as it was later understood. The theory that the ruler should dictate the religion was generally accepted. Protestant leaders failed to agree on doctrine at the Colloquy

of Marburg (1529). But for Lutherans a general confession of faith was issued at Augsburg in 1530. In 1531 Protestant princes formed a political confederacy, the Schmalkaldic League.

Luther lived until 1546, but his main work was now done. He had married a former nun, Katharine von Bora, and became the father of a large family. He continued to preach and write, and on his death-bed corrected proofs of the German translation of the Old Testament.

The attempt to reform the Church had resulted in division, and the inability of the Protestants to agree amongst themselves. The Holy Roman Empire had now certainly come to an end. There followed a terrible period of religious wars and persecutions.

But there were good results. The tyranny of the clergy had been broken, and with it went much superstition. The religious value of other occupations, and of married life, could now be acknowledged. Men could worship and read the Bible in their own language, and for many, like Luther, Christian faith became a more living, intimate and confident experience.

Stemming the tide of reform

As the tide of Protestantism swept relentlessly across northern Europe and calls for change were heard within the Church itself, the Counter Reformation arose to meet the challenge.

THE SIXTEENTH CENTURY saw the end of the Middle Ages and the beginning of the modern world. In Europe, growing nationalism brought a breakdown of old political loyalties. New learning and the new spirit of inquiry in the Renaissance brought a questioning of accepted ideas and institutions.

The Roman Catholic Church suffered from the political changes and the critical spirit. Just after the middle of the century it had lost much political power, and the Protestant Reformation had weakened its spiritual prestige. Some changes in both areas were permanent. The popes were never again the secular or spiritual powers they had once been. Yet, in spite of the permanent establishment of Protestantism, the Church of Rome was perhaps healthier at the end of the century than at the beginning.

Abuses in Rome

That there had been abuses which needed reforming could not be denied. The Renaissance popes were more concerned with the political power of the papacy than the spiritual well-being of the Church, and were involved in ceaseless intrigues and changing alliances with European rulers in order to maintain their own position. Appointments to high positions in the Church were bought and sold; new ones were created to pay civil servants; men employed at Rome were appointed as bishops in lands they would never visit; pluralism was common, where many drew incomes from several offices at once. Monks and lesser clergy were equally open to criticism.

Demands for reform were widespread. Many felt that the Church should be a spiritual not a political power. Good men in the Church were grieved by the corruption of the clergy and the lack of pastoral care for the laity. There were reform movements fermenting in the monastic orders, which became important later on. Rulers, moved more by political than religious motives, resented the buying and selling of offices which took so much money to Rome. There were calls for a General Council of the Church. The time was ripe when any movement towards reform would find a ready response.

A movement came from the Protestant leader Martin Luther, whose criticisms were at first supported by many faithful Catholics. But Luther wanted doctrinal changes as well as moral and administrative ones, and this movement led to the division of the Western Church. Soon after the middle of the century, Lutheranism had spread throughout northern Europe.

The Roman Church owed its recovery, which history has termed the Counter

1 The religious intolerance which found its outlet in the Inquisition was the dark side of the Counter Reformation.
2 By contrast, the Jesuits were a strong force for good. By the end of the sixteenth century, they had preached in most parts of the world.
3 Cardinal Contarini was present at the Colloquy of Ratisbon (1541) where a vain attempt was made to establish common ground with leading Protestants Melancthon and Bucer.

Reformation, to several forces. Reform movements, in motion before Luther's action, gained strength; the appeal for a Council was met by the Council of Trent; the Inquisition brought discipline to the Church; the Jesuits introduced new missionary zeal and combated Protestant doctrine; and the end of the century saw a succession of reforming popes, who, by their lives as well as their actions, helped to erase the worldly reputation which earlier popes had earned. Such movements were aided by Protestant divisions and the political situation at the end of the century.

Protestantism did not gain a firm hold in Spain nor in Spanish territories in Italy. This was only partly due to the more settled politics of Spain compared with the fragmented rule of the electors in Germany. Spanish Catholicism was more austere. Spanish rulers had taken some control of the Church from the popes, and from 1478 had exerted it through the Inquisition. Abuses found elsewhere in Europe were absent from Spain. Bishops were often ascetic and learned men, demanding high standards from clergy and people. Francisco de Cisneros (Cardinal Ximenes), Archbishop of Toledo (1495–

1517), carried out a thorough reform. He compelled clergy to live in their parishes, dissolved unsatisfactory religious communities, and founded the university of Alcalá to raise the educational standards of the clergy.

It was mainly through Spanish influence that a number of attempts were made to deepen devotion and return to a simpler way of life through religious orders. An attempt to reform the Franciscan order of friars by returning to the rule of St Francis ended in the formation in 1529 of a new order, called Capuchins after their pointed hoods. At a time when parish priests rarely preached, they won a reputation for their preaching and helped keep the Italian peasants loyal to Rome.

Dissatisfied with the Church

Other orders were new. The Theatines, founded in 1524, were an order of secular clergy trying to improve the spiritual and moral standards of parish priests. Similar orders followed. Normally gatherings of priests, dissatisfied with the life and work of the Church, formed associations which were later raised to the dignity of orders. The Paulines began to meet in the early thirties and changed their name to Barnabites in 1545. The Somaschi formed an association in 1540 and became an order in 1568.

One of the most influential groups, though it never became an order, was the Oratory of Divine Love. It included clerical and lay members who met for discussion, prayer and devotional exercises. It began about 1517 and included several future cardinals and popes.

Some of this group, at the request of Pope Paul III (1534–49) drew up a plan for the reform of the Church. It was produced in 1538. It asked for reforms in administration, in the choice, training and conduct of the clergy, and particularly in the conduct of the popes and their advisors. But it was never published and not acted upon. The man chiefly responsible, Cardinal Contarini, was sent by the pope to the

Colloquy of Ratisbon (1541) to debate with Protestant leaders Melancthon and Bucer. A formula was worked out to incorporate the important Protestant doctrine of Justification by Faith, but no reconciliation was finally possible.

Eventually a Council was called. It met at Trent in three sessions – 1545–8, 1551–2, 1562–3. For those who hoped for reconciliation with Protestants it was disappointing. Definitions of doctrine took place at the first session when no Protestants were present.

The Council declared that tradition should be given equal authority with scripture. Since Protestants appealed to scripture alone, reconciliation was now virtually impossible. Some other doctrinal definitions were repudiations of Protestant views. Faith alone was declared insufficient for Justification; there were declared to be seven sacraments, all normally necessary for salvation, though not all of equal rank; the Mass was declared to be a sacrifice in which the substance of the bread and wine were changed to the substance of the Body and Blood of Christ 'which change the Catholic Church calls **transubstantiation**'.

There were also administrative and moral decisions which affected the future of the Church. Allowing the laity to drink the consecrated wine at the Mass, and the possible marriage of priests were not accepted; neither was the belief of the Spanish bishops that all bishops derived authority from God, not from the pope. The office of indulgence-seller was abolished, and the Council demanded that bishops and clergy should preach, that synods (ecclesiastical councils) should be held, and that simony – the buying and selling of ecclesiastical offices – should be punished. Perhaps the most effective reforming step was the demand that bishops should set up seminaries for the training of priests.

The Council was a victory for the conservative elements in the Church, and the position of the pope was strengthened,

1 St Ignatius Loyola, founder of the Jesuit order, hung up his sword at the altar of Our Lady and changed clothes with a beggar. His aims were to reform the Church, to convert the pagan world and to fight against heresy. This painting by Rubens exemplifies the splendour of Baroque painting which adorned many of the churches.
2 The Council of Trent was held as a response to pleas for reform. Doctrines were defined for simple people to understand, but no compromise with Protestants was possible.
3 *The Fight Between Carnival and Lent* by Pieter Brueghel is a symbolic portrayal of the conflict between Catholics and Protestants.
4 Painted in 1618, this allegory of Catholics and Protestants fishing for souls represents the struggle for converts.

since all decisions were formally sent for his approval. But the Council had good positive results. It framed Catholic beliefs in such a way that in future the faithful should know clearly the mind of the Church. The vagueness which had helped the growth of Protestantism would be less prevalent in future. The definite moral reforms, influenced by the line of reforming popes which began as the Council was ending, fashioned the character of the Roman Church for the next 400 years.

The victory of the conservative element at Trent reflected a stronger, less conciliatory line which had gained the upper hand at Rome. Its chief exponent was the ascetic Cardinal Caraffa, a member of the Oratory of Divine Love and one of those who had produced the plan for reform in 1538. Later he became Pope Paul IV (1555–9).

Caraffa persuaded Pope Paul III to set up the Roman Inquisition. The use of force against heresy was not new. Its avowed purpose was to save the soul of the heretic by forcing him to give up false doctrines, and it would in any case prevent false teaching from spreading. It had been used at Rome at least from the twelfth century, but had since declined. In Spain, however, it had flourished. It was its success in Spain which impressed Caraffa.

3

4

By a Papal Bull of 1542 the Inquisition was given authority to proceed against anyone, ordained or lay, suspected of heresy. The authority of the Inquisition overruled that of bishops, and from 1562 even bishops could be called before it.

Caraffa, the first Inquisitor General, ordered that Inquisitors must punish on suspicion, must have no regard for social class, but rather be more severe on any who tried to use social position as a shield. Finally they were to show no mildness 'least of all to Calvinists'. Thus Protestantism was suppressed wherever the pope had sufficient power for the Inquisition to be recognized.

Parallel with this went control of the press. In 1543 Caraffa ordered that no book should be printed without papal permission. In 1559, as Pope Paul IV, he issued an Index of books which the faithful were forbidden to read under threat of punishment. It included not only Protestant works, but the works of Erasmus and vernacular translations of the New Testament. The Index was also published by his successors.

Soldier of Christ

A more positive, and ultimately more effective, force was the Society of Jesus founded by Ignatius Loyola. Loyola, a former soldier, dedicated himself to Christ and the Church in 1521 while recovering from wounds suffered in the defence of Pamplona. At first he doubted his own sincerity, but he found spiritual peace by complete obedience to the Church. Henceforth obedience was the keynote of his thought. It is expressed most clearly in his *Spiritual Exercises*. These cover a month and are aimed at reducing human pride, showing the soul's dependence on Christ, and leading to complete obedience to the Church. In 1534 he formed a small brotherhood which in 1540 became an order. Novices entering the order perform the Spiritual Exercises and members perform a modified version annually. Its distinguishing marks are the vow of total obedience to the pope made by fully professed members, and the demand that this obedience should be exercised in the world, not in a monastic order.

The Society spread rapidly and became one of the greatest missionary forces the Church has known. In 1542 Francis Xavier, one of the original brotherhood, went to India as the personal representative of the king of Portugal as well as papal *nuncio* – a representative of the Holy See. Later he went to Japan and Malaya. He died in 1552 trying to enter China. Wherever he went he left a church behind. He brought a new approach to missionary work by trying to understand the culture of the people to whom he preached and incorporating the best of it into Christianity. Previous missionaries had denied all value to pagan cultures. By the end of the century, Jesuit missionaries had preached in most parts of the known world.

The Jesuit Peter Canisius (1521–97) produced a number of catechisms rivalling those of the Protestants as vehicles of simple instruction. He also gained political influence as adviser to the Emperor Ferdinand. In 1554, instructed by Ignatius, he

advised Ferdinand to wage open war on heresy, not to allow a Protestant to hold high office, and to make it plain that no promotion or wealth could be expected by anyone even suspected of heresy.

More than any other single force, the Jesuits halted or turned the tide of Protestant advance. They used political influence when possible, but their success was due more to their dedicated lives and the clarity of their teaching. Before the end of the century they had been largely instrumental in re-establishing Catholicism in eastern Europe, France and Southern Germany.

Jesuit influence may be seen in the character of many leading churchmen at the end of the century. After the Council of Trent there were several reforming popes. Pius IV (1559–64) ordered a revision of the Breviary and Missal (books containing the Roman Catholic form of service) and enforced the Council's decisions about the training of the clergy. Pius V (1565–72) increased the power of the Inquisition and enforced stricter discipline among the clergy. Gregory XIII (1572–85) completed the liturgical reforms and founded many colleges. Meanwhile,

1 There was continuous civil war in France between the Catholic majority and the Protestants. The Massacre of the Huguenots on St Bartholomew's Eve in 1572 was the most terrible incident. 2 The Jesuit Peter Canisius gained political influence as adviser to the Emperor Ferdinand of Spain. Under his tutelage, Ferdinand assumed open hostility towards Protestants.

saintly men such as Charles Borromeo (1538–84) and Philip Neri (1515–95) achieved greater influence in the Church.

Further evidence of spirituality is the amount of devotional literature which appeared. Probably the best example is *The Introduction to the Devout Life* by Francis de Sales, which appeared early in the next century. This book provided guidance on devotion and meditation for the use of lay people, urging them to spend an hour a day in spiritual exercise to make their faith more meaningful.

Massacre of the Huguenots

The politics of the time also assisted. In 1547 Charles V (1520–55) defeated the Protestants at Muhlberg, and in 1555 the Peace of Augsburg allowed rulers to decide the religion of their own land. This ensured religious peace in Germany until the beginning of the Thirty Years' War in 1618, the name given to the series of religious and political wars between Catholic and Protestant powers. Philip II of Spain, the most powerful ruler in Europe, was a champion of Rome and opposed Protestantism in the Netherlands. The tangled politics of France led to the massacre of the Protestant Huguenots on St Bartholomew's Eve, 1572. England, now Protestant, was generally uninvolved, though Pius V formally excommunicated Elizabeth in 1570.

By the end of the century, Rome had regained much lost ground. It was a less corrupt Church than it had been a century earlier. Clergy and laity were better disciplined and better instructed. The Counter Reformation recovered not only territory and prestige, but to some extent, the practice of true religion.

Rise of the nation-states

As a result of the Protestant break with Rome and the growth of a powerful middle class, the people of Europe came increasingly to see themselves as members of particular 'nations'.

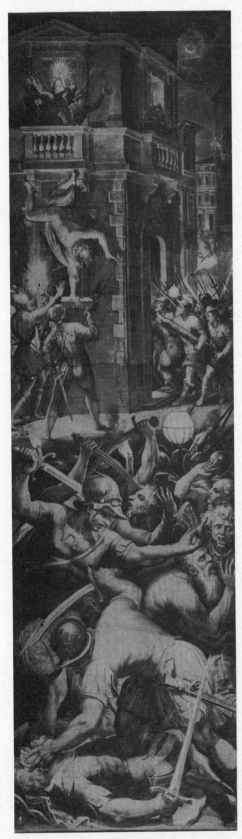

UNTIL WELL into the thirteenth century almost all the monarchs of western Europe acknowledged – even if grudgingly on occasions – that they owed allegiance to the Pope. But the fourteenth century began with a violent reaction against the whole idea of the Pope's overlordship. The first clash came between two obstinate and ambitious men, Pope Boniface VIII and Philip IV of France.

Boniface, an Italian cardinal of noble birth became Pope in 1294. He was a professed sceptic in religion, more interested in political power than in spiritual matters. He became Pope by the ingenious trick of installing a concealed megaphone in the room of his saintly but simple predecessor, Celestine V. Voices in the night advised Celestine to resign and, when the aged Pope did so, his successor promptly imprisoned him. 'I am Pope, I am Caesar' was the motto of Boniface, and he occasionally wore imperial, rather than papal robes to make the point. This arrogant and unspiritual man determined to uphold and extend the power of the Papacy over the monarchs of Christendom.

In 1296, Boniface issued a bull (*Clericis Laicos*) forbidding the clergy to pay any taxes on their incomes or ecclesiastical property to secular rulers without the Pope's authority. At the same time, he forbade any ruler, under threat of excommunication, to receive such payments.

This peremptory interference was especially irksome to the kings of England and France whose perpetual and costly wars could be financed only by taxation. Moreover, the Church was becoming wealthier, and thus more capable of paying the taxes that the native sovereigns in-

creasingly heaped upon it. Torn between the prospects of possible damnation in the future or loss of a war – and possibly a throne – kings increasingly preferred to save their crowns rather than their souls. Edward I of England defied Boniface's bull and supported by his parliament won the day.

Philip IV of France took more violent measures. He burnt the bull outside Notre Dame in Paris and threw the papal envoy into prison. Undeterred, Boniface countered with another bull (*Unam Sanctam*), asserting the papal supremacy in extreme terms. Philip's patience was at an end.

The Pope is kidnapped

In 1303, he sent his agent, Guillaume de Nogaret, into Italy with orders to kidnap the Pope. Nogaret and a companion seized Boniface in his own apartment where he lay in bed quivering with fright, clutching a Cross. Although the Pope was liberated by local people a day or two later, he was again imprisoned almost immediately. Throughout these ordeals he was threatened, cuffed and insulted freely, and the shock to his dignity brought the unfortunate old man to his death within a few weeks.

All over Europe men of power saw the point that Philip had proved: the authority of the Popes had vanished. Henceforth monarchs might expect support from their subjects when the interests of the State were threatened, and they could rely on national armies to enforce their wills.

Philip's ruthless and decisive action won him respect. The papal throne was briefly occupied by Benedict XI – a good and saintly Pope believed to have been poisoned

Henry of Navarre, the leader of the Huguenots, became king of France in 1589. He was only able to secure Roman Catholic toleration of the Protestants by becoming a Catholic himself!

An influential political writer in Italy during the Renaissance was Niccolò Machiavelli. He advocated the use of any means, however immoral, to maintain power in the interest of the State.

Above is an Italian version of one of the massacres of the Huguenots, the Protestants of the French Reformation. Thousands of martyrs were made before they gained religious toleration.

– and then lay unoccupied for nearly a year. In 1305 the cardinals elected as Pope a Frenchman, Clement V, who resided in Avignon, in the south of France, and became a mere puppet of the French king. In Avignon, seven Popes reigned before Gregory XI restored the Papal See to Rome in 1377.

The Avignon Popes were mainly undistinguished. One of them, John XXII, vainly urged the old high-handed papal claims against Louis IV, the Holy Roman Emperor. But the bitter quarrel that followed between them was really little more than a nationalistic dispute between a Frenchman and a German, each representing the interests of his own country.

The end justifies the means

Louis IV was supported in his controversy with John XXII by one of the most notable of later medieval writers on politics, Marsilius of Padua (c. 1278–1343). As an Italian, Marsilius was distressed by the chaos of Italy and the collapse of the power of the Italian city-states, which he blamed on papal tyranny and interference. He was strongly opposed, therefore, to ecclesiastical power, but he also had no regard for the pretensions of the Holy Roman Emperors.

In 1324 he published his *Defensor Pacis*, in which he insisted that all rulers derive their authority from the people and must exercise it subject to popular control. Marsilius also insisted that the clergy should restrict themselves to their spiritual functions and not meddle in secular matters. He thus attacked the very foundations of the Church's authority and he was the first political writer to demand the subordination of the Church to the State.

Two centuries of dramatic change followed the death of Marsilius. The European discovery of America at the end of the fifteenth century revealed the smallness of Christendom in relation to the rest of the

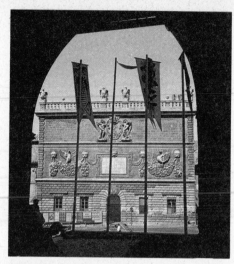

Part of the Papal Palace in Avignon. In 1305 the cardinals elected a Frenchman, Clement V, as Pope; after this seven Popes reigned in France before the Papal See was restored in 1377.

world. Simultaneously the observations of astronomers revealed the paucity of the thinking that once falsely elevated the world to the central point of the Universe. The development of trade further enlarged men's ideas, bringing them into contact with new peoples and alternative faiths. New towns sprang up, with a new middle class that grew wealthy, ambitious and independent.

Spreading from Italy, the Renaissance – that great revival of art and literature – liberated men's minds so that many ideas once gravely discussed and argued over became merely ridiculous. Finally came the tremendous impact of movable-type printing – an earlier Korean invention exploited in Europe only in the fifteenth century. All these events came like hammer

This engraving shows the Spanish Armada lying at anchor off Calais. Sent against England by Philip II of Spain, the Spaniards were routed when the English sent fire-ships among them.

blows to weaken the political power of the Church and strengthen the State.

This situation produced another important Italian political writer, Niccolò Machiavelli (1469–1527), whose subtle and devious thoughts caused the adjective 'Machiavellian' to be added to the vocabularies of the world. Machiavelli, a member of an old Tuscan family, had once tasted power as secretary to the council of the Republic of Florence. He had also suffered torture and imprisonment at the hands of the Medici family, who regained power in Florence in 1512.

It was thus with first-hand knowledge of the ruthlessness he advocated, that Machiavelli wrote *The Prince,* a treatise that came to have a profound influence – even if indirectly – on the course of government. Machiavelli's immediate purpose in writing his book was to persuade the new Medici ruler to reinstate him to an official position out of regard for his usefulness. In his limited purpose Machiavelli was disappointed, but in his larger aim – to instruct rulers how to keep their power – his treatise proved brilliantly successful.

He advised rulers bent on keeping power, to employ any means to achieve their ends, however immoral or ruthless. He regarded religious and moral considerations as mere sentimentality, which the ruler should disregard in pursuance of the supreme interest of his State. No ruler can enjoy the luxury of a private conscience, said Machiavelli. Whereas, an ordinary individual can afford to tell the truth and suffer for it, because he suffers alone, a ruler cannot. If he weakens, his subjects, to whom he has a prime responsibility, will suffer as a consequence.

'It is necessary,' Machiavelli wrote, 'for a Prince wishing to hold his own to know how to do wrong and to make use of it or not according to necessity.' Machiavelli saw no reason for a ruler to have virtues, but he should appear to have

them. On the other hand, a reputation for cruelty was to be sought rather than avoided, and one might be feared without being hated. A ruler should avoid being judged a monster, not because popularity is pleasant but because people do not willingly obey monsters.

In short, Machiavelli's advice was practical rather than moral, realistic rather than sentimental. Medieval chivalry in rulers had no place in Machiavelli's concept. Whether or not the monarchs of powerful states such as England, France and Spain had heard of Machiavelli, they came, by the end of the sixteenth century generally to share his views. Were they more unscrupulous than their predecessors – or merely less hypocritical?

The rise of the secular rulers was speeded by religious dissensions. These already troubled the Church in the fourteenth century and in the sixteenth century they exploded into the Reformation. This great split in the Church divided Christians into those who still acknowledged the authority of the Papacy, and those who belonged to rival, Protestant churches.

The complete bureaucrat

But whether a state was Roman Catholic or Protestant, its political development was essentially the same. By the sixteenth century, rulers claimed supremacy over all the churches within their territories, and the right to control the beliefs and consciences of their subjects.

The strongest power in the sixteenth century was Spain, which had recently come into possession of a vast overseas empire and had defeated France in a struggle for supremacy in Europe. A firmly centralized, comprehensive administration was established by the Spanish monarchy during the long reign of King Philip II (1555-1598).

Philip was the complete bureaucrat of his day. A slow-thinking, dedicated man, he sat in a small office in the heart of his huge palace, going through the state papers minutely and controlling as closely as he could the activities of his realm. In religion he was a fanatic, determined to stamp out Protestantism within his own country, and spread Roman Catholicism in others. But his was a peculiarly Spanish brand of Roman Catholicism, and Philip had more control over the Church in Spain than the Pope had. One of his ministers even went so far as to declare there was no Pope in Spain.

But while Philip used religion as a tool to unite Spain, religious wars tore France apart. The French Protestants, the Huguenots, too strong to be eliminated, formed a militant political force. After a series of battles and political assassinations, the

211

Protestant leader, Henry of Navarre eventually became king as Henry IV in 1589. An able and far-sighted ruler, Henry secured religious toleration for his supporters, and in turn gained the support of the Roman Catholics by becoming one himself, remarking cynically as he did so, 'Paris is worth a Mass.' (He had already renounced his Protestant faith once before to save his life at a time when the Huguenots were being massacred.) By wise administration Henry brought peace to France, but then became obsessed with the idea of uniting 15 European countries into a 'universal Christian republic'. Before he could do anything about it he too was assassinated.

The defeat of the Armada

England like Spain, was united enough to manage its own political destiny without civil war. But while Spain ignored the Papacy, England broke with it completely. Before the coming of the Tudor dynasty in 1485 the English Crown had two powerful rivals – the feudal barons and the Popes. But the fearful slaughter of the nobility during the Wars of the Roses (1455–85) freed the way for the growth of a powerful English middle class.

This new class supported the Tudors in their determination to achieve power over Church and barons alike. Under Henry VIII, a self-willed man whose limited patience was tried beyond endurance by the efforts of Pope Clement VII to control his matrimonial affairs, the Crown took over all authority previously exercised in the kingdom by the Papacy. The English Church became a state Church with the king at its head.

The Tudors were a despotic family, who appealed to popular patriotism to bolster their authority. They harnessed the growing nationalist spirit to make England a power of consequence in Europe. The efficient Tudor government was served by a new nobility drawn from the middle class and enriched by lands seized from the Church.

The last serious attempt by a foreign power to invade England came in 1588, when Philip II of Spain (who had briefly been King of England as husband of Mary I between 1554 and 1558) launched his Armada against the English coasts, following a quarrel with England about the Netherlands. The disastrous end of the Armada (most of its ships were wrecked due to bad seamanship) marked the rise of England to great-power status as much as it marked the decline of Spain.

New nation-states did not develop everywhere – even in western Europe. Italy and Germany, for example, remained little more than geographical expressions until the second half of the nineteenth century. But Roman Catholic Italy enjoyed at least religious unity, even if the whole peninsula was divided into a number of separate and independent states dominated by the distant power of Spain.

In central Europe, the Holy Roman Empire – now enfeebled – was quite unable to establish a central authority over its domains. The Empire had become no more than a patchwork quilt in which hundreds

of petty princes pursued independent policies. It looked for a time as though Protestantism would gain the whole of the German lands and bring some kind of unity to central Europe, but this was not to be. The Roman Catholics, with foreign aid, regained control in parts of Germany and the result was war and even greater division.

The terrible Thirty Years' War (1618–48) turned central Europe into a desert through which starving refugees fled or were callously slaughtered by the ravaging armies, both Protestant and Catholic, that perpetually came and went. The end of this disastrous war left a ruined Germany even

The development of trade in Europe brought with it a new and wealthy middle class. In this late-medieval market scene notice the leisurely passers-by and the play going on in the background.

more divided politically than it was religiously. Of the German princes that survived, each gained complete control of their own territories and pursued their own individual policies.

Thus, hastened by religious differences, the medieval European system vanished, and with it went the political power of both the Papacy and the Holy Roman Empire. Soon after the Thirty Years' War Sweden, Russia and (later) Prussia were also hammered into strong nation-states by dynamic rulers. To an increasing extent the people of Europe came to see themselves as members of this or that 'race' or 'nation'. The urge to found new nation-states continued unabated into the twentieth century. The peace treaties of 1919 that followed the First World War, for example, created or resurrected no less than seven new nation-states by a few strokes of the pen.

Nor has this drive for nationalism been confined to Europe. In our own time, for example, the situation in Islam has paralleled that of medieval Christendom. The whole brotherhood of the Arabs may be Moslem, but it is also split into Algerians, Egyptians, Syrians and a host of national groups with widely differing loyalties. Islam in the twentieth century has proved no more capable of checking nationalism than the Catholic Church in medieval Europe.

A fanatical Roman Catholic, Philip II attempted to unite Spain by stamping out Protestantism.

Three young kings of Europe

Charles V, Francis I and Henry VIII were the three monarchs of sixteenth-century Europe whose reigns saw the end of the outworn medieval traditions and the birth of a new royal absolutism.

THE FIFTEENTH CENTURY is marked by the final decay of medieval feudalism, by the disintegration of a society based on a pyramidal lord-vassal relationship. Mutual rights and obligations were gradually replaced by the cash bond; hereditary ties and territorial dependence succumbed to the fluctuations of personal and group interests.

Against this background of transition during which medieval concepts still played a major role, we ought to look at the monarchs who dominated the first half of sixteenth-century Europe: Charles V, Francis I and Henry VIII.

The basic problem of medieval government, of making a decision and getting it put into effect, was one which did not affect the king alone. Countless mutual advantages and services to lord and vassal could be secured by mutual consent, a process which the Imperial Diet of the Holy Roman Empire, the *parlements* in France and the English Parliament all served to institutionalize. Thus, the successful or unsuccessful relationships between monarch and barons or estates (nobility, clergy and the major towns) point to a factor of overriding importance in medieval politics; the personality of the monarch. Only under a strong monarch could the balance between king and the estates of the realm be maintained.

Charles V's achievement

None of the monarchs under consideration here possessed a weak personality – on the contrary – but their fortunes were influenced by at least two factors. One, geography, was beyond their control; the second, the Reformation, could either be utilized for the benefit of the dynasty or combated by persuasion or by force.

The achievement of Charles V (1500–58) lies in the fact that in spite of being geographically hampered through the very size of his possessions in an age when the problem of administration was one of communications, he managed not only to retain, administer and enlarge his possessions, but uphold and assert for the last time in European history the universalism of the Holy Roman Empire.

Born in Burgundy, Charles was the product of three dynasties: Austria, Burgundy and Spain. As such, the number and extent of his possessions seemed almost to suggest the reincarnation of Charlemagne's Empire. In Germany he possessed the Austrian duchies; on the shores of the North Sea, the Low Countries; with the exception of Portugal, the Iberian Peninsula; and in the Mediterranean, the Kingdom of Naples and Sicily. And with these family heritages went the claim of Austria to the Empire, to Bohemia and Hungary; the claims to the remains of the old Duchy of Burgundy (i.e. the Low Countries and Franche-Comté), as well as claims to the heartland of the old Burgundian Duchy around Dijon. Added to this must be Spain's claim to Italy, the coasts of Barbary and her overseas territories in the Americas.

Called upon to unify the territories of the Iberian Peninsula and to rule over them at the age of 16 on the death of his maternal grandfather, Ferdinand of Aragon in 1516, Charles was initially handicapped by his ignorance of the Spanish language, and the nobility of the Spanish regions at first proved intractable. With the death of the Emperor Maximilian in 1519 their hostility reached danger point, for now Charles became the head of the House of Habsburg, King of Germany, and thus the logical successor to the throne of the Holy Roman Empire. They feared he would pay less attention than ever to Spanish interests, and that the Peninsula would become merely an outpost of his wider domains.

During his absence in Germany for his coronation, the smouldering discontent in Spain flared into open rebellion culminating in the demand that Charles return to Spain and make his permanent residence there. Moreover, all foreigners (particularly his Flemish countrymen) were to be barred from Spanish offices. Although the revolt failed because of divisions within the rebel camp, Charles, after his return, partly acquiesced in these demands, and his subsequent marriage to Isabella, daughter of the King of Portugal, lifted him to unexpected heights of popularity. The union of the entire Iberian Peninsula seemed, for the time being, to have been achieved.

Had this been his only aim, Charles might have been successful, but his attempt to make Spain dominant in Europe, as well as governing an empire, ensured that either one or the other would fail.

The two main events which affected both his domestic policy in the Empire and his foreign policy, were his election as Emperor of the Holy Roman Empire and the Reformation. In spite of its diminished material value the imperial title was still the most coveted in Europe, and Charles's main rival was Francis I, the Valois King of France. The latter enjoyed the support of the papacy but Charles obtained the support of the German electors by huge bribes and by the signature of a deed in which he promised to respect

1 Henry VIII and Cardinal Wolsey. The cardinal's greatest ambition was to become pope and have England win equal footing with France and Spain. But the king's divorce put an end to his plans.
2 Charles V rides at the head of his troops against the Lutheran princes in the Schmalkaldic War. Despite the victory he won, he failed to suppress the Protestants.

1 Van Dyck's portrait of Charles V, the Holy Roman Emperor. He was the last emperor to pursue the medieval idea of universal empire, but the very size of his empire defeated him.
2 Francis I: his reign was spectacular for the rise of royal absolutism. Without his achievement, the monarchy of Louis XIV could never have evolved.
3 The riding party for the coronation of Charles by Pope Clement VII in the imperial city of Aachen. Charles rides on the pope's nearside beneath the panoply.
4 On becoming involved in conflict with the papal power Henry VIII created a national Church separate from Rome, with himself as supreme head.

their rights and privileges, to confer all offices on native Germans, to call no meeting of the Reichstag, the Imperial Diet, outside the limits of the Empire, and to bring no foreign troops into Germany. In October 1520, in the imperial city of Aachen, Charles was crowned emperor.

His election made conflict with Francis I virtually inevitable. Personal factors apart, France was now bordered in the south by Spain and in the east by the Empire. Moreover Francis laid claim to the neighbouring Navarre, part of which had been annexed by Charles's predecessor. He also claimed the Kingdom of Naples and Sicily. Charles's immediate objectives were his native Burgundy, which Louis XI had appropriated, and northern Italy where Francis, at the beginning of his reign, had seized the Duchy of Milan. A series of wars began in 1521 which intermittently continued until 1559. It is important to note that Francis set the precedent, to be followed by French foreign policy for centuries thereafter, in making an alliance with a power to the east of the Empire, in this case the Turks, thus bringing pressure to bear on it from two directions.

The confrontation with Luther

The second event, the Reformation, was one which Charles ultimately failed to cope with. The spread of Lutheranism threatened to disrupt the entire political and social order of the Empire and Charles was too preoccupied with affairs in Spain and the wars against France until too late. By 1521, when Charles first intervened, Luther could no longer be suppressed and almost triumphantly justified his position before Charles at the Diet of Worms. That Luther was subsequently put under the ban of the Empire by the Edict of Worms did little to keep in check the tendencies to disperse inherent in the Holy Roman Empire and ensured that not only could Francis I exploit the religious dissension, but that the German princes under the religious pretext could assert their own territorial sovereignty. Charles was fully prepared to reconcile the contending parties, but the Catholic princes, actively encouraged by Francis I, insisted upon the execution of the Edict of Worms and the re-assertion of the primacy of Roman Catholicism. The Lutheran members of the Imperial Diet drew up a statement of their beliefs to be read before the Diet which was to meet at Augsburg in

1530. But this essentially conciliatory statement known as the 'Confessions of Augsburg' failed to bridge the division in the face of the 'all or nothing' attitude of the opposing Catholic princes.

Fearing that the emperor would now forcibly suppress Lutheranism, a number of Lutheran principalities and cities formed a defensive union called the Schmalkaldic League and in 1546 the Schmalkaldic war broke out. In the final analysis Charles failed to suppress the Lutherans, and at the Peace of Augsburg in 1555, each prince of the Empire was granted the right to decide which of the two faiths was to be permitted in his territory and to be imposed upon its inhabitants. Dejected and disillusioned, Charles turned over the rule of the Low Countries to his son Philip. A year later he relinquished the imperial crown in favour of his brother Ferdinand and abdicated the Crowns of Spain and his Italian possessions in favour of Philip. An exhausted man, he retired to the monastery of San Geronimo de Yuste in Spain where he died in 1558.

The last of the medieval emperors had disappeared from the scene. While succeeding in giving some coherence to his vast conglomeration of possessions, Charles had failed in his chief ambition to regenerate the universalist imperial idea based on the preservation of the unity of the Roman Catholic Church. He was a prodigious administrator who attended personally to the minutiae of administrative detail, but, religious divisions apart, the very size of his empire defeated him.

By contrast, the task of Francis I (1494–1547) was easier. The main theme of his reign was his conflict with Charles V, and the growth of French territorial and national consciousness was as strongly influenced by its conflicts with the Habsburgs as it had been before by the Hundred Years' War with England. In spite of individual grievances, the French population at large admired and supported Francis, who continued vigorously the policy of administrative centralization already initiated by two of his predecessors, Charles VIII (1470–98) and Louis XII (1462–1515). His success in securing the title to Burgundy from Charles by the Peace of Cambrai in 1529 removed the threat of imperial influence extending into the very heart of France. And his annexation of Brittany rounded off the territory of his kingdom.

The Hundred Years' War had seen the beginning of a policy of the French Crown which on the one hand managed to levy sizable taxation without any form of consent, while on the other it issued edicts carrying the force of law. Although there existed a variety of representative assemblies, none of them took any part in the process of legislation. Their function was restricted to airing grievances.

The superior law courts, the *parlements*, such as that of Paris, were meant to register royal edicts before they could become effective. Hence, one of Francis's early steps was to subordinate them to the royal will by creating central courts out of the royal council which at first duplicated the *parlements'* functions and finally, to all intents and purposes, replaced them.

This decline in the authority of traditional medieval institutions was helped by administrative reforms which successfully improved the collection and management of the revenue and transferred local government from magnates to royal officials. Wherever the aristocracy did not become part of the bureaucracy, the latter replaced the former in the course of time. Thus the foundations were laid for the rise of the absolute monarchy in France.

Both as a diplomat and as a soldier Francis remained inferior to Charles throughout their long drawn-out contest, but the conduct of his domestic policy clearly shows him to reflect the dawn of a new age while Charles was no more than the last glimmer of a bygone era.

As on the continent of Europe, in England too, the feudal system was in the throes of disintegration. The great climax was reached in the Wars of the Roses: afterwards government was only reasserted gradually and the 'over-mighty subject' subdued by the revival of strong personal government, first by Edward IV and then by Henry VII. To some extent this meant the return to medieval methods whose great weakness had been the dependence not upon a self-operating administrative machinery, but upon the personal action of the Crown. Consequently the fate of the sound heritage which Henry VII left very much depended on the strength of personality and political skill of Henry VIII (1491–1547). Initially unwilling to burden himself with the task of government, Henry nevertheless showed sound sense in the choice of his chief administrators – first Cardinal Wolsey and then Thomas Cromwell. In their hands medieval institutions such as Parliament, and the offices of the king's household such as the Exchequer, were adapted to meet the changing needs and increasing complexity of royal administration.

England's break with Rome

The chief event in Henry's reign, the Henrician Reformation, culminated in the king's claim to supremacy in both temporal and spiritual matters clearly stated in the Act of Supremacy (1534) which represented the final break with the papacy. The real issue underlying the Reformation in England during the reign of Henry VIII was the matter of the king's marriage. Cardinal Wolsey's failure to obtain the king's divorce from Catherine of Aragon, the aunt of Charles V, made the statutory assertion of royal supremacy a very practical response to a highly volatile political problem; the problem of the royal succession.

Catherine had failed to produce a male heir. Only one of her six children, Mary, had survived infancy. And the rule of a woman was without precedent in England. Besides, the marriage of a woman ruler was bound to raise serious problems. If she married an English noble, the jealousy of the other nobles might give rise to civil war; if she married a foreign prince, England might become the appendage of

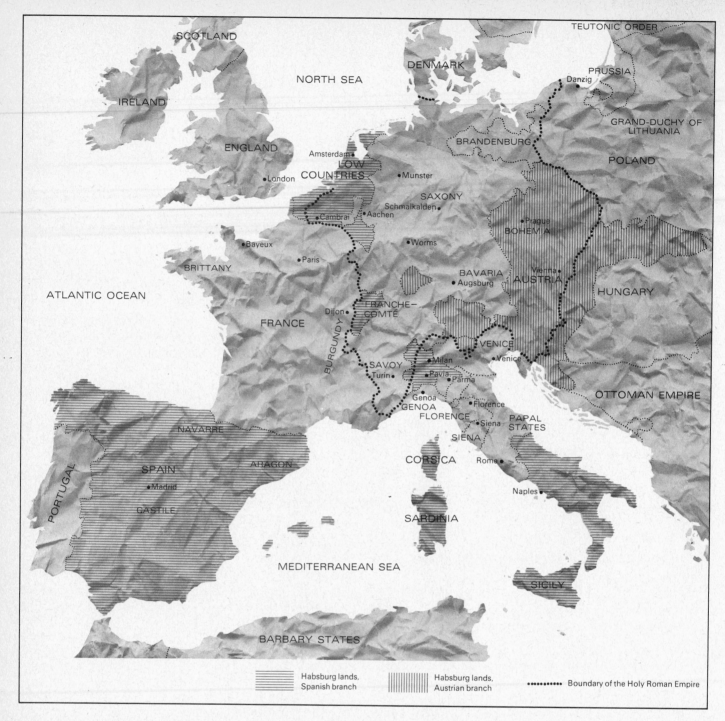

| | Habsburg lands, Spanish branch | | Habsburg lands, Austrian branch | •••••••••• Boundary of the Holy Roman Empire |

A map of Europe in the mid-sixteenth century showing the extent of Charles's lands, and the areas where his territorial claims conflicted with the claims of Francis I.

another nation; if she did not marry at all the civil conflicts over the succession might break out afresh. The shadows of the 'over-mighty subjects' were ever-present in Henry's political consciousness, turning his desire for a male heir into an obsession.

Although the king was strong-willed and impetuous, for him as well as for Thomas Cromwell, his chief minister, the break with Rome was a last resort, and in an age when Christianity was still part and parcel of the fabric of society it was politically wise to sanction the separation from Rome through the one relatively representative body of England and Wales – through Parliament. Although the summoning of Parliament was no more frequent between 1509 and 1603 than between 1372 and 1485, the novel feature was the

deliberate establishment of a community of interest between Crown and Parliament which the king did his best to secure by the dissolution of the monasteries. By this action the wealth of the Church in England was first transferred to the Crown, from where it spread out to nobility and gentry. This process, taking place within a century, brought about a permanent shift of economic power away from the Crown to its subjects, a shift which found its expression in the growing ascendancy of Parliament. Over the long term this was to have consequences in England which fundamentally differed from those in Europe. There forces of modernity made for a stronger administrative centralization which favoured the emergence of absolutism at the expense of representative assemblies. These forces were at work in England, too, but here the shift of economic power, increased by England's growing overseas trade, to the royal subjects in Parliament made the latter

into an effective check against monarchical absolutism. Perhaps it may be said – even at the risk of greatly oversimplifying the issues – that Henry VIII and Thomas Cromwell laid the steps to the scaffold upon which Charles I was to die.

Henry VIII's character and achievements are the subject of heated controversy to this day. There is little doubt that he laboured to make England great, but whether for love of his people or self aggrandisement remains an open question.

Yet like his royal contemporaries, he too reflected his time. In central Europe, in Spain, France and in England, the new absolutism was welcomed with relief by the great mass of people as deliverance from the most fearful domestic feuds. The feudal system had outlived itself and dissolved into an anarchy of wilfulness. The strong monarchy was able to claim that its demands were at one with the general interest and thus prepared a fertile soil for the emergence of dynastic absolutism.

Catherine – devil or diplomat?

Catherine de Médicis steered France through one of the most dangerous periods of its history, but controversy still rages as to whether she was a monster of duplicity, or a truly wise woman.

1

2

QUEEN JEZEBEL, Madame Serpent, Madame Satan, the 'Florentine shopkeeper' – a variety of names, all full of loathing or contempt, were applied to Catherine de Médicis in her own lifetime. Yet after her death her worst enemy, her son-in-law Henry IV, spoke of 'the wise conduct of that intelligent woman'. And historians have ever since been divided between those who see her as a cold, calculating monster of viciousness, who planned the Massacre of St Bartholomew months ahead and disposed of her enemies by subtle Italian poisons, and those who see her as a great queen who, by her patience and devotion to duty, saved the Kingdom of France from foreign domination or total anarchy at one of the most turbulent times in its history.

Any examination of Catherine must first go back and look at the family from which she came. Two of the unforgivable things about her, in the eyes of many of the French nobility, were that she was born into a distrusted race and a despised family. Honoured and respected throughout Europe as brilliant businessmen and patrons of the arts the Médicis might be, but they were still Italian, not French, and their blood was not royal. The taunt of 'the Florentine shopkeeper', heard so frequently in Catherine's lifetime, indicated a division between herself and her most powerful subjects which she was unable to repair.

Her family had a long political tradition of affiliation with France. When Renaissance Italy was torn by the quarrels between the party of the Guelfs – who supported the Papacy and its ally France – and the Ghibellines, who favoured an alliance with the Holy Roman Empire, Florence supported the Guelf side, and emphasized her allegiance by becoming banker to the Roman Curia (the Papal court). This made her automatically a notable European power; and gradually

3

1 Catherine de Médicis: crafty, cultured and intelligent, her abiding object was to preserve the authority of her sons.
2 The beautiful château at Chenonceaux, presented by Henri II to his mistress, Diane de Poitiers. On Henri's death, Catherine forced Diane to exchange it for another.
3 All manner of evil practices were attributed to Catherine in her lifetime, not least being that she consorted with magicians and sorcerers. This print shows her seeing the future rulers of France through an enchanted mirror.

the Médicis family could be seen to be under-propping the whole system of European credit. They formed alliances with great houses; Lorenzo – named after his ancestor, Lorenzo the Magnificent, most generous of Renaissance patrons of the arts – married Madeleine de la Tour d'Auvergne, daughter of an old and distinguished French family. Their daughter Catherine was born on 13 April 1519. A fortnight later her mother died of puerperal fever, and barely a week afterwards

her ailing father died, too. She was the last legitimate Médicis, and the civil strife which was to bedevil her whole life began to gather as she lay in her cradle.

Her childhood passed in an atmosphere of intrigue and revolt. Her cousin Giuliano, bastard great-nephew of Lorenzo the Magnificent, became Pope Clement VII in 1523; he allied himself with Francis I of France, both declaring that their aim was 'to put an end to the wars that were desolating Christianity'. The Emperor

Charles V, however, invaded and sacked Rome itself – and at this time of unrest the Florentines rose against their rulers. Little Catherine was sheltered in a convent while outside the streets ran with blood and churches were sacked and desecrated. (It was seriously proposed by the Ghibelline faction that she be sent to a brothel, as the pope could not then bring about a French alliance by marrying her off.)

This childhood memory of the horrors of civil war had a most profound effect on Catherine; she came to feel that whatever were her means, the end of preventing such war was in itself sufficient to justify them. All her life she was an ardent disciple of Niccoló Machiavelli (a fellow Florentine who died in 1527). His 'political recipes' were the result of his experiences as an astute observer of the struggles around him; above all, he envisaged unity as the prime aim of a ruler, and this unity was what Catherine later sought as she coped with the violent factions of France.

Machiavellian practice

Machiavelli's 'handbook for rulers' is a disillusioned work; he brought the humanist common-sense of the Renaissance to a world still trying to rid itself of the worst legacies of the Middle Ages – religious passion and intolerance. He saw that in the jungle which was Italy, only the most efficient rulers survived, and he prescribed maxims to ensure such survival, based on self-interest rather than on idealistic motives: 'Men ought to be either well treated or crushed, because they can avenge themselves of lighter injuries; of more serious ones they cannot; therefore the injury that is to be done to a man ought to be of such a kind that one does not stand in fear of revenge.' It was this kind of thinking, rather than the innate villainy imagined by romantic novelists, which led Catherine to instigate the 1572 Massacre of St Bartholomew which sought to eliminate the French Protestants as a political force.

Pope Clement – a master of Machiavellian practice – finally did exactly what his enemies had envisaged: he cemented the alliance with France by marrying the 14-year-old Catherine to Henri, second son of the King of France. By a strange irony of fate, Francis I signed the marriage contract at the castle of Anet, which belonged to the old Seneschal of Normandy and his beautiful 32-year-old wife Diane de Poitiers – a woman who was to cause the new bride long years of bitter, repressed jealousy, and to be publicly treated as Queen of France in all but name.

Catherine brought to France her dowry of 100,000 gold crowns, countless magnificent jewels and all her mother's lands in Auvergne – but the wily pope managed to avoid handing over 'three inestimable gems, greatly but vainly desired by three kings' – namely Naples, Milan and Genoa, for which Francis I had been angling. This was probably why he later said that in accepting Catherine as a daughter-in-law, he had taken a girl 'as naked as a newborn babe'.

On the death of his elder brother in 1536,

1 A court ball in 1570: Catherine stands in the centre, the figure at the rear in the white turban is the future Henri III, and Charles IX stands directly behind Catherine's daughter Marguerite who is kneeling before the Duc de Guise.
2 Henri III and Catherine: he was the only one of her sons whom she was never able to dominate.

Henri became heir to the throne of France. At about the same time his liaison began with Diane, now a widow and nearly 20 years older than her royal lover. But she was still a startlingly beautiful woman, and one who knew how to correct, advise, and at the same time flatter the prince, who found few attractions in his ugly, intellectually gifted, barren little wife. In her childlessness lay Catherine's great peril. She dared not draw attention to herself for fear of being repudiated and returned to Florence. For ten years she waited; then the miracle occurred. In 1544 she gave birth to a son. Whatever malformation had previously been present in her body may have naturally corrected itself; certainly she had no further difficulty in bearing children. She produced ten in 12 years; the last two – twins who did not survive – nearly killed her, but all the others lived to make glittering

For 26 years Catherine had to endure Henri II's infatuation for the beautiful Diane de Poitiers, right. Had she shown her resentment, she would probably have lost her position at court

marital alliances.

In 1547 her husband at last became King Henri II. Loving politics as she did, longing for power, wanting to feel the reins of government in her capable fingers, these years of being 'Queen Cinderella', as one historian has described her, were torment to Catherine. But that impenetrable mask did not falter. Had she shown hostility to Diane, she would have lost her husband's respect and her position at

court which secured her the dignity and the appearance of being queen, though she ranked only fourth behind the king, Diane, and her own friend and confidant, the great soldier Anne de Montmorency, Constable of France. The latter had become the queen's ally in disgust at the sight of innumerable rights and monopolies, and even the crown jewels themselves, being poured into Diane's lap by the besotted monarch. Diane herself encouraged the Constable's enemies – the splendid, ambitious Guises, Princes of Lorraine, one of whom described the Médicis as 'tradesmen who are not fit to call themselves our servants'. A weak

king who loved to be dominated, two skilful women, two powerful, arrogant families; these composed the uneasy equilibrium by which the government of France was maintained.

No woman who was basically evil could have endured the situation for so long without giving some hint of her true nature. Catherine reveals herself in her correspondence as longing for peace and friendship. She went out of her way to be pleasant to Diane, although she never ceased to resent the favourite's supremacy; Diane responded by nursing Catherine devotedly when, in 1552, she nearly died of scarlet fever. As queen mother,

1 The Place des Innocents, Rue St Denis, Paris. It marks the burial place of 1,100 Huguenots who fell in the Massacre of St Bartholomew instigated by Catherine to eliminate the Protestants.
2 A sixteenth-century medallion struck with a portrait of Henri III. His curious morals were ignored by Catherine who called him 'my dear eyes' and openly adored him.

Catherine used torture on prisoners only in the last resort; she never forgot a kindness shown to her; the 7,000 letters of her voluminous correspondence which survive contain innumerable recommendations of her own servants and those of her friends. She was kind, generous, genuinely submissive to her husband – but not involved. The quality in Catherine which survives most strongly down the centuries is her detachment, her self-sufficiency.

Her sons, Francis II (1544–60), Charles IX (1550–74) and Henri III (1551–89), respected and feared her. Their kingdom was ruled as she thought best, only Henri III ever daring to oppose her. In their interest she delicately played off Huguenots against Catholics, endeavouring to prevent the ultimate tragedy of civil war, which might turn her sons off the throne as she had been turned out of Florence.

Family relations

She terrified her daughters whom she thought (in the case of Marguerite with good reason) to be thoroughly immoral, and hence in danger of failing to make good matches. When she discovered that Marguerite was in love with Henri de Guise and that the Cardinal of Lorraine, head of the Guise family, was contemplating their marriage, she allowed her half-insane son Charles to beat his sister until she was left half dead on the carpet of his room. When her sense of political expediency was outraged, as in the case of Marguerite, she was ruthless in her anger. But her son Henri's curious morals did not disturb her; these she regarded with disinterested tolerance. He was the only person for whom she ever showed love – as opposed to gratitude or friendship – calling that curious blend of kingly genius and infantile degenerate 'my dear eyes'.

It is not the purpose here to recount the history of her 30 years' rule of France as the widowed queen mother guiding three

sickly, neurotic sons; or her hand in the Massacre of St Bartholomew. More important is a consideration of her achievement during this time. She was in the almost intolerable position of having responsibility without power. Both Protestants and Catholics in France persistently suspected her efforts at peace-making; they could not believe that she was not possessed by the same fanaticism which possessed them, and each therefore assumed that she had been suborned by the other side. Her interest was above all to procure a state of peaceful compromise, not mutual devouring, provided that the safety of the throne was maintained. But she could not enforce her will, because her forces were simply never great enough to bring the opposing sides to heel.

With the Crown in such a position, the most likely danger was that of foreign intervention. This was what she feared and dreaded, and spent 30 years of Machiavellian negotiation trying to avoid. Both Elizabeth of England and Philip II of Spain were only too willing to step in and 'protect' France. By alliance with Philip, who married her daughter Elizabeth, and by the possibility of alliance with Elizabeth Tudor, who kept the Duc d'Anjou (later Henri III) dangling at her heels for 13 years by endless patient diplomacy – by enduring the sneers of foreign diplomats who knew her powerlessness – she staved off the tragedy of a foreign war.

Neither Spain nor England could ever find legitimate cause for interfering in French affairs. She inflicted a heavy defeat on Spain without firing a gun by

contriving the election of the then Duc d'Anjou as King of Poland. This gave him, together with her reigning son Charles IX, the 'two ends of the strap' which could be tightened round Austria to prevent the Holy Roman Emperor from joining with Philip II of Spain to attack France. One French historian writes of this election: 'Such was Catherine's great work – to lose all the ground gained by two years of intrigues and labour in a single day (that of St Bartholomew), to break so many hard-won alliances, and then to turn this Europe, simmering with indignation, inside-out like a glove: this was indeed the most striking triumph of her diplomacy!'

A triumph of diplomacy

But perhaps the most striking of her triumphs was the fact that after 30 years of hatred and slaughter, there still existed, as one entity, a country unconquered by the greedily watching powers of Europe. She could not save it for her line; the degenerate blood of the Valois had failed to provide an heir. But France still held together. It came, however, perilously near total disintegration in the last months of her life when she was deserted by her capricious son, Henri III, and deprived of power. As Catherine lay on her death-bed Henri made what she knew was the disastrous mistake of assassinating the Duc de Guise and the Cardinal de Lorraine, Catholic leaders in the pay of Philip of Spain, who wanted France neutralized by internal wars while he sent the armada against England. It had been a desperate attempt to assert his authority as king, but the Catholic Guise faction reacted immediately and rose against him while the Spanish ambassador poured in gold to keep the strife stirring, and the Huguenot army, in its turn, advanced into France from the north. 'This is the end of the kingdom', wrote the Venetian ambassador; the king's dominions were reduced to three loyal towns: Tours, Blois, Beaugency. They had never been so small since the English heyday in France before the appearance of Joan of Arc. Just in time, Henri III sought an alliance with the Huguenot leader, Henri of Navarre, his oldest enemy. The treaty which they signed six months after Catherine's death, in 1589, saved the monarchy. It wiped out – at least politically – the memory of St Bartholomew, and in the nick of time preserved France whole for a king whose aim was religious toleration and strong government.

'Every other consideration being set aside,' Machiavelli had written when Catherine was a little girl, 'that course alone must be taken which procures the existence of the country and preserves its liberty.' As a political morality it is limited in its concept and short on ideals: but it was Catherine's morality and she lived by it. Her reward was to die alone in her château at Blois. Even there, where she was adored and venerated, little sorrow was felt at her death. As much respect, it was said, would have been shown for a dead goat. Catherine's subtle and elusive genius took its secrets to the grave. They have not yet been fathomed.

On the Eve of St Bartholomew

The massacre of the Huguenots was instigated on the night of 23 August 1572 by a ruthless and selfish woman, Catherine de Médicis. But even this desperate measure failed to save her line.

IT WAS a hot, tense August night. The old city of Paris – in 1572 a rabbit-warren of narrow streets hemmed in by tall wooden houses – stank and sweltered. Always crowded, it was more so than usual, for six days earlier the Queen Mother's daughter Marguerite had been married to the French Protestants' leader, young King Henri of Navarre, a little independent kingdom in the Pyrenees. The city's inns were filled with his followers, while the many nobles and country squires who supported him had come with their retinues to fill the houses of their relatives and the royal palace of the Louvre. There should have been music and dancing on such a night; but few were in a mood for this. The air was heavy with suspicion and fear.

Two days earlier, on 22 August, an unknown assassin had unsuccessfully tried to kill the admiral Gaspard de Coligny, the Protestant leader, whom the Queen Mother was known to regard as the most dangerous man in her kingdom. Nobody doubted that her authorization had been given to the sniper who fired at the Admiral from the window of a house. The Queen Mother knew that the Protestants – in France called Huguenots – would not rest until they discovered who was behind the attempted murder, and that when they did so, the civil wars of religion which had been tearing the country apart for the last ten years, would break out once more. Moreover Charles IX, the king of France and a neurotic youth of 22, usually dominated by his mother and the great Catholic nobles, had a dangerous admiration for the forceful Huguenot Admiral. He had already been heard to declare that vengeance should seek out the would-be murderers.

Fatal persuasion

Secretly, on St Bartholomew's Eve, 23 August, the Queen Mother, Catherine de Médicis, went to her son's room. She could see only one way out of this intolerable situation if the crown of France were to be saved for her family. It was a simple lethal solution which she had in mind. Far into the night, Catherine talked: of Huguenot plots to murder the king, to take over the crown, to sell France to her enemy, England. She talked until the king, in a state of hysterical subjection, agreed to the order which only he could give – the order to execute 'those who intend to rise against the state'.

Within minutes the bell of the church of St Germain l'Auxerrois was clanging out the tocsin, the alarm-bell which for centuries had signalled the citizens of Paris to take up arms. Catherine's plans were thoroughly organized. Soldiers scoured through the palace, pulling Huguenot

1

nobles and their wives from bed and killing them on the spot. One man broke away and rushed shrieking into the room of the newly-married Princess Marguerite, pushing her in front of his naked body as a shield. Another was dragged away and murdered before her eyes. A party of soldiers set off for the Admiral's house; this time they made no mistake about their task.

Out in the streets the citizens were awake, and ready to pay off old scores. To them the Huguenots were both blasphemers and traitors, enemies of God and of the crown alike. Killing them was to do a favour to both. Couriers had ridden out from the Louvre as soon as the king signed the warrant, warning the provinces to demonstrate their loyalty in the same manner as the people of Paris, and within the next few days similar massacres took place in many cities where the Huguenots were in a minority. When the Pope heard he assembled his cardinals to chant a Te Deum, and a special coin was struck to commemorate the event.

But what was it that had placed the government of France in such an impossible position, that the threat of civil war could be resolved only by mass murder? To answer the question, we must go back to the moment in 1559 when King Henri II, husband of Catherine de Médicis, died of the wound he had received during a ceremonial joust, leaving as his successors four boys, the eldest of whom was only 15.

2

1 Catherine de Médicis (1519–89). Ruthless and intelligent, it was she who persuaded the sickly Charles IX to order the massacre of the Huguenots on the night of 23 August 1572. He died less than two years later, a complete mental wreck.
2 Despite all her efforts, Catherine could not save her line. In 1589 the last of her sons, Henri III, was struck down by a maniac. In came Henry IV (above), the 'Gamecock from Navarre'.

In the sixteenth century, monarchy was an intensely personal thing; it was to the king, not the state, that the people's loyalty was given. But only if the king had personal power as well as this loyalty could a stable rule be assured. With a young king, therefore, the ruler's power in effect went to the highest bidder. Catherine, guarding her son's rights, found she had three families to contend with.

Three rivals for power

The *Bourbons* were princes of the blood, claiming descent from Louis IX. Their leader was Prince Louis de Condé, not yet 30, a restless, ambitious, able soldier and a Huguenot convert. The *Guises,* a brilliant Catholic family from Lorraine, had been raised to favour by previous kings of France. The third family was that of the highest soldier in France, the Constable, Anne de *Montmorency,* and also Catholic.

Because of events in the recently-ended Italian wars, this family hated the Guises, particularly the Constable's three nephews, all of whom had been converted to the Huguenot faith. The eldest of these was Gaspard de Coligny, the Admiral: brave, loyal, of noble spirit, he was the only man to emerge without reproach from the whole sorry tangle.

As these three families competed for influence over the young king, the religious teaching of Calvin made steady progress throughout France. It offered a strict discipline in contrast with the licence of the Court, and earnest, hard-working pastors instead of absentee priests. It was organized in a logical way which appealed to the temperament of the French middle-class professional men (lawyers, doctors, etc.) and the country gentry who became its main adherents. At a time of persecution, when tales of Queen Mary's martyrs were coming from England with every boat, it gave to its followers the inestimable comfort of knowing that they were elect, predestined to salvation, fighting those already condemned to eternal damnation.

Gradually, as the new religion took force, local disorder spread. Condé fomented it by an attempt, the conspiracy of Amboise, to kill the king and the two Guise lords, and take over power himself. When this failed he joined his brother, the king of Navarre (father of Henri) and

1

3

4

2

1 The marriage of Henri II to Catherine de Médicis. For 30 years, she stirred up wars between the Huguenots and Catholics, siding with either as her selfishness dictated.
2 *La St-Barthélemy* by François Dubois shows all the horror of the Huguenot massacre. Yet in Rome the Pope applauded and Philip II of Spain sent his personal congratulations.
3 Millais's famous painting, *The Huguenot*, in which a girl vainly tries to persuade her lover to wear the white scarf of the Catholics, embodies the awful dilemma so many faced.
4 Gaspard de Coligny, Admiral and leader of the Huguenots, renowned for his courage. But his influence over Charles IX was his death-warrant; his murder was authorized by the Queen Mother.

raised an army to march on the Court. The Guises fell upon this Bourbon uprising; the king of Navarre hastily abandoned his brother, and Condé was arrested. At the same time, however, King François became dangerously ill. His next brother was not yet ten; an official Regent would have to be appointed, and by his birth the king of Navarre held the best claim to this post. Catherine could foresee the turmoil into which a Huguenot Regent would

throw the country. Pursuing the policy of appeasement which she followed throughout her life – until circumstances overtook her – she promised a bargain: Condé's life for Navarre's rejection of his claim to be Regent. On 5 December 1560, she received Navarre's agreement to this in writing; on the same night the young king died, and his sickly, unstable brother succeeded him as Charles IX.

The uneasy peace

Catherine appeared to have achieved a sort of peace; she had brought Bourbons and Guises together at Court and persuaded them to be apparent friends; she had issued amnesties which calmed the outbursts of Catholic-Huguenot violence in the provinces. Now she faced the task of settling the religious problem, and chose to do it by arranging debates between the leading clerics and scholars of the two Churches, herself entertaining two leading Calvinist theologians at Court along with Coligny, whom she personally admired.

The talks failed – not surprisingly to anyone but the Queen Mother, who oper-

ated from expediency rather than principles and could not realize just how passionately held were the principles which divided the two parties. An Edict of Toleration which she issued in 1562, and which permitted, under certain conditions, liberty of worship to the Huguenots, might have brought peace, but the king of Navarre decided at this point to 'rat' on Catherine and his co-religionists alike. Abjuring his beliefs, he sought the help of the Catholic leaders, the Guises and the Constable, in deposing her and establishing himself as Regent after all – 'to save the country from the Huguenot threat'. In panic, she asked Coligny to find out what forces the Huguenot Churches could raise in defence of the monarchy – since her two Catholic factions with Henry of Navarre had now allied against her. So the Huguenots abandoned the policy of passive resistance which their preachers had been urging, mustered their arms and prepared to fight – for the Queen Mother.

To this potentially explosive situation, François Duc de Guise set light. Coming across a barnful of Huguenots worshipping in a town called Vassey (against the

terms of the edict, which said they must be outside the city wall), he ordered his soldiers to attack. Some 30 of the peaceful congregation were killed, over 100 wounded. The civil war blazed into being.

Coligny's 'unfortunate honesty'

For Catherine it was a good war, for all the trouble-makers were either killed or captured; the tiresome king of Navarre died, the ambitious Duc de Guise was assassinated, the Constable and Condé were each taken by the opposing side.

She promptly let the captive leaders make the peace treaty, which they did efficiently, although the terms were severe enough to dissatisfy many of the Huguenots, since they granted freedom of worship for the Protestant aristocracy only. Guise's assassin, however (before he was torn apart by four wild horses), swore that Coligny had employed him. Coligny at once published a firm denial, but added with what one historian calls 'unfortunate honesty' that he was glad Guise was dead, as he was an enemy of God and the king. From then on the Admiral's days were numbered. Both the unsuccessful attempt on his life just before the Massacre and his final murder, though authorized by the Queen Mother – whose admiration for the Admiral never blinded her to the expediency of his removal – were carried out by the Guise family and their men.

After four years of uneasy peace, the failure of another Huguenot plot against the king provoked a flare-up of the war, this time with singular ferocity. Atrocities were committed on both sides; Montmorency was killed in 1567; two major battles were fought at Jarnac and Montcontour, both Catholic victories, and in the first – or rather, after it was all over and the Huguenots had surrendered – Condé was shot in the back. Coligny could, for the first time, assume unchallenged leadership of the Huguenots and in 1570, despite his military defeats, he negotiated a favourable peace which recognized more fully than ever before the importance of the Huguenots as a distinctive new force in the kingdom.

Intervention abroad

It was at this time, as the exhausted country licked its wounds, that Coligny decided to strengthen the Huguenot position by engaging in alliances outside France. In April 1572 he signed – together with the late king of Navarre's exuberant young heir, Henri – a defensive treaty with England, and produced a plan to combine with the inhabitants of the Netherlands (who had been trying to gain independence from Spain for years) and free the provinces of Artois and Flanders from Spain by adding them to France. Again Catherine took fright. Spanish troops lined the Franco-Netherlands border, commanded by the terrible Duke of Alva, and only waiting to move in if France threatened Spanish territory. She knew that Elizabeth of England might support Huguenot help for the Netherlands, but would not extend this to watching quietly while a slice of the country became absorbed into France – even Huguenot France. Catherine had arranged a marriage between

Leader of the Catholics was the ambitious Henri Duc de Guise. He actively participated in the St Bartholomew Massacre, and met his own death at the hand of an assassin in 1588.

Henri, the little, rough Southerner from Navarre and her own elegant (though somewhat depraved) daughter; as a piece of statecraft it might work – 'peaceful co-existence' might just be achieved – if only the dominating Coligny could be removed from the scene.

The Guises, their blood-feud against Coligny still unsettled, all chafing at the sight of the king under his influence, were the obvious people to turn to for help. Had their servant's shot from the window succeeded in killing Coligny, it is possible that the Massacre might never have happened.

1 During the Massacre, which lasted in Paris from 24 August to 17 September, and until 3 October in the provinces, the English Embassy was a refuge for all fortunate enough to escape.

It did not profit the Queen Mother. After the wretched Charles IX died raving, his brother Henri III succeeded – a potentially able man who was also an exhibitionistic homosexual, given to fits of morbid penitence when he would organize processions of flagellants through the streets of Paris. From La Rochelle the Huguenots who had survived defied the king, and once more war broke out. Humiliated again and again by the Guises, whose power was no longer checkmated by Coligny, Henri III too sought refuge in the deadly solution of the knife: his men surprised and hacked to death both the Duc de Guise and his brother the Cardinal of Lorraine. 'Now I am King of France,' said Henri. 'I have killed the king of Paris.' It must have seemed the final irony to many Frenchmen when a few months later a maniac struck down the king and the long Valois dynasty was ended.

In came the little 'game-cock from Navarre', cynical enough (or tolerant enough) to renounce his Huguenot faith for the sake of assuming the throne, loving his people, intelligent, humane, eager to repair the wrongs of 30 years' warfare, which had turned half France into a desert. Henry IV abandoned his own religious preferences, but he did not forget his old friends. By the Edict of Nantes, in 1598, he gave the Huguenots freedom of conscience throughout his kingdom, liberty to hold services wherever established and in at least one place in each district, an absolute equality with Catholics in all employments. He made France, which had seen so much misery in the name of religion, the first country in Europe to have religious liberty. Henceforth, prejudice was legally powerless; he had taken the first, the most difficult and the greatest step towards integration of Protestant and Catholic into one nation.

2 With the first light of dawn on 24 August, soldiers of the Guise family attacked Coligny in his house. Blow after blow was struck before he was thrown from a window and killed.

Ivan the Terrible

He is notorious for his cruelty and misdeeds, but Ivan IV had the vision and intelligence to recognize Russia's great potential, and his reforms went far to achieving its realization.

1

2

3

IVAN THE TERRIBLE must be judged one of Russia's most outstanding but strangest leaders. His reign saw war and destruction, countless bloody executions of his enemies, many of them innocent, and acts of cruelty barbarous even by the standards of the sixteenth century.

His title, Ivan 'Grozny' – literally meaning 'the Dread' – was well deserved. In character he was brutal and capricious, plagued by suspicion and distrust of almost everyone around him. Yet he was also a man of intelligence, with the vision to see ahead to the greatness and power of Russia, and with the vigour and determination to lead his people to the beginnings of nationhood. And on his death his people grieved for him, to an extent never before seen in Russia.

The kernel of Russia

When Ivan was born in Moscow in 1530, most European countries were already well advanced in the process of becoming nation states. England was flowering under Henry VIII, and later Elizabeth. Despite the strife of the Reformation, England was clearly a nation, reasonably secure from its enemies, expanding its trade overseas, and with a degree of culture and civilization acknowledged throughout the world. By contrast Ivan's principality of Muscovy, the kernel of the disunited lands occupied by the Russian peoples, was backward and undeveloped. Moreover, these lands had for two centuries been ravaged by the Tartars.

By the fourteenth century the Tartars had retreated and by Ivan's reign Muscovy had emerged as the strongest principality. But it was surrounded by enemies. With no

fixed borders there were constant wars and skirmishes. In the south and east there were the Tartars, continually raiding Russian territory. To the west, Lithuania and Poland were determined to deny Muscovy access to the Baltic. And semi-independent city-states like Novgorod and Pskov were thorns in the side of a Muscovy which wished to extend its rule over all the Russian people.

Most Russians wanted the creation of one, strong state. After centuries of devastation by war and plague they desired security and stability; above all they needed a powerful leader.

Ivan the Terrible's father, Vasily, and his grandfather, Ivan III, had already

1 When he was barely 17, Ivan astounded Moscow by announcing that he would be crowned Tsar of all Russia. For his crown he chose one of gold and jewels with sable trim.

2 After his return from Alexandrov, Ivan was a changed man. He instigated a rule of violent terror, and when the Metropolitan Philip bravely protested Ivan had him strangled.

3 A scene from Eisenstein's film, *Ivan the Terrible,* showing Ivan looking down on the long trail of Muscovites come to Alexandrov to plead with him to return to his city.

laid the foundations of strong, centralized government. But when Vasily died, in 1533 Ivan IV, heir to Muscovy at this crucial time in its history, was barely three years old. Within a few years his heritage was in a state of anarchy and chaos, and Ivan himself went through a tormented childhood. For a time his mother Elena, an ambitious and forceful woman, maintained order as regent, but when Ivan was only seven she died, believed poisoned by one of the groups of boyars (Russian aristocracy) plotting to seize power. After his mother's death Ivan was on his own. He had a nurse and one or two boyars he trusted and liked, but they were taken from him. He was neglected, often cold and hungry. 'What suffering did I endure through lack of clothing and through hunger', he was to write later.

For the boyars, the rule of a child presented an opportunity to regain some of the power they had lost as Muscovy grew stronger and more centralized. They might have stood some chance of restraining the growth of rule by one all-powerful man had they been at all united as a class. But instead, they were bitterly divided. Faction fought faction in a desperate, greedy struggle for power. Little thought was given to their country's problems; they were too concerned with their own selfish interests. Their irresponsibility was to lead Ivan to believe that only by ruling alone and crushing the boyars could he save Russia from their stranglehold.

Ivan himself could hardly escape the influence of the brutality and violent conflict around him. The boyars even fought and killed each other in the halls of Ivan's Kremlin palace. He was encouraged to indulge a taste for cruelty and one of his pastimes was to gallop with his boyhood friends at full speed through the streets of Moscow, knocking down any citizens in their way. The people themselves protested little; coarseness and savage brutality were accepted parts of their lives.

Before long the quarrelling boyars found that the field of power was no longer theirs alone. In 1543, at the tender age of 13, Ivan struck. After lecturing the boyars for their misdeeds he suddenly ordered the arrest of the most powerful boyar at that time, Andrei Shuisky. Ivan then had him thrown to a pack of savage dogs, to be torn limb from limb. Thirty of his supporters were hanged on roadside gibbets. It was Ivan's first gesture of the dictatorial power he was later to wield. His people welcomed it – to them Shuisky's faction had run the state like selfish tyrants. And from this time the boyars were aware that their grand prince was no longer just a boy, but a force to be reckoned with. Suddenly he was respected and feared.

Russia's first Tsar

By the age of 17, Ivan had decided to be crowned, not simply as Muscovy's grand prince but as Ivan IV 'Tsar of all Russia'. This was unheard of – no previous ruler of Muscovy had been crowned as Tsar, originally the Russian title for the Byzantine Emperor. Ivan was proclaiming to the world that Muscovy was the heir to Byzantium as the defender of the Orthodox Christian faith. More than this, Ivan wished it understood that his power and authority came from God and could not be challenged.

For Ivan was nurturing great dreams. He had not spent all his early years playing barbaric games. Left alone, he had turned to books. He hungrily devoured Greek and Roman history, and what the chroniclers had written about the past of his own land. Impressed by the great heroes he read about, he came to see himself as the divinely ordained all-powerful ruler of Russia, an insecure and divided land he intended to mould into a great nation.

The new Tsar had had little experience of his people, and shortly after his crowning he received a rude shock. After a great fire in Moscow, Ivan was confronted by an angry mob who believed the fire had been started by one of the ruling boyar families close to the Tsar. Although he dispersed the mob by executing its leaders, Ivan was disturbed that much of

his people's anger had been directed at him personally. He had no wish to offend his people, and he needed their support against the boyars.

In the early years of his rule, barely out of his teens, Ivan relied heavily on his advisers. To them fell the responsibility of running the state and introducing reforms. It was significant that Ivan's closest advisers were not aristocratic boyars but men of the middle classes, like Adashev, his chamberlain, a man from the minor gentry, or the monk Sylvester, the court chaplain and Ivan's leading adviser. To have these humble men as his ministers was a definite break with Russian tradition and a rebuff to the boyars. But reforms were most necessary. For almost a century Muscovy had been expanding; its system of government, unable to keep up, creaked and groaned.

For the ordinary people the most needed reform was in the administration of justice. This was largely in the hands of local governors with enormous powers which they often abused. Unpaid, they lived by 'feeding' off their people, extorting as much money as they could, and there

Ivan IV of Russia (1530–84) as portrayed in a contemporary ikon. He led his people to the beginnings of nationhood and ranks as one of Russia's first and most far-sighted statesmen.

were no appeals against governors' decisions. But in the 1550s a new legal code was drawn up and the powers of local governors restricted. A special petitions office – virtually a high court of appeal – was set up for the people's complaints. Later the governors were replaced by less powerful sheriffs, and the system of 'feeding' abolished. With a new system of central departments, Moscow began to run the whole country.

If Russia was to survive, let alone defeat its numerous enemies, it needed not only stronger government but a more efficient military system. Ivan's reforms extended his grandfather's system of military fiefs. To men who entered into a bond of service he granted land, thus creating a new class of serving gentry, a counter to the unreliable boyars and more directly tied to Ivan himself. One of the biggest problems with the boyars was their wretched tradition of 'precedence'. Able commanders could not be promoted except in strict order; rival officers squabbled over their appointments, even on the battlefield. Seeing the effects of this ludicrous system for himself, Ivan passed new laws to give junior officers more responsibility and tighten up discipline. He also introduced a regular army: previously all soldiers had been haphazardly recruited as needed.

1 The Cathedral of St Basil in Moscow is an outstanding monument to Ivan IV. But legend tells that Ivan later had the architect blinded so he could never again create anything so beautiful.

2 A print of an Easter festival in sixteenth-century Moscow with the Kremlin in the background. Ivan began the process of unification which ultimately made it the capital of all Russia.

3 When the English captain, Richard Chancellor, discovered the sea route to Russia through the White Sea, Ivan was delighted. But his subsequent plans for an alliance with England all failed.

Military matters had become of increasing importance to Ivan himself. At the precocious age of 15, eager to arouse popular enthusiasm, he had launched his first military campaign against Muscovy's enemies in the west, the Tartars of Kazan. After several abortive campaigns Ivan returned in 1551, determined to subdue his stubborn enemy. This time, after days of savage fighting and using explosives to blast Kazan's walls, Ivan was triumphant. He returned to Moscow amid wild celebrations, a conqueror and a hero. Not long afterwards he brought Astrakhan, the Tartar land to the south, under his control. Muscovy had at last taken the offensive against its neighbours, whose defeat opened the way for further colonization.

Fearful of treachery

Flushed with the plaudits of the people for his triumphs in war, Ivan felt ready to rule alone and he began to push his advisers aside. Sylvester wanted another war in the south, against the Crimean Tartars. Ivan disagreed; more interested in gaining an outlet to the west, he attacked Livonia. Before long both Sylvester and Adashev had lost their power and left Ivan's court. But fearing all kinds of plots and treachery, and growing increasingly hostile to criticism, Ivan rounded up some of their supporters and had them executed. As his personal power grew he resorted more to harsh violence. The death of his wife Anastasia in 1560 saddened him, and it removed the one calming influence from his life.

He grew more and more suspicious of his boyars. When he suddenly fell gravely ill, all their petty rivalries were exposed once more over the question of the succession. Then in the middle of the war with Livonia, one of his most trusted commanders, Prince Kurbsky, defected to the enemy. More than that, he incited all Muscovy's enemies to attack her. Then he turned on the Tsar, writing bitter letters expressing a burning and highly personal

As Ivan grew older he became increasingly irascible and suspicious. In one terrible frenzy he fatally struck his eldest son Ivan, leaving the succession open to the feeble-minded Fedor.

hatred for Ivan himself.

To Ivan, such disloyal treachery unleashed all his suspicions and fears of the boyars generally. He believed they hated him and were plotting the downfall of his state. He decided to 'abdicate'. In 1564, without any warning, he left Moscow for Alexandrov in the country.

After a month he sent messages back to Moscow, telling the people that his anger was not against them but against the boyars. But the people, by now thoroughly alarmed at the strange absence of their leader, wanted Ivan back. Some set out for Alexandrov to persuade Ivan to return. Ivan agreed, but only on certain conditions – that he should be free to rule as he thought necessary, and to punish traitors as he thought best.

Ivan returned to Moscow a changed man. Physically he was stooped, haggard and unkempt. He had apparently been through some kind of nervous breakdown. Changed in himself, he proceeded to alter the structure of the state. He set up the Oprichnina, the Tsar's independent private state within the country, his own personal realm. On this state he was to withdraw, secure from all traitors, surrounded by his own special guards, who swore allegiance to Ivan personally. The purpose of this seems partly to have been Ivan's desperate need for personal security, partly a plan to crush the boyars.

The creation of his realm brought incredible confusion and suffering. Land was needed. Many boyars were simply dispossessed of their estates. Some were given other lands; others had to search for them, stranded, with their families, in the bitterly cold winter of 1565.

Meanwhile, under Ivan's guards, the 'Tsar's men', a vicious reign of terror began. Muscovy became virtually a police state. Ivan's raging fury selected vast numbers of victims; his men, in special black uniforms, put them to death in various barbarous fashions. Merchants and townspeople were plundered. All law broke down – there was no justice, no appeal against the Tsar's men. Metropolitan Philip, Ivan's own choice for the post, was strangled for daring to criticize. Fearing treachery from Novgorod, Ivan plundered, tortured and massacred its

inhabitants. Sixty thousand died. Famine and plague devastated the country. Only after eight years of savage chaos did Ivan abandon the Oprichnina and his ruinous policy of terror.

Despite these internal troubles, the war in the west had continued. Ivan saw that access to western Europe was Russia's only chance to break out of her backwardness, but her western neighbours, Poland, Lithuania and Sweden, feared a strong Russia and tried to prevent her trading or learning from the west. Ivan had therefore been delighted when British adventurers discovered a route to Russia through the White Sea.

By granting English traders privileges, he planned an alliance with Elizabeth I. But in vain; the English queen was far too shrewd to embroil herself with Russia's enemies. Nor, in the end, was he able to gain his foothold on the Baltic, despite 28 years of fighting in Livonia. It was to be left to Peter the Great, nearly 150 years later, to achieve Ivan's Baltic ambitions.

Both feared and loved

When Ivan died in 1584, his people mourned as if they had lost a favourite son. Many years earlier an English visitor had written: 'no prince in Christendom is more feared of his own than he is, nor better beloved.' Not all the trouble and misery of his reign could turn the people against him. To them he was a leader, their defender against Russia's enemies, including the treacherous boyars.

For the next century at least, Ivan was remembered not as 'the Terrible', but as a conqueror. For above all Ivan cared about Russia as a nation; he had defended and expanded her frontiers in all directions, even in his last years into Siberia. And despite all the strife he brought a degree of stability which became most apparent after his death. Ivan had believed his boyars were incapable of governing his country; as Russian history entered the time of the Troubles, events justified his fears.

In 1584, whilst playing a game of chess, Ivan suffered a severe stroke, and in the last moments before his death assumed the monastic hood, dying as the monk Jonah.

Queen without master

Elizabeth I, Queen of England and Ireland, was an outstanding sovereign and woman in whom strength of character, ingenuity and cunning were combined with an innate talent for rule.

NO SINGLE PERIOD of the story of England is more dazzling for its wealth of individual characters than the second half of the sixteenth century. In those 50 pulsating years lived seamen like Raleigh, Frobisher and Drake, politicians like Howard, Burleigh and Walsingham, writers like Shakespeare, Jonson and Spenser.

Over this history-making group of men ruled a woman whose own individuality was even more impressive. Elizabeth I was a woman of violent temper, with a brilliant gift for courting popularity. She was cunning, excitable and vain; a slave to excessive fashion. She dabbled in alchemy yet was a brilliant scholar, able to speak six languages fluently. Undoubtedly the rough, unscrupulous and talented men who peopled England in the Elizabethan age took their lead from their sovereign.

Elizabeth was born at Greenwich Palace, the favourite home of her parents, Henry VIII and his second wife Anne Boleyn, on 7 September 1533. At three months she was sent to Hatfield House, where she was educated and grew to womanhood while her capricious father went through the gamut of marriage and remarriage which enlivens the pages of Tudor history.

Shadows of danger and death

When Elizabeth was only three years old her mother was executed and the little princess branded with the stigma of illegitimacy. Neglected by the king, her life at Hatfield was hard and loveless. When she was in her teens, Tudor gossips revelled in the addresses made to her by Sir Thomas Seymour, the Lord Admiral of England, who was much her senior in years. Rumour-mongers declared that Elizabeth was guilty of all sorts of infamous conduct with the elderly admiral, and the malicious were eagerly watching for any signs of emotion she might show when news of his execution was brought to her in 1549. Instead, the young princess, who had no doubt been extremely fond of the admiral, showed some of the self-command which was later to endear her to her subjects by remarking, 'This day died a man with much wit and very little judgement.'

Death and danger punctuated Elizabeth's youth at Hatfield with frightening regularity. Her sickly brother Edward reigned only very briefly after the death of her father before he died in 1553. To her good fortune she played no part in the Duke of Northumberland's subsequent struggle for the Crown through Lady Jane Grey, and when Elizabeth's elder sister, Mary Tudor, won her rightful crown from the scheming duke, Elizabeth, then 20 years old, rode by Mary's side as the new queen made her triumphant entry into

1 A view of London in the sixteenth century, with London Bridge, centre. London was the heart of activity in Elizabeth's England, and one of the most glittering capitals of the time.
2 Philip II of Spain (1527–98), husband of Mary Tudor, later suitor for Elizabeth's hand. His intervention on Elizabeth's behalf saved her from almost certain execution.

London to begin her rule.

This manifestation of sisterly tenderness was not to last. Mary had been raised as a Catholic and her intention of restoring the Mass and other Catholic ceremonials filled the Protestants with alarm. They saw in Elizabeth, whose upbringing was Protestant, their rallying point, and soon the court was alive with plots to put Elizabeth in Mary's place. The plots could not fail to come to the ears of Mary, and Elizabeth attempted to escape them by retiring to the country.

This prudent move failed to minimize the danger to Mary. On 12 February 1554, shortly after Sir Thomas Wyatt's abortive rebellion, Elizabeth was summoned to London by her sister the queen. Eleven days later, ill from worry and a prisoner of state, she arrived in the capital, which was 'covered in gibbets, and the public buildings crowded with the heads of the bravest men in the kingdom'. The crowds lining the London pavements to watch the arrival of the young Princess Elizabeth were certain that another royal execution was about to take place.

Elizabeth was sent to the Tower of London, where she was kept a close prisoner while the Great Council debated her fate. Without doubt, the future queen's life hung on a thread during that year and without doubt, too, her liberation came as the result of an unexpected intervention. When Philip of Spain, husband of Mary Tudor, realized that his wife was unlikely to provide him with an heir to the English throne, he saw that if Elizabeth were removed there would be no barrier to Mary Stuart, Queen of Scots, becoming queen in her stead. Mary Stuart was also the daughter-in-law of the King of France, Philip's greatest rival, and if she were to become Queen of England the balance of power would be heavily weighed against Philip's Spain. Philip saw then the importance of Elizabeth's life, even if she were a Protestant. The result was that Mary released Elizabeth and allowed her to return to Hatfield.

On 15 November 1558, Mary Tudor died and Elizabeth was summoned to London to begin, at the age of 25, one of the most momentous reigns in English history. It had, however, an inauspicious beginning. Plague and famine had decimated London, the nation was dispirited by the loss of

1 Lord Burleigh, the originator and director of much of Elizabeth's policy. As Secretary of State, he organized a network of spies to detect plots against the queen.

2 The death of the armada. In 1588 Philip II sent 130 ships to invade England. But a storm shattered the fleet before it arrived, and Spain suffered a humiliating defeat.

3 The triumphant entry of Mary I with the Princess Elizabeth into London in 1553. Elizabeth soon became a rallying point for the Protestants, who wished to make her queen instead.

Calais, the Exchequer was empty, and religious strife ran high enough for the contemplation of civil war. Nor was the new queen's personal life free from difficulty. Having rejected the pressures of half a dozen suitors for a marriage while still a princess, she was now pressed to become the wife of Philip of Spain, her sister's widower. In rejecting him too, she knew that she was losing the friendship of Spain, her only strength against a hostile France and Scotland.

Philip's suit ended with his marriage to Elizabeth of France, leaving the field for Queen Elizabeth's hand open to all the princes of Europe, most of whom were zealously enthusiastic to marry her, as well as all the eligible Englishmen with any claims to nobility and quite a few without any such claims. Her choice for court favourite fell upon Lord Robert Dudley, her Master of Horse. When Dudley's wife died in mysterious circumstances the queen's interest in him appeared to quicken. She made him Earl of Leicester and Baron of Denbigh, and foreign ambassadors to the English court sent back word to their princes that the English queen was certain to marry the handsome Earl of Leicester.

Elizabeth, however, was ever quixotic. While Leicester was at the height of her favour and a marriage was the talk of the court, the queen told the French ambassador, 'I will never concede to a husband

Tall, with reddish-gold hair, Elizabeth I was an impressive figure. Yet she refused to marry declaring: 'I will never concede to a husband any share of my power'.

any share in my power. For the sake of posterity and the good of the realm, I will not marry.'

Such determination did not please the Protestant faction. The birth of a son to the Catholic Mary Queen of Scots, who had married Henry, Lord Darnley, and was regarded as England's rightful queen by most of the Catholics in Britain, gave them more cause for alarm about the succession. They sent 20 peers to Elizabeth, entreating her either to choose a consort or name a successor, to whom the queen scornfully replied, 'You are hair-brained politicians, unfit to decide such matters.'

Typically, Elizabeth was contemptuous of Parliaments. She governed for years without one; then, when the Exchequer was empty, summoned a Parliament to whom she declared, 'You are not called together to make new laws or lose good hours in idle speeches, but to vote a supply to enable her Majesty to defend her realm against the hostile attempts of the King of Spain.' When the members asked for freedom of speech, the queen rejoined that they should have that freedom, but it was not to extend beyond 'yes' or 'no' – adding all manner of threats if either reply was against her own wishes.

Elizabeth could be just as capricious in matters of government and intrigue. On a number of occasions, she answered the rough language of the individual, noisy, unscrupulous and scheming members of

her cabinet in similar terms, calling one a fool and another a madman. When her cousins, the Ladies Mary and Katherine Grey, incurred her displeasure by secret marriages she had them both strictly confined in the Tower. But undoubtedly the blot on her reign was her treatment of Mary Queen of Scots, who, having fled to England in 1568 for refuge after an uprising in Scotland, was kept by Elizabeth in a state of imprisonment.

By a succession of arranged plots and planted spies it took Lord Burleigh, her Secretary of State, Leicester, Walsingham, and their colleagues in Elizabeth's cabinet, 18 years to convince the queen that Mary was so dangerous to her, her government and her Protestant subjects, that she must

be tried for treason, with execution as the inevitable result.

As, by Tudor standards, Elizabeth entered the valley of her years, she grew more unpredictable. At 49 she was playing at romance with the 23-year-old Duke of Anjou, drawing up a marriage contract and giving him a ring. At the eleventh hour Elizabeth began talking to the bewildered duke about her conflict of feeling between love and duty. The duke, tearing off the ring, declared that, 'The women of England were as changeable and capricious as their own climate, or the waves that encircled their island.' There is little doubt that Elizabeth used the duke as she used most of her royal wooers, as a tool for embarrassing others, and with his departure for France the hope of her probable marriage was finally abandoned.

But if, in her daily dealings, Elizabeth seemed an indecisive monarch, history has shown that she knew how to bide her

231

time wisely, that her caution often acted as a valuable counter to the wilfulness of her courtiers. Certainly, few of her near kinsmen at court matched her shrewdness, intelligence and ability to rule. When she gave an audience, said an eye-witness, 'her eye was set upon one, her ear listened to another, her judgement ran upon a third, to a fourth she addressed her speech; her spirit seemed to be everywhere and yet so entire in her self, as it seemed to be nowhere else.'

In no direction was Elizabeth's shrewdness of judgement more valuable to England than in foreign affairs. In this field she was governed by a profound dislike of war and of needless expense. Although she encouraged a covert war against Spain, she held back from the final provocation that would have compelled Philip to open war until 1587, when Mary Stuart was executed. The Catholic powers were incensed, and a year later the rupture between England and Spain had become so complete that Philip II openly claimed the English throne for himself, and sent his armada of 130 men-of-war to invade England.

Every sovereign has his finest hour and Elizabeth's was undoubtedly at Tilbury on a summer's day in 1588 when the armada was sailing into the English Channel. All along the coast, men and ships were gathered to repel the Spaniards, and it was typical of Elizabeth's courage that she wanted to travel to the coast to be among the first to come to grips with the invaders. Instead, the queen went in royal and martial pomp to the army camp at Tilbury, where she harangued the soldiers with her most famous speech.

'I have come amongst you . . . being resolved, in the midst and heat of the battle, to live and die amongst you all. . . . I know I have the body of a weak, feeble woman, but I have the heart and stomach of a king.'

No such sacrifice was called for, however. The armada foundered, Sir Francis Drake became a national hero and only Leicester was disappointed in the round of promotions and honours which followed.

Robert Devereux, Earl of Essex, and one of Elizabeth's favourites. He was sent to quell a rebellion in Ireland, but his attempted insurrection forced her to order his execution.

With the passing of time, new courtiers and new favourites came upon the scene to flutter like butterflies around the rose. The young ambitious Sir Walter Raleigh first came to the queen's notice through his military talents, and brilliantly furthered his career by laying his new plush cloak at the feet of Elizabeth when she was obliged to cross a muddy pool. Raleigh was introduced to Elizabeth by Sir Edmund Spenser, who courted success by eulogizing the queen with his poetry. But the Adonis among the new men who most caught the queen's eye was the young, graceful, and utterly impetuous Robert

Elizabeth shown watching a performance of a work by the dramatist, William Shakespeare. In an age crowded with talent, she lent her patronage freely and generously.

Devereux, Earl of Essex, and 33 years Elizabeth's junior.

Like the old favourites, the new ones were querulous and place-seeking to the exclusion of all principle. But fulfilment of their ambition was always made difficult by the unpredictability of their sovereign, who would pardon a would-be royal assassin caught red-handed in her presence and then endorse the burning or hanging, drawing and quartering of churchmen for 'promulgating erroneous opinions'. More than once the English army abroad was short of ammunition as a result of the queen's parsimony. Yet throughout her reign she lavished rewards on a long succession of selfish favourites who were never content. During frequent bursts of temper she swore at her ministers and struck her maids of honour. In church she would shout from her pew at the preacher if his sermon was not to her liking; then, outside, would present an entirely different and endearing face to the people, replying 'God bless you all, my people', to their cheers. The same queen who delighted in bear and bull baiting, and slew deer confined in a paddock with a crossbow, was the easiest of victims to unsubtle flattery and was prepared to forgive all for a word of praise.

Despite the favourite place he held, inevitably the impetuous Earl of Essex ran foul of the royal temper, until, in 1598, exasperated beyond the bounds of self-control by his vehement obstinacy, the queen 'gave him a sound box on the ear and bade him go and be hanged'.

Elizabeth as statesman

Rather than reconsider his words, Essex swore, uttered some words about 'a king in petticoats', and grasped his sword hilt with a menacing gesture. The upshot was that he retired immediately from the court and began to testify his resentment whereever possible. His arrest came after he had attempted an insurrection with 300 of his partisans.

Elizabeth's qualities of statesmanship were most evident during her declining years. Now that the danger of an insurrection, which had always been likely if she had named a successor, was passed, she made it known that James VI of Scotland, the son of Mary Queen of Scots, should succeed her. She spoke at length about the importance of maintaining the balance of power in Europe by restoring liberty to Germany through its own imperial elections, by making the United Provinces of the Netherlands an independent republic, and by annexing to them some of the German states.

In January 1603, in the forty-fifth year of her reign, the aged and enfeebled Elizabeth caught a cold, which added to the number of complaints already afflicting her. She gradually weakened and died on 24 March. She was interred the following month in Westminster Abbey, when a saddened England had had time to reflect upon the great age associated with her name, for, says a contemporary, 'There was such a general sighing, groaning and weeping as the like hath not been seen or known in the memory of Man.'

Overlords of Europe

At the height of its power the House of Habsburg could boast a pan-European empire, unprecedented grandeur and the title of Holy Roman Emperor: how did it achieve such eminence?

WHATEVER BELIEFS the Habsburg family may have cherished across the centuries they certainly did not share the age-old romantic adage that 'marriages are made in heaven'. Throughout their dynasty the Habsburgs proved themselves matchmakers *par excellence*. The very basis and driving force of their dynastic aspirations and eventual eminence was a meticulously calculated matrimonial policy. By pursuing it unremittingly the Habsburgs forged an empire which held sway in Europe for over 600 years.

The Habsburg ancestral home was Habichtsburg – hence the name of Habsburg – built by Werner, Bishop of Strasbourg, about 1020 A D at the junction of the Rivers Aar and Rhine in the canton of Aargau. His descendants styled themselves Counts of Habsburg and the great Habsburg saga began in 1273 when the comparatively insignificant Count Rudolf of Habsburg (1218–91) was elected Emperor of the Holy Roman Empire, a confederation of German princely states founded by Charlemagne in 800 A D.

Victory at Marchfeld

When the imperial electors, seven of the most important German princes, conferred the Holy Roman Crown on Rudolf they chose him in preference to the powerful Ottokar II of Bohemia in the hope that Rudolf would prove more pliable to their wishes and interests. Rudolf I, however, very soon revealed unsuspected martial and diplomatic qualities, much to Ottokar's discomfiture, and the armed confrontation which followed in 1278 at Marchfeld, near Vienna, ranks as one of the decisive combats in European history. The Bohemian king lost the battle as well as his life and the victorious Rudolf took possession of the Duchy of Austria, originally one of the bastions set up on the eastern fringe of Charlemagne's territories. Rudolf proclaimed the conquered duchy a hereditary Habsburg possession in 1282 and it represented the modest nucleus of the great administration of the House of Habsburg which was to endure until 1918. Another legacy inherited from the first of the Habsburgs was the famous protruding lower lip, a notable feature throughout the history of the family.

Gradually, additional territories were added to Austria by successive Habsburg dukes, promoting the Habsburgs to one of the most powerful German princely families of the time. Their prestige soared to new heights in 1438 when the crown of the Holy Roman Empire was bestowed on one of Rudolf's successors (Albert V), and from then on it remained in Habsburg possession almost without break until 1806.

Archduke Frederick V – the archducal

1 A contemporary cartoon of the 1815 Congress of Vienna showing the European powers dividing up the remainder of Napoleon's empire. The same congress saw the replacement of the Holy Roman Empire by the German Confederation with Austria accorded the leadership in perpetuity.
2 Rudolf I, the first Habsburg to be elected Holy Roman Emperor.

dignity was created by Rudolf IV who ruled from 1358 to 1365 – became Holy Roman Emperor in 1452 as Frederick III. This remarkable Habsburg had an obsessive belief in the inevitable destiny of Habsburg glory and grandeur. He invented the mystic initials A E I O U, variously interpreted as proclaiming to the world: 'All the Earth is subject to Austria' – and he caused the device to be inscribed in all his books and engraved on all public buildings.

Frederick engineered the marriage between his son Maximilian and Maria, the heiress of Charles the Bold of Burgundy, bringing within the Habsburg orbit the rich province of Flanders and large parcels of modern France. And although the alliance triggered off the armed conflict between the Habsburgs and the French which was to be a feature of European history for centuries to come, it was one of the most important stepping-stones to the Habsburgs' European eminence. Maximilian I did even better for his family by betrothing his son Philip to Joanna, the heiress of Spain, while his grandson Ferdinand, by an adroitly manoeuvred double matrimonial coup of Maximilian, netted the kingdoms of Bohemia and Hungary in 1526. In a way, the acquisition of the two kingdoms was the inception of the Austrian monarchy but it altogether

altered the character and complexion of the Habsburg realm, for the additions resulted in the incorporation of several nationalities of totally different tongues and traditions. This crucial factor eventually proved the principal cause of the disintegration and fall of the Habsburg empire.

The one monarch of world stature produced by the House of Habsburg was Charles V (1500–58) – the offspring of Philip and Joanna. Charles was the greatest European potentate of the sixteenth century and with his reign the Habsburgs reached the zenith of their grandeur. He became the pan-European overlord of a huge empire embracing the Netherlands, Burgundy, the Austrian crown lands, Spain and all her possessions in Italy, as well as vast territories in the New World.

Throughout his reign he was engaged in wars with Francis I of France for the retention of his Italian possessions. The other major conflict of his life was with Martin Luther and his teachings. On becoming Holy Roman Emperor in 1519 on Maximilian's death, Charles V relinquished the sovereignty of the German and Austrian territories to his brother Ferdinand I, and the two brothers ruled from Spain and Austria respectively. In 1556 Charles V abdicated and retired to his favourite monastery. His son, Philip II (who married Mary Tudor, Queen of England), took over Spain, the Netherlands, Sicily and Sardinia. Ferdinand I kept the German lands and received the imperial crown.

Austria also took over from Spain the fiercely militant spirit of the Counter-Reformation, and throughout his reign as emperor (1556–64), Ferdinand I had to grapple with the twin tasks of defending the Catholic Church against the Protestant Reformation and the defence of Central Europe against the menacing spread of Turkish power. The latter preoccupied the Habsburgs for almost two centuries while the religious conflict resulted in the pernicious Thirty Years' War, (1618–48). It was eventually resolved with the Peace of Westphalia, marking an appreciable decline in Habsburg prestige.

The Turkish menace reached its most critical point in 1683 when Vienna was besieged by a huge Turkish army. The starving and exhausted city was on the brink of surrender when the imperial forces with Saxon, Swabian, Bavarian and Bohemian units joined hands with those of King Sobieski of Poland near the walls of the beleaguered city and inflicted a crushing defeat on the enemy. The Battle of Vienna saved Austria, as well as Europe, from the Turks, and although the victory was a continental rather than a national triumph, it served as a timely boost to the fluctuating prestige of the Habsburgs.

By a curious quirk of history both the Spanish and the Austrian branch of the dynasty became extinct at the same time, around 1700. In Spain the absence of a 2

1 Emperor Leopold I (1658–1705) disguised as a shepherd for a court theatrical. During his reign imperial forces helped to inflict a decisive defeat on the Turkish army besieging Vienna.
2 A royal banquet in honour of the marriage of first cousins, Leopold I and Margaret Theresa, daughter of the King of Spain. Such unions linked Europe in a network of imperial power.

male heir brought in its wake the long embittered War of the Spanish Succession (1701–14) embroiling nearly all Europe. The result was that the Bourbons replaced the Habsburgs on the Spanish throne, and the Habsburgs had to content themselves by gaining possession of the Spanish Netherlands, Belgium, Milan and Sicily.

In Austria, Charles VI, having no male heir, succeeded in persuading the estates of his various lands to accept his famous decree of 1713, the Pragmatic Sanction. This enabled his daughter Maria Theresa to succeed him and established for the first time the principle of the indivisibility of the territories under Habsburg sovereignty. Charles VI also obtained guarantees from the various foreign powers for the acceptance of his daughter's accession under the Pragmatic Sanction.

Despite these guarantees, Frederick II of Prussia used the accession in 1740 of a woman to the Habsburg throne to invade the rich industrial province of Silesia. The sequel was the arduous War of the Austrian Succession which, in effect, turned out to be the prologue to the long struggle for supremacy in Central Europe between the two great dynasties. Harassed by enemies invading all her dominions with the exception of Hungary, and lacking adequate military strength to defend her realm, Maria Theresa revealed remarkable resilience during the ordeals of the long war. Though Austria lost Silesia, she managed to save the cohesion of her empire from utter disaster and when she married Francis of Lorraine in 1736, the House of Habsburg became the House of Habsburg-Lorraine. Maria Theresa is the only female monarch in the annals of the

famous black and yellow colours of the defunct empire, as well as the double-headed eagle as the national emblem of the Austrian imperial crown.

Perhaps one of the greatest humiliations ever suffered by the Habsburgs was in the turbulent days of the Napoleonic wars. In order to maintain his realm and to buy temporary peace, Francis II submitted to the indignity of assenting to the marriage of his favourite daughter, Marie Louise, to the divorced Corsican general who was yearning for a legitimate male heir.

This gesture of appeasement was the handiwork of the Austrian statesman, Prince Clemens Metternich, who dominated European politics from 1809 to 1848. In 1812 Austria became an ally of Napoleon for a brief spell, but after his débâcle in Russia, and following the historic victory at Leipzig in October 1813 of the Allied forces, Francis I joined the Grand Alliance against his son-in-law.

Due largely to the adroit diplomatic machinations of Metternich, Austria emerged from the troublesome Napoleonic period with her former territories restored and even gained some new ones – Dalmatia and Venetia, important outlets for foreign trade.

Meanwhile, the Congress of Vienna (1814–15) replaced the discarded Holy Roman Empire, with the German Confederation, a body which embraced all German Europe and the parts of the Habsburg realm which had belonged to the Holy Roman Empire.

Austria was accorded the leadership of the Confederation in perpetuity – a dignity she enjoyed until it was swept away in the aftermath of Austria's crushing defeat at Königgrätz in 1866 at the hands of the Prussians. In 1815, the monarchs of Austria, Prussia and Russia, concluded in Vienna the Holy Alliance, designed to guarantee and maintain the peace and *status quo* in Europe. In effect, this grandiose instrument was used to uphold and promote absolutism in their own realms and abroad and to root out reform movements of all kind.

During the period 1815–48 Austria was a

3 The last real emperor of the Habsburg empire, Francis Joseph I, photographed with his family. He ruled on a basis of strict personal autocracy for 68 years until his death in 1916.
4 Organization and discipline were passwords to victory in Habsburg armies. In a military exercise imperial pikemen fix their weapons through a rail to help form a barrier.

Habsburgs, and many historians rate her as a great empress, ranking on a par with Catherine the Great of Russia.

When Maria Theresa was succeeded in 1780 by her son Joseph II, the new monarch tried to rush through a spate of measures aimed at the modernization of almost every facet of life throughout the Empire. He was regarded as an 'enlightened despot', 'the revolutionary emperor'. Flouting deep-rooted traditions, he strove to remove the shackles of serfdom, feudalism and religious bigotry but his reform schemes were wrecked on the inflexible opposition of the Church, the army and the nobility. Joseph II was described by an anonymous French chronicler as having 'possessed a thousand fine qualities which are of no use to Kings'. He died in 1790 a profoundly disillusioned man, echoed by the epitaph he composed himself for his tombstone: 'Here lies Joseph II, who failed in all his enterprises.'

With the advent of Napoleon, Austria once more became involved in a series of wars with France. Following his brilliant victory at Austerlitz, Napoleon had himself crowned Emperor of the French, and a number of German princes seceded from the Holy Roman Empire to join the Confederation of the Rhine he created. Lest the dignity of the Holy Roman Crown be overshadowed. Francis II, the incumbent Holy Roman Emperor, proclaimed its demise in 1806 and under the style of Francis I, he assumed the hereditary title of Emperor of Austria. By discarding the elective imperial crown, with ten centuries of history and glamour attached to it, Francis I became the first hereditary Habsburg emperor, and adopted the

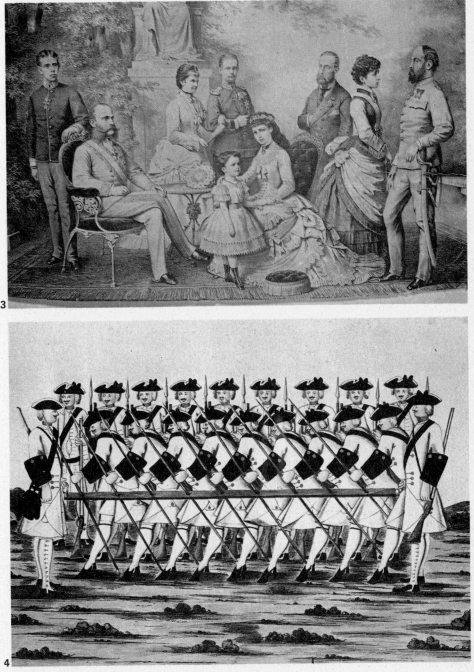

hotbed of reaction, ruthlessly suppressing every vestige of liberal thought or movement. However, by 1848 the revolutionary current engendered by the French Revolution had permeated the entire Continent and the various European capitals were seething with political unrest. There were widespread upheavals due to nationalistic tendencies and anti-authoritarian manifestations. In Vienna it was realized that the good-natured but sickly and feeble-minded Ferdinand I, was unequal to the task of coping with the explosive situation.

He was induced to abdicate in favour of his youthful nephew, Francis Joseph I, who presided over the affairs of the Habsburg empire for 68 years – a period fraught with his almost ceaseless personal tragedies and national disasters, culminating in the First World War in 1914. His rule was largely a personal one, based on strict autocratic principles, totally oblivious of Austria's most urgent need to unite the 11 different nationalities (Germans, Hungarians, Czechs, Slovaks, Moravians, Poles, Serbo-Croats, Slovenes, Ruthenians, Romanians and Italians), which made up the Habsburg amalgam. Yet, despite the chauvinistic dissensions amongst the component nationalities of the empire, the reign of Francis Joseph represented for Austria economically and culturally a golden era.

'Swan song'

The status of Austria was completely altered when Prussia, under the vigorous leadership of Otto von Bismarck, the 'Iron Chancellor', with the connivance and support of France and the newly established Kingdom of Italy, provoked a war with Austria in 1866. A short and effective campaign, forerunner of the modern *blitzkreig,* ended with the decisive Prussian victory at Königgrätz. The triumph settled forever the long drawn-out tussle between the two dynasties for the hegemony over German Europe. For Austria, the debacle at Königgrätz marked the beginning of the end as far as the Habsburg's European eminence was concerned.

In a desperate attempt to resuscitate some

1

of the lost Habsburg prestige, Austria evolved with Hungary the famous 'Compromise of 1867' creating the dual Austro-Hungarian monarchy. But in doing so, the interests and aspirations of the empire's national minorities, and the necessity of evolving in the multinational empire a unifying conception, were totally ignored. As David Lloyd George, British prime minister from 1916 to 1922 remarked, the Habsburg monarchy was a 'ramshackle realm' – an empire without an idea.

Only the heir to the throne, Franz Ferdinand, recognized how vital it was that the authority and power of the central government be strengthened. He was resolved particularly to curb the excessive influence of the Magyars at the expense of the other nationalities of the monarchy, but his assassination at Sarajevo in 1914 robbed him and the monarchy of any chance of confronting the empire's most burning problems.

The ensuing years brought in their wake the dramatic disappearance of Europe's three oldest and most illustrious dynasties: the Romanovs of Russia were the first to vanish followed in quick succession by the Habsburgs and the Hohenzollerns of Germany. Francis Joseph I was the last real emperor of the Habsburg empire. He died in 1916 at the age of 86.

His successor Charles I, published a manifesto on 6 October 1918 envisaging a federal Austrian state with full autonomy for all the subject nationalities of the dual monarchy, patterned on the United States or Switzerland. But it was much too late: the revolution swept him off the throne in mid November and with him vanished all the Habsburg glories and the heartaches of six and a half centuries.

Opening up the Russian hinterland

From the time of Ivan the Great, traders and adventurers pushed their way across the vast lands of what is now Russia. They began an age of exploitation which is still going on today.

TWO CENTURIES of Tartar domination over the small Russian state of Muscovy were broken in 1480 when Ivan the Great, Grand Duke of Muscovy, refused to pay further tribute to his Mongol suzerain, and toppled the Khanate of the Golden Horde. Ivan swept the Tartars out of Muscovy, and pushing northwest annexed the neighbouring principalities of Tver and Novgorod.

Thus began 300 years of expansion which was to spread the Russian Empire into three continents covering one-sixth of the world's land mass. Ivan the Great's grandson, Ivan the Terrible (reigned 1533–84), turned the expansion southwards and conquered the Tartar states of Kazan and Astrakhan. He ruled an empire that extended from the Arctic to the Caspian Sea eastwards to the Urals, and was the first to be crowned 'Tsar of all the Russias'.

Yet the achievements of this stirring century of Russian history, spanned by the reigns of the two Ivans, were dwarfed by the conquests of the next two centuries. These conquests extended the Russian Empire 7,000 miles eastwards of Moscow to the site of present-day San Francisco.

Unlike the annexation of Tartar lands west of the Urals, the colonization of Siberia was largely carried out by private enterprise.

Conquest by Cossacks

Russian Asia was taken not so much by advancing armies as by the infiltration of hunters, traders and explorers.

The prize that lured them to that cold, bleak wasteland was not national glory but furs, which brought high prices west of the Urals. Such battles as were fought in Siberia seldom involved more than a few hundred men and little blood was shed. This was because the few scattered inhabitants were primitive hunters and fishermen who had neither firearms nor an integrated social organization. The drive across Siberia began in 1581 when the wealthy merchant family Stroganov employed Yermak, a Cossack pirate from the River Don, to explore the country east of the Urals in search of furs.

With 800 men Yermak stormed the Tartar stronghold of Isker on the River Irtysh, and in the following year utterly routed the forces of Kuchum, the Khan of Siber (Siberia). After 400 years the tide was on the turn. The Moslem Tartars, descendants of the irresistible hordes that had once spread the Mongol Empire from the Sea of Japan to central Europe, fled from the Christian Cossacks.

Yermak's brisk conquest of western Siberia established a private empire for his masters, the wealthy Stroganovs. Almost immediately, the Russian government joined in the drive to the east. It

1 The Cossacks first appeared in the fifteenth century as bands of wild mercenaries and later led Russian expansion to the east. This fierce horseman is a Cossack from the Don River.
2 Ivan IV, who earned the name of 'the Terrible', was the first to be crowned 'Tsar of all the Russias'. His empire stretched from the Arctic to the Caspian Sea and west to the Urals.
3 Tsar Paul I, who ruled from 1796 to 1801, signed a charter in 1799 setting up the Russian-American Company and giving it the monopoly of mining and hunting on the North American mainland.

reversed the policy it had pursued in the northern territories, which had generally aimed at preserving and protecting the interests of native peoples, and granted trading rights and privileges exclusively to Russians. The bitter memories of the recent past prevented the Russian government granting to Tartars the protection given to other conquered peoples.

In 1584, the year of Yermak's death, the Russian government sent a force of 500 men under Prince Bolkhovskiy to the River Irtysh. He was quickly followed by Ivan Mansurov, who in 1585 built Obskiy Gorodok at the confluence of the Irtysh and the Ob Rivers. This was the first Russian town to be built in Siberia.

Long after Yermak's death, Kuchum, together with his son, remained a threat to Russian aspirations. In order to be able to contain Kuchum, and other local chiefs who resisted their advance, the Russians built more and more fortified posts including the present-day city of Tobolsk, which became the administrative centre for western Siberia. From here the Russians pushed south eastwards and in 1604, at the request of a local chief, the Russians constructed another fortress, Tomsk. Kuznetsk, built to the south of Tomsk in 1618, became the base for the conquest of the nomadic Kirghiz people, now permanently settled in the Kirghiz Soviet Socialist Republic in Central Asia.

Meanwhile, another advance was in progress far to the north of Tobolsk. Pushing 800 miles eastwards along stormy waterways that branched from the lower reaches of the Ob, hunters sought the sable whose fur could make men rich. In 1601 yet another fortress, Mangazeya, was built on a cabin site where hunters had for many years spent the icy winters.

From Mangazeya, Russian authorities controlled the surrounding area, imposing customs duties on products sold or bartered by nomadic tribesmen who hunted, fished and herded reindeer for their living. Mangazeya, a walled town guarded by Cossacks, was built not only to control the

1 A band of Zaporozhye Cossacks write a defiant letter to Sultan Mohammed IV of Turkey (1648–87) refusing to submit to his Moslem rule.
2 Catherine the Great who, in 1789, claimed as Russian territory the North American coastline and islands explored by Vitus Bering.
3 The wooden fort at Bratsk, on the River Angara, was built in 1631 as a centre for the collection of fur tribute for the tsars.

tribesmen, but also to 'show the flag' to foreign interlopers who were then interested in northern Russia. The Dutch and the English were thought to be especially dangerous, and James I of England, acting through the Russia Company in London, looked covetously at northern Russia.

Mangazeya prospered as a garrison town and wintering centre for about 60 years after which it declined as new centres sprang up to the east. In 1672 Mangazeya's garrison was withdrawn; it became a ghost town and its timber buildings disappeared without trace.

The early Siberian settlements, particularly those near to the Urals, were mainly capitalist enterprises organized along the lines of the Stroganovs' settlements established by Yermak. But as colonization extended further east, the development of Siberia became more and more the concern of the state. The government organized its eastern territories through *voyevodas* (military governors) based on administrative centres like Tobolsk. The voyevodas commanded small regular military forces, called *streltsy*, but more important were the irregulars – the Cossacks.

The Cossacks first appeared in the fifteenth century as wild mercenary horsemen who defended the emergent state of Russia against the Tartars. The name *Cossack* is thought to derive either from the Tartar word meaning *free labourer* or the Turkish word meaning *to wander*.

The original Cossacks were not so much an ethnic group as bands of nomadic adventurers who survived the Tartar invasions because they lived in inaccessible swamplands. They were known as the Don Cossacks, the Astrakhan, Kuban, or Ural Cossacks, according to the place which they came from.

Shrewdly, the Russian government refrained from laying too heavy a hand on the fierce Cossacks; they organized them into quasi-independent 'hosts', granted

them special privileges, and employed them as frontier defence forces against marauding Tartars. The boisterous Cossacks never quite lost the urge to be on the move and they formed a stock of adventurers ever ready to join in the push to the east. Their number were swollen by many Russian hunters and traders who joined the Cossack bands to avoid being treated as inferiors in Cossack-controlled areas.

Throughout their history the Cossacks remained surprisingly loyal to the Tsars – an allegiance that was to bring them into disastrous clash with the Bolsheviks in the Revolution of 1917. The Cossacks became to some extent the 'policemen' of Russia – and were in addition the most important colonizers of the east.

As well as being accomplished horsemen, the Cossacks became competent sailors. They pioneered exploration of the waterways to the Arctic Sea north of eastern Siberia, and reached the Sea of Okhotsk, north of Japan, in 1641.

In 1648 Semen Dezhnev, a Cossack

seaman, sailing with 90 companions in six open boats, rounded the easternmost extremity of Asia, since called Cape Dezhnev. He was the first man to prove that the continents of Asia and America were separated by sea.

An account of an official's life in Siberia has been left by Petr Beketov, a Cossack in the service of Tsar Mikhail Fedorovich, who in 1627 set out with a small armed guard to collect fur tribute from the Tungus, a tribe living near Mongolia. In his report, written on birch bark, he told the Tsar that the Tungus had not only refused to pay their dues, but had also beaten his soldiers and driven Russian traders from their territory.

Submission of the tribes

Beketov, beginning each paragraph of his report to the Tsar with 'Sire, I your slave', also reported that he and his men spent the whole of 1628 collecting fur tribute from the people living near Bratsk, a settlement about 300 miles northwest of Lake Baikal.

His party travelled along the river routes collecting tribute all the way until they reached the land of the Buryat people – a territory which Beketov claimed no Russian had previously visited. He forced the Buryat people to accept the authority of the Tsar, and they took their regular tribute of furs to the Russian *ostrog* (fort) at Yeniseyskiy.

Life was not easy for poor Beketov; in another part of the widespread Buryat lands people refused to pay any tribute. Beketov's report contained the following lament from the heart – perhaps included to excuse his failures: 'Sire, I shed my blood for you, Sire, and . . . defiled my spirit, and ate mare's meat and roots and

1 In 1582 Yermak, with a band of 800 Cossacks, defeated the Tartar stronghold of Isker on the River Irtysh and a year later drove the last of the Moslem Tartars from Siberia.
2 The map of the Soviet Union shows the extent to which the Russians spread across Siberia to the Pacific, colonizing North America as far south as present-day San Francisco, 7,000 miles eastwards of Moscow.

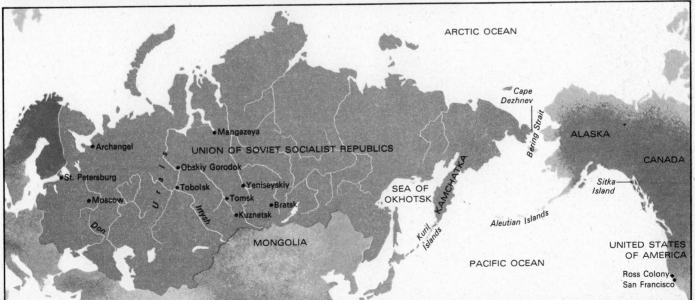

1 On the Alaskan island of Sitka, the Russian-American Company built a fortress in 1799 as a base for hunting and mining.

2 A group of Russian fur-hunters camp in the woods of Alaska. By 1839 Russian expansion had reached its peak and begun to recede.

bark and all kinds of filth, and many times had scurvy.'

In 1725, the great shipbuilding tsar Peter the Great dispatched Vitus Bering, a Danish sea captain, to the Kamchatka Peninsula, north of Japan. There, Bering built boats to explore the Arctic Ocean and he discovered the strait, later named after him, which separates Asia and North America by 56 miles. Between the years 1733 and 1741 Bering led a second expedition.

Death of Bering

The crew of one of his two ships spent the winter of 1740 exploring the Aleutian Islands and the coast of Alaska. Meanwhile, Bering's own ship started back to the Kamchatka Peninsula, but fog forced the exhausted crew to put into an uninhabited island near the peninsula. Bering, who had scurvy, died there in December 1741. The island was later named after him and so was the surrounding sea.

Peter the Great died shortly after sending Bering on his first expedition, but that Tsar's enthusiasm for exploration was shared by his successors. While Bering's voyages were in progress, other Russian mariners were braving the rigours of the Arctic, mapping the coast all the way from Archangel to the Bering Strait.

Russian activity in the extreme northern Pacific did not go unchallenged by other European powers, particularly Britain. Although Captain Cook did not venture so far north, his voyages indicated British interest in the whole area of the Pacific Ocean.

Defiantly, Catherine the Great claimed for Russia in 1789 the American coastline north of latitude 55° 21′, together with the Aleutian and Kuril islands. But because of wars then being fought against Turkey and Sweden, Russia was unable to maintain in the east the naval squadron which alone could have enforced the claim.

What could not be enforced politically might be achieved commercially. In 1799, Tsar Paul I set up the Russian-American Company, granting it a monopoly of hunting and mining in the areas claimed under Catherine the Great, and the right to explore beyond those areas. For the next half century Russian governments pursued their political ambitions and even waged war under cover of the Company.

In 1799, Alexander Baranov became the Company's first Governor of Alaska, which he administered from the fortress of Mikhaylovsk in Sitka Island, off the southern mainland of Alaska. Alaskan Indians seized Mikhaylovsk in 1802, probably with British assistance, but in 1805

Baranov recaptured it and extended its fortifications.

Russian hunters and traders penetrated southwards along the Alaskan coast and into the offshore islands in search of fur seals, sea otters, walruses, and small fur land animals. Many of the tough Russian fur-seekers took native wives and by the 1820s about 600 Russian or part-Russian people were settled in the area. The southernmost settlement was Ross Colony near the site of present-day San Francisco, which a northbound Spanish expedition had reached in 1769.

An important motive for the continued push southward was the Russian desire to possess fertile land where sufficient food could be grown to feed more settlers. Attempts by the Russians to push their border even further south were eventually abandoned for diplomatic reasons. The Tsar Alexander I wished to avoid incurring the enmity of Britain and of the United States, whose nationals were at that time actively engaged in opening up the 'wild west' of North America.

The Russian Governor of Alaska made a half-hearted attempt to keep California by winning Mexican support in exchange for Russian recognition of Mexico's independence from Spain, but Tsar Nicholas I vetoed the proposal.

Withdrawal from America

In 1839 Ross Colony was abandoned, and the southernmost part of present-day Alaska was leased to the British Hudson Bay Company. In time, the tsars came to regard their North American territories as bargaining counters in their diplomatic negotiations in Europe.

At the Tsar's request the Governor-General of Siberia drew up a report on the Company's activities admitting that the Company was economically unsound. The idea grew in St Petersburg that it would be better to sell Russia's North American possessions before they were either seized by the British or Americans, or that they should be abandoned in order to reduce the drain on the Russian economy.

The best price for the territories would probably have come from Britain, but Russian foreign policy after the Crimean War (1854–6) was anti-British and directed to winning American diplomatic support. Negotiations for the sale began in 1857, but were delayed by the American Civil War.

Ten years later the deal was done and the United States bought all Russian North America for $12.30 a square mile. The purchase was unpopular in the United States because most Americans thought that good money had been squandered on useless land.

At the turn of the century (1896–1903), gold was discovered in Alaska and in the neighbouring Yukon territory of Canada. The population of Alaska leapt from a few hundred to 63,000 in 1900, and in 1959 the territory became America's forty-ninth state. Had Tsar Alexander II not reversed Russia's Far Eastern policy, both Alaska and California might be Soviet Socialist Republics.